# GALLA PLACIDIA
# AUGUSTA

# GALLA PLACI

# DIA AUGUSTA

## *A Biographical Essay*

STEWART IRVIN OOST

THE UNIVERSITY OF CHICAGO PRESS · CHICAGO & LONDON

*Library of Congress Catalog Card Number: 68-25090*

THE UNIVERSITY OF CHICAGO PRESS, CHICAGO 60637

The University of Chicago Press, Ltd., London W.C. 1

*Published 1968*

*Printed in the United States of America*

*In Loving Memory of*

*"My Favorite Proofreader"*

*and the Others Who Sleep at Coopersville,*

*Awaiting the Coming*

*of the Lord*

*Rev. 22:20–21*

# PREFACE

The late A. J. A. Symons once wrote that a biographer had the privilege of assuming omniscience about his subject, and that full knowledge of a person is quite possible if one has available the subject's letters and those of his contemporaries, his (written) work, and documentary sources for the external facts of his life.[1] According to such a standard it would be impossible to write biographies of most of the leading figures of ancient Greek and Roman history, with such possible exceptions as Cicero, Caesar, the Emperor Julian, the sophist Libanius, and various Fathers of the early Church who have left large amounts of written materials which survive to our day. Above all, it is impossible to write a real biography according to this standard of political personages living in the fifth century, for the history of which our sources of information are, far more than is usually the case, scattered, incoherent, and sparse.

Yet many of the external events in the life of Galla Placidia Augusta are so startling and peculiar that our curiosity is more than ordinarily engaged to find out what can be known about her. To my knowledge there is in English no full-length account of her life, although such accounts do exist in other languages. In attempting to supply this omission I have been painfully aware of the omissions and lacunae in our sources; it is for this reason, to give the reader fair warning ahead of time, that I have subtitled this interpretation *A Biographical Essay.* In trying to put together and explain the scattered and disparate data that survive concerning Galla Placidia I have found myself obliged to construct bridges of inference to a degree well beyond what is customary in other areas of history where the evidence is much thicker, as it were. In all such cases I have been careful to use qualifiers in the text, and

[1] A. J. A. Symons, *The Quest for Corvo: An Experiment in Biography*, Penguin ed., p. 116.

vii

sometimes to warn the reader of the tentative nature of what is being said by explicit statements in the notes.

An attempt is made in this narrative to avoid the opposite defects of presenting a history of the West Roman Empire in the first half of the fifth century under the guise of a biography, and of recounting in a vacuum a life lived in a generally unfamiliar age. My purpose has been to describe as much of the background of the history of the West in the fifth century as should make the life of Placidia intelligible to the general reader and, it is hoped, to advance our knowledge of her life in terms of her interaction with her environment. It is primarily for this reason that the first and last chapters have been added; the first to outline the character of the world into which Placidia was born, the last to sketch the conclusion of various matters whose earlier development it had been necessary to describe in interpreting her life. Like most professional students I indulge the pious, but sincere, wish that others than my professional colleagues may be interested in reading this book. For such general readers I have tried to keep mention of technicalities concerning the administration and life of the Later Roman Empire to a minimum, and simply or roughly to define or explain those whose mention seemed unavoidable. It should be possible for the general reader who is uninterested in the minutiae of scholarship or the polemics of scholars to read the book without any reference to the notes. On the other hand, it seemed impossible to write an account where the very existence and relationship of events themselves are in doubt, not to mention attempts to understand the meaning of such events, without indicating the evidence on which the account is based and the reasons for adopting the views presented in the text. Hence the inclusion of the footnotes for those interested in such matters; the notes are bulky indeed, but the student will at once perceive that they are far from exhaustive. I have been at pains to document the life of Galla Placidia itself quite fully in the primary sources (whether ancient or medieval); for the rest I have tried to refer to accounts that are most helpful or perspicacious, or sometimes merely most recent. Résumés of the general course of events are sparsely documented; for these summaries I refer once and for all to the general histories of Seeck, Stein, Bury, and Jones, as cited in the bibliography.

Writing an account of this nature makes one realize how much any success a writer can attain is owing to the instruction he has received from his teachers, students, and colleagues, as well as from those who stand in no formal educational or professional relation to him. It is with the warmest gratitude and affection that I here express my debt to the late Professor Einar Joranson, who with the customary twinkle in his eye outlined the more striking vicissitudes in the life of Galla Placidia to a rapt undergraduate class more than a quarter of a century ago and thus first attracted my interest to her; more, I can only hope that his own highest standards of meticulous scholarship would not be outraged if he were able to read this account. It is also with great pleasure that I acknowledge assistance in the shaping and revising of this book from various of my colleagues: Professor Richard T. Bruère, who as my editor has so frequently in the past saved me from committing all sorts of errors in public print, was always willing to discuss puzzling or ambiguous Latin passages with me, and also graciously consented to go over the manuscript of this work with his keen editorial eye. Professor Benedict Einarson, as he has done so frequently, unstintingly placed his vast knowledge of the Greek language at my disposal in trying to solve cruxes in the frequently crabbed Greek of late antiquity and the early Middle Ages; he also read the whole manuscript critically. My former teacher, Professor Blanche B. Boyer, cheerfully put her knowledge of late Latin language and literature at my disposal, even as she had firmly guided a younger tyro through the difficulties of the same tongue. Professor Edward L. Bassett also discussed Latin cruxes with me, and drew my attention to some choice items of recent bibliography. Naturally, however, only the ignorance or the indurated obstinacy of the writer is responsible for the faults that remain. I am particularly happy also to recognize the assistance I have received from students in my seminar in late Roman history for the past several years, especially from Mr. Briggs Twyman and Mr. Frank Clover, whose specific contributions are acknowledged at the proper places in the notes. I also appreciate grants from the Division of the Humanities of this institution, which enabled me to consult in eastern libraries books not available in Chicago, as well as meet other expenses involved in the preparation of this work.

Finally, and first of all, my debt to those referred to in the dedication cannot be expressed in any words I know how to write; I hope they would be aware of what I would put here if I could

The University of Chicago
*25 April 1967*

# CONTENTS

# ILLUSTRATIONS

# 1

# PROLOGUE:
# THE ROMAN EMPIRE

Galla Placidia was born in the Christian city of Constantinople, the second capital of the Roman Empire, or possibly in Thessalonica, the scene of her parents' marriage, either in the year 388 or in the first few months of the year 389 of the Incarnation of Christ as we number the years today.[1] She was the first child of the Emperor Theodosius the Great by his second wife, Galla; she was also the granddaughter and the half sister of Roman emperors, and in time to come she would be the wife and mother of other emperors. She was also destined for a brief time to be the consort of a king of the Visigoths and bear him a son, while one of her granddaughters would be the consort of yet another Roman emperor, and the other granddaughter the mother of a king of the Vandals. During a goodly part of the first half of the fifth century Galla Placidia would play an important role in the politics of the Western half of the Roman Empire in the critical age when it was approaching its final dissolution. Her name was to be indelibly associated with the city of Ravenna in Italy, but when she died she was interred with the funereal pomp befitting a Christian Roman empress in a mausoleum adjacent to the church built by Constantine the Great for the Prince of the Apostles at Rome, where whatever is mortal of her may well still to this day rest beneath the transept floor of Michelangelo's mighty basilica.

---

[1] The marriage of her parents occurred in autumn, 387. Galla died in childbirth in 394 together with her child (Eun. Frag. 61 [*FHG,* IV, 42. N.B.: Hereafter fragments of the late Greek historians will be cited by number, followed by the relevant page and volume (IV) number in Müller's *Fragmenta Historicorum Graecorum*.]; Zos. 4.

In Placidia's father's reign, to the uncritical eye at least, the Roman Empire still spread its imposing bulk over parts of the three continents of Europe, Asia, and Africa, its frontiers still "guarded by ancient renown and disciplined valour."[2] The former provinces of Dacia (much of modern Rumania) had been abandoned to the barbarians in the third century; the angled territory between the upper courses of the Rhine and the Danube, known mysteriously (to us) as the "Tithed Lands," had been lost during the same troubled age; similarly, by the close of that century the imperial government had had considerably to retrench its frontiers in the westernmost parts of North Africa, so that the nomads of the desert roamed at will where imperial peace and order had been imposed under earlier emperors.[3] Nevertheless the whole civilized Mediterranean world lived, more or less, under one law, and at the death of Theodosius in 395 the emperor's will ruled men among the mists of distant Britain as along the fertile narrow valley of the Nile, the

57. 3; Joh. Ant. Frag. 187 [IV, 609]). The period 388 to Nov. 391 may be excluded (together with the following nine months), for at that time Theodosius was in the West, while Galla remained at Constantinople (Marcell. *s.a.* 390, 2 [Mommsen, *Chron. Min.,* II, 62. N.B.: Hereafter the minor Latin chronicles of late antiquity and the early Middle Ages will be cited by the appropriate item number followed by the relevant volume and page numbers of this edition: I, II, III = respectively *Monumenta Germaniae Historica: Auctores Antiquissimi* (i.e., *MGH: AA*), vols. IX, XI, XIII]); in view of the just cited passage from Marcell. and the general tenor of what else is known about Galla, the passage of Zos. (4. 45. 4; cf. 46. 1) indicating that Galla returned to Italy when her husband marched west is to be regarded as a confusion with her sisters. The *Paschal Chronicle* (I, 563 [Bonn]) refers to Placidia as of 385; probably the correct date is Nov. 391, for it mentions an entry of Theodosius into Constantinople. The argument that the *Chronicle* confuses Placidia with her mother involves considerable logical contradiction. The poet Claudian (*IV Cons. Hon.* 207–9) refers to Placidia as of Jan. 393 in terms which imply that she was more than a babe in arms at the time. Hence probability points to her conception at the time of Theodosius' first sojourn with Galla rather than later. Ambrose, in a letter written to Theodosius when the latter was in Italy before his return to Galla, refers to the Emperor as the "father of Gratian" (*Ep.* 51. 17). One of the children of Theodosius was named Gratian, but the reference is ambiguous, for this remark could be a courteous reference to the late Emperor of that name. Indeed, it makes good sense for Ambrose, long associated with the Emperor Gratian, thus to refer to the man whom Theodosius had avenged. Cf. the note in the Migne ed. *ad loc., PL,* XVI, 1214, although it is not very well informed about Theodosius' offspring. Note that in *Ep.* 53. 5 Ambrose refers to Valentinian II as Theodosius' son, and the former's sisters as the latter's daughters, and there is no question that the relationship is not literal. The question of Theodosius' children is argued at length in "Some Problems in the History of Galla Placidia," *CP,* LX (1965), 1–10, at 1–4.

2 E. Gibbon, *The History of the Decline and Fall of the Roman Empire,* Chap. I, *init.*

3 There had also been some fairly extensive losses along the eastern frontier because of military failures against the Sassanid Persians in the fourth century.

fisherfolk by the shores of the limitless western ocean as well as men consecrated to God in the monasteries erected by the pious devotion of ascetics and mystics in the barren hills of Judaea. It was the last moment in history when this was true.

For although at that moment the Roman cities still stood in the marble grandeur of their porticoes and public baths, their libraries and even the abandoned temples of the ancient gods, and the poor still huddled together in crowded squalor behind city walls frequently hastily repaired amid the turmoil of the third century or later, although the great roads which united the Empire were still kept in passable repair, at least to the penetrating aftereye of history, the signs and symptoms that Rome was not in fact eternal, as the court panegyrists so regularly informed the emperor, crowded upon every side. In fact, in every department of life—trade, agriculture, learning and education, social relations, law and justice, and above all in the minds of men—great changes were preparing, indeed, had long been in process beneath the straining fabric of imperial greatness. Probably in 395 the overwhelming majority of the Empire's subjects was still theoretically loyal to it. Yet gradually, hardly realizing the fact themselves, many of them, whether in desperation and hunger or in greed and self-seeking, or because they had come in fact to put the service of God and the salvation of their souls above their loyalty to the state, were pursuing courses of action which overtly or implicitly were inimical to the welfare of state and society as they then existed. Whether, or how far, whole blocks of the population in some areas had begun to be dissatisfied with the imperial regime to such a degree that they experienced a sense of difference from it or oppression by it which can usefully be described as "nationalism" by twentieth-century men is a matter of considerable discussion today.[4] In all probability while certain aspects of such revulsion from the Empire or some part of it are similar to some aspects of modern nationalism, so many other aspects of nationalism are missing from these ancient

4 For an able recent discussion which rejects "nationalism" as a relevant concept, see Ramsay MacMullen, *Enemies of the Roman Order: Treason, Unrest, and Alienation in the Empire*, pp. 192–241, with the cautionary remarks in my review, *CP*, LXIII (1968), 169–70. On the other hand, M. Lichtheim, "Autonomy versus Unity in the Christian East," in *The Transformation of the Roman World*, ed. Lynn White, pp. 119–46, esp. 139, sees in the religious movements in the Eastern half of the Empire the "primacy of religious motivation," but an "autonomy of conscience," which was "the nucleus around which national and other communal structures were formed."

protests that it is better to avoid the term as misleading at best. Similarly a subject of controversy today, not unrelated to the biases of the modern historian himself, is the question whether whole classes were alienated from society, with which they were engaging in a "class struggle."[5] Certainly there appear to have been approximations of such a conflict in many times and places in Greek and Roman history. Unfortunately history is never simple, and in all ages, those which the historian regards as epochs of success as well as those he considers periods of decay, there are always those who reject the prevailing regime,[6] or at least hold that circumstances are bad or even intolerable. Thus Livy,[7] writing in or on the verge of what is regarded by many historians as the most glorious or successful period of Roman history, yet refers to his time as one when men can bear neither the ills by which they are afflicted nor their remedies. Many men, perhaps most, have a tendency to look on the past as good, and the present as less so in varying degree according to their temperaments. The historian must, accordingly, discount such statements belittling the present in terms of the past. What he usually does, however, is to view them in the light of the history of their time as he knows it. If he thinks the time evil, then such statements not only attest to knowledge of the fact among the people concerned, but become part of the corpus of evidence proving the fact itself. If the time appears to his aftersight as relatively good, then the statements are regarded as isolated individual curiosities, or part of a literary commonplace. Indeed the latter is frequently the case in Greco-Roman antiquity, for one of its prevailing commonplaces is of the Golden Age in the past. An anthology of pessimistic statements about the late fourth and fifth centuries could easily be compiled; unfortunately so could a collection of optimistic views; eternal Rome and a new Golden Age do not appear exclusively in the writings of court poets and rhetoricians. Hence the historian cannot really trust overt statements of alienation or rejection as proof of the tendency of the Late

[5] That they were is the thesis of almost all eastern European discussions touching on the subject; consult the historical sections of *Bibliotheca Classica Orientalis* at random.

[6] See the whole of MacMullen's *Enemies;* he considers only the Empire, but similar data could be assembled for the Republic. Cf. also H. Fuchs, *Der geistige Widerstand gegen Rom in der antiken Welt.*

[7] *Praef.* 9.

Empire, but must try to interpret the course of events themselves.

Certainly there is evidence of such overt acts of rejection: peasants, crushed by intolerable burdens, joining brigands or barbarians; townsmen fleeing all but the greatest cities (in the latter they were supported by the government)[8] to the countryside; the pious choosing the socially acceptable asceticism of the desert to please God, to reject the (Roman) world and its penetration into the church, and, in quite human and natural fashion, to find a solution for their personal dilemmas.[9] The upper classes wrote history and other things; we are best informed about them. The Roman aristocracy of the Empire throughout its history probably placed a greater value on literary culture than any other ruling elite in European politics. At the end of the Empire in the West, Roman literary tradition, Roman greatness, and the Roman state, as embalmed in that tradition and commemorated by their own privileged position, were fiercely defended by the nobles; yet the spirit of personal self-sacrifice, the core of that tradition, was commonly absent from their overt behavior. Imperial legislation continually attests the nobles' self seeking and their disregard of the needs of the state; the vast wealth which they freely expended to obtain ancient, meaningless, but traditionally Roman honors for themselves or their families was all too successfully guarded from serving the real needs of the state. This is particularly true of the great nobles of the City of Rome itself.[10] And such an attitude is also an example of effective, although probably unconscious, alienation from the state and what it really meant.

It has recently been suggested, with much point, that in the fourth (and fifth) century the most altruistic, most able, most public-spirited men chose like an Ambrose or an Augustine to serve God in his Church rather than in the organization of the imperial state or society. Such acts are also unconscious rejection of or withdrawal from the state, and of the most serious character, for obviously the state cannot continue its success or greatness if the

8 S. Mazzarino, *Aspetti sociali del quarto secolo,* pp. 256–57.

9 Cf. M. Rostovtzeff, *SEHRE*[2], pp. 479, 742, n. 28.

10 Historians have frequently pointed this out; esp. cf. Olympiod. Frag. 44 (IV, 67) (great wealth) and Zos. 5. 29 (unwillingness to use a small part of it to buy off Alaric). For a concise summary of withdrawal and rejection on the part of the upper classes, see Lucien Musset, *Les invasions: Les vagues germaniques,* pp. 229–30; and pp. 230–32 on centrifugal tendencies in the Empire.

ablest minds and the natural leaders produced by successive generations tend to use their gifts for other purposes.[11] There is considerable truth in the belief that the Church helped promote the decline and fall of the Roman Empire, but perhaps not in the way Gibbon thought.

But one may well counter this statement with the observation that quite possibly the Church better deserved victory in this silent competition than the state. Rome in her millennial history had brought death, slavery, starvation, ill-being of every kind to thousands, perhaps millions of people. On the other hand, she had conferred peace, order, prosperity, law and justice, on perhaps hundreds of millions, despite the sometimes perfidious, more frequently brutal methods she had employed in her conquests. In her great days Rome had ruled with justice, equality, and the allowance of considerable liberty to her subjects. As such she still presents to subsequent ages the realized ideal of one world for all men of that world. It is an ideal which sometimes even inspires the present as it did the Middle Ages, although the temper of our times makes most of us reluctant to face the implications of the fact that this peace was originally imposed by naked, brute force. On balance, it seems fair to say that the phenomenon of Roman history was a greater good than evil. Yet in the last stages of its existence the Empire's beneficent aspects were more and more overshadowed by the destructive effect exerted upon the sum total of the happiness and welfare of its subjects.[12] Certainly we, living in a prosperous age and in countries which are relatively orderly and free, find it easy to regard the Late Empire as a vast prison house where the rank and file were exploited for the benefit of the guards, that is, the ruling classes, but where even the latter were horrifyingly subject to the most destructive vicissitudes of circumstance and ill fortune. And to us the fact that even the curative efforts of the emperors themselves, when not thwarted by one agency or an-

[11] A. Momigliano, *The Conflict between Paganism and Christianity in the Fourth Century*, pp. 9–12; cf. Gibbon, ed. J. B. Bury, III, 156; suggestive and perspicacious is G. B. Ladner, "The Impact of Christianity," in *Transformation of the Roman World*, ed. White, pp. 59–91. Eventually in different ways and at different times East and West would create an alliance of church and state which would partially supply the destruction of the pagan unity of these two institutions, but in the Later Roman Empire that time was not yet.

[12] Cf. C. W. Hollister, "Twilight in the West," in *Transformation of the Roman World*, ed. White, pp. 179–205, at 186–87, 204, summarizing the ideas of W. C. Bark, *Origins of the Medieval World*.

other, all too frequently worsened the evils that they tried to remedy is no excuse.

Certainly it is quite easy to understand the phenomenon of withdrawal or alienation under the conditions prevalent in the Later Roman Empire. Economic and social misfortunes are regularly blamed on the government of the time,[13] even though most governments in history have understood the basic workings of economy and society even less than do the governments of our own day. Presumably the long continuation of such difficulties, especially when conjoined with a high degree of corruption among the agents of the government at worst, and at best with measures aimed at remedying those conditions but thwarting the plans of individuals who were attempting to escape to safety by their private devices, would cause such disaffection to spread from the government of the time to the whole fabric of society. As early as the second century A.D., even in the gracious days of the Antonine emperors, the last golden Indian summer of the classical Greco-Roman world, disquieting symptoms of economic change had begun to appear. The beginning of the century, for example, had seen grandiose ideas of urban expansion in Britain, but the end of the same century witnessed the beginning of the decline of British towns.[14] This decline of towns, shortly to be found in most parts of the Empire, is especially striking, since the Greek *polis*, the Latin *urbs* or *civitas*, was the central institution of Greco-Roman antiquity; the towns provided the nodes or focal points for the economic, social, political, and cultural life of the ancients. It is no accident that the Latin word *urbanitas* means "urbanism," and therefore culture or civilization, "urbanity." That such evidence first appears in a place like Britain is characteristic; gangrene is more likely to set in first at points farthest removed from the centers of circulation. There is evidence of decentralization of manufacture and consequent decline both in volume of trade and in quality of goods produced in the second century, perhaps even late in the first. Agricultural products as articles of trade, grown not for immediate consumption but for exchange, appear to have had much the same history. The population of the towns, sup-

---

13 Cf., e.g., Am. Marc. 28. 5. 14; J. G. Frazer, *The Golden Bough* (1 vol. ed.; New York, 1922), p. 168; in the United States one also remembers the "Hoover depression."

14 R. G. Collingwood and J. N. L. Myres, *Roman Britain and the English Settlements*, 2d ed., pp. 201–2.

ported directly or indirectly by trade, could not fail to be affected adversely; with the economic basis for their existence being thus slowly eroded, the towns' activities as focal points for the other aspects of society also tended to diminish. And it must surely be true that in terms of the corresponding failure of an ever larger group of individuals to achieve what they had come from the experience of the near past to think of as reasonable goals of life, disappointment and disillusionment prepared the way for a more or less dumb dissatisfaction with the quality of life, and eventually for attempts by individuals to better their lot which were tantamount to withdrawal of cooperation, active or passive, in the maintenance and continuation of their society.

For in the next century, the third, things became grim indeed for the overwhelming majority of the population of the ancient world, which in primitive technological conditions, with only rudimentary devices for the control of nature and of man, lived even at the best of times on the slender margin of subsistence and destitution, except in the greatest cities, such as Rome itself. Here the state, not primarily from humanitarian concerns, but from well-founded fear of the faceless urban mass, living in squalid tenements which pressed on all sides upon the palaces of the great and the offices of the government, attempted by its dole and its amusements to divert the populace and support it at a subsistence level. Most of Rome's subjects were not so lucky, and were exposed without protection to the rising tide of disasters which burst upon the Empire from every quarter. Wars, civil and foreign—with their ravaging of field and town and their progressive destruction of the economic margin, which in its slenderness was the chief characteristic of material existence in antiquity—famine and plague, the incursions of the barbarians, the harrying of imperial subjects by mutinous and undisciplined troops, which seemed worse than the attacks of overt foes and sometimes was; all these things continued for the lives of generations of men. The finances of the imperial government could not stand the strain. In the best days of the Empire its income had barely sufficed to meet usual expenses; the fact that it did not raise taxes further must surely mean that it could not with safety; in turn that fact again testifies to the low level of the Empire's material resources.

The structure of credit and banking was far too rudimentary to permit the government to borrow the huge sums it needed to meet the emergencies of the third century; the accumulated savings of frugal emperors were regularly dissipated by the reckless extravagance of spendthrift monarchs who sooner or later succeeded to the throne, and whose personalities could not withstand the suggestion that their power was unlimited, divine. Hence the only resort available was repeated debasements of the coinage, until by the middle of the third century it was composed of slugs of billon washed with gilt or silvering. The consequences of the resulting inflation are obvious, for they have recurred more than once in modern times. Large numbers of the middle classes were reduced to penury, while the dislocation of trade prevented their making good their losses. The poor, save in the sheltered enclaves of government support, starved in town or country, or fled to the hills and forests and became brigands, actively attacking the society they had fled, and augmenting the disasters that had created them. The great rich, those who managed to escape the political storms, conspiracies and treasons, or the direct attack of armies or barbarians on their persons, as usual survived, since their wealth, securely invested in land, for the most part was inextinguishable, and their estates, scattered throughout the whole Empire, were seldom exposed to destruction at the same time. Their numbers were increased by adventurers who managed by shrewdness and luck to become wealthy in the midst of the general misfortunes, frequently through the state, whose power was more and more commonly diverted from its legitimate objects to exploit helpless subjects of the Empire for the benefit of bureaucrats. Much of the aristocracy of the fourth and fifth centuries was composed of the descendants of such persons, who nevertheless also frequently claimed to derive from the noble houses of the illustrious past. Attempting, for the most part without success, to dominate and reunite the disintegrating state and society, emperors came and went with amazing rapidity. Some ruled for only a short time, even only a few days, over only a small territory; yet arrogating to themselves the proud titles of universal dominion. Others managed to reign over much of the Empire for some years. In any case, violent death, sometimes in its ugliest forms, was their common lot, whether they ruled for little or for long. Yet many of those who succeeded for a time were truly great men; it required a combination of shrewdness, political skill, hard-handed ruthlessness, and a talent for conniving—traits raised to a degree approaching genius—to manage to ride the

wounded tiger for even a few years. For the same withdrawal from
the ideals of selfless service to the state that the past had imposed
and sometimes practiced, that turned too many bureaucrats into
more or less petty tyrants, easily convinced any general with a few
troops that he might as well inspire, or accede to, the demands of
his soldiers that he become Caesar Augustus. Since the soldiers
under arms amid a disarmed population could easily read the
lessons of self-interest in the world about them, and since for generations the emperors had taught them that the accession of a new
Caesar meant a splendid gift to each man . . . . The time when the
Emperor Antoninus Pius in the golden sunlight of an Italian
morning could join with his dependents in the vintage at his
country villa, while his heir pondered in his bedroom the rules of
rhetoric or the precepts of the Stoic philosophy, seemed gone
forever.

For most of the population of the Empire, however, the vintage
had never been an occasion merely for the emulation of the ancient
Roman virtues of frugality and simplicity, or for the modified im-
personation of Cincinnatus. The long-lasting effects upon the
general population of the disruptive factors, which reached a sort
of culmination in the third century, were to constitute a basic element in the changed world of the Late Empire, a world which,
especially in the West, was already beginning to show quite
obviously the character of the early Middle Ages. We have no real
means of knowing the size of the population of the Roman Empire.
Even the most careful and informed guesses vary widely. It seems
certain, however, that even at its maximum in the Early Empire the
number of people inhabiting the circle of the Mediterranean lands
was far inferior to what it is today; the technology of the ancient
world was simply incapable of supporting anything like such a
number even at the subsistence level. This pressure of population
upon the means of subsistence had been the root causative factor
of such ancient pagan practices as the exposure of unwanted children, and probably of the toleration, which sometimes amounted
almost to approval, of homosexuality, first in Greece and later at
Rome and in the West.[15] In the third century, however, the population drastically declined from its previous levels; war and disease

---

[15] The basic work on ancient population is the still unreplaced K. J. Beloch, *Die
Bevölkerung der griechisch-römischen Welt* (Leipzig, 1886).

directly killed thousands or tens of thousands; the widespread destruction of the material means of human support slew hundreds of thousands more. Such carnage is made good with the passage of time in healthy societies and economies; witness the regrowth after the ravages of the Black Death in the later Middle Ages. But for reasons which are poorly understood, if at all, this is not true of a declining society. Fewer children are born, or carried to term; fewer survive the perils of childhood. The fact is almost certain; the reasons, apart from certain obvious considerations of lack of proper nourishment for mother and child, are unclear.[16] At a time when as never before the government and society needed people to create wealth in order to support the Empire's efforts against its external and internal foes, to supply soldiers to fight its enemies, to maintain the oriental luxury of the imperial courts of the Late Empire, to support the vastly increased bureaucracy (these latter two measures were themselves primarily designed to end the civil wars, and to mobilize all the Empire's available resources to combat the evils which were afflicting it)—at a time when the Empire needed ever more hands and strong-muscled backs, the ultimate of all human resources was failing it badly.

What population, in its millions, the Empire still possessed was undergoing important cultural changes. In effect, in varying degrees, society was in the process of becoming simplified, germanized, and orientalized. In earlier days ancient society had been a relatively complicated organism. Economically, for example, there had been a considerable specialization of labor with attendant sophistication of the products of that labor, of the necessities and amenities of life: one carpenter made a door, for example, another hung it.[17] Socially, there had been an imperial, Empire-wide aristocracy, subdivided into senators and knights (so-called); there had been a local aristocracy of the towns (we would perhaps call them upper middle class), and beneath them the artisans and shopkeepers. In the towns and countryside there had been free labor; in the towns, at least, this had been organized in benevolent associa-

[16] With some caution see A. E. R. Boak, *Manpower Shortage and the Fall of the Roman Empire in the West;* on plagues, endemic and epidemic, as a cause in the third century, see now the important article by J. F. Gilliam, "The Plague under Marcus Aurelius," *AJP*, LXXXII (1961), 225–51.

[17] W. W. Tarn, *Hellenistic Civilisation* (3d ed. with G. T. Griffith; London, 1952), p. 3.

tions (*collegia*) in which the members took great pride, and which engaged in more or less snobbish rivalry among themselves. Beneath these were sharecroppers, still free, on country estates, and small farmers with their own land; and at the bottom, of course, were the slaves. And there were many subtle variations and cross-strata of population; the pampered slaves of a rich man were frequently better off than many a proud free man, and freedmen, commonly despised—in order to bolster their own self-respect—by many people in all classes except, presumably, the very slaves, were found at every economic level; some of them became very rich and powerful, sometimes far more so than the richest and bluest-blooded aristocrats. Not uncommonly the descendants of some of these freedmen attained the highest positions in politics and society. It was a society of notable social mobility within the forms of a much more rigidly stratified system of class and status, inherited, like so many of the forms of the Early Empire, from the Roman Republic. But from the third century onward society was in the process of simplification; eventually it would become the early medieval society of those who fought (nobles), those who worked (mainly in agriculture), and those who prayed (the Christian priesthood and the monks). That time was not yet, or near, but society was tending in that direction. The emperors of late Rome, striving desperately to avoid change, since their experience seemed to tell them that nearly all change was bad for the state (particularly, its much needed revenues were likely to be diminished thereby), attempted, with quite imperfect success, to halt what social mobility still remained. Their failure is demonstrated by the need for constant repetition of prohibitory legislation.[18] At least by the fifth century in Gaul the aristocracy was beginning to desert the cities for the countryside,[19] where it was to remain for most of the Middle Ages; the trend may have been even earlier in Britain;[20] in Italy apparently the change did not occur, at least in the same degree.[21] Indeed, town and countryside were never to be so absolutely

[18] See the salutary and needed remarks by Ramsay MacMullen, "Social Mobility and the Theodosian Code," *JRS*, LIV (1964), 435–55, which upset a common generalization on the subject.

[19] Ap. Sid. *Epp. passim.*

[20] The villa system; e.g., Collingwood and Myres, *Roman Britain*, p. 210.

[21] Esp. L. Ruggini, "Vicende rurali dell' Italia antica dall' età tetrarchica ai Longobardi," *Riv. stor. ital.*, LXXVI (1964), 261–86.

divided in medieval Italy as elsewhere in western Christian Europe. The wealth and influence of the numerically small, but vastly powerful, uppermost class of society was to increase still further as time went on, until in the fifth century in the Western Empire it had become such a collective force that the emperor himself must frequently yield to its wishes, its greed, and its prejudices. We shall see both Galla Placidia and her son forced to try to placate this power.

Society was also becoming orientalized. The Early Empire had, officially at least, and in circles of the ruling classes which professed to wish to follow the ideals of old Rome, frowned upon Greeks to some extent, and on non-Greeks, or only partially hellenized easterners even more. But the effect of these prejudices wore away more and more. Easterners, even Egyptians and Jews, made their way into the governing classes and the aristocracy. Gradually the etiquette of the court and the protocol surrounding the emperor took on an ever more eastern character, as with the passage of time the mask of republicanism which had clothed the power of the early Caesars fell away. The Emperors Aurelian, Diocletian, and Constantine, at the end of the third century and the beginning of the fourth, merely accelerated and codified such changes that had long been in progress.[22] Eastern magic and astrology, above all eastern religions, had won a firm foothold at Rome as early as the last generations of the Republic. More and more during the Empire even stanch Romans, like the Hellenistic Greeks before them, yielded to the allure of eastern religions; their splendid ritual, their offer of communion with the divine which relieved human insecurity and, in a vast world, ruled by the distant emperor and moved by incomprehensible forces, gave assurance and support to the individual personality, won over the souls of men. The terrors of the unknown and the unforeseeable future cease to exist for man when God is with him. "If God be for us, who can be against us?" Mithra, Isis, the Great Mother, Adonis, the Syrian Goddess, and all the rest, were savior gods; but the greatest of all, because the most uncompromising of all in demands and assurances, was Christ. "What is truth?" asked Pilate (John 18:38). The

---

[22] A. Alföldi, "Die Ausgestaltung des monarchischen Zeremoniells am römischen Kaiserhofe," *Röm. Mitt.* XLIX (1934), 1–118; *idem,* "Insignien und Tracht der römischen Kaiser," *ibid.,* L (1935), 1–171.

answer of Christ (John 14:6) best satisfied the needs of the ancient world in its search for emotional security. Yet a person of Greek or Roman culture who reverenced Christ, or the Ephesian Artemis of the many breasts (or whatever the objects on the front torso of her cult statue are supposed to be), was by that fact partially withdrawing from the traditional society of the classical past. And the implications of Christianity are such that the Christian was withdrawing the more.[23] Christianity, however transformed and developed by Greek thought, Greek philosophical methodology and conclusions, was of the East. Yet the simplicity and assurances of its faith comforted the uneducated; the profundity of the mysteries propounded by the union of Hebraic revelation and Greek thought satisfied the learned.

In yet other ways the Late Empire was also a world that was becoming germanized. Germans are found in the Early Empire as imperial bodyguards; toward the end of the second century Marcus Aurelius settled large numbers of them on devastated lands; gradually they immigrated, ordinarily with the consent of the government, in ever greater numbers. Good fighters in an age when most inhabitants of the Empire were becoming ever less warlike, partly because of the government's careful restriction on the bearing of arms by imperial subjects, they served in Rome's armies and rose to the highest military office, especially in the fourth century. In particular the reigns of Constantine the Great and Theodosius the Great marked important advances in this process of germanizing the imperial armies. These "Roman" Germans were frequently used to fight the free German enemies of the state. German slaves in great households and German habits also became more common among the Romans. Soap, a barbarian invention, began to replace olive oil for cleanliness.[24] Trousers, previously thought of as barbarian or effeminate dress, became common as an article of apparel; the Emperor Severus Alexander in the early third century is said to have preferred white trousers to red; in the late fourth century the Emperor Honorius indignantly prohibits wearing them in public in Rome.[25] Angels in Christian art began to be blue-eyed

[23] The best work by far is still A. D. Nock, *Conversion* (Oxford, 1933).

[24] F. S. Taylor, in *A History of Technology,* ed. by Charles Singer *et al.,* II (New York, 1956), 355–56.

[25] *SHA Alex.* 40. 11 (contrast Tac. *Hist.* 2. 20; Quintil. *Inst.* 11. 3. 144); *CTh* 14. 10. 2; S. Dill, *Roman Society in the Last Century of the Western Empire,* 2d ed., p. 297 with n. 4.

blondes, and ladies on earth came to sport blond or red hair or wigs.[26] The private armies of the great generals of the fifth century and later, the *bucellarii,* are probably related to the German institution of the *comitatus,* the group of warriors which a successful German war chief gathered about himself.[27]

While some Romans had no particular misgivings about accepting Germans, or at least peaceful Germans, others were not so charitable. Their dislike ranged from complaining that the Germans stank to more radical extremes.[28] Using modern concepts many historians have not been slow to see nationalistic or even racial phenomena here. But the ancients had little or no racial prejudice as such; although Negroids and Mongoloids were known to them, examples were so rare as to excite only curiosity, or at most perhaps derision. The peoples of the Mediterranean belonged to many subvarieties of Caucasoids, but thanks in large part to the intermarriage of countless migrations that had occurred over hundreds of centuries of dim prehistoric time, individual differences were so wide-ranging in these groups as largely to obviate the anti-otherness reflex which in primitive prehistoric time may have had some value as protection. As previously remarked, nationalism has far too many erroneous connotations of other, later, ages to be a useful concept for comprehension. What the ancients did have was an emphatic cultural prejudice; non-Greco-Romans were despised because of their lack of the graces, the education, the fluent polished Greek or Latin which the Greeks and Romans considered absolute prerequisites for a valuable person. Since this feeling of superiority did exist, it could unconsciously be used to rationalize fear of otherness proceeding from economic, or social, or political competition by other peoples, in a pattern only too well known in later ages. Fear could frequently be rationalized on religious grounds also, for while the fourth century became the fifth and paganism gradually died, and more and more of the Empire's in-

26 J. W. Thompson and E. N. Johnson, *An Introduction to Medieval Europe 300–1500* (New York, 1937), p. 81; on the whole subject, Lynn White, "Technology and Invention in the Middle Ages," *Speculum,* XV (1940), 141–56, at 143–44.

27 O. Seeck, *s.v.* "Bucellarii," *RE,* III (1899), 934–39. See the contradictory theory of the origin of the *bucellarii* expounded by P. Guilhiermoz, *Essai sur l'origine de la noblesse en France* (Paris, 1902). The subject is treated by many of the twentieth-century discussions of the origin of feudalism.

28 Salvian *Gub. Dei* 5. 21; Prudent. *Symm.* 2. 816–19. J. Straub, "Die Wirkung der Niederlage bei Adrianopel auf die Diskussion über das Germanenproblem in der spätrömischen Literatur," *Philologus,* XCV (1943), 255–86, makes out anti-German feeling too strongly.

habitants became orthodox Christians, most of the Germans became Arian heretics, in part because of historical accidents of conversion, in part, perhaps, because the barbarians were less able to understand, or less accustomed passively to accept, such subtle distinctions as those implied in the concept of the Triune God. One God with a Son, divine, but less than the Father, was easier to comprehend, even although the ultimate implications of such a belief might be unsatisfactory. Such prejudice had existed in the past against other groups, but in the past the Greeks and the Romans had been far more sure of their superiority over the barbarians, East or West, militarily or otherwise, to produce really strong and overt hostility. The unchanging otherness of the Jews, of course, especially in the Greek East, had provoked hatred which on occasion had expressed itself in riots, burnings, and murder.[29] Yet it would be very easy to overestimate anti-Germanism as a motive force in Western society and politics in the Late Empire.

As far as the cultural or intellectual life of the late ancient world is concerned, decline, or at least change, is as marked as in other spheres of human activity. In the plastic arts the standard example is the Arch of Constantine at Rome, executed to commemorate that Emperor's triumph over his rival Maxentius at the Battle of the Milvian Bridge (A.D. 312).[30] The monument was apparently erected in some haste; much of the sculpture attached to it was taken from older monuments—by no means a novel procedure at the beginning of the fourth century, it must be admitted. Some of the sculpture on the arch, however, was commissioned fresh for the purpose. Earlier generations of historians have denounced without qualms the crudity and barbarousness of these figures, especially when they were thrust into such close juxtaposition with more "classical" work. Today students are cautious, and tend to see in this work of the fourth century rather a change in the ideals of art to the conventions which were to be typical in much of the Middle Ages, in contrast to the "naturalism" and "fluidity" of earlier classical art; such things as the positioning of figures in a square, frontal manner, hieratic and rigid, formal; the importance of some

[29] On such classical prejudices see T. J. Haarhoff, *The Stranger at the Gate* (Boston, 1951 [= London, 1948]); A. N. Sherwin-White, *Racial Prejudice in Imperial Rome* (Cambridge, 1967).

[30] Recent arguments to change this date have not met with general acceptance among students.

figures shown by increased relative size, and so on, are nonclassical. Note also that this is one of the last great Roman triumphal arches, which once adorned the City in great profusion; in the future triumphal arches were to be reserved for the interior of God's churches, to separate the nave from the apse.[31] The last great classicizing "renaissance" in the fine arts had taken place in the middle of the third century under the high patronage of the Emperor Gallienus. This change to nonclassical modes of artistic expression, barbarous or not, obviously also constitutes withdrawal from, or abandonment of, a major corpus of ancient standards. Such changes can be seen in the coins; in the Late Empire these cease to carry even idealized portraits of imperial personages;[32] instead the coins frequently show lay figures decked out as possessors of imperial rank (cf., e.g., Pl. VI) and differentiated now mainly by the stamping of the appropriate name on the metal. Accordingly, although various coins and medallions (cf., e.g., Pl. I) commemorating Galla Placidia are extant, there is no cogent reason to believe that any of them displays even an idealized likeness of her. The fact is doubly unfortunate, since representations of her likeness in other forms of plastic art, such as certainly once existed, have not come down to us; although scholars have argued that various anonymous likenesses of girls or women, dating from the fifth century or thereabouts, actually represent her, all such attributions are doubtful at best.[33] One can argue that this cessation of

31 In general see, e.g., G. M. A. Hanfmann, *Roman Art,* pp. 123–24 with corresponding illusts. and further bibliography. A concise summary will be found in Albert Hoxie, "Mutations in Art," in *Transformation of the Roman World,* ed. White, pp. 266–90. For an example of the decline of artistic taste even among the wealthy in late antiquity, see, e.g., J. E. Packer, "The *Domus* of Cupid and Psyche in Ancient Ostia," *AJA,* LXXI (1967), 123–31, at 130.

32 Cf., e.g., J. B. Bury, "Justa Grata Honoria," *JRS,* IX (1919), 1–13, at 5; A. Alföldi, *Die Kontorniaten,* pp. 98–99; Felix Burckhardt, "Galla Placidia," *Schweizerische Rundschau,* XXV (1925–26), 409–19, 481–89, at 484.

33 For some possibilities see, e.g., Richard Delbrueck, *Die Consulardiptychen und verwandte Denkmäler,* Lief. 2, pl. 2, with text, pp. 87–93. A portrait on glass of three personages in a cross now at Brescia has been referred to her (sometimes the woman, sometimes the girl depicted); cf. Pier Desiderio Pasolini, *Ravenna e le sue grandi memorie,* pl. facing p. 44; Joseph [i.e., Giuseppe] Fattorusso, *Wonders of Italy,* p. 76; J. E. Crome, "Il vetro dorato della croce di Desiderio," *Felix Ravenna,* LXXXI (1960), 117–23; for large color reproductions of the glass picture, see Hanfmann, pl. LII; W. F. Volbach, *Early Christian Art* (New York, 1961), pl. 61 (pl. 60 shows the whole cross in black and white). For coins with portraits, see, e.g., R. Delbrueck, "Portraets byzantinischer Kaiserinnen," *Röm. Mitt.,* XXVIII (1913), 310–52, at 331 with fig. 8; George Ostrogorsky, *History of the Byzantine State,* pl. facing p. 16; Luigi Salvatorelli,

the practice of stamping recognizable likenesses on the coins was due to technical decline, or one can argue, or rationalize, with some art historians that the reason was a transferral of interest from individual emperors and empresses to the abstract idea of imperial power, of emperor/empress in general. This last seems doubtful, however, for in other art forms true representations of persons do occur in the Late Empire, and certainly in literature there is no reason to suspect any diminution of interest in the minutiae and particularity of individual imperial personages.

One can argue that much more indicative, because much more typical or representative of ancient culture than art, was literature. While plastic arts in later antiquity were left in the hands of not very highly regarded professionals, literature, or what purported to be literature, was practiced in all its branches not only by professionals, the most famous of whom by virtue of their skill easily found entry into the highest circles and even into the immediate imperial entourage itself, but by enthusiastic amateurs, including many personages of the highest levels of society. Most of this "literature," however, was not fit to read, whether by modern standards or by those of earlier antiquity. "Poets" composed poems which formed pictures on the page; verses were produced which obeyed all the rules of composition, codified by the assiduity of centuries of study, and which were characterized by a vapidity of content that must be sampled to be believed. Form was all, content almost nothing; the point is that almost all the mythological references had been made so many times, the cola and antitheses balanced and artfully variegated so often in centuries past, the "proper" subjects of declamation had so long engaged the attention of schoolboys and their elders, that there was very little left to

---

*L'Italia medioevale dalle invasioni barbariche agli inizi del secolo XI* (Milan, n. d.), p. 16, fig. 10; Walter Dennison, "A Gold Treasure of the Late Roman Period from Egypt," in *Studies in East Christian and Roman Art*, by Walter Dennison and Charles R. Morey, pp. 104–5 with fig. 3 = Gnecchi, *I medaglioni romani* [3 vols.; Milan, 1912], pl. XX, 2 (see here, pl. I); H. Cohen, *Description historique des monnaies frappées sous l'Empire romain*, VIII (2d ed.), 195, no. 7 (with A. Grabar, *L'empereur dans l'art byzantin*, p. 24); M. Minuzzi, "La spilla di Ténès con ritratto di Aelia Flaccilla," *Felix Ravenna*, LXXXIII (1961), 99–108 (N.B.: p. 104, the author erroneously identifies Placidia's mother); A. Chabouillet, "Observations sur deux médaillons d'or d'Honorius et de Placidie," *Rev. num.*, 3d ser., I (1883), 70–91, at 75–76. Another possibility: C. Diehl, *Ravenne: études d'archéologie byzantine*, p. 18, n. 1. On Placidia's portraits in general: J. B. Bury, *History of the Later Roman Empire*, I, 264; W. Ensslin, *s.v.* "Placidia" (1), *RE*, XX: 2 (1950), 1910–31, at 1930.

say. From time to time poets and panegyrists touched on current events to arouse the attention of modern historians, but it is ordinarily astonishing how many words are expended to convey the simplest thought. Such was the bitter end of the great traditions of classical literature. Bombast was the order of the day; imperial laws were so full of it that their very meaning was sometimes obscure even to contemporaries, as well as to modern historians. Ammianus Marcellinus in the fourth century was the last great ancient historian, in his still relatively "scientific" approach the distant heir of Thucydides, but in his style addicted to the excesses of his day—a style which amuses when it does not perplex.[34] The rhetorical tradition of the ancients was worn out and played out. It is significant, then, that the Christians still had something to say; that it was frequently theology, from which most men today turn in boredom, is irrelevant. The Christians could and did write with conviction, and were easily understood by readers or auditors who had the same interests; they were writing in order to communicate ideas, not in order that they and their friends in some precious circle might admire their mastery of all the rules and all the proper allusions. Increasingly they came to "plunder the Egyptians,"[35] to use pagan literary devices to communicate after their own purposes; Christian preachers-to-be, for example, came to study under the pagan rhetorician Libanius, himself perhaps not so bored as many of his contemporaries. The cleverness of the pagan Emperor Julian the Apostate in forbidding the Christians to frequent such pagan schools was attested by the storm of obloquy with which the Christians condemned his prohibition. Thus literature witnessed withdrawal from classical tradition in its outworn pagan form; from the classical, pagan point of view it was perverted to serve purposes which in a sense were closer to those of the original creators of those rules: the use of language to carry ideas and to sway and mold the minds of men. In particular one may note that the Greek Christian historiography so well represented by Eusebius in the fourth century was continued in the fifth. Even in the West, where education and literature were

[34] On the style of Ammianus, M. L. W. Laistner, *The Greater Roman Historians* (Berkeley, 1947), pp. 146–48.

[35] Cf. E. K. Rand, *Founders of the Middle Ages* (New York, 1957 = Cambridge, Mass., 1928), pp. 34–68.

slipping along an ever more precipitous decline, good Latin secular history was produced in the fifth century. Again, history is never simple; there are always back eddies running against the main current, and we wish we had more of the histories of Renatus Profuturus Frigeridus and Sulpicius Alexander than the brief, tantalizing excerpts preserved by their sixth-century successor, the ecclesiastical historian Gregory of Tours. Yet the most characteristic historical productions of the fifth century are the laconic and artless chronicles that we do have, and which in their concision are, unfortunately, the principal sources of our information about Galla Placidia, as about other matters, once the first decades of the century are past.

It was the great imperial crisis of the third century, then, that, more than anything else, shaped the world into which Galla Placidia was born—part of which she would try to govern for a time, as far as government was possible. But even so, the third century was not the fifth. The Roman Empire not only managed to avoid the dissolution that for a time had seemed inevitable; another century of partial, and, as it turned out particularly in the West, temporary recovery intervened.[36] In part this recovery was brought about by reaction in men's minds against the excesses of the third century; in part, presumably, by still existing strength or momentum in the weary, ancient culture of the Mediterranean world; in part, finally, by the harsh remedies imposed upon the Empire by the two strong men who reigned at the end of the third century and in the first decades of the fourth, the Emperors Diocletian and Constantine the Great. Some of their reforms worked toward halting the headlong rush to dissolution of state and society; some aggravated the maladies they were intended to cure, whether immediately or eventually. Unfortunately the imperfect state of our knowledge of the mechanisms of society and history does not permit us to be sure which reforms fell into which category. But for better or for worse the reforms were to help shape Galla Placidia's world. In typical Roman fashion ("make haste slowly"), however, they were mostly not original, but the regularizing and codifying of

---

36 The great capital losses of the ancient world in the third century, at least in the West, were never regained; Musset, *Vagues*, p. 246, n. 3, underlines the fact that the invasions of the third century stimulated the burial of vast masses of treasure on the part of the still prosperous provincials; those of the fifth rarely had the same result, presumably because of the degree of relative impoverishment.

procedures which had been used extraordinarily and irregularly to meet specific situations in the third century or even earlier. Some of them were merely the product of forces that had been at work in Roman history for centuries. The most obvious and pressing emergencies of the third century and later were military; it is not surprising that emperors who managed to confront them, including Diocletian and Constantine and their fellows, were primarily military men. In almost any age the first response of a government to a problem or difficulty is to attempt to legislate and regulate it out of existence; in any age the military way of life necessarily involves regulation of almost any aspect of existence. Small wonder, then, that emperors trained in the "army" way should have seen in the regimentation of society and a militarization of the government far beyond what had already existed in the Early Empire the main answer to the difficulties of the state.[37] Precedents for what was in fact done can be found in the traditional Roman past, as well as in institutions of German and oriental peoples in contact with or subjection to the Empire; but that military men regulated society and favored the growth of a hierarchy of class and rank seems to explain much as the application of the "army way" to the difficulties of the time.

In the Early Empire there had been two levels of the ruling class: the senators, and members of the equestrian order, or "knights" as they are frequently but anachronistically called. These latter had regularly discharged governmental duties which were usually inferior in power to those performed by senators and always inferior in terms of outward symbols of status and prestige. Senators had formed a class from which the highest administrative personnel of the Empire was recruited, although their corporate body, the Senate—also always possessing great prestige and status —rapidly lost in the Empire even the small de facto powers which it had retained from Republican days under the first Emperor, Augustus Caesar. The emperors had always tended to be jealous of the great prestige (*auctoritas*) of the Senate and its members; in the later third century emperors had been inclined to remove senators from positions of military power and entrust equestrians with such posts. What had been accomplished by the middle of the

[37] As suggested by Ramsay MacMullen, *Soldier and Civilian in the Later Roman Empire*, pp. 173–77.

fourth century, however, was not the displacement of the senators by the knights, but the absorption of the latter into the senatorial order by the conflation into one hierarchy of offices the positions formerly segregated into two groups. Senators of the Late Empire formed a class of great landowners and officeholders, whose estates were found throughout the Empire. In the Late Empire only the greatest senators regularly attended Senate meetings at Rome and spent much time in the City. It was this group above all which was most tenacious of ancient traditions, including paganism, and most conscious of the ancient power and dignity of their class. There was a strong tendency for members of great families in the West to secure a monopoly of high civilian office, although persons of low birth, adventurers, even Germans, came frequently to hold the highest military offices and to rank technically with the most exalted senators.[38] For centuries senators had borne the honorary title of *clarissimus* ("most distinguished"); in the Late Empire holders of higher offices were also called *spectabiles* ("looked up to") and, highest of all, *illustres* ("illustrious"). By the end of the fourth century several of the highest officials of the state possessed this last title of honor. It was ancient Roman custom that important decisions, public or private, should be taken only after consultation with one's friends. The emperors had naturally followed this custom; this consultation with their friends came gradually to approximate the deliberations of an executive with a council of state. In the Late Empire this imperial council came to be known as the Sacred Consistory (the "standing together," since men ordinarily stood in the Imperial Presence). The emperor, of course, could deliberate with whom he pleased, but regularly he did so with the greatest officers of state, who attended the Consistory: the principal generals of the army, or Masters of the Soldiery; the two treasurers, the Counts of the Sacred Largesses and of the Privy Purse; the Quaestor, or principal law adviser of the emperor; the Master of the Offices, or head of the imperial secretariat; and frequently the Provost of the Sacred Cubicle, or head of the imperial household, whose private and continual access to the emperor's

---

38 In general, cf. most recently, A. Chastagnol, *La préfecture urbaine à Rome sous le bas-empire.* More research into the minutiae of the relations of these two types of senators to each other is needed to clarify our understanding of the real political history of the Late Empire.

person made him a figure of great importance and power. We shall see the eunuch chamberlain Heraclius become the principal adviser of Galla Placidia's son Valentinian III.

Among the most important of the great officers of state and members of the Consistory when they were serving at the domicile of the emperor were the Praetorian Prefects; originally commanders of the household troops of the emperors, they had in the course of centuries been delegated various administrative and judicial tasks, so that they came in effect to be almost vice-emperors. In the Late Empire they were entirely removed from all command of troops and became purely civilian officers of great power. A common Latin word for the chief assistant of any official was *vicarius,* "substitute." In the course of time many of the functions of the Praetorian Prefects were necessarily delegated to their vicars. Under Diocletian these vicars were attached to various territories called dioceses, which included several provinces, such as those of Spain, for example. Constantine took the next step and also delimited the functions of the Praetorian Prefects territorially. The precise delimitation of such Praetorian Prefectures varied rather frequently in the fourth century, but there was a tendency for them to be four in number, each controlling two or more dioceses: the group farthest west, Spain, Gaul, and Britain (plus the westernmost tip of northwest Africa) was the Prefecture of the Gauls; the easternmost dioceses and provinces, curving from Thrace around to Egypt and Cyrenaica, made up the Prefecture of the Orient; the Balkan peninsula to the Danube, the smallest of the four, comprised the Prefecture of Illyricum; the rest, from the upper Danube southward, including Dalmatia, Italy, and most of northwest Africa, formed the Prefecture of Italy. Within the dioceses were the provinces ruled by provincial governors with various titles; a common term used for governors in the laws of the Late Empire was "judge," for judicial functions were an important duty of the governor. Appeals went upward, by paths which varied according to legal and historical technicalities, to the vicars, to the prefects, to the emperor himself. Sometimes the emperor tried cases himself; more often in the press of business the function was delegated to a substitute said to be "judging in sacred substitution" *(vice sacra iudicans)*. Emperors had always, and with reason, been jealous of the power of provincial governors; Augustus himself had divided the greater part of Gaul which Caesar the Dictator had conquered into three provinces and two military districts (the Upper and Lower Germanies along the Rhine, which later became provinces themselves) and had placed various restrictions on the governors of the immensely wealthy province of Egypt. Septimius Severus (193–211) had significantly divided the provinces of Britain and Syria, which had previously served as the power bases of his two rivals for the imperial throne. Diocletian and Constantine carried this process much further, so that the provinces of the Late Empire were only small fractions of the provinces of the first centuries. Their successors made further subdivisions; although sometimes two provinces might be united for administrative convenience, the basic motive remained the same, the removal of possible power bases for revolt, in accordance with the bitter lessons of the third-century chaos. There was probably another motive as well: the multiplicity of provinces, with the attendant reduction in their size and the accompanying increase in the number of officials, the emperors probably hoped, would increase the efficiency of the central government's control of the provincials. In the Early Empire the basic unit of administration had been the city, and the transformation of noncity districts, such as tribes, into cities had been favored, although not forced, by the imperial government. These cities had enjoyed a considerable degree of local autonomy, so long as they did not get into financial trouble, or so long as they did not quarrel overtly with their rival cities or act against the interests of the imperial state. In those good days the provincial governor had been seen mainly as a sort of benign umpire whenever his services were needed, and as a local agent stationed in the province to act when matters arose with which an individual city was incapable of coping. But the cities did get into trouble, above all, at first, in their basically healthy rivalry to keep up with their neighboring cities in splendor and magnificence. With the best of intentions the paternalistic government began to send in agents to unsnarl their affairs. But as the signs of the decline of the cities multiplied as the second century wore on, and of course above all in the third, the emperors came more and more regularly to interfere. The iniquitous publican or tax-farming system of the Republic had gradually been substituted by collection of taxes by the curials, the municipal aristocracy (roughly, upper middle class). But as their economic base declined, the curials became more and more prone to shirk the heavy responsibility the collection of taxes entailed, as well as the large financial outlay for the cities which the holding of municipal office (without salary, of course) necessitated. But the Empire had to collect its taxes to supply the ever more pressing needs of the state in the third century, as well as to see to it that the cities, its basic units of administration, were governed. Hence the curials came to be compelled to serve, and to make good deficiencies in the tax collections in the Late Empire. To insure their performance of these functions became a prime objective of late Roman government; there are more laws regulating the curials in the codes of the Late Empire than on any other subject. The piety of Christian emperors was compelled to restrict narrowly, if not to deny completely, even entry into the ranks of the clergy or the monks. Such was the end of the freedom of the cities of the earlier ancient world; such was almost certainly a motive of the emperors in dividing the provinces and multiplying the bureaucracy—to keep a closer eye on local matters.

Fear of rebellion also dictated another basic reform, the separation of military and civil authority. Although union of high military command with high civil magistracy had for centuries been one of the most characteristic features of Greek and Roman constitutions, Diocletian and Constantine and their successors strictly segregated the two kinds of function in fact, although in theory nearly all servants of the state were regarded as serving as soldiers. Provincial governors, vicars, and prefects did not command troops. Instead separate military commands were entrusted for the most part to military careersmen. A basic military need of the Empire had long been for a mobile military striking force. Instead of ready troops such forces had been made up ad hoc whenever a military expedition was planned, by detaching units from the frontier garrisons where most of the imperial armies were stationed in the Early Empire. This procedure had the obvious disadvantage that it required considerable time, frequently time that was spent by an invader in ravaging the provinces after he had broken through the perimeter defenses; besides, the weakening of the frontier forces in this fashion was itself an invitation to Rome's frequently restless neighbors to attack. In mid-third century the Emperor Gallienus, although the last scion of the ancient aristocracy to sit upon the throne, had perceived the difficulty and created a mobile striking cavalry force. The Late Empire, profiting from this experience, divided the army, which it raised from about three hundred thousand to about four hundred thousand men (an amazingly small army in any case for so vast an Empire with such lengthy and exposed frontiers), a necessary but further heavy burden on the diminished human and material resources of the state, into two parts: mobile field forces (*comitatenses*, "comrades" of the emperor or his generals), commanded by counts (also "comrades" of the emperors), and frontier guards (*limitanei*), lower quality troops stationed on the perimeter as the whole army had been in the past, and commanded by dukes (i.e., leaders). The legions of this remodeled army, which also included other, comparable units with a bewildering variety of names, were no longer five to six thousand men strong like those of previous centuries; instead they came to number only about a thousand effectives. Like most of these reforms, and again in typical Roman fashion, this change in size of the legion was not put through at a stroke, but gradually over many decades. The whole army was commanded by Masters, variously of Horse, Foot, Soldiers, or Both Branches, under the supreme authority of the emperor, who still in the fourth century ordinarily took personal command of major military undertakings. Those Masters who served in immediate conjunction with the emperor were named *Praesentales* ("in the Presence") and were superior in prestige or rank to their colleagues who, deprived of the divine aura, served at a distance. It will be seen later that the differing arrangements regarding these high officers in the East and the West had a considerable effect on the different destinies of the two parts in the lifetime of Galla Placidia.

By the latter part of the third century the economic chaos of the time, combined with the debasement of the coinage, had almost destroyed the traditional system of imperial taxation, created as it had been for a relatively prosperous society with a relatively stable money economy. To bypass the monetary system, property taxes were collected in kind in the Late Empire. The collection of the tax on the returns of the earth was entrusted to the chain of command of the Praetorian Prefects down to the municipal level where the hard beset curials were ultimately responsible. The subjects of the Empire were thus further burdened by the necessity of transporting large amounts of bulk goods to the warehouses of the state and from them to their ultimate destination, their consumption by the imperial troops and bureaucracy; obviously such a system offered many opportunities for graft, corruption, and chicanery. Elaborate checks, tallying and countertallying for the receipt and distribution of grain and other bulk commodities to and from the warehouses of the state, were employed, frequently in vain, to prevent the obvious opportunities for abuse. The drawing of rations (or pay) for nonexistent troops, for example, is far from unknown in the history of the armies of modern states, and the American army in the twentieth century has to take elaborate precautions against it. Tax assessments of landed property for the purpose of the equitable distribution of the annual quotas of taxes occurred only every fifteen years, and apart from the fact that this was probably too infrequent for the continuing equitable assessment of agricultural land's real value, it was in itself, in an age when a very large proportion of the servants of the state was amenable to bribery, a source of unjust hardship. The curials were caught between the upper and lower millstones; the great landowners, by corruption, or by the use of force or the threat of force from the bands of armed retainers they kept, or from the procurement of unrighteous indulgences from the helpless emperors of the West in the fifth century, were able to escape paying their proper share. The curials, therefore, to make good such tax delinquencies, had to press the less powerful to make them pay more than their share, under penalty of making good the deficiencies themselves. In the fifth century the priest Salvian would write that "every curial is a tyrant"; the observation is probably true, but the fact is that the curials were as much oppressed as oppressing. The result was, inversely to the situation in most modern states, that those least capable of paying paid the most, while the most capable paid the least. With the partial economic revival of the fourth century, more and more these taxes in kind were commuted into money payments once again (*adaeratio*). Whether it was the bureaucrats or the taxpayers who favored this commutation,[39] we may be sure that, one way or another, it was the common taxpayers rather than the bureaucracy who suffered.

Commutation to money payments was rendered possible in the

[39] See Mazzarino, *Aspetti, passim*, for a discussion of this aspect of the matter, with bibliography; see also A. Piganiol's review of Mazzarino's book, *Journ. des savants*, 1955, pp. 5–15, at 6–7.

fourth and fifth centuries in large part by the monetary reforms of Diocletian, whose efforts in this direction were revised by Constantine to such good effect that the state possessed once again a sound and stable coinage, which for many centuries merited and received the respect even of peoples far removed from the Empire, whether Roman or its medieval eastern Byzantine successor state. And some subsidiary taxes in fact were always collected in money, or precious metal, levied upon towns, the merchants and artisans in them, and upon the senatorial order. It was these taxes which fell mainly to the competence of the Count of the Sacred Largesses and his own bureaucracy throughout the provinces. The Count of the Privy Purse on the other hand obviously supervised the vast crown lands of the Empire, but historical accident distributed to each department a motley array of functions which, aside from their historical development, had no other apparent connection among them. And the bureaucrats of both services, the laws of the Late Empire tell us with emphatic repetition, also abused their position to exploit and to rob the taxpayer, and to corrupt other officials of the state who might be tempted to denounce them. The state and emperor owned mines, factories for the manufacture of arms or cloth, stud farms for the breeding of horses; these were erratically distributed between the departments of the two great treasurers. But whether through their offices or those of the Praetorian Prefects, the revenues of the state, as a historian once remarked of the Old Régime in France, were carried in a leaking bucket. Statistics are lacking, as is usual for antiquity, but one gains the impression that a very large portion of the revenues collected on behalf of the state never reached the disposition of the government.[40]

In an age requiring great expenditures for military, bureaucratic, and courtly costs (these last by no means merely due to the emperors' love of luxury and ceremony), when the general economic level of the Empire was trending more or less rapidly down-

---

[40] In general see A. H. M. Jones, *The Later Roman Empire,* chap. 13 and *passim.* There seems to be no recent monograph on the general financial administration of the Later Roman Empire; one must make do with the old book of Léon Bouchard, *Étude sur l'administration des finances de l'empire romain dans les derniers temps de son existence;* see also A. Piganiol, *L'impôt de capitation sous le bas-empire romain;* F. Lot, *Nouvelles recherches sur l'impôt foncier;* A. Déléage, *La capitation du bas-empire* (Macon, 1945); and another old book: Rudolf His, *Die Domänen der römischen Kaiserzeit.*

ward, it is little wonder that a major preoccupation of the imperial
government was revenue, so much so that historians can speak of
the fiscality of the policy of the later emperors. The question arises,
as in the similar case of the fat man, whether the Empire survived
to tax, or taxed to survive. Economics affected foreign policy; if
the Empire's enemies were bought off instead of fought, frequently
the decision was based on the fact that the buying off was fiscally
preferable. Above all, the domestic policies of the Empire were
drastically affected. Not only did the emperors decree ever more
ferocious penalties against malfeasance in financial administration
—measures whose repetition proves their inefficacy—almost their
entire social policy seems largely dictated by fiscal considerations.
The number of taxpayers must not be reduced; hence before the
end of the reign of Constantine the sharecroppers are attached to
the soil they till; like the serfs of the Middle Ages they may not
leave their farms. Since this sort of sharecropping has become the
principal means of the exploitation of the land, agricultural slaves
tend in fact to be assimilated to the same condition. The curials
must stay on to assure the collection of taxes. Like the peasants their
status has become hereditary, and they are forbidden with ever
more stringent desperation to change. The state requires manu-
factured products; the peace of the great cities of the Empire, above
all Rome and Constantinople, must be assured by keeping their
people content; hence those responsible for furnishing crucial
goods and services, bread-baking, grain transport from Africa or
Egypt, must suffer their activities to be regulated in detail, must
be forbidden to change occupation, and finally, in order that the
supply of such persons may not decline from natural attrition of
their numbers, their marriages and the occupations of their children must be regulated to the same end. The theoretical, un-
expressed ideal is one of no change in such matters, forever. Again
the repetition of legislation attests the failure of the government
to control natural economic and social processes by mere fiat.
Everyone, it almost seems, steals, cheats, lies; secret police under
the Master of the Offices, stationed in government agencies, must
watch and spy on officials and bureaucrats; administrative em-
ployees must be made responsible for delicts along with the magistrate they serve.

And regularly, despite all this regulation of more and more

facets of human life, this attempted wholesale destruction of the individual liberties of past ages, people did find it possible to change.[41] Bureaucratic as the late Roman state became relative to what had gone before (with the possible exception of Ptolemaic Egypt in the last three centuries B.C.), it simply did not possess the technological resources to regiment the acts of men and regulate their thinking which twentieth-century states have used much more successfully, although still imperfectly, to attain these ends. In all probability, also, it lacked both a sufficient supply of sufficiently educated persons to serve as bureaucrats,[42] and sufficient financial resources to pay them, to make it economically feasible to use enough personnel for regulation rather than in directly productive occupations. The failure to use bureaucrats exclusively, hence the need for municipal curials (themselves taking the place of tax-farmers), to collect taxes is probably significant. We cannot think that for many centuries the Roman government failed to perceive the obvious disadvantages of the curial system, or that it would not have employed professional servants of the state to collect taxes, had the practice been feasible. So the curials, in theory, collected the taxes in their spare time while they, again in theory, supported themselves and directed their private socially productive affairs as their main business. Yet the state tried mightily to regulate; unfortunately the end result, largely, was that its regulatory efforts were felt as tyranny and the thwarting of individual hopes of betterment and the good life, while the relatively good purpose aimed at—the stabilization of economy, society, and politics—did not come about, and in its attempts the government merely stimulated more alienation, more withdrawal, active or passive, from the ideas and ideals it was trying to serve.[43] While the state became ever less successful at procuring the peace and order which the ruling classes had for centuries considered to be its prime purpose, the masses of its subjects, suffering from the oppression entailed by its attempts to do these things with dwindling means and with

41 See above, n. 18.

42 On the education of bureaucrats in the Late Empire, see esp. Ramsay Mac-Mullen, "Roman Bureaucratese," *Traditio*, XVIII (1962), 364–78.

43 "Confucius said, 'Guide the people with governmental measures and control or regulate them by the threat of punishment, and the people will try to keep out of jail, but will have no sense of honor or shame . . . ,' " *The Wisdom of Confucius*, ed. and trans. by Lin Yutang (New York, 1938), p. 198. "Mavult quilibet inprobus execrari legem quam emendare mentem," Salvian *ad Eccles.* 4. 49.

at best superficial understanding of the problems it really faced, more and more easily embraced heresies which revolted from the state's religion, or barbarian rule which rudely ended the state's torments, or secession movements which threw off alike its laws and its ruling classes.[44]

It has been remarked above that Christianity in important respects afforded a socially respectable, accepted avenue of withdrawal, even though the emperors in many cases found it necessary to shut, or almost close, the more obvious and open means of withdrawal to God. Whether Constantine the Great, first Christian emperor, accepted his new faith out of conscious statecraft, to use Christian unity and strength as props to his throne and as a resource against his rivals, or whether he became convinced that Christ was more powerful in this world and the next than were the ancient gods is a subject of controversy today.[45] However that may be, it is fairly certain, as has been remarked, that "there were no freethinkers in the fourth century." Indeed, the pagan world had been trending toward monotheism for some time. The ancient gods of the traditional religion of Greece and Rome had long been dying; even Plutarch, long before Constantine, had observed the phenomenon with some dismay. Plutarch records that a traveler had heard voices crying out, "Great Pan is dead!"[46] Syncretism, the identification of one god with another, and the teachings of Platonic philosophy, the leading non-Christian system of thought in late antiquity, with its theory of the ultimate unity of real existence, had largely converted pagan believers to acceptance of monotheism under diverse external divine forms; modes of thought not dissimilar to the Christian had thereby unwillingly been favored.

Some of Constantine's predecessors had emphasized one god or one aspect of the divine at the expense of others. A common choice

[44] What those peasants involved in the movement of the Bacaudae thought of the much vaunted Roman law is well expressed in the play *Querolus*, p. 58 (Hermann).

[45] N. H. Baynes, *Constantine the Great and the Christian Church* (London, 1930); and A. Alföldi, *The Conversion of Constantine and Pagan Rome* (Oxford, 1948) among many others in a large monographic literature; for a concise summary of the problem, see H. M. D. Parker, *A History of the Roman World from A.D. 138 to 337*, pp. 291–304.

[46] *Defec. orac.* 419C–D; whether this report rests on a misunderstanding of something quite different, as has ingeniously been conjectured, is irrelevant here; Plutarch understood it as indicated in the text, where it is used symbolically.

was the Unconquered Sun; before his acceptance of Christianity Constantine himself had been attracted by Sol Invictus. But Christ, in Constantine's belief, had shown his power by defeating Maxentius at the Milvian Bridge. Constantine proclaimed toleration of Christianity, not quite the first emperor to do so, and in the latter years of his reign became more and more convinced by his new faith. On his deathbed he was baptized a Christian, unfortunately by an Arian heretic (the fact was resolutely overlooked by most of his successors who at Constantinople continued for more than a thousand years to venerate the memory of the first Christian Emperor). In fact, most of Constantine's successors in the East were more or less of Arian sympathies in the fourth century, until at its end Galla Placidia's father, Theodosius the Great, inaugurated a series of firmly orthodox Caesars. Theodosius also made Christianity the sole acceptable religion of the state. Students have variously evaluated the Christianization of the emperors. Certainly the small fraction of the Empire's inhabitants already Christian before Constantine was joined by a stampede of timeservers who wished to profit by association with this group newly rejoicing in imperial favor, and the Church thereby lost something of the pristine fervor and purity of faith of early times (although every persecution of the past had shown that not all the members of even the early Church had been willing to witness their faith in their blood). Did the Church serve even in part to support, to animate the dying Empire? Did it not, rather, offer the opportunity for withdrawal previously mentioned, and did it not distract the Christian emperors by stridently involving them in its ceaseless disputes, usually about extremely abstract and at least obviously impractical questions? No final answer can be given these questions in terms of objective proof; Christian historians will, presumably, if their curiosity continues, have an opportunity to interrogate Ultimate Authority for the answers. At least, however, the Roman government in the fourth and fifth centuries became ever more oriented toward favoring the Church; gradually as time passed more and more men became Christian in varying senses and degrees of fervor, conviction, and accuracy of response to the teachings of Christ. More and more men came to find in their faith a security which armored them against the misfortunes of their lives and their age; for many Christians this continuing process far outweighs the fate of the transient phenomenon which was the Roman Empire, state, society, and culture.

Theoretically, and as far as one man can be supreme over his fellows, at the terrestrial summit of all human hopes and ambitions was Our Lord the Emperor—Imperator, Invictus, Augustus, among other things. However one may analyze the real motives and purposes of the first Emperor Augustus, he had seen fit to conceal his real power, more or less, behind a facade of the continuing constitution of the Old Republic. But even in China, England, or Rome, with all their conservatism, appearances eventually catch up with reality. The stresses of the third century completed the exposure of the Republican sham, or rather, completed the process of making it irrelevant to the prejudices of men; insofar as there was hope of escape from that crisis in this world, men naturally found it in the source of real power. The Greeks had always forthrightly referred to the sovereign of Rome as *basileus,* king, in preference to the translation of Latin *Imperator* by *Autokrator.* In the Late Empire Latin *rex* (king) and *regnum* (reign, kingdom), in Republican usage reserved for foreigners or for the vilification of one's domestic enemies, were applied without malice to the emperor and his regime.[47] But something more was needed; the early emperors had reigned by a power based partly on law, partly on their own prestige (*auctoritas*) and that of their exalted position. But the third century, at the same time it had largely destroyed the last vestiges of real respect for the abstract traditions of the law and constitution of the Republic, had also cheapened and debased the imperial position itself. Divine emperors who were made and unmade almost over night, whether by the dagger of an assassin or the insurrection of a greedy and contemptuous soldiery, inspired less and less respect. Men had too often seen the prince, despite the ever more splendid titles of power and majesty attributed to him in the third century, dragged from his throne, the pinnacle of human greatness, and trampled, sometimes literally, in the dust. To preserve himself and the Empire from this dangerous cheapening Diocletian sought a new resource or mystique of power, a new means of establishing the charisma of

---

47 E.g., W. Suerbaum, *Vom antiken zum frühmittelalterlichen Staatsbegriff.* On the position of the Late Roman emperors in general, see M. A. Wes, *Das Ende des Kaisertums im Westen des römischen Reichs,* pp. 25–51.

awe and respect by which monarchs more or less consciously impose upon the mass of their subjects the pretense that they are basically different from ordinary men; such pretenses seem to be a necessary part of the apparatus of all higher political authority. Again, conservative Illyrian-Roman that he was, Diocletian seized upon a tendency and drew it to its logical conclusion. Almost from the beginning the emperors had come gradually to surround themselves with the pomp and circumstance of ancient royalty, drawing regularly upon the usages of the ancient and contemporary Orient for procedure and protocol.[48] Diocletian and Constantine after him installed the full apparatus of eastern royalty at the Roman court, even although by virtue of the emphasis on things military in the Late Empire it was frequently referred to as "the camp" (*castra*). The emperor's Person became Sacred; by extension all things about him were Sacred, or Divine Imperial. He dwelt in a Sacred Palace; he took counsel with his Sacred Consistory. Those fortunate enough to be admitted to the Sacred Presence for a Silence (i.e., imperial audience, for ordinarily one did not speak in the Presence), performed deep obeisance, prostration, before the imperial throne, and were graciously allowed to kiss the purple, that is, the hem of the Sacred Robe. Constantine took the logical step of adding the diadem, no longer the mere ribbon that had bound the locks of ancient Greek kings, but an elaborate headdress adorned with pearls and other precious stones. When the emperor signed his name or jotted a note on the margin of a document he did so with his divine hand; the precious fact was duly noted in subsequent copies of the document. The imperial purple, worn originally by eastern kings, the gods of Rome, the triumphing generals of the Republic, and by the early emperors for state purposes, was now richly embroidered with gold thread (this addition had already been made in the later Principate) and sewn with precious gems. Ceremonies of the court involved the presence of serried

---

48 The standard articles of A. Alföldi cited above, n. 22, are supplemented by O. Treitinger, *Die oströmische Kaiser- und Reichsidee nach ihrer Gestaltung im höfischen Zeremoniell: Vom oströmischen Staats- und Reichsgedanken;* W. T. Avery, "The *Adoratio Purpurae* and the Importance of the Imperial Purple in the Fourth Century of the Christian Era," *Mem. of the Am. Acad. in Rome,* XVII (1940), 66–80; much relevant material in Delbrueck, *Consulardiptychen;* and *idem,* "Der spätantike Kaiserornat," *Die Antike,* VIII (1932), 1–21; cf. *idem, Spätantike Kaiserporträts.* See now, esp. Francis Dvornik, *Early Christian and Byzantine Political Philosophy: Origins and Background.*

ranks of officials in appropriate costumes and other symbols of rank and function, and centered upon the imperial person like the solemn hieratic rites of a religious cult. The Christian emperors by no means ceased to be "divine" or "sacred"; they were no longer gods, but the representatives of God on earth; they would come to be regarded officially, at least in the Byzantine East, as *isapostoloi*, the "equals of the apostles."

Thus the imperial majesty was restored, and the effect intended was apparently attained; at least, attempted or successful usurpations never again in Roman and Byzantine history became so common as they had been in the third century. Since men are ruled by words and symbols, one may safely attribute this desirable result in some part to this system, a system which was more or less adequately copied by all succeeding courts of Europe, and in fading splendor and formality persists in such courts to our own day. Nevertheless a price was paid for sacred grandeur; emperors once again were undoubted objects of veneration and awe to most of their subjects, but of their own will they necessarily walled themselves off from those they ruled. For the most part they saw only their ministers, the members of their court, and the servants of their luxury and their persons. They tended to know and see their Empire only through the eyes of such individuals and the reports of their administrators. But these ministers and servants held office in a day when the servants of the state commonly dispensed with integrity as an outmoded habit. Even the strongest and most forceful monarchs had difficulty in penetrating the web of glozing deceit woven about them by their courtiers. At all times "absolute power" as attributed to one man is a laughable misnomer for the numberless limitations under which his theoretically unlimited authority is exercised; even the most honest and courageous of courtiers hesitates to tell unpleasant truths to a man whose frown can ruin a career. The emperors themselves regularly tried in vain to remedy the multitude of abuses and injustices in their dominions; the colossal weight or inertia of bureaucracy was too much for one man, or one woman, to move—even at best, that is when that bureaucracy is composed of a majority of honest and conscientious civil servants. And this condition did not obtain in later Rome. The insulation provided by the walls of his palace made the emperor's hopeless task more hopeless still. The emperor must always fear lies, self-seeking, treason, insurrection, assassination. Whom could he trust? The emperor was like a blind man who knows that many of the guides on whom he must rely many times lie to him about his environment. But which ones at which times? Persons whom the emperor came to fear not uncommonly met terrible deaths. But the object of politics in an absolute monarchy is the manipulation of the monarch. The penalty for failure could be death, but success would bring wealth and power almost without end; business at court was regularly conducted amidst intrigues, lies, slander, libel, and corruption. Some such cases were scandalous enough to be detailed in written history. The classic example is that of Count Romanus, who through his "friends" at court and additional corruption caused the sincere but choleric Emperor, Valentinian I, Galla Placidia's maternal grandfather, to punish in frightful fashion the innocent victims of the Count's oppression in Africa for making a "malicious" accusation against a person the Emperor had been made to believe was merely doing his duty.[49] Galla Placidia was to have to cope with this kind of politics with the added handicap of being a woman, the mother of a child emperor, and the de facto successor of her brother who had rarely, if ever, tried to govern for himself, but had supinely left the conduct of affairs in the hands of his ministers and favorites. If the latter were sometimes able and dedicated men the fact reflected little credit upon the Emperor Honorius. We shall also see that in Galla Placidia's day the power and selfishness of the great aristocratic landowners of the West was increasing to an alarming extent which further limited the effective exercise of imperial authority.

Like many another Roman or Byzantine imperial dynasty, the family of Galla Placidia was not of ancient lineage, but rose to prominence only in the middle of the fourth century. The Emperor Constantine the Great died in 337, leaving his power to be inherited by his sons, after the latter had profited by a massacre of nearly all the other relatives of their late father who might prove dangerous. Of the three sons, the cold, reserved, and suspicious Constantius II survived his two brothers who had perished from

---

49 The Case of Count Romanus is well summarized by N. H. Baynes, *CMedH,* I, 227–28, where the scattered passages, mainly from Ammianus Marcellinus, are brought together.

mutual rivalry and from rebellion. Sole Emperor, Constantius was succeeded, not without various difficulties, by his only surviving close male relative, the short-lived pagan, Julian the Apostate. From his own several marriages Constantius left only a posthumous daughter. Julian was slain doing battle with the Persians (363), and his successor Jovian purchased a disastrous retreat by the ignominious cession of no small extent of Rome's eastern territories. But the next year, on the march across Asia Minor, the new Emperor died suddenly, apparently suffocated by fumes from a faulty stove, and the imperial throne once again was vacant (16 February 364).

After considerable deliberation, not without its intrigues among the commanders and generals of the army, the choice fell upon an officer named Valentinian, the son of a Pannonian peasant named Gratian, who had risen by his merit to high military rank. By his ability and caution Valentinian had managed to weather Constantius' suspicions of Julian as well as the latter's devotion to the ancient gods, despite his own obvious acceptance of Christ. His firm and resolute character was bespoken on the very day of his accession. When the soldiers urged him to name a colleague, he proudly reminded them that by their own act he alone now possessed the right to command. Nevertheless when in his continuing westward march he reached Hebdomon, a suburb at the seventh milestone west of Constantinople, he raised his brother Valens to share the imperial throne (28 March 364). Shortly thereafter Valens, who never forgot that his brother was his senior and his benefactor, was given the East, while Valentinian I assumed the government of the West. Both Emperors were Christians with some aversion to pagans which, however, they did not erect into a policy. Yet in orthodox Christian eyes Valens was disgraced by his favoring the Arian heresy; right-thinking Christians were to see in his terrible end divine retribution for his falling away from the true faith of Christ. The Eastern Emperor, although having to face further difficulties from Persia, unsuccessful rebellion, and treason which his own sour suspicion largely precipitated, was to rule until 378. The reign of Valentinian was marked by the successful defense of the western frontiers against the barbarians, and, domestically, by a savagery which tried to repress the abuses of the time. On 17 November 375, the Emperor was so enraged by the freedom of speech which some barbarian envoys presumed to use to his face, that he suffered a stroke of apoplexy and expired shortly thereafter.

By a first marriage Valentinian had had a son, born in 359 and named Gratian after his grandfather. When Gratian was eight years old a serious illness of Valentinian prompted the latter to proclaim the boy Augustus. At his father's death Gratian was sixteen years of age. Valentinian, however, also had another surviving son. By a somewhat irregular union with Justina, the relict of a man named Magnentius who had unsuccessfully usurped the imperial dignity in the reign of Constantius II, he had had several children—Justa, Grata, Galla (the future mother of Galla Placidia), and a boy named Valentinian.[50] Although Gratian was already Emperor in law at his father's death, the boy Valentinian, a child of four, was also proclaimed Emperor in Illyricum where he was living with his mother Justina. The purpose was presumably to secure the loyalty of the Illyrian army; Gratian accepted the accomplished fact and the theoretical reign of Valentinian II also began. During the latter's short lifetime, however, even after Gratian's death, he was seldom if ever in reality to exercise the uncontrolled power of an Augustus, even at a time when he was the senior Emperor in precedence, as inscriptions listing imperial honors dutifully record by putting his name and titles first. The Emperor Gratian had married as his first wife the posthumous daughter of Constantius II;[51] she bore him no children who lived, nor did his second wife, Laeta, who survived him. But this first marriage connected, however remotely, the house of Valentinian with the family of the revered Constantine the Great;[52] later Galla Placidia would not forget this distinguished connection as a source of the legitimacy and prestige of her family.

Shortly after the accession of Gratian and Valentinian II events occurred in the East which were suddenly to terminate the reign of Valens and, much more importantly, to initiate a series of calamities which in the sequel were to bring about the collapse of the

---

50 Soc. *HE* 4. 31. 19.

51 Am. Marc. 21. 15. 6, 29. 6. 7.

52 Note how Ambr. *Ob. Theod.* 40, consoling, remarks that not only will the dead Emperor be reunited with previously deceased members of his family, but he will also be united with Constantine; cf. also *ibid.* 41–51 in praise of Constantine and especially of his mother Saint Helena.

Western half of the Roman Empire. These same events in the East were to elevate Galla Placidia's father, Theodosius, to the imperial throne as the successor of her great-uncle. In the year 376, to the north of the imperial frontier along the lower reaches of the River Danube dwelt a German tribe, the Visigoths, and to the east of them the closely related people of the Ostrogoths. These Gothic peoples had been domiciled in this region for some generations, after a migration which in the lapse of centuries had brought them from northern Europe. A few years before this there had come to the Empire and its neighbors in Europe news of a new kind of barbarian—little yellow men who gashed their faces with scars to make them seem more ferocious to their foes, and who were said to spend almost their whole lives on their wiry steppe ponies, which in turn gave them great mobility as a striking force. Thus the Huns first appear in European history, although they may, centuries before, have been among the causes of the building of the Great Wall of China to keep them out of that empire at the other end of the earth. They met the Ostrogoths in battle and completely overthrew that people; the Ostrogothic chief Hermanric committed suicide. The Visigothic chieftain Athanaric, whose people had been involved in various hostilities with the Roman Empire in the past, seemed unable to cope with the situation; in their terror of the Huns many of his people petitioned Valens for permission to cross the Danube into the apparently safe haven of the Empire; in return they would serve in the imperial armies and help defend the Empire against its foes. Valens and his ministers were flattered by this appeal and the promises of military support that came with it, and gave permission to the Visigothic chiefs, Fritigern and others, to cross the frontier and settle in Thrace. In the autumn of 376 the Visigoths crossed the Danube. Some were safely dispersed to service in other parts of the Empire, but the majority remained in the European provinces of the East, south of the Danube. When, because of the supply difficulties involved in victualing so large a number of people, hunger and outright starvation began to be felt among them, the Roman officials concerned, in a fashion much too characteristic of their kind, mercilessly exploited the misery of the Goths, selling them dogs at the rate of one dog in exchange for one Visigoth given over into slavery; among the persons thus sold into servitude by their un-

Boundaries of The Roman Empire
Boundaries of the Prefectures
Other Boundaries

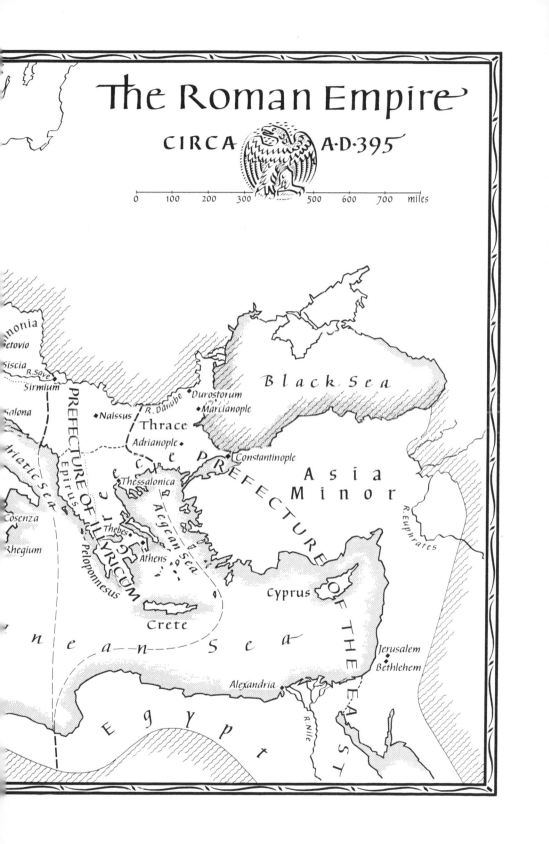

# The Roman Empire

## CIRCA A·D·395

0   100   200   300   500   600   700   miles

Pannonia
Petovio
Siscia
R.Save
Sirmium
Salona

PREFECTURE OF ILLYRICUM
Epirus

Naissus
R.Danube
Durostorum
Marcianople

Thrace
Adrianople

Thessalonica
Aegean Sea
Thebes
Athens
Peloponnesus
Crete

Constantinople

PREFECTURE

Black Sea

Asia Minor

R.Euphrates

Cyprus

PREFECTURE OF THE EAST

Adriatic Sea

Cosenza
Rhegium

Mediterranean Sea

Jerusalem
Bethlehem

Alexandria

R.Nile

Egypt

fortunate parents there were, we are told, even some children of the highest ranking personages among the Goths.[53]

Unfortunately for the Roman Empire, it was one thing for its greedy officials to exploit its docile, unarmed subjects, quite another to oppress a free people practiced in the use of arms. In the resulting disturbances and confusion more barbarians crossed the river, including some Ostrogoths under their own chiefs. When several Visigoths were massacred at a banquet given by the Romans at Marcianople, the Goths rose in open revolt against the tyranny and cruelty of the Romans; slaves, including Goths sold into servitude, joined the insurrection. When the local forces of the Empire, even reinforced, were unable to restore what the Romans understood by peace and order, the Emperor Valens himselm left Antioch in the spring of 378 and marched to Thrace. Assistance had also been asked from Gratian in the West, and was on its way. This force, hampered by various intrigues as well as the incompetence of some of its commanders, was too late. Valens was eager to enjoy the unshared glory of a Gothic triumph; in a tactical situation adverse to the Roman army and aggravated by the cleverness of the Gothic commander, battle was joined near Adrianople (9 August 378). Valens himself paid the penalty for his vainglory, as did many high officers; the Emperor may have been burned alive in a hut in which he had taken refuge, but the precise manner of his death is not certainly known. His army was annihilated as a force in being; so great a military disaster had not befallen the Roman arms since the Battle of Cannae, six centuries before. From this time onward the Roman Empire was never to be free, at least in its western parts, of armed, organized bands of barbarians within its frontiers. The process which would in a century witness the disappearance of the imperial state itself in all its western dominions had begun. The vigorous manpower of the Republic after Cannae had eventually been able to expel Hannibal, a military genius, from the soil of Italy and to defeat him decisively. The resources of declining Rome were incapable of such a feat, even against foes so inferior to Hannibal as were the Gothic chiefs. It is to be emphasized that the strength of the barbarians was a mortal menace only to the weakness of Rome; in the

[53] Am. Marc. 31. 4. 11.

heyday of her strength and power she had decisively vanquished foes far more able, far better organized and disciplined, and far more numerous than the barbarian hordes which now preyed upon her.[54] Even in this last agonized century of her life as Empire, and despite the decay of her military system, given ordinarily competent command, Rome was still capable of beating the barbarians when her armies met them under conditions of approximate parity in the field.

Some of the remnants of the Roman army, together with those surviving officers who retained their wits, took refuge behind the impregnable walls of Adrianople. A Gothic move against Constantinople failed; the barbarians remained masters of the open countryside, but in their ignorance of the art of siege warfare were unable to take the walled cities of the land. The Emperor Gratian was wise enough to realize that amidst the necessities of government and defense of the West against its own barbarian foes, he could not simultaneously rule the East. In this emergency he turned to a soldier from Spain, named Theodosius, who despite his previously exhibited military talents was rusticating on his estates, under a cloud because of court intrigues. At Sirmium (near modern Belgrade), on 19 January 379, Gratian raised Theodosius to the Empire in the East. The new supreme commander reopened organized warfare against the Goths with what troops he could scrape together as well as some contingents transferred to his command by his Western colleague. Our sources give us only the most doubtful and fragmentary information about these operations, but apparently the new Emperor was able to hold his own, although without being able to gain a decision. The aged Athanaric, who had quarreled with Fritigern, was welcomed in truly royal fashion at Constantinople by Theodosius; when he died shortly thereafter his funeral was conducted with all the pomp and circumstance of which the Roman court was capable. Apparently this gesture won Theodosius considerable favor among the Goths, and eventually in 382 a peace was agreed upon between the barbarians and the Empire. Seemingly, although the precise terms of the treaty are doubtful, the Goths received lands in Thrace along the Danube

---

[54] On the futility of the attempt to establish statistics for the numbers of the Germans, see Musset, *Vagues,* p. 235, although he may be perhaps a bit too pessimistic about the efforts of modern scholars.

and again agreed to serve in the armies of Rome—but not as individuals, rather in units commanded by their own chiefs, contingents in effect sent by an allied power which was domiciled within the borders of the Empire. This was the first time that any barbarian people had ever been granted a position of such relative independence on imperial soil; probably, however, it was the best Theodosius could do in terms of the gravely weakened resources available to him. The future was mercifully hidden from his sight. His achievement, however, was typically praised in the most fulsome tones of victory and glory, of wisdom, and of charity to the vanquished, by a contemporary panegyrist. At least, Theodosius had consolidated his position on the throne and was able to found a new imperial dynasty.

# 2

# THEODOSIUS
# THE GREAT
# AND STILICHO

The Emperor Theodosius the Great was a Spaniard, the son of a like-named general of the Emperor Valentinian I. The elder Theodosius had performed a task of great military distinction when he restored peace in the British provinces after their ravaging by assorted barbarians This done, he had forestalled a possibly dangerous conspiracy and reorganized the defenses of the Diocese of Britain. Thereafter he was assigned the task of suppressing the rebellion of a Moorish prince named Firmus in the African Diocese. Here too Theodosius was victorious; in despair the rebel Firmus committed suicide. Unfortunately the victorious general was accused of some crime; it is today impossible to tell exactly what the charge was, for contemporaries or near-contemporaries, writing in the reign of Theodosius the Emperor, were not anxious to discuss the offense, real or probably imaginary, of the Emperor's father. We may be entitled to see in this attack on the general the activities of some court coterie, with possibly some connection with an alleged magical attempt in the East to divine the name of Valens' successor.[1] At any rate the accusation was successful; at his request Theodosius was baptized to enter into glory with Christ, and was then beheaded at Carthage

---

[1] Hieron. *Chron.*, p. 330 (Fotheringham); Oros. 7. 33. 7 (note "instimulante et obrepente invidia" on the cause of Theodosius' execution); recent literature: E. Stein, *Histoire du bas-empire,* I (2d ed. by J.-R. Palanque), 511, add. n. 121; add A. Piganiol, *Les empereurs romains d'Espagne: Madrid-Italica 31 mars-6 avril, 1964* (Paris, 1965), p. 267. On the intrigues at court see also the suggestion of N. H. Baynes, *CMedH*, I, 228–29.

(376). The situation of course was not without peril for the future Emperor himself; his father's enemies, we are told, also plotted his destruction;[2] but he was allowed to retire to his estates in Spain,[3] whence he was summoned to mount the Eastern throne in the critical aftermath of Adrianople. His age at this juncture is uncertain, for the evidence about the time of his birth is conflicting;[4] but he was probably born around 346, and was thus in his early thirties at his accession. We are told that he was moderately well educated, and, incidentally, interested in Roman history.[5]

At the time of his accession Theodosius was married to the pious, clement, and orthodox Aelia Flaccilla, the daughter of Flavius Claudius Antonius, whom his son-in-law honored with the consulship in 382.[6] In 377 Flaccilla had borne her husband a son named Arcadius; a second son, Honorius, was born 9 September 384. A girl, Pulcheria, died in childhood a short time before her mother. The infant Honorius received the consulship, which he entered on 1 January 386 (a year after his elder brother, Arcadius, who had already been promoted to the nominal rank of Augustus in January, 383), but shortly after Honorius' entry upon his office Flaccilla died and left Theodosius a widower.[7] Less than two years later, the misfortunes of Theodosius' Western colleague Gratian and his family were to bring another empress-consort to the New Rome on the Bosporus.

The youthful Emperor of the West had become more and more unpopular with his subjects; he was said to be excessively devoted to the chase, to the neglect of affairs of state. Some circles averred that he was also too partial to the barbarians among his troops, to the disgruntlement of his Roman soldiers; various other policies applied in his administration of the state and army also gave offense. A devout Christian, he had refused (in this Theodosius may

---

2 Ambros. *Obit. Theod.* 53.

3 *Ibid.*; Pac. *Pan. Theod.* 9.

4 *Ca.* 346 seems the most likely date for Theodosius' birth; see A. Güldenpenning and J. Ifland, *Der Kaiser Theodosius der Grosse,* p. 52 and n. 21; G. R. Sievers, *Studien zur Geschichte der römischen Kaiser,* p. 292.

5 *Ep. Caes.* 48. 11.

6 Them. *Or.* 16, p. 293 (Downey = p. 249 Dindorf).

7 The evidence on Flaccilla and her children is collected by O. Seeck, *s.v.,* "Flaccilla" (3), *RE,* VI: 2 (1909), 2431–33, at 2432; see also L. S. Le Nain de Tillemont, *Histoire des Empereurs,* V, 192; *CP,* LX (1965), 9, n. 16.

have acted first) the title of Pontifex Maximus, which for centuries had conferred upon the emperors of Rome supreme authority over the pagan religion of the state; he aroused even more dislike among the senatorial aristocracy of the City by his order removing the Altar of Victory from the Senate House at Rome. In the spring of 383 the Spaniard Magnus Maximus, a distant relative of Theodosius, was acclaimed Emperor by the troops of Britain after his victories over the Picts and Scots. Maximus speedily crossed to the continent to do battle with the legitimate Emperor, but when the two armies came into contact in Gaul nearly all of Gratian's troops deserted to the side of the usurper. Gratian himself fled, hoping to gain the comparative safety of Italy, while the cities of Gaul closed their gates against their sovereign; at Lyons, however, he was overtaken by officers of Maximus and treacherously slain. Maximus sent embassies to his two imperial colleagues, Gratian's surviving half brother Valentinian II, at the age of twelve now by anteriority of title technically the senior Augustus, but for whom his mother Justina in effect carried on the government, and to Theodosius. At Milan Justina had acted with decision to bar the Alpine passes with loyal troops. To both courts Maximus professed to be satisfied with Gaul, Spain, and Britain, and to entertain no further ambitions for dominion beyond the Alps. After some hesitation Theodosius recognized Maximus; whether he intended merely to gain time for adequate preparations to fight the usurper and to secure his rear against the Persian foe in the East, or whether he was content indefinitely to accept the murderer of the man who had raised him to the Empire, are questions to which no certain answer can be given, and which in fact historians have answered variously according to their estimate of the personality and competence of Theodosius. Justina and Valentinian were not strong enough to act without the Eastern Emperor, and could only hope that Maximus' fear of provoking Theodosius might induce him to abide by his assurances.

This uneasy truce endured less than four years, during which even in Valentinian's part of the Empire inscriptions[8] honoring the emperors dutifully listed Maximus along with his three col-

---

8 *ILS*, 787; cf. Zos. 4. 37, there cited.

leagues (including Theodosius' son Arcadius). In 387, however, Valentinian's government made a mistake such as Maximus doubtless had been patiently awaiting. Indeed, the attitude of Maximus as he consolidated his authority in the Gauls became ever less conciliatory; he rebuffed the request, personally transmitted by Saint Ambrose, the great Bishop of Milan, to allow the body of Gratian to be taken to Italy for burial. In 387 barbarians were again troubling the province of Pannonia, and Valentinian's government asked Maximus for military assistance to restore order. Maximus sent troops, but followed on their heels to Italy. The Empress Justina was strongly in favor of the Arian heresy; she had struggled in vain with the orthodox Ambrose over this question. Now Maximus came, righteously protesting his Christian duty (in Gaul he had become the first Christian emperor to execute heretics) to support orthodoxy and true religion.[9] Before his coming the Emperor Valentinian, together with his mother and sisters, fled from Milan, and then by sea from Aquileia at the head of the Adriatic to Thessalonica (summer, 387).[10] This latter city was at that time included in the dominions of Valentinian.[11]

The orthodox Theodosius had written to Valentinian even before he learned of the latter's arrival at Thessalonica, sharply rebuking him for his Arianism, and attributing the ill fortune of the Emperor of Italy as well as the successes of Maximus to the effect of their different religious persuasions.[12] On the arrival of the fugitives from the West in Thessalonica they sent an embassy to Theodosius asking his assistance in punishing Maximus for his wrongdoing. The former came in person in response to this appeal.[13] A pagan historian, hostile to Theodosius, tells us, however, that the Eastern Emperor vacillated even at this juncture, but

9 Cf. *Coll. Avell.* 39.

10 On the chronology, see S. Mazzarino, *Stilicone: La crisi imperiale dopo Teodosio,* p. 47; O. Seeck, *Geschichte des Untergangs der antiken Welt,* V: 2, 521.

11 The question of to which emperor all or part of the Illyrian Prefecture in which the city of Thessalonica was situated belonged is controversial, but had it been Valentinian's and Justina's intention to flee to Theodosius, they would almost certainly have continued to his court at Constantinople instead of halting at Thessalonica. There is considerable discussion of the point by modern scholars; purely by way of example, see V. Grumel, "L'Illyricum de la mort de Valentinien Ier (375) à la mort de Stilicon (408)," *Rev. ét. byz.,* IX (1951), 5–46, at 11–14; Mazzarino, *Stilicone,* pp. 47–51.

12 Theod. *HE* 5. 15. 1–2.

13 Zos. 4. 43. 2; Theod. *HE* 5. 15. 3.

that Justina besought him not to leave the murder of Gratian, his benefactor, unavenged or to deprive his relatives of hope. Furthermore, the same historian says, Justina was quite aware of Theodosius' susceptibilities to feminine charms, and she dramatically exhibited to the Emperor her mourning daughter Galla, a girl described as of surpassing beauty. Under these circumstances Theodosius was much struck by the force of Justina's appeal. He asked for Galla to wife, and when he was told that in return he must avenge Gratian, the much smitten Emperor agreed to these terms, married Galla, and began wholehearted preparations for war.[14] The story thus recounted in so crass a form is clearly akin to the Greek prose romances so much beloved by the secular reading taste of late antiquity, as well as to the historian's attempt to show that even the war against Maximus, interpreted according to the most simplistic motives of personal and moral causation, proceeded from unworthy emotions on the part of the Christian Emperor. The words chosen by the historian to describe the conduct of Theodosius emphasize the weakness, sensuality, and cowardice of his character. The Christian Saint Augustine[15] more convincingly stresses the Christian piety and affection shown by Theodosius toward Valentinian. The fact remains that Theodosius did marry Galla (autumn, 387) and immediately set on foot preparations for the war against Maximus.[16] It has been pointed out that the very coming of Theodosius to Thessalonica indicates that he had determined to assist the refugees; in any case, he may very likely have seen Galla before, as early as 384 on the occasion of a visit to the West.[17] In any event, even apart from any proper feelings of gratitude and respect to Gratian and Valentinian and their family, Theodosius could not with safety allow the larger part of the Roman Empire by the overthrow of Valentinian to come into the control of Maximus. If the latter were allowed to consolidate such power, it was to be feared as likely that he would not leave Theodosius in undisturbed possession of the East.[18] There can be little

[14] Zos. 4. 43. 2–44. 4.

[15] *CD* 5. 26.

[16] Cf. Joh. Ant. Frag. 187 (IV, 609); Soc. *HE* 4. 31. 20; Marcell. *s.a.*, 386, 2 (II, 62); Philostorg. *HE* 10. 7; on the date see Seeck, *RE*, VI: 2 (1909), 2432; *idem, Gesch.*, V: 2, 521–22; W. Schild, *Galla Placidia*, pp. 8–14.

[17] Stein, *Hist.*, I, 205, 528, n. 85; J.-R. Palanque, "L'empereur Maxime," in *Les empereurs romains d'Espagne*, pp. 255–63, at 262–63.

[18] Cf. Bury-Gibbon, *Decline and Fall*, III, 163–64.

doubt, however, that the religious sentiments of Theodosius were sincere; he must deplore the Arianism of Valentinian and his family. The agreement between them must have included the renunciation of their false religious beliefs, certainly by Galla before her marriage.[19] Surely also, however, it is not to sink to the level of pagan polemic to observe that the lonely widower did not find it any the less pleasant to do his duty and protect his future because of his marriage to Galla.

Theodosius and his new wife remained at Thessalonica with Valentinian and Justina during the winter of 387/88, while the arms and resources of the East were being collected to meet Maximus. On 19 April 388, the two Emperors in all Christian piety and trepidation presumably celebrated the holy feast of Easter.[20] As spring advanced and the snow disappeared from the mountain passes of Illyricum and Italy, Theodosius set forth to the West.[21] Justina and her other two daughters, Justa and Grata, took ship for Italy and Rome; Galla remained behind in the East.[22] Apparently she was pregnant. She was not to be fortunate in her childbearing save this first time; her subsequent children were to die at birth or in infancy,[23] and she herself was to die in childbirth. It seems a fair conjecture that the reason for her being left behind was illness attendant upon a possibly difficult pregnancy. At the term of this pregnancy in 388, or possibly the beginning of 389, she gave birth to a healthy child, a daughter, who was given the name Galla after her mother, and the additional name of Placidia,[24] quite likely in honor of some relative of her father's. The family of Theodosius regularly named children after older relatives, and while neither

19 See W. Ensslin, *Die Religionspolitik des Kaisers Theodosius d. Gr.,* p. 56; with the sources cited above, n. 13.

20 Ensslin, *Religionspolitik,* p. 58; Theodosius' presence at Thessalonica is attested on 30 April (*CTh* 9. 11. 1).

21 Philostorg. *HE* 10. 8.

22 Zos. 4. 45. 4 (cf. 46. 1) certainly (in view of 43. 1) means to say that Galla accompanied her mother to Italy, but he must be mistaken (and he is not noted for his meticulous accuracy), since there is evidence (see below) that Galla was at Constantinople during her husband's absence in the West. While the sources which describe Theodosius' Western stay are relatively detailed, there is nowhere the slightest hint of the presence of his consort. In general, see Seeck, *Gesch.,* V: 2, 523; *CP,* LX (1965), 1–2.

23 *CP,* LX (1965), 9, n. 16.

24 Philostorg. *HE* 10. 7.

the name Placidia nor a variant is attested for earlier generations of the Theodosian family, variations of the name do occur in Spain.[25] In the Eastern portion of the Empire, at least in later times, she was also officially known as Aelia Placidia, apparently in honor of her father's first wife, Aelia Flaccilla;[26] the relations of Galla with her stepson Arcadius were anything but friendly; it is possibly for that reason that the coins of the East commonly suppress the name Galla, and Placidia appears on them as Aelia Placidia.[27] The fact strengthens the assumption that Placidia as well as Aelia was a name from the family of Theodosius. Presumably Theodosius was consulted (according to Roman law) about the name to be given his daughter, whether after her birth or by previous arrangement before he left his bride to undertake his western campaign.[28] We know that later on Galla lived in or near Constantinople while awaiting the return of her husband; it is not clear whether she had journeyed there before the birth of her daughter or not. It is quite possible, however, that the same presumptive condition of delicate health which dictated her remaining behind in Thessalonica instead of accompanying her husband or her mother to the West may also have required her to remain in the same city until after she had borne her child. At least a distinct possibility remains that Galla Placidia was born in Thessalonica rather than in Constantinople or its environs.[29] Before leaving for the West Theodosius had arranged that the (nominal) power in the East should be exercised by his elder son Arcadius, then a child of eleven years of age.[30] When Galla arrived to take up her residence in Constantinople, apparently she and Arcadius took a dislike to each other; or, at

[25] See the indexes of *CIL*, II, and Supp., *s.vv.* "Placidius" (*nomen*) and "Placidus" (*cognomen*); on the date of Placidia's birth, see above, Ch. I, n. 1.

[26] The name Aelia is known from Eastern coins honoring Galla Placidia: e.g., Cohen, VIII, 193, 197 (no. 14); cf. Ensslin, *RE*, XX: 2 (1950), 1910. Later Greek sources display a tendency to confuse Galla Placidia with Aelia Flaccilla; cf. Güldenpenning and Ifland, *Kaiser Theodosius*, p. 55, n. 30; A. Güldenpenning, *Geschichte des oströmischen Reiches unter den Kaisern Arcadius und Theodosius II*, p. 23, n. 2.

[27] Cf. A. A. Boyce, *Festal and Dated Coins of the Roman Empire*, p. 60.

[28] Schild, *Placidia*, p. 15 and n. 1, concludes from the language of *Chron. Pasch.*, p. 563 (Bonn) (from Galla "he [Theod.] had a daughter of the same name as her mother Galla whom he also called Placidia") that it was in fact Theodosius who gave his daughter the name Placidia.

[29] The possibility was not entertained in the argument, *CP*, LX (1965), 2.

[30] Soc. *HE* 5. 12. 9; Soz. *HE* 7. 14. 1.

least Arcadius disliked his stepmother. As a man and emperor, the kindest epithet one can apply to Arcadius is "weak," but he also possessed the petulant stubbornness and capacity to hold petty grudges which are a common characteristic of the weak. A chronicler writes rather vaguely, under the year 390, that Arcadius expelled his stepmother.[31] Whence she was expelled is not clear, but apparently either the palace or the city, or both, are meant. That there was a faction in the palace politics of Constantinople that regarded with displeasure, the pretensions, real or presumed, of the new Empress is nowhere stated, but it is by no means impossible. At least the boy Emperor was allowed to have his way in the absence of his father, and that seems hard to understand unless he had interested support at court. Whatever the actual situation may have been, it apparently did not hasten the return of Theodosius from the West, where he was making a protracted stay.[32]

In 388 Theodosius had defeated the usurper's forces at Siscia on the Save and at Poetovio. With Theodosius in close pursuit Maximus retreated into Italy and encamped at Aquileia. After another clash the pretender was forced to shut himself up in Aquileia where, however, he had no recourse but to surrender. He was hurried before the throne of the Emperor, but, possibly anticipating the clemency of Theodosius, the soldiers put Maximus to death (28 August 388). Most of the fallen rebel's partisans were amnestied; the actual assassin of Gratian committed suicide. Valentinian was restored to nominal control of the Western Empire; the death of his mother Justina, which probably occurred about this time, largely removed any fear of a lapse into Arianism on the part of the young Emperor. Despite the restoration of Valentinian, to whom Theodosius was technically junior as Augustus, the latter proceeded to legislate for the entire Empire, and was in fact hardly more superior to Arcadius than he was to Valentinian. (See Pl. II).[33] Immediately after the downfall of Maximus, Theodosius had

31 Marcell. *s.a.* 490, 2 (II, 62). One cannot be absolutely sure of the year, for sometimes by their own errors, more frequently by the errors of scribal transmission, entries in the late annals are not uncommonly misplaced; on this subject see the demonstration in the case of Hydatius by C. Courtois, "Auteurs et scribes: Remarques sur la chronique d'Hydace," *Byzantion*, XXI (1951), 23–54.

32 Certain obvious speculations about the character of Galla present themselves in this connection, but it would be profitless to discuss them without fuller information about the circumstances of this quarrel.

33 Cf. J.-R. Palanque, *Essai sur la préfecture du prétoire du bas-empire*, p. 74.

sent for his five-year-old son Honorius from Constantinople.[34] In the summer of the next year, 389, father and son paid a lengthy state visit to Rome where Theodosius, like other visiting Caesars before him, was duly astonished by the magnificence of the ancient capital, and where in turn his affability and condescension won great popularity among the people. The fact has suggested to modern scholars that as early as this time Theodosius was thinking of a day when Honorius would succeed him in Italy; presumably Valentinian would be content to rule in Gaul. At any rate, thither he was sent in 389; at his side was stationed the Frankish general Arbogast, a trusted officer of Theodosius, to exercise the talent for government and military affairs which Valentinian did not possess, or in his youth under the surveillance of his mother had never exhibited.

Theodosius was a good family man, devoted to even the more distant relatives of his house. Among the most favored members of his family was his niece, Serena, the daughter of the Emperor's brother Honorius. After her father's death Theodosius had brought her up and treated her as his own daughter, although he never legally adopted her. So great was his affection for her that, it was said, she alone could quiet the paroxysms of savage rage that could seize upon him and formed, perhaps, the worst fault of his character as a man. Theodosius had no compunctions about using barbarians in his service, even in the highest posts; after the terrible destruction that the Roman army had suffered at Adrianople his troops were more and more composed of Germans. One of these Germans was a young officer named Stilicho; Stilicho's father was a Vandal, his mother may have been Roman. At any rate Stilicho attracted the favorable attention of Theodosius, who about 384 married him to Serena, who a year or so later bore him a daughter named Maria after her own mother; thereafter the young officer's rise through the hierarchy of military command was rapid and certain.[35] Serena, evidently of a less delicate makeup than Galla, accompanied her uncle and cousin on the visit to Rome; quite possibly it was under her care that Honorius had been fetched from

34 O. Seeck, *s.v.* "Honorius" (3), *RE*, VIII: 2 (1913), 2277–91, at 2278, with the evidence.

35 On the early lives of Serena and Stilicho see the evidence collected and summarized by O. Seeck, *s.vv.* "Serena" (2), *RE*, IIA (1923), 1672–73, at 1672; "Stilicho," *ibid.*, IIIA (1929), 2523–24, at 2523.

the East.[36] Serena was again pregnant and during this Roman visit she bore a son named Eucherius after the uncle of the Emperor. We may well believe in the Emperor's delight in his grandnephew, the son of his favorite niece, as recorded several years later by the poet Claudian,[37] who draws a striking, though conventional, picture of the August Emperor, purple and all, as he dandled the baby. Some years later Serena was delivered of a third child, another girl, named Thermantia—also a family name.

From Rome Theodosius returned north to Milan at the end of summer; there even the majesty of the Emperor could be overawed by the Christian firmness of Ambrose the Bishop. Not long after the defeat of Maximus Theodosius had yielded, against his better judgment, to the demand of Ambrose that he not order the damage done the Jewish synagogue at Callinicum by Christians to be punished. The condescension of Theodosius at Rome had led the pagan senators to hope that he might consent to the restoration of the Altar of Victory to the Senate House; after some hesitation by the Emperor the influence of the saint again procured a decisive refusal. In the spring of 390 the mob of Thessalonica had lynched one of the Masters of the Soldiery for a trifling reason. Theodosius had flown into one of his famous rages and ordered a massacre of the citizens in reprisal; the order was carried out before the better sense of the Emperor could countermand it. Not until Theodosius at Christmastime publicly proclaimed his repentance in church was he readmitted by the stern and conscientious Bishop to the communion of the faithful. Such power of Christ through his church over the consciences even of the mighty announced the approach of the Middle Ages. Although she was never to be required to exhibit the spirit of Christian humility in so dramatic or public a fashion, Galla Placidia would, especially in her later life, demonstrate that she was the true daughter of the pious Emperor. And from this time onward the policy of Theodosius grew ever more severe toward the pagans.

In the summer of 391 Theodosius finally journeyed eastward to his own dominions. On the way to Constantinople the Emperor

36 When she joined her uncle is unknown; but she accompanied Honorius when he was summoned West again in 394, and somebody must have accompanied the small boy in 388/89 also.

37 *Cons. Stil.* 3. 176–81.

was compelled in Macedonia to take military action against bands of barbarian brigands who were ravaging the countryside with impunity.[38] In the company of Honorius he entered Constantinople 10 November 391.[39] Here, of course, he had to confront the difficult situation posed by the quarrel between his wife and his elder son.[40] A Byzantine chronicle tells us that, presumably on this occasion, "Placidia, having entered Constantinople with her father Theodosius, founds the household of Placidia."[41] Since Galla had been expelled by Arcadius, there can be no doubt that the infant Placidia had shared in the expulsion. One infers, therefore, that Galla, with her daughter, presented herself to her husband before his official processional entry into the city (this would be true even if the chronicler had confused Galla with her daughter) to complain of her treatment by Arcadius. And whether, as is sometimes suggested, Placidia is mentioned by error for Galla as entering the city with her father on this occasion,[42] we may fairly safely assume that mother and baby daughter were together in such circumstances, especially since the child had never before been seen by her father.

[38] Zos. 4. 48–49, a picturesque but unclear account.

[39] Soc. *HE* 5. 18. 13; cf. Zos. 4. 50. 1.

[40] Although Seeck, *Gesch.*, V: 1, 234, followed by Stein, *Hist.*, I, 210, connects the quarrel closely with Theodosius' homecoming, in view of the lapse of time between Galla's "expulsion" and the return of her husband, at least if Marcell.'s dating of the former be accepted (and even if it may be doubtful, we have no means of correcting it), it seems unlikely that it was a principal motive for not staying longer in the West. Presumably Theodosius left the West because he thought he had arranged its future satisfactorily.

[41] *Chron. Pasch.*, I, 563 (Bonn), accepted by Schild, *Placidia*, pp. 16–17. Many scholars have dismissed the statement of the chronicler as valueless; the date under which it is recorded is erroneous (hardly fatal in itself, since this sort of mistake is found in otherwise indisputably accurate entries in the *Chron.*; the entry into Constantinople in 391 is the only one which falls in the lifetime and possible presence either of Galla or her daughter), and just before, a number of quite erroneous statements are made by the author. But criticism has been centered on the supposed confusion between Placidia and her mother, despite the fact that the chronicler expressly and pointedly distinguishes between the two. Under the circumstances the rejection of the passage quoted seems arbitrary and hypercritical on that ground. And there can be no doubt about the existence of the household of Placidia which is quite independently attested in several other places. For a more detailed discussion, see *CP*, LX (1965), 2–3, with relevant notes, p. 9. For a recently published reference (6th/7th century) to the "divine house[hold] of Placidia," that is, either of Galla Placidia or her granddaughter Placidia the Younger (in the history of the property "Placidia" could well mean both), see *P. Ant.*, III, 188. 3–4.

[42] On the assumption that she had already been born, for which this passage, although important, is not the only evidence; see above, Ch. I, n. 1.

It is also difficult to avoid the inference that the establishment of a household (or house, or estate) for the child immediately after is also connected with the difficulties which had arisen between the Emperor's second wife and his son. It is to be expected that an aversion for the mother would also be extended to the daughter. It has been suggested that this estate, or part of it, was originally settled upon Galla;[43] that may well be, and there is some inherent probability that she would have an establishment of her own, like Flaccilla, the Emperor's first wife.[44] Nevertheless Galla Placidia had her own establishment, for it is referred to a few years later at a time when she was in Italy;[45] hence, apart from the chronicler's statement, Placidia probably received this establishment between the end of 391 and, at the latest, the beginning of 395, for it is improbable that she would have received property after her father's death, especially while Arcadius was still alive. It was of itself prudent that emperors provide for the economic security and well-being of their children, especially children who in the normal course of events could not be expected to succeed to the throne, for there was always a strong tendency in Roman administration for the private estate of an emperor to be absorbed after his death into the imperial domains, to the injury of his nonimperial heirs.[46] At any rate it was probably in this fashion that Theodosius attempted to keep his wife and son apart and at the same time provide for the future of his daughter and, quite likely, for his second wife as well.

43 Particularly, as seems improbable, if there be confusion between mother and daughter in this passage; cf. Ensslin, *RE*, XX: 2 (1950), 1920–21, who thinks that the *palatium Placidianum* (cf. *Not. urb. Const.* 2 [p. 230 Seeck]) may have belonged originally to Galla. This is by no means impossible, but cannot be proved or disproved.
44 *Not. urb. Const.* 12. 8 (p. 238 Seeck).
45 Synes. *Ep.* 61; it continued to exist as a separate entity within imperial properties for centuries; for references and discussion, see *CP*, LX (1965), 9, n. 14; C. du Cange, *Historia Byzantina*, II, 141–42; add the inscription *CIG*, II, 2712, better ed. by K. E. Zachariae von Lingenthal, "Ein Erlass des Praefectus Praetorio Dioscurus vom Jahre 472 oder 475," *Monatsberichte Akad. Berlin*, 1879, pp. 159–69; and cf. above, n. 41, *fin*. The term *oikos* followed by the name of its original owner is a regular description of property that has come into the estates of the emperor; cf. H. Grégoire, "Miettes d'histoire byzantine," in *Anatolian Studies Presented to Sir William Mitchell Ramsay*, pp. 151–64, at 160–64. In fact this practice goes back to the Early Empire, as Egyptian papyri demonstrate.
46 In this connection see the important remarks of H. Nesselhauf, "Patrimonium und res privata des römischen Kaisers," *Historia-Augusta-Colloquium, Bonn, 1963*, 73–93, at 80–81; the discussion is particularly directed to the circumstances of Antoninus Pius, but the remarks apply with equal validity to any Roman emperor who had children not destined to succeed him on the throne.

Theodosius thus made provision for his daughter when she was still a small child; it is not surprising that he should do so in view of the public honors, if not powers, conferred upon his sons Arcadius and Honorius. Although the latter had held the consulate when he was a baby, unlike his brother he had not yet been elevated to the imperial throne itself. On 23 January 393, when he was only eight years old, Honorius received the ultimate promotion at the hands of his father.[47] By the later fourth century Hebdomon, named from the seventh milestone from the center of Constantinople along the coast road running westward along the Sea of Marmora, had become the common scene, as it was to remain for centuries, of great imperial ceremonies, especially those requiring the presence of large numbers of troops and civilians, for which even the great churches and fora of the Eastern capital were too small. Here in particular new emperors were invested with the purple, to have the investiture ratified by the acclamation of the army. Here there was a permanent imperial tribunal to accommodate the sovereign himself; other buildings had been erected for the convenience of both imperial personages and their suites. In 393 the complex of imperial buildings, although splendid, was still quite modest in comparison with what was to rise there in subsequent centuries, but Valens had apparently constructed a small palace; Constantine the Great had erected a church in honor of Saint John the Evangelist, and Theodosius himself built another, dedicated to Saint John the Baptist.[48] Here Theodosius and his court repaired for the solemnities of the proclamation of Honorius as Augustus; years later Honorius' court poet Claudian, honoring the fourth consulship of his patron, described the ceremonies in some detail.[49] Upon the conclusion of the fortunate event the three Augusti returned in solemn pomp to the palace in Constantinople. It was a great day for the child Honorius; it was also a great and dazzling day for the little Galla Placidia, now about

[47] Soc. *HE* 5. 25. 7; Philostorg. *HE* 11. 2; Soz. *HE* 7. 24. 1; Marcell. *s.a.* 393 (II, 63); *Fast. Vind. Prior.* 521 (I, 298). The sources vary as to the precise date; I have followed O. Seeck, *Regesten der Kaiser und Päpste für die Jahre 311 bis 476 n. Chr.,* p. 281.

[48] On Hebdomon, see esp. R. Demangel, *Contribution à la topographie de l'Hebdomon;* A. Van Millingen, *Byzantine Constantinople: The Walls of the City and Adjoining Historical Sites,* pp. 67, 316–35; R. Janin, *Constantinople byzantine,* 2d ed., pp. 139–40, 446–49. Van Millingen showed long ago that the old theory that it was situated near Blachernae and the Golden Horn is quite untenable.

[49] *IV Cons. Hon.* 169–212.

four years old, for along with her brothers she rode in triumph to the plaudits of the crowd. If the letter of the description is to be trusted, like her brothers Placidia was arrayed in robes of gold and wore some sort of imperial radiate headdress,[50] although doubtless inferior in splendor to those of the Augusti, for the day when she would attain supreme rank as an Augusta was not yet. The purpose of the poet is to convey a picture of united imperial magnificence; surely it is not too fanciful to infer that the impressionable memory of a child retained the recollection of that day through the long years ahead when she would struggle so proudly and determinedly to secure imperial power and prerogatives for herself and her children. At least, the association of his small daughter with his sons on this day attests the affection and pride which Theodosius felt toward her; it was probably not solely for reasons of state policy that she in turn was to name her own firstborn child Theodosius. It was customary at this time for imperial children who had not yet received a higher imperial title to be awarded the designation, "most noble girl (boy)" (*nobilissima puella, nobilissimus puer*); at some time in her life before she became Augusta, Placidia received this title. The date is nowhere recorded, but it seems very likely that it was her father, who had thus honored her with her brothers in public and had made careful provision for her future material welfare, who also conferred this honorific upon her,[51] perhaps about this time.

One notes the absence of any mention of Galla in connection with these ceremonies at Hebdomon in 393; many reasons could be suggested, but among them is the possibility that she was again pregnant at the time. In the few years of her life remaining after the return of the Emperor from the West in November, 391, there was time for her to have borne him three more children; in fact apparently she bore him two, both boys, the one named Gratian, the other John; both children died at birth or shortly thereafter.[52]

50 *Ibid.* 203–8.

51 *ILS*, 8953, with Ensslin, *RE*, XX: 2 (1950), 1912.

52 The "Gratianus nep." of *ILS*, 818. 4 is almost certainly a child of Galla and Theodosius, for his existence is confirmed by Ambrose (*Obit. Theod.* 40); the other "Ioannes nep." is best accounted for on the same supposition (see Dessau's note *ad loc.;* note that the two names stand together). Ensslin's suggestion (*RE*, XX: 2 [1950], 1915) that "nep" as transmitted and printed in this no longer extant inscription is a mistake of the copyist for "n(obilissimus) p(uer)" must be right; it is the only remotely feasible possibility that presents itself, for "nep(os)" makes no sense.

# The family of Galla Placidia Augusta *

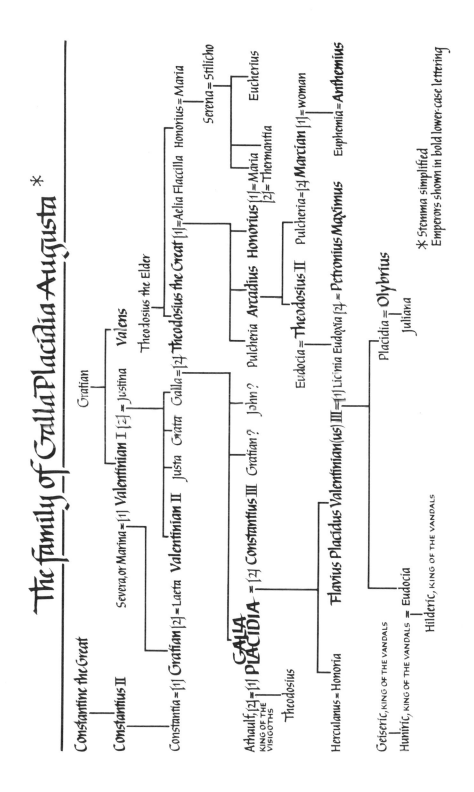

* Stemma simplified
Emperors shown in bold lower-case lettering

Galla herself died in childbirth, together with her last child,[53] about April, 394.[54] Since in his funeral oration for Theodosius[55] Saint Ambrose speaks of Gratian, the fact may mean that that child lived for a time, and that John died at birth, quite possibly the child who died with his mother in 394. Thus Galla Placidia's small triumph of 393 was followed in little more than a year's time by the loss of her mother, a loss which she was at an age to feel keenly. In the meanwhile, however, events in the West were underway to affect her future life even more decisively.

Her uncle, Valentinian II, resided in Gaul with Arbogast at his side, placed there by Theodosius presumably in order to guide the young man; perhaps, as some modern scholars have suggested, to control him. Certainly in these years Arbogast dealt energetically and successfully with German attacks across the Rhine frontier. These successes of course greatly strengthened the power of the Frankish Master of the Foot; at the same time he inaugurated a policy of favoring the pagans despite the Emperor's conscientious Christianity. Once again the latter refused the request of the Roman Senate for the restoration of the Altar of Victory, although Arbogast wished the request granted. Relations between Emperor and general progressively deteriorated; the barbarian slew an adherent of the Emperor in the latter's very Presence and despite his protection. Arbogast even contemptuously tore up an imperial order dismissing him from his post. Suddenly on 15 May 392, Valentinian was found dead. It is impossible to tell whether the crime was murder or suicide. Roman feeling might tolerate a German as the de facto ruler of the Empire; it could not be reconciled to a German emperor—at least not for centuries to come. Arbogast was shrewd enough to realize he could not ascend the throne himself; for a time he may have hoped that he might be allowed to remain the ruler of the West under the overlordship of Theodosius,[56] but

[53] Zos. 4. 57. 3; this must be the meaning of Zos., despite Güldenpenning, *Arcad. u. Theod.*, p. 309, n. 21; and T. Hodgkin, *Italy and Her Invaders*, I: 1, 2d ed., 819 n. 1.

[54] Zos. 4. 57. 3–4; Eun. Frag. 61 (IV, 42); Joh. Ant. Frag. 187 (IV, 609); cf. Stein, *Hist.*, I, 216; Seeck, *Regesten*, p. 283.

[55] *Obit. Theod.* 40; here surely the real son of Theodosius is meant in a context describing the Emperor's reunion in Heaven with his loved ones, rather than the Emperor of that name. Note that *ILS*, 818. 4, mentions both the Emperor and this boy; hence there is no doubt of the latter's existence; on Theodosius' children in general, as far as the literary evidence goes, see Tillemont, *Empereurs*, V, 192.

[56] Stein, *Hist.*, I, 211.

the silence of the Eastern Emperor was unpromising. Arbogast and his pagan friends were further alarmed by the continuing, energetic antipagan policy of the Eastern government. Accordingly, on 22 August 392, Arbogast took the fatal and irreversible step of elevating a new emperor to the throne to serve as his instrument. His choice fell upon a certain rhetorician and civil servant named Eugenius. The latter, nominally a Christian, attempted by a policy of religious neutrality to gain the support of both pagans and Christians as well as of Saint Ambrose, the redoubtable leader of the latter. Theodosius assumed the consulate for 393 with one of his subjects, rather than with Eugenius; since it was customary for a new emperor to hold the consulship for the year following his accession, this constituted public notice that the Eastern Emperor did not recognize the claims of Eugenius, who nevertheless entered upon the consulship in the West on his own authority. That Theodosius clearly understood that the pagan party in the West was behind the elevation of Eugenius was made apparent when on 8 November 392, he issued an order which forbade any celebration of pagan cult by any person of any kind, sort, or degree.[57] This law, especially when taken in conjunction with the other antipagan laws which Theodosius had been uttering during these years, is commonly and rightly taken as marking the final legal victory of Christianity in the Roman Empire. Constantine had granted official toleration and recognition of Christianity; Theodosius thus in effect made the cult of Christ the sole legal religion of the Roman state. As the Emperor Julian the Apostate is reported to have exclaimed when he lay dying a generation before, the Galilaean had conquered. It was also quite characteristically Roman that this vast legal change was brought about not by a sweeping doctrinaire pronouncement, but as an ad hoc policy devised to meet a given situation. The Greeks had exercised their quick minds by discussing first principles and had failed to govern themselves or find peace. The Romans sought practical solutions for specific problems, and administered the world.

It was in these circumstances that early in 393 Theodosius elevated his son Honorius to the purple. There can be no doubt that by this time, if not already some years before when he had inter-

[57] *CTh* 16. 10. 12.

vened in the West against Maximus, Theodosius intended that the boy should be the next Emperor in the West, if God so willed. Once again great military preparations were set on foot for a western expedition to lay low another tyrant—the epithet is almost technical language in the Late Empire for any unsuccessful rebel. Once again Arcadius was left the role of supreme power in the East, this time with a capable, although apparently unscrupulous, Rufinus, the Praetorian Prefect of the Orient, at his side. The army contained a large contingent of Visigoths with their young chieftain, Alaric, while among the Roman generals, although not in the highest command, was the Emperor's trusted relative by marriage, Stilicho. Once again the army would march to the West, where Arbogast, with smaller forces, waited on the defensive. Just before the departure of the expedition in the spring of 394 the Empress, who had been much affected by her brother's death, died in childbirth, as we have seen.[58] Honorius,[59] Galla Placidia, and Serena were also left behind in Constantinople. To judge by the sequel, Serena was probably entrusted with the care of the two children.

The armies of East and West met on the banks of the little River Frigidus (Wipbach) in northeast Italy, for gilded statues of Jupiter had been unable to prevent the army of Theodosius from defiling through the passes of the Julian Alps into the plain below. The battle was fought on both 5 and 6 September 394; the forces of the East were worsted on the first day and the Goths especially suffered heavy losses, but after a night of prayer to God Theodosius sent his troops into the battle the next day with the Bora, the savage wind, well known in these parts, falling from the mountains at their back and blowing the dust and their own weapons back in the faces of the foe. With this help from God who thus rewarded the piety of Theodosius and smote the enemies of his own Son, so the Christians triumphantly reported, and not without the intervention of various saints as well, the victory belonged to the arms of Truth. Eugenius was captured and slain by a band of soldiers; Arbogast fled the field into the mountains and two days later per-

---

[58] Eun. Frag. 61 (IV, 42); Zos. 4. 57; Joh. Ant. Frag. 187 (IV, 609).

[59] Soz. *HE* 7. 24. 1; Claud. *III Cons. Hon.* 88–89, 109–13; *IV Cons. Hon.* 385–87; *VI Cons. Hon.* 88–91. Zos. 4. 58. 1 says that Honorius accompanied his father to Italy; in the light of the reiterated contemporary testimony of Claudian, certainly known to Honorius himself, he is wrong, as not seldom, on such a detail. The ambiguity of Marcell. *s.a.* 394, 1 (II, 64) is probably unintentional.

ished by his own hand. In a time when the pagans and many ex-pagan Christians estimated divine power by its presumed practical effect on the affairs of earth, the blow to paganism, if not mortal, was staggering. Theodosius used his victory wisely, and extended clemency to most of his former foes.[60]

The Christian historians tell us that before the campaign against Eugenius and Arbogast the Christ-loving Emperor sent to a holy monk of Egypt to learn the outcome; he was told that he would triumph, but shortly thereafter lose his life.[61] And so in fact it turned out, for Theodosius survived the Battle of the Frigidus by less than half a year. Apparently in the fall of 394 the health of the Emperor began visibly and rapidly to decline. As the realization came to him that his end was not far off, he desired to see his son Honorius present in the West and, though still a child, at least nominally in possession of the power which should be his in the Western Empire, without any dangerous de facto interregnum and the ever present danger of usurpation. Entirely apart from reasons of state, however, we may be sure that the father wished to see his son[62] and his small daughter.[63] As previously remarked, it would be quite natural for the animosity of Arcadius toward Galla to have extended to her daughter; she would be much better off in any event in the charge of the beloved Serena than left to the sole care of servants in the East.[64] Hence, probably in accordance with Theodosius' instructions as well as out of her own desire to see her uncle for probably the last time, Serena brought the two children by land from Constantinople to the Emperor's residence at Milan.[65] Theodosius was greatly moved by his children's arrival; as a Christian and a ruler he had felt responsibility for the deaths of those

[60] A question debated among scholars is whether Theodosius visited Rome again after his victory; so Zos. 4. 59. 1; Theod. *HE* 5. 23. 8; Prudent. *Symm. or.* 1. 410–506; accepted, e.g., by Stein, *Hist.*, I, 217. The counterarguments against such a visit in 394 advanced by W. Ensslin, "War Kaiser Theodosius I. zweimal in Rom?" *Hermes*, LXXXI (1953), 500–507, seem convincing.

[61] Soz. *HE* 7. 22. 7–8; Rufin. *HE* 11. 32; *Hist. Laus.* 35; Theod. *HE* 5. 24. 1–2, etc.

[62] Soc. *HE* 5. 26. 1–2; Philostorg. *HE* 11. 2; Soz. *HE* 7. 29. 3–4; Claud. *VI Cons. Hon.* 90–96; *III Cons. Hon.* 110–25.

[63] Ambr. *Obit. Theod.* 34 ("filiorum"); Paulin. *V. S. Ambr.* 32 (*PL*, XIV, 39; "filiis"); cf. Mazzarino, *Stilicone*, p. 106, n. 3; Ensslin, *RE*, XX: 2 (1950), 1912; Sievers, *Kaiser*, p. 447; Schild, *Placidia*, pp. 18–19; G. Gigli, *Il regno dell' Imperatore Teodosio*, II, 60; Seeck, *Gesch.*, V: 1, 258; V: 2, 544.

[64] Schild, *Placidia*, pp. 18–19; Ensslin, *RE*, XX: 2 (1950), 1912.

[65] Claud. *VI Cons. Hon.* 90–96.

who had fallen in battle against him, but he saw in the safe arrival
of Honorius and Placidia while he was still living a manifestation
of God's grace to him, and took communion, from which he had
abstained since the battle.[66] It remained for him to put his house in
order: Honorius was officially designated Emperor in the West (if
this step had not been taken before);[67] the children were placed in
the care of Stilicho and, for their private upbringing, Serena,[68]
while their souls were entrusted to Saint Ambrose. Whether now
or earlier Stilicho was promoted to be Master of Both Branches of
the Soldiery in the West, becoming thereby commander of all the
armed forces of the Western Empire.[69]

In January the Emperor prepared to entertain the people of
Milan with horse races. Early on the appointed day he felt quite
ill and sent for Honorius, but when the latter came he felt much
better and during the morning presided over the races. But again
after lunch he suddenly became very ill and dispatched his son in
his stead to attend the races in the afternoon. The Emperor felt
worse and worse and repeatedly asked for the spiritual comfort of
the presence of Saint Ambrose; he urged his sons to cling to the
true faith. And during the ensuing night he fell asleep in the Lord;
the cause of death was stated to be dropsy. It was 17 January A.D.
395;[70] the last strong emperor who had ruled the whole Roman
Empire, serving God in orthodox piety according to his lights, had
gone to his reward, and Galla Placidia was left an orphan in her
seventh year. Forty days after the Emperor's death Saint Ambrose
delivered a solemn funeral oration in his honor, attesting the piety,
the wisdom, the success of Theodosius, and the security and tran-
quillity which he had given the Roman world, while painting a
picture of the arrival of Christ's servant in Heaven. For the repose
of Theodosius' soul he prayed:

Thou, Lord, Who art the guardian of even the smallest in this humility,
save those who hope in Thee. Give perfect peace unto Thy servant

[66] Ambr. *Obit. Theod.* 34.

[67] Cf. Cedrenus, I, 563 (Bonn).

[68] Claud. *VI Cons. Hon.* 94.

[69] Ambr. *Obit. Theod.* 5; Paulin, *V. S. Ambr.* 32; *CTh* 7. 4. 18, 7. 9. 3 (29 July,
393); *ILS*, 1277, 1278; W. Ensslin, "Zum Heermeisteramt des spätrömischen Reiches,"
II, III, *Klio*, XXIV (1931), 102–47, 467–502, at 145.

[70] Ambr. *Obit. Theod.* 35; Rufin. *HE* 11. 34; Soc. *HE* 5. 26. 3–5; Soz. *HE* 7. 29. 4;
Theod. *HE* 5. 25; Hyd. 25 (II, 16); *Fast. Vind. Prior.* 525 (I, 298); Malalas, p. 348
(Bonn); *Chron. Pasch.*, I, 565 (Bonn); Theophanes, p. 74 (de B).

Theodosius, that peace which Thou hast prepared for Thy saints. Let his soul be returned thither whence it did descend, where it cannot feel the sting of death, where he may know that this death is not the end of nature, but of fault; "For in that he died, he died unto sin" [Rom. 6: 10], that there can be room for sin no longer; but he shall rise again that his life may be restored more perfect by renewed gift.[71]

Honorius, the new Emperor of the West, was of course present to hear this discourse, as were Stilicho, Serena, and Galla Placidia. Honorius could not restrain his tears; we may be sure that his little sister was hardly more successful.[72] After this final farewell to the Emperor his body was transported by gradual and solemn stages to the East, to Constantinople,[73] where it was reverently received by the Emperor Arcadius, and on or about 8 November 395, interred among the imperial sepulchers in the Church of the Holy Apostles,[74] where also lay the body of Constantine the Great.[75] Traveling as escort with the body of Theodosius, Serena journeyed to the East, taking with her her children.[76] Placidia, however, since she was presumably not a welcome sight to the Emperor Arcadius,

---

[71] Ambr. *Obit. Theod.* 36.

[72] Honorius present and weeping: Ambr. *Obit. Theod.* 3, 54, 55; Stilicho present, *ibid.* 5. J. Straub, "Parens Principum: Stilichos Reichspolitik und das Testament des Kaisers Theodosius," *La nouvelle Clio*, IV (1952), 94–115, at 100, n. 1, denies that "praesenti" has this meaning here, probably wrongly; so also J. Koch, "Claudian und die Ereignisse der Jahre 395 bis 398," *RhM*, n.s., XLIV (1889), 575–612, at 593, on general grounds that seem inadequate. Nevertheless, apart from the meaning of the word, it is almost inconceivable that he was not present. The presence of Serena and Placidia is nowhere attested, but they must nevertheless have been in attendance. Saint Ambrose's remarks are directed primarily to Honorius, for as the son of Theodosius, even although a child, he must be the Emperor's successor in piety, duties, and responsibilities.

[73] Ambr. *Obit. Theod.* 55, 56; Zos. 4. 59. 4 in characteristic half-truths says that Theodosius returned to Constantinople and died there.

[74] Soc. *HE* 6. 1. 4.

[75] Cedrenus, I, 574 (Bonn); cf. Const. Porphy. *Caer.* 2. 42 (p. 642 Bonn).

[76] This is not directly attested, but Serena was in Constantinople with her children before the death of Rufinus (27 Nov. 395), for she was able to send her husband messages about the Prefect's plots (Claud. *Laus Ser.* [*Carm. Min.* 30] 232–36; cf. *Cons. Stil.* 1. 297; *Ruf.* 2. 95); this would be the most reasonable explanation of how she came again to be in Constantinople in 395, although she had just completed the reverse journey at the end of 394. For it seems eminently probable that some close member of his family would have accompanied Theodosius' body on its long journey to its final resting-place. We are explicitly told that Honorius could not accompany the corpse (Ambr. *Obit. Theod.* 55), but the emphasis of Ambrose's *ipse* applied to Honorius may well intend that someone else would. There is no real basis for conjecture whether Placidia accompanied her father or not, but in the view of the presumed dislike of Arcadius she may well have been left behind in the charge of her nurse as indicated in the text, although Eucherius and Maria went along with their mother on this hypothesis. This evidence about Serena's presence in Constantinople in 395 has perplexed various scholars, e.g., E. Demougeot, *De l'unité à la*

may very well have been left behind in the care of her nurse Elpidia, of whom we hear later.[77] In any event Serena returned once again to the West, probably in 396, at least before the death of Saint Ambrose in 397.[78] In her household and under her care Placidia was to pass her girlhood;[79] undoubtedly this arrangement was in accordance with the wishes of Placidia's late father. We are told that Serena acted as a mother to Honorius;[80] she surely served in the same capacity, or tried to, to Placidia (see Pl. V).[81]

The sources have very little to tell us about the life and education of a little girl growing up in relative obscurity in her cousin's house and in the shadow of her brother the Emperor and his master Stilicho, but they do vouchsafe an occasional glimpse. It is a fair assumption that Placidia was trained much as Serena's own daughter Maria was. Maria was taught the ancient Roman as well as Christian virtues; we may also assume for both girls a thorough grounding in the principles of the Christian religion and morality, more or less as outlined about this time by Saint Jerome for another young girl.[82] On a more worldly level Maria, and probably Placidia too, was taught both Greek and Latin literature from

---

*division de l'Empire romain 395–410*, p. 154 and n. 184; Stein, *Hist.*, I, 229, 541, n. 57. As the beloved foster daughter of the late Emperor and the foster sister of Arcadius, Serena was in little danger, as long as she was circumspect, from the intrigues of Rufinus. While the ceremonies of interment of Theodosius took place in Nov., the body may actually have arrived in Constantinople sometime before; hence Serena would have had reason to discover what Rufinus was actually about and warn her husband, before the Prefect's end on 27 Nov.

[77] Olympiod. Frag. 40 (IV, 66).

[78] F. Bücheler, *Carm. Lat. Epig.*, 907 (= *CIL*, V, 6250), with nn. *ad loc.*; cf. also E. Nischer-Falkenhof, *Stilicho* (Vienna, 1947), p. 61; Bury, *Hist.*, I, 118–19; Demougeot, *Unité*, p. 158 and nn.

[79] Claud. *Carm. Min.* 48; cf. title ". . . a Serena" with vv. 1–2, 11–12; on the interpretation of these lines, see Ensslin, *RE*, XX: 2 (1950), 1912. The presence of Placidia in Serena's household is generally admitted; cf. M. Assunta Nagl, *Galla Placidia*, p. 11 (but there is no reason to believe with Nagl that any considerable part of this upbringing occurred in Constantinople); E. Kornemann, "Galla Placidia," in *Grosse Frauen des Altertums*, 4th ed., pp. 314–54, at 324; V. A. Sirago, *Galla Placidia e la trasformazione politica dell' Occidente*, p. 45.

[80] Claud. *Epithal. Hon. Mar.* 41–43.

[81] Under these circumstances we should not apply to Placidia's early life, at least, the confused statement of Cedrenus (I, 573–74 [Bonn]) (who makes her the daughter of Gratian), the statement that she resided at Rome while Honorius lived at Ravenna (as does, with some reservations, Schild, *Placidia*, p. 21 and n. 5; cf. E. Hutton, *Ravenna*, p. 36); as a child she almost certainly lived with Serena. The further theory that she lived with her aunts Grata and Justa (Schild, *Placidia*, p. 19; cf. Kornemann, *Grosse Frauen*, p. 324) is purely gratuitous, quite inadequately supported by the fact that she eventually named her daughter (Justa Grata Honoria) after them.

[82] *Ep.* 107, esp. 4.

Homer downward.[83] The versifying Claudian, who tells us this, naturally emphasizes the poets, but this emphasis was in fact characteristic of ancient Greek and Roman education. Surely Virgil was included too, although he is not specifically mentioned in the curriculum. And there must have been some prose authors. Certainly when she was a grown woman Placidia more than once manifested an acquaintance with basic Roman ideas about law and order and the functions of an ideal ruler.[84] Nor, apparently, were the housewifely arts, considered appropriate in all ages for the future Roman or Christian matron, neglected. We are told that Placidia helped Serena weave or embroider a girth or cinch for her brother's horse, and Serena dispatched the gift to Honorius.[85] Household tasks of this sort were part of the traditional education of Roman girls, and of the ancestral activities of Roman women. Placidia was receiving an education of both a conservative and an advanced nature. Sometimes teachers are actively disliked by their pupils, for whatever reason. The sequel will amply demonstrate that sooner or later Placidia must have come to detest her mentor.[86] Possibly she found comfort and the affection she needed from her nurse Elpidia.[87]

While Placidia was thus being trained to be a good, Christian, reasonably learned woman, she was also growing to an age when she could not fail, as the daughter and sister of emperors, to be either an actor or a pawn in political affairs of high moment. Her brother Honorius was still hardly more than a child himself; his affairs were administered largely by his general-in-chief, the Master of the Soldiers, Flavius Stilicho (See Pl. IV). The passive, rather dull personality of the Emperor would be controlled by one principal minister or another all his life. Only rarely would unintelligence and fear, played upon by the intrigues which were contin-

---

[83] Claud. *Epithal. Hon. Mar.* 231–37, including the poems of Sappho? Is this merely poetical fancy, or were these verses carefully edited for juvenile Christian consumption?

[84] See "Galla Placidia and the Law," *CP*, LXIII (1968), 114–21, and below, Ch. VI.

[85] Claud. *Carm. Min.* 47–48, or does the poet possibly mean that the gift was a saddlecloth? In 47 Claud. praises the gift of Serena to the skies, in accordance with his glorification of his patrons; in 48 he refers to a small gift of a sister. Because of the different reference to this gift, the sister of 48 must be Honorius' (half) sister Placidia, rather than his (foster) sister Serena, especially since in 47. 14 Serena is referred to in her capacity as (foster) mother. Cf. also Ensslin, *RE*, XX: 2 (1950), 1912.

[86] So, e.g., Hutton, *Ravenna*, p. 36.

[87] Olympiod. Frag. 40 (IV, 66).

ually woven about the power vacuum on the throne, move him to drastic action or interference. For the present, for the first thirteen years of Honorius' reign, Stilicho was the de facto regent of the Empire, the real ruler of the West in the name of a boy and a man who in some respects mentally, and possibly physically as well, never ceased to be a child.[88] Since the legal position of the emperor was rooted in a largely forgotten (save by historians and other useless antiquaries) quasi-Republican past of the early Principate, since by ancient fiction of the law the imperial power was that of a theoretically temporary, extraordinary magistrate, the Empire could never develop the legal theory of a regency.[89] Stilicho owed his power to the extralegal last wishes of Theodosius the Great, to his position of supreme commander, to the ascendancy of his personality and that of his wife over the Emperor, and to his success in manipulating the Emperor as the latter grew older and in preventing other ambitious courtiers from effective interference. To these factors during most of his tenure of power must be added the prestige of his military successes against the external foes of the Empire. But as time went on and Stilicho for practical purposes tried to please all sorts of groups and individuals, Christians, pagans, Germans, anti-Germans, landholders, and others, while trying to administer the needs of a declining state and society, he perhaps inevitably encountered more and more jealousy, which had an easy excuse or reason in his German ancestry, and thus made more and more enemies.[90] And Honorius, though dull, was human; there was always the danger that he might become too restive in the leading strings; that he might recall too clearly—and there would never be wanting those eager to remind him—how many times in the past emperors had met a violent or ignominious end through the treasonous ambitions of the powerful and the

[88] A somewhat more favorable opinion of the personality of the Emperor emerges in Sirago, *Placidia*, esp. pp. 47, 242–43. For the more traditional view, see, e.g., Hodgkin, *Invaders*, I: 2, 643.

[89] F. Martroye, *Bulletin de la Soc. Nat. des Antiquaires de France*, 1916, pp. 202–6; Mazzarino, *Stilicone*, pp. 106–7. It is unlikely that Stilicho legally even had private *tutela* over Honorius and Arcadius; cf. R. Keller, *Stilicho*, p. 66. When Olympiod. Frag. 2 (IV, 58) refers to Stilicho's position as *epitropos* (guardian), he is speaking of fact, not law.

[90] Especially on these aspects of the matter, see Mazzarino, *Stilicone*, by far the best statement of the perennial vexed questions of Stilicho's policies, ambitions, and hopes. A concise summary of Stilicho's policies to different groups is in Stein, *Hist.*, I, 227.

successful. Thus further to consolidate his influence over the Emperor Stilicho arranged for him successively to marry his two daughters, first Maria (in 398 when she was about thirteen years old—a not unusual age for Roman girls to marry;[91] see Pl. III) and then, when she died, her younger sister Thermantia (late 407 or early 408). We are told, and the information may well be correct, that the Emperor did not consummate his marriage with either of his wives;[92] some rumors at least said that he was sterile or impotent, although we owe this information to an account prejudiced both against Stilicho and Serena and against the pious, orthodox[93] Honorius.[94] Indeed, that the latter was impotent is probable; there is no reason to believe that Honorius was in fact so pious as to enter into a pact of chastity with his wives, or so strong of character that, a young man, he would have wished and found it possible to enter upon and maintain any such undertaking. And such matters, intimate though they may be, would be quite difficult to conceal from the malice of court gossip.[95]

Thus, in January 395, the Empire came nominally into the hands of Arcadius in the East and Honorius in the West, but since Arcadius' character was not unlike that of his younger brother, in the East real power devolved on the Praetorian Prefect Rufinus as in the West it had upon Stilicho;[96] it was the first time that the sovereigns of Rome were *rois fainéants*.[97] A prime question that arose at once, however, was the matter of the relation of Stilicho

91 W. Ensslin, *s.v.*, "Maria" (3), *RE*, XIV: 2 (1930), 1712–13, at 1712. Claud. *Epithal. Hon. Mar.* 29 apparently means to say that the marriage had been arranged by Theodosius the Great. Even though the statement of Stilicho's protégé may be suspect, the assertion may be true.

92 Marcell. *s.a.* 408, 1 (II, 69); Jord. *Get.* 154.

93 Cf. Oros. 7. 36. 3, 37. 11; Soz. *HE* 8. 1. 1; Theod. *HE* 5. 25. 2; Orosius praises Honorius' chastity.

94 The rumor, repeated by the Arian Philostorg. *HE* 12. 2, accuses Honorius of being rendered incapable of having children because of a drug administered to him by Stilicho. Cf. the pagan malice of Zos. 5. 28. 2–3, who declares the Emperor neither willing nor able to consummate his marriages. F. Gabotto, *Storia della Italia occidentale nel medio evo (395–1313)*, I, 64, thinks Honorius was probably impotent, and rightly dismisses as unlikely the story that either Serena or Stilicho wanted these marriages to be childless; obviously the birth of children would only confirm their hold on Honorius.

95 Compare the similar difficulties encountered by Louis XVI in the first years of his marriage. The allegations made about Honorius' attitude toward his sister near the end of his life are psychologically quite possible for a man possessed of such a disability.

96 Cf. Eun. Frag. 62 (IV, 42).

97 Stein, *Hist.*, I, 225; possibly, however, the Emperor Gordian III in the third century might also be so classified.

to Arcadius. On this matter, as on almost every other fundamental question concerning Stilicho, scholars have disagreed; but since at Theodosius' death Stilicho was the supreme commander of almost the entire mobile force of the Roman Empire (for most of the mobile forces of the East were still in the West),[98] it seems correct to think that Theodosius, who could have changed this but did not, meant that Stilicho's extralegal guardianship should extend to Arcadius as well as Honorius.[99] Certainly, whatever the desires of Theodosius, Stilicho wished to extend his control over the East, but he was balked, first by the rival ambitions of Rufinus in 395, and after the latter had been lynched by German troops, by the similar ambitions of his successor in the real power of the Eastern Empire, the eunuch Eutropius. Stilicho's loyalty to the dynasty, or to the memory of Theodosius, proved beyond all question by the manner of his death in 408, forbade him to establish his control at Constantinople by force of arms, at least for several years; for a leading principle of his policy was the maintenance of the Empire's unity under its two sovereigns.[100] Of particular importance in this regard was the question of the Prefecture of Illyricum. Since Theodosius had arranged all matters concerning the future government of the Empire before his death, he must certainly have determined the boundaries between the spheres of the Eastern and Western governments—that is, the question of the control of Illyricum.[101] Unfortunately the evidence is quite unclear as to what the disposition of Illyricum was, but it seems likely that Stilicho, for whatever motive, recognized by the end of 395 that eastern Illyricum (the dioceses of Macedonia and Dacia) pertained to the sphere of the East.[102]

[98] Cf. Zos. 5. 4. 2.

[99] Ambr. *Obit. Theod.* 5; cf. Jones, *Roman Empire,* I, 174; E. Demougeot, "Note sur la politique orientale de Stilicon de 405 à 407," *Byzantion,* XX (1950), 27–37, at 27–29; Straub, *Nouvelle Clio,* IV (1952), 115; for another view, e.g., N. H. Baynes, "A Note on Professor Bury's 'History of the Later Roman Empire,'" *JRS,* XII (1922), 207–29, at 212.

[100] W. Ensslin, "Das Römerreich unter germanischer Waltung von Stilicho bis Theoderich," in *Das neue Bild der Antike,* II, 412–32, at 415; Straub, *Nouvelle Clio,* IV (1952), 94–95.

[101] Ambr. *Obit. Theod.* 5, as interpreted by Grumel, *Rev. ét. byz.,* IX (1951), 25, against Demougeot, *Unité,* p. 145, n. 138; and Mazzarino, *Stilicone,* p. 57; among the many discussions of the history of the administrative control of Illyricum, see esp. F. Lot, "La 'Notitia Dignitatum Utriusque Imperii,'" *RÉA,* XXXVIII (1936), 285–338, at 332–33.

[102] Palanque, *Prétoire,* pp. 84–85, following E. Stein, "Untersuchungen zur spätrömischen Verwaltungsgeschichte," *RhM,* LXXIV (1925), 347–94, at 351–54; Demougeot, *Byzantion,* XX (1950), 27.

A great part of the attention of the supreme military commander of the Western Empire was necessarily engaged in defending the frontiers and, in the case of the Goths, the interior of the Empire against the almost incessantly recurring attacks of the Germans and other barbarians; nor were these external matters by any means unrelated to internal affairs. The hostile government of the East was believed, rightly or wrongly, to have directed the barbarians against the West, as a means of self-defense or as an instrument for its anti-Stilicho policy. At the death of Theodosius the Goths were already restive; they believed, with or without reason, that their heavy losses at the Frigidus were the result of a set policy of decimating their ranks; their chieftain Alaric was disgruntled because he had not received a high military position in the Roman army; possibly the agents of Rufinus were busily intriguing among the Goths. In any event in the same year, 395, they elected Alaric their paramount chief (whether he received or took the title of King at this juncture or later is arguable) and commenced to ravage the Balkans. Stilicho marched against them with an army a goodly part of which was composed of the troops of the East under his command. He had maneuvered Alaric and his people into a strategically inferior position when he received the command of Arcadius (that is, Rufinus) to return the troops of the East to Eastern control and to vacate the dominions of the Eastern Emperor. Stilicho obeyed, probably to avoid the disloyalty of refusing the overt command of the senior Augustus, and Alaric escaped. The Eastern troops, however, commanded by the Goth Gainas, when they reached the environs of Constantinople, lynched Rufinus. From the Eastern capital Serena had informed her husband of the intrigues there in progress against him. The fall of Rufinus had already been put in train by the conspiracies of the eunuch Eutropius, who succeeded him in the real control of affairs. If Stilicho had hoped or expected that the latter would be more amenable to his control, he was to be rudely disillusioned. In 397 Gildo, Master of the Soldiers in Africa, revolted openly against the Western government; his attitude toward Eugenius had already been treasonable, or at least ambiguous, although he apparently had earlier been sent by Theodosius to seize his native land from the control of Maximus.[103] Stilicho used Gildo's brother

---

[103] For this interpretation of Gildo's career, see "Count Gildo and Theodosius the Great," *CP*, LVII (1962), 27–30.

and enemy Mascezel to defeat him (398); shortly thereafter the victorious commander was perfidiously assassinated. In the same year Stilicho himself managed handily to defeat various barbarian inroads across the frontiers of the Western Empire. In the East, however, Alaric had again started harrying the Balkans, this time penetrating into Greece itself, where he ravaged Boeotia, except Thebes, seized the Piraeus, but was repelled by the strong walls of Athens (repaired in the third century) which, so the pagans retorted against claims of similar divine intervention in emergencies made by the Christians, were guarded by Athena Promachos herself.[104] Nevertheless Alaric as an individual was received as a guest within the trembling city; Attica was ravaged and the great shrine of the ancient mysteries of the goddesses at Eleusis was plundered. Thence the Goths crossed the Isthmus into the Peloponnese; in 397 Stilicho again intervened against Alaric, this time crossing by sea, but apparently as a result of the intrigues of Eutropius the Goths were able to retreat into Epirus, and Stilicho returned again to Italy.[105] Eutropius, however, fell from power largely because he had incurred the wrath of the Empress Eudoxia, but the government of the East continued to be hostile to Stilicho, especially since the opponents of the Germans, a group more powerful in the East and more clearly distinguishable than in the West, attained control of the government.

In 401 Alaric and his Goths moved against the West, not without the encouragement of the Eastern government. Stilicho found it necessary to summon troops from Gaul and even distant Britain to meet the emergency.[106] This weakening of the Western garrisons had been in progress for some time, but in the successive military emergencies with which Stilicho had to cope the process was greatly accelerated. For reasons that are imperfectly understood today, the

---

[104] Zos. 5. 6. 1; Philostorg. *HE* 12. 2 errs when he says that Alaric took Athens itself.

[105] These events are obscure, and there are not wanting historians, ancient and modern, who accuse Stilicho of so frequently letting Alaric escape for his own evil motives, notably the desire always to remain indispensable.

[106] The weakening of the Western garrisons is beyond question; on the gradual character of the process, not assigning the sole responsibility to Stilicho, see J. J. Hatt, *Histoire de la Gaule romaine (120 avant J.-C.–451 après J.-C.)*, p. 348; E. Demougeot, "Notes sur l'évacuation des troupes romaines en Alsace au début du Ve siècle," *Revue d'Alsace*, XCII (1953), 7–28, at 7. Stilicho tried to make good these withdrawals by entering into treaties with the adjacent tribes as *foederati* to protect the frontier; cf. *ibid.*, 17–18. The policy was not entirely unsuccessful, as the opposition offered by the Franks to the great invasion of 31 Dec. 406 shows.

Western government was finding it ever more difficult to raise troops in numbers adequate to defend its dominions. Recruits served in the army more and more unwillingly; the great land-owners were reluctant in the manpower shortage to see their peasants impressed into military service, and frequently evaded the demands of the government by fraud or force. Stilicho himself had found it necessary to conciliate the great magnates by reducing demands on them for the manpower without which their lands would be valueless. And it is quite probable, although occasionally denied, that the declining economic conditions of the West, especially in comparison with the East, made it more and more difficult to pay and support armies. Certainly this was to be true as the fifth century advanced, and it is difficult to believe that this situation had not begun to obtain even in the last years of the fourth century.

Emperor and court at Milan were thrown into a panic by Alaric's approach, and the walls of Rome itself were thoroughly repaired and strengthened.[107] Commonly hereafter Honorius was to reside in Ravenna, guarded by its swamps and morasses, rather than in Milan in the midst of its too accessible plain. Barely in time Stilicho was able to confront Alaric at Pollentia where victory on Easter Sunday, 402, inclined, but not decisively, to the Roman side. Another battle in 402 or 403 near Verona went more decisively in favor of the Romans. Once again, however, Stilicho did not move in for the kill, but may have negotiated a treaty with Alaric which allowed the Goths to settle in Pannonia along the Save. One's view of Stilicho's motives depends in the last analysis on one's general evaluation of him as man and statesman.[108]

According to the technical letter of the Roman law this triumph of Stilicho's belonged to his military superior, the Emperor Honorius; at the end of the year 403, at the request of the Senate and the Roman People,[109] the Emperor, Stilicho, Serena, their son

107 *ILS*, 797; cf. *CIL*, VI, 1188–90; with I. A. Richmond, *The City Wall of Imperial Rome*, pp. 30–36, 257–62.

108 The sketch of these events offered here is so lacking in detail that it is probably correct; almost all details are controversial. The writer, however, would opt for 403 as the date of the Battle of Verona. Demougeot, *Unité*, p. 281 and nn. 275–76, argues that Stilicho concluded no treaty with Alaric after the battle; so V. Costanzi, "La rivolta di Pavia e la catastrofe di Stilicone," *Bollettino della Soc. Pavese di Storia Patria*, IV (1904), 481–523, at 506–9.

109 Claud. *VI Cons. Hon.* 332–33, 356–60.

Eucherius, the Empress Maria, and the rest of the court proceeded from Ravenna to Rome. There Honorius entered the City in the solemn procession appropriate to the Advent of the Emperor and on 1 January 404, accepted the fasces of his sixth consulship. As he had so frequently in the past, Stilicho's protégé, Claudian, composed a verse panegyric in honor of the great and auspicious occasion, for great was the relief and joy felt in the City and throughout all Italy at the deliverance from the terrible Goth. Perhaps to most of the people, as in the flattering lines of Claudian, the power and majesty of eternal Rome seemed as great and splendid as ever; in the poet's tired imagery all the mythical lore of the classical past adorned the glorious event. The City had been festively decorated, and rain which had fallen the night before ceased with the morning sunshine. The streets were lined all along the route of the sacred procession from the Milvian Bridge, historic scene of the triumph of Constantine and Christ, through the Flaminian Gate (Porta del Popolo) along the Via Lata (the Corso) to the Palatine. The entry gate itself had recently been sheathed with marble as part of the reconditioning of the Walls of Aurelian.[110] The condescension of the Prince forbade the welcoming delegation from the Senate to march on foot before his chariot, although Eucherius did so march, in ostentatious humility, like a simple soldier at the behest of his father. At the Circus Maximus the Emperor received the plaudits of the crowd from the imperial box, and presided over races and other spectacles such as that of a drilled team of soldiers who completed their complicated evolutions by falling on their knees before the throne. The court took up its residence in the ancient palaces of the Caesars upon the Palatine Hill.[111]

Galla Placidia must have accompanied her brother on his triumphal progress to Rome, but Claudian makes no mention of her, although he insinuates that Eucherius (see Pl. V) was the brother of the Emperor.[112] This failure to mention Placidia (the

[110] Richmond, *Wall*, pp. 260–61.
[111] Claud. *VI Cons. Hon.* 495–644; Prudent. *Symm. Or.* 2. 731–38.
[112] Claud. *VI Cons. Hon.* 552–53. This passage has commonly been misinterpreted: Demougeot, *Unité*, p. 373, n. 115, cf. 284, n. 293; Sirago, *Placidia*, p. 45, n. 4; Bury, *Hist.*, I, 108, n. 1, think that Placidia is mentioned in 552–54, but this is a mistake; the verses mean: "although even Eucherius, whose blood is royal on both sides and (whose) sister is the Empress [Augusta, i.e., Maria], renders the obedience of a (common) soldier to his brother [Honorius, referring to the position of Stilicho and

Empress Maria is referred to instead) is particularly noteworthy, since a few years before, writing in honor of Stilicho's consulship (A.D. 400) he had expressed the hopeful prophecy of a marriage between Placidia and Eucherius, and boasted that the house of Stilicho bore empresses and the husbands of empresses. The implication of course is that Galla Placidia would become an Augusta (*regina* here).[113] But, significantly, in the earlier poem the "prophecy" about Eucherius and Placidia is immediately preceded by another in which the Empress Maria is depicted in childbirth, bearing a future emperor.[114] We may be sure that in these political poems the appearance of such ideas reflects the plans or hopes of Stilicho. Evidently about 400 Stilicho intended to marry Eucherius to Placidia, but four years later there is no hint of this. Whether the general had changed his mind is uncertain, but it seems likely that he did not wish to press a marriage between his son and Placidia when his daughter had so far left the Emperor childless. To do so would be at least impolitic, for as long as Honorius was childless, Eucherius if married to Placidia would too obviously be in the line of imperial succession. Especially in the light of what had been written in 400, it were better not to mention Placidia at all. The mission of Claudian was to glorify Stilicho and his family,[115] even when celebrating Honorius; the latter's family is irrelevant when it does not serve this purpose. One probably should not conclude, however, that Stilicho had abandoned his project of a marriage of Eucherius to Placidia,[116] only that it would be impolitic to lay himself open to charges of imperial ambitions for Eucherius, such as would certainly offend the Emperor. The fact that Eu-

---

Serena as foster parents of the Emperor]. . . ." The reference in 554–55 to *parentis* is to Stilicho; that in *pignora* to Eucherius and Maria. Placidia cannot be described as an Augusta, a rank she was not to hold until many years later. It is one thing to refer to her in a "prophecy" as *regina* (*Cons. Stil.* 2. 361) and another to describe her in the present by the legal and official title of Augusta which she did not possess.

113 Claud. *Cons. Stil.* 2. 354–61.

114 *Ibid.* 342–49.

115 Straub, *Nouvelle Clio*, IV (1952), 96, rightly points out that Claudian praises Stilicho in a way that earlier would have been regarded as treasonable utterance when referred to a subject rather than to the emperor.

116 Kornemann, *Grosse Frauen*, pp. 324–25, suggests that Stilicho wanted to promote this marriage to ensure that the imperial house continue despite the childlessness of Honorius. And surely he would not have been unwilling in those circumstances to see his son succeed to the throne by virtue of such a union; cf. G. Romano, *Le dominazioni barbariche in Italia (395–1024)*, pp. 59–60; Sirago, *Placidia*, p. 52; Schild, *Placidia*, p. 21 and n. 3.

cherius walked humbly on foot, as well as the underlining of his dutiful *obsequium* to his "brother" the Emperor by Claudian, one suspects, was a deliberate attempt to scotch rumors that Eucherius was destined for imperial honors. That Eucherius received only the relatively low rank (it was frequently conferred on those of eminent birth as a presage of things to come) of *tribunus et notarius*[117] is further evidence of Stilicho's caution, stimulated by envy of him and his family.[118] But had Stilicho really wished to put such rumors about his intentions absolutely at rest, it seems likely that another candidate would have been found for Placidia's hand. The latter went unwed far longer than was customary for Roman girls, and there is no suggestion anywhere that she was being devoted to Christian chastity as a means of removing the possibility of a politically awkward marriage—a fate that was to befall many a princess of this imperial house in the future. We may conclude that she was being held in reserve to marry Eucherius whenever and for whatever reason it might be desirable to do so. One is tempted in the general silence about Placidia after 400 in the publicity given the imperial family to see a set policy of Stilicho, and to think that the daughter of Theodosius was being deliberately kept in the background, as long as it was impolitic for her to marry Eucherius, for her marriage to anyone else would also affect the imperial succession as well as the general's presumed plans for his son. One notes that the golden locket of the Empress Maria, found in her sarcophagus, mentions Honorius and all members of the (Western) imperial family except Placidia.[119] The foregoing argument is possible and plausible, it may even be probable, but the fact remains that Placidia continued unmarried. True, she may have disliked Eucherius; but she was to dislike marrying her second husband Constantius, yet marry him she did at the Emperor's command.

What Placidia thought of the situation we cannot know; there

---

[117] Zos. 5. 34. 7; on the potentialities of the rank see E.-Ch. Babut, "Recherches sur la garde imperiale et sur le corps d'officiers de l'armée romaine aux IVe et Ve siècles," *Rev. hist.,* CXIV (1913), 225–60; CXVI (1914), 225–93; at CXVI, 258–59, 258, n. 2; C. Lécrivain, *Le sénat romain depuis Dioclétien à Rome et à Constantinople,* p. 52; K. Hopkins, "Eunuchs in Politics in the Later Roman Empire," *Proceedings of the Cambridge Philolog. Soc.,* no. 189 (1963), 62–80, at 75; Jones, *Roman Empire,* I, 572–73.

[118] Cf. Sirago, *Placidia,* pp. 52–54.

[119] *ILS,* 800.

is no reason to believe that she looked with favor upon a life of Christian virginity and retirement; most young girls wish to be married when their contemporaries are. It is not unlikely that she resented the situation, and that she also was irritated by being kept in the background while the less exalted family of Stilicho was preferred to her in the limelight. This visit of the court to Rome beheld a clear example of the power and majesty of Serena, who was less closely connected with the imperial house than Placidia, and whom the latter quite likely secretly detested. In the summer of 404 Melania and Pinianus, a young married couple, sought and obtained an interview with Serena.[120] The two young people, wishing to lead a life of Christian poverty and consecrate themselves to God, desired to sell all they had and give the proceeds to the poor. But both of them belonged to the most wealthy and most exalted circles of the Roman aristocracy, and their relatives were much opposed to their literal interpretation of the injunction of Christ. Yet Serena, they thought, would be able by her power and influence to override family opposition, and so it turned out. Serena was able to persuade Honorius to interpose his authority in favor of the two. But the entire account of this transaction is evidence of the power and splendor of Serena, who is referred to as empress (*basilissa, regina*); although the title is technically incorrect, in every way her power and magnificence reflect the majesty of the imperial court. She has her own chamberlain, for example, for whom as well as for Serena the young couple thought it wise to bring rich presents. Serena's intervention of course springs from her Christian piety. It is difficult to avoid the impression that Serena, the niece of Theodosius, has put his daughter quite in the background and out of countenance, and that the increasing dislike for her that Placidia was presumably coming to feel was probably in part caused by sheer jealousy.

In these years Stilicho and his family were indeed at the zenith of power, even although the death of the Empress Maria, probably in 404, cast some shadow on their splendor. The late Empress was interred near the Prince of the Apostles in the imperial mausoleum,

---

120 *V. greca S. Mel. Iun.* 11–14 (pp. 146–57, ed. D. Gorce [Paris, 1962]) = *V. lat.* 11–14 (*Anal. Boll.*, VIII [1889], 28–31). See P. Courcelle, "Les lacunes de la correspondance entre Saint Augustin et Paulin de Nole," *RÉA*, LIII (1951), 253–300, at 272; P. R. L. Brown, "Aspects of the Christianization of the Roman Aristocracy," *JRS*, LI (1961), 1–11, at 8; Demougeot, *Unité*, pp. 287–88; H. Grisar, *History of Rome and the Popes in the Middle Ages*, I, 60–61.

a round building connected with the south transept of the Constantinian basilica of Saint Peter in Rome.[121] But the peace of Rome, Italy, and the Western Empire was never really to be reestablished in the time of anyone then living, and Stilicho in his generation was to be made the scapegoat responsible for the unwelcome fact. Apparently the general was never to give up his hope of extending his control over the government of the East, or at least over Illyricum. His plans to use Alaric and the Goths for this purpose, however, never matured because of the reiterated calamities which burst upon the Western Empire in the remaining years of Stilicho's government and life. In 405 a large horde of mixed barbarians commanded by a chief named Radagaisus crossed the Danube and the Alps and fell upon the terrified provinces of Italy; despite his inferiority in numbers Stilicho was able to shut up and blockade the barbarians in the mountains of Etruria near Faesulae (Fiesole). Radagaisus was captured and executed; his horde was destroyed or sold into slavery. Italy was saved for the time being, but on 31 December 406 another mixed horde of barbarians, including Asding and Siling Vandals, Alans, Sueves, and others, crossed the frozen Rhine,[122] largely denuded of its garrisons in previous years in order to defend Italy, and spread over the devoted lands of Gaul, harrying, burning, destroying, killing as they went.[123] Stilicho was blamed for the event, and even accused later of having provoked it.[124] A characteristic feature of the history of the fifth century is the habit of making some individual responsible

---

[121] On the date, Demougeot, *Unité*, p. 373 and n. 112; on the burial and the sepulcher, *ILS*, 800 with nn.; O. Fiebiger and L. Schmidt, *Inschriftensammlung zur Geschichte der Ostgermanen*, ad no. 19 (p. 22); M. Armellini, *Le chiese di Roma*, 3d ed., II, 934–35; on the discovery of the sarcophagus and remains of Maria, see the sixteenth-century accounts printed by F. G. Cancellieri, *De secretariis veteris Basilicae Vaticanae*, II, 995–1002, 1032–38; a more accessible account is in R. Lanciani, *Pagan and Christian Rome*, pp. 202–5.

[122] Both Radagaisus' horde and this one were apparently pushed by the pressure of the Huns in their rear: Oros. 7. 37. 3; cf. E. A. Thompson, *A History of Attila and the Huns*, p. 28; F. Altheim, *Attila und die Hunnen*, p. 82.

[123] The economic interests of the state, apart from all the rest, were directly and immediately affected, since there was a heavy concentration of state factories along the Rhine frontier; cf. A. R. Lewis, *The Northern Seas*, pp. 23–24 with nn. On the general destruction: Salvian *Gub. Dei* 6. 82–84, 7. 50, 52; Prosper [?] *Prov. Div.* 15–60; Orient. *Common.* 2. 165–84; Hieron. *Ep.* 123. 16; in general: Demougeot, *Unité*, pp. 521–25; but cf. F. Vercauteren, "Note sur la ruine des villes de la Gaule d'après quelques auteurs contemporains des invasions germaniques," *Mélanges Bidez*, II, 955–63, on the danger of taking statements about the destruction of cities too literally.

[124] Cf. Hieron. *Ep.* 123. 16–17, who piteously describes the calamities of the Empire from 407, and then in an access of rage blames it all on Stilicho.

for the successive disasters which befell the Roman Empire. This was both very human,[125] and quite in accord with the theories of historical causation which prevailed in antiquity. Impersonal historic forces were hardly conceived of; instead great events were laid to the credit or guilt of some man or small group whose motives were interpreted on moral grounds.

In Britain, itself under continual attack by the German and Irish pirates who came by sea, as well as by the Picts from Scotland who came by land from the north, in 407 after two ephemeral rebels had been put up and pulled down before him a certain Constantine was proclaimed Emperor, in large part because of his auspicious name.[126] Not content with his remote island, about to be sundered from the human race as Tennyson was to put it, Constantine crossed into Gaul, taking with him the larger or better part of the troops garrisoning the British Diocese. In vain the communities on the island implored help from the central government, which could do no more than recognize their right to protect themselves under arms (otherwise forbidden by longstanding imperial legislation against their use). In much the same way, at the same time that the peninsula of Armorica was receiving so many refugees from Britain that it came eventually to be known as Brittany, that area of Gaul was also effectively detached from the Empire, which in the midst of catastrophes in or near its heartlands could no longer protect or govern its outlying provinces. At about the same time there broke out in Armorica and the adjacent regions of Gaul from the mouth of the Loire to that of the Seine the greatest of all risings of the peasant Bacaudae, which lasted for some ten years.[127] In Gaul Constantine was well received by a people and army desperate for succor and leadership from any quarter, and feeling themselves abandoned by the central government.[128] Officials loyal to Honorius fled to Italy[129] or elsewhere. But despite some successes against the barbarians infesting his new domain, the usurper was

125 On the search for scapegoats in the fifth century see P. Courcelle, *Histoire littéraire des grandes invasions germaniques,* pp. 30–31; G. Morosi, *L'invito di Eudossia a Genserico,* pp. 61–64.

126 By far the best treatment of these British usurpers is C. E. Stevens, "Marcus, Gratian, Constantine," *Athenaeum,* n.s., XXXV (1957), 316–47.

127 E. A. Thompson, "Peasant Revolts in Roman Gaul and Spain," *Past and Present,* II (1952), 11–23, at 16.

128 K. F. Stroheker, *Der senatorische Adel im spätantiken Gallien,* p. 45.

129 *Ann. ép.,* 1953, 200, with H.-I. Marrou, "L'épitaphe vaticane du consulaire de Vienne Eventius," *RÉA,* LIV (1952), 326–31.

unable to halt their ravages to any important extent. In spring, 408, the government sent an army commanded by a Goth named Sarus against Constantine; after some successes Sarus was forced to fall back on Italy, able to purchase his passage through the Alps from the Bacaudae of the region only by the surrender to them of all of his booty.[130] Thereupon Constantine closed the Alpine passes and took up or resumed his residence with all due pomp in the pleasant imperial city of Arles, whither some years before the seat of the Gallic Prefecture had been transferred from the much more exposed frontier city of Trier. Here he elevated his son Constans from the cloister to the subordinate imperial rank of Caesar and sent him with a general named Gerontius to seize the Diocese of Spain. This task was successfully accomplished despite some initial setbacks caused by the stalwart attempts of some Spanish relatives of the Emperor to organize a defense against both the usurper and the barbarians (408).

In the third century what was to become the Gallic Prefecture in the fourth had in effect seceded from the central government of the Empire, accepting the rule of local emperors who were better able to organize defense against the barbarians. That century had also seen outbreaks of the peasant Bacaudae; these examples of withdrawal, economic-social, or political, or military, or cultural (Armorica and much of Britain, particularly among the lower classes, had never been thoroughly romanized)[131] after the lull of the partial recovery of the fourth century now recurred with renewed vigor. The magnates of Gaul, even if not wanting to secede from the Empire, conceived a corporate interest in rivalry with the Italians, sometimes for control of the central government, regularly for the control of the imperial administration in their own homeland.[132] The government showed its awareness of the existence of these ambitions among the Gallic magnates, as well as its own weakness, by the adoption of a policy adverse to the maintenance of imperial unity, that is, by its regular appointment of Gallic aristocrats to administer Gaul. Around many of its edges,

130 On this incident of the Bacaudae revolts see Béla Czúth and Samu Szádeczky-Kardoss, "Bagaudák az Alpokban" ["The Bagaudae in the Alps"], summarized in *Bibliotheca Class. Orient.*, IV (1959), 280–81.

131 On the separation of Britain and Armorica (and adjacent parts of Gaul) from Roman rule in 409–10, see below, Ch. III, n. 25.

132 Stroheker, *Adel*, with the cautions once again of MacMullen, *Enemies*, pp. 192–248, esp. 211–13; and A. H. M. Jones, "Were Ancient Heresies National or Social Movements in Disguise?" *Journ. Theolog. Stud.*, n.s., X (1959), 280–98.

its frontiers, the West Roman government was drawing back toward its Mediterranean heartlands, and losing effective control on its fringes to barbarians or local magnates, or local peasant rebellion against any source of exploitation whatever, or some combination of these. Much the same process can also be seen in Pannonia, for example, in the lands near the great bend of the Danube, while Africa was bedeviled by "Circumcellions," bands of brigands recruited mainly from peasants and acting more or less in connection with the Donatist heresy.[133]

Meanwhile in Italy the central government was distracted by further difficulties with the Goths and by a growing disagreement over basic policy between Honorius (or persons who tried to manipulate him to the disadvantage of the minister) and Stilicho, and even between Stilicho and Serena. Profiting by the difficulties occupying the government's attention in the Gallic Prefecture, Alaric entered Noricum and demanded four thousand pounds of gold in recompense for his efforts of preparation, in accordance with instructions from Stilicho, for obtaining control of Illyricum for the West.[134] The matter was brought before the Roman Senate, which demurred at paying such a sum (easily within reach of the huge incomes received by many senators);[135] one senator cried out that "this is not peace, but a pact of servitude."[136] The senator who had thus boldly expressed his opinion at the conclusion of the sitting took refuge in a church, for Stilicho was still powerful enough to gain his way. Then on 1 May 408, the Emperor Arcadius

133 See S. Mazzarino, *La fine del mondo antico*, pp. 158–59; A. Alföldi, *Der Untergang der Römerherrschaft in Pannonien*, I, 18–19, II, 70–71 (but see W. Ensslin's review, *Philolog. Wochenschrift*, XLV [1925], 121–24; XLVII [1927], 842–52, at XLVII, 847–50): Musset, *Vagues*, p. 74; Bury, *Hist.*, I, 166 with nn.; details and exact chronology may be obscure (cf. Jones, *Roman Empire*, notes, p. 351 [= Am. ed., p. 1421]). On Africa, see E. Tengström, *Donatisten und Katholiken;* W. H. C. Frend, *The Donatist Church;* P. R. L. Brown, reviewing Tengström's book and discussing the differences between the latter and Frend, *JRS*, LV (1965), 282; J.-P. Brisson, *Autonomisme et christianisme dans l'Afrique romaine*, esp. pp. 7–8, 337–39, 343, 356–58, 413–14; all of these discuss the question whether the Donatists and the Circumcellions are to be considered a "national" movement or not.

134 There is considerable discussion by modern scholars of these Eastern plans, especially of when the first signs that Stilicho had conceived them occur; cf. Demougeot, *Unité*, pp. 366–70; *idem, Byzantion*, XX (1950), 33–34; Grumel, *Rev. ét. byz.*, IX (1951), 42–43; with anterior bibliography.

135 The sum equalled only the annual income of a senatorial family, as has frequently been pointed out; cf. e.g., H. Dannenbauer, *Die Entstehung Europas von der Spätantike zum Mittelalter*, I, 260.

136 Zos. 5. 29; cf. Olympiod. Frag. 5 (IV, 58). For a plausible explanation of the opposition thus dramatically underlined by the remark about "servitude," see Mazzarino, *Stilicone*, p. 246.

died in the East, leaving three daughters and a seven-year-old son, Theodosius II, Augustus since 402, now nominal ruler of the Eastern Empire. Stilicho at once planned, despite the difficulties in which the West found itself, to go to the East and fulfill his long-cherished ambition by assuming the government for the new Emperor; at the same time a plan was put forward to use the Goths against the usurper Constantine. Although Honorius for some time stubbornly resisted, since he was set on going East himself, and although in this matter Stilicho was also opposed by no less a person than his own wife Serena,[137] Honorius finally gave in and Stilicho once again was to have his own way. Malicious tongues were gossiping, however, that Stilicho's real motive was to put his son Eucherius on the Eastern throne; this interpretation was of course busily insinuated into the ears of the Emperor by the general's enemies, who also viewed with great alarm, real or pretended, the growing importance of Germans in the army and the government, as a menace to the rightful control of the Roman Empire.[138] Presumably, however, Stilicho hoped that Honorius' marriage, early in 408 or at the end of 407, to his younger daughter Thermantia, would be of critical importance in keeping the sovereign from being too much impressed by the accusations of the general's many enemies at court.[139] If so, he was mistaken, for during a re-

[137] Probably Serena was primarily concerned lest Stilicho's Eastern project give another handle to his enemies to attack him; she may also have more disinterestedly been averse to a project amounting to civil war between the two parts of the Empire, especially at a time when the Western government was in such difficulties in its western provinces (Zos. 5. 29. 8). See Keller, *Stilicho*, p. 60; Demougeot, *Byzantion*, XX (1950), 35, 37; *idem, Unité*, p. 372; S. Mazzarino, *Serena e le due Eudossie*, p. 12; *idem, Stilicone*, pp. 282–83.

[138] The most detailed exposition of the anti-German position is found in Synes. *De regno*, apparently pronounced (it is so outspoken that it is hard to believe that anyone would have dared thus bluntly to lecture the August Emperor) before the Emperor Arcadius at Constantinople some years before Stilicho's downfall. Dannenbauer, *Entstehung*, I, 201, points out that the accusation against Stilicho, that he was *semibarbarus*, was quite illogical, for Theodosius II and his sisters were also *semibarbari* (or at least quarter-barbarians), for their mother was the daughter of the Frank Bauto, but prejudice, or malice using prejudice for its own ends, is seldom logical.

[139] Apparently Stilicho was originally opposed to the marriage, but Serena was in favor of it (and probably inspired Honorius' request for his sister-in-law's hand) (Zos. 5. 28). The disagreement was probably whether it was politic to conclude such an alliance, Serena holding that thus their control of Honorius would be assured, Stilicho doubting whether that advantage might not be offset by the additional evidence it would give his enemies of his presumed imperial ambitions for his family, especially since such a marriage was considered incestuous by Christians (cf. *CTh* 3. 12. 4 [Constantinople, 415] and the discussion of Tillemont, *Empereurs*, V, 557).

view of the Roman troops at Pavia on 13 August 408, while Stilicho was at Bologna, the soldiers suddenly attacked the high dignitaries in the imperial entourage and slew them; thereafter they raged through the city, massacring any one else, whether Roman or German, they suspected of being friendly to Stilicho. The white-faced Emperor himself was unharmed.[140] At first Stilicho, informed of these events only by rumor, was uncertain whether Honorius himself had been slain, but he soon learned the truth, that Honorius was safe, but had in his fear made common cause with the general's enemies, anti-German or whatever. Stilicho refused the advice of his barbarian supporters to march on Pavia; thereupon they deserted him. In his indecision the general moved to Ravenna, where he took refuge in a church. Here a ruse, suggested by the Emperor's new principal adviser and Stilicho's former protégé Olympius,[141] drew him out of sanctuary; since he still refused the armed assistance of his friends and proudly declined to resist the commands of his sovereign, however perfidious, an officer named Heraclian[142] struck off his head (22 August 408). The profound loyalty at that supreme hour which he exhibited to the Roman Empire and the Roman Emperor should, but has not, have silenced those critics ancient and modern who have accused him of various kinds of conspiracy or treason.

Among other results, the anti-German opposition had triumphed in the West as it had previously in the East; for forty years hereafter the armies of Western Rome were headed principally by Romans.[143] The version of Stilicho's policies and career which prevailed in the histories written in the next generation was that of his enemies; he was depicted as a traitor in collusion with Goth and

---

[140] Sirago, *Placidia*, p. 43, holds that Honorius took an active part in the conspiracy against Stilicho, rather than merely being a subject for manipulation. Courcelle, *Hist. litt.*, pp. 29–30, may be closer to the truth when he portrays Honorius' sacrificing Stilicho out of fear for his own safety. It is difficult to believe that Honorius was not thoroughly terrified and cowed by the massacre carried out in his presence. Obviously the anti-Stilicho, antibarbarian, faction had been assiduously at work among the soldiers; cf. Mazzarino, *Stilicone*, pp. 290–92. Since Stilicho's power had rested in large part on the army, it was evidently necessary to turn the army against him, if his downfall were not to have dangerous repercussions among the military; cf. Dannenbauer, *Entstehung*, I, 200–201.

[141] Olympiod. Frag. 2 (IV, 58); Zos. 5. 35. 1.

[142] Zos. 5. 37. 6, cf. 34. 5; by way of reward he was made Count of Africa, *ibid*. 37. 6.

[143] J. Sundwall, *Weströmische Studien*, p. 6; R. Grosse, *Römische Militärgeschichte von Gallienus bis zum Beginn der byzantinischen Themenverfassung*, p. 265.

Vandal, a man who faithlessly designed to set his son Eucherius on the throne in lieu of the legitimate Emperor. Most modern scholars rightly reject these allegations outright, and limit their attention to trying to form a coherent idea of Stilicho's policy within the compass of his loyalty to the Roman state and the family of Theodosius the Great.[144] The fall of the minister was followed by the confiscation of his property and that of his friends,[145] and the witch-hunt common after the downfall of a great minister of state was set on foot in order to apprehend his "accomplices."[146] The fright and consternation at all levels of the government and administration must have been acute;[147] the precipitous decline in morale was the more undesirable in the midst of the turmoil and confusion of the immediately following months. At least, however, the removal of Stilicho meant a period of renewed good relations between the Eastern and Western governments, an amity which was to have its value for the West in the next difficult years.[148]

Among the first to suffer after the death of Stilicho, naturally, were the members of his family. Thermantia, married less than a year to Honorius, was repudiated that autumn and, still a virgin it was said, sent back to her mother.[149] Otherwise she was not molested, apparently, but died in obscurity in the summer of 415. She was probably buried in the imperial mausoleum by Saint Peter's, for she had after all been the wife of an emperor.[150] But

---

[144] Note: that Stilicho may have planned, under certain conditions, to marry Eucherius to Placidia and thus acquire for his son some title to the succession was ambitious, but not treasonable as long as the plan did not include the overthrow of Honorius (or Arcadius, or Theodosius II), as there is absolutely no evidence that it did. On the accusations against Stilicho, see Oros. 7. 38. 1; Soz. *HE* 9. 4. 7, 8; Marcell. *s.a.* 408, 1 (II, 69); other references and discussion in Demougeot, *Unité*, pp. 414–15; cf. *idem*, *Byzantion*, XX (1950), 29. See also E. von Wietersheim, *Geschichte der Völkerwanderung*, II, 2d ed. by F. Dahn, 145; Mazzarino, *Stilicone*, p. 289 (Eucherius).

[145] *CTh* 9. 42. 20 (24 Sept. 408), 21 (25 Oct. 408); Zosimus (5. 35. 4) exaggerates when he says that the confiscation extended to all who held office during Stilicho's regime; to have carried such a program into execution would have brought the government to a standstill after the long tenure of power by the general; other laws against Stilicho's partisans: *CTh* 9. 40. 20, 7. 21. 4, 9. 42. 22 (all of 22 Nov. 408).

[146] Zos. 5. 35. 3–6, 44. 2, 45. 3–4.

[147] Cf. G. Kaufmann, *Deutsche Geschichte bis auf Karl den Grossen*, I, 322.

[148] J.-R. Palanque, "Collégialité et partages dans l'empire romain aux IVe et Ve siècles," *RÉA*, XLVI (1944), 47–64, 280–98, at 290, seems to go a bit far in postulating a period of "no relations" between East and West after 408.

[149] Zos. 5. 35. 3, 37. 5; Marcell. *s.a.* 408, 1 (II, 69).

[150] Death: *Chron. Pasch.*, p. 572 (Bonn); burial: H. Koethe, "Zum Mausoleum der weströmischen Dynastie bei Alt-Sankt-Peter," *Röm. Mitt.*, XLVI (1931), 9–26, at 10, n. 3.

this inviolability did not extend to her brother Eucherius. Upon Stilicho's fall his son was taken under the protection of some of his father's barbarian troops. They fled south, but when they neared Rome, the youth took refuge in a City church. His barbarian friends meanwhile lived by plundering the countryside in the vicinity of Rome and eventually joined up with the Goths. Honorius had meanwhile ordered that a general search for Eucherius be instituted, and that he be put to death when found. But when those sent to seize him discovered him in sanctuary at Rome, they thought it best to let him go for the present.[151] Apparently thereafter he left the church and the City, for sometime later he fell into the hands of the Emperor's men outside of sanctuary; by imperial order the same eunuchs who conducted Thermantia to her mother at Rome also brought Eucherius there, where in compliance with the wishes of Honorius or his advisers he was put to death, doubtless on the charge of treason. If thus Olympius and his coterie thought to escape vengeance by destroying the person who could be the natural rallying point of their enemies, time was to prove them mistaken. These events occurred some months after Stilicho's death, for at the time of Eucherius' execution Alaric's Goths were already pouring over the Appenines on their way to Rome. Communications with Ravenna had been interrupted and the two eunuchs had to find their way back to their master by a circuitous route, partly by sea.[152]

The storm so many times feared by Rome and Italy in recent years, so many times turned aside at the last moment by the efforts of Stilicho, was about to burst upon Italy. As Alaric advanced southward at the end of the year 408 there ensued scenes of near-chaos such as, unhappily, many men of the twentieth century are too well acquainted with. Orderly government and communications were breaking down; for the first time in centuries a foreign foe was about to appear before the walls of Rome, fortunately recently repaired by Stilicho. Nevertheless now as in the next years masses

---

151 Zos. 5. 34. 5, 35. 3–4; Philostorg. *HE* 12. 3.

152 Zos. 5. 37. 4–5; cf. Oros. 7. 38. 6; Olympiod. Frag. 6 (IV, 59); Soz. *HE* 9. 4. 8; Marcell. *s.a.* 408, 1 (II, 69). There seems to be some confusion in the details given by the epitome of Philostorg. *HE* 12. 3; perhaps the latter originally wrote that Eucherius left sanctuary on the ground that immunity still attached to him, but Honorius issued commands to the effect that he be arrested since he had left sanctuary.

of refugees poured out of the City in all directions, while others will have striven to gain the protection of the walls before the approaching deluge broke over their heads. In the City itself reigned panic and desperation. The ironic pathos of the situation is underlined when one reflects that these scenes took place among the serene monuments of past imperial splendor and power. At this time Galla Placidia was in residence in the City; apparently she had remained in Rome after the Emperor departed the previous spring.[153] For whatever reason, she did not now flee. The barbarians were between her and Ravenna; perhaps she calmly disdained to yield to panic, remembering whose daughter she was. Whatever the motive, it probably reflects a considerable amount of courage, coolheadedness, and resolution on her part.

She was about to take the first important public step of her career; one may wish she had fled from Rome instead. For also residing in the City at this time was Serena, Placidia's cousin and Stilicho's widow, who had just been joined by her repudiated daughter, and whose son Eucherius had just been ignominiously put to death by the Emperor to whom Serena had once acted as a foster mother. Since Honorius had expressly returned Thermantia to her mother's keeping, he obviously did not intend to execute either one of them. After all, whatever Stilicho and Eucherius were, Serena was his cousin and his father's beloved niece. By this time his sister Placidia was a young woman of about twenty years of age. Although unmarried, she doubtless had her own household, supported by the private means which her father had left her, for we are fairly safe in assuming that she would have left the household of her cousin and foster mother as soon as the opportunity presented itself, at the time of Stilicho's death at the latest.[154]

In the frenzy of apprehension and terror which gripped the City the wildest rumors flew about. In view of the circumstances of Stilicho's downfall, his German ancestry, his policy of favoring Germans (that is, of using them extensively in the service of Rome,

153 Cf. Seeck, *Regesten,* pp. 312, 314.

154 Nagl, *Placidia,* p. 14, says Placidia and Serena were both living in the imperial palaces on the Palatine, but there is no evidence, and as far as Serena is concerned it seems unlikely after her husband's downfall and death; nor would Honorius rid himself of Thermantia by consigning her to her mother if the latter were living in his own house.

a policy which was in direct continuation of that of his mentor Theodosius the Great), the uncontested fact that he had let Alaric go more than once when he had had the Goth and his people more or less at his mercy; all these things combined to produce an absolute conviction that Alaric had been in collusion with Stilicho against Rome, and that now he was in collusion with Stilicho's widow in his march on Rome.[155] We do not need the assurance of the narrator of these events to conclude that Serena was completely innocent of the charge.[156] Yet by a really not surprising leap in the logic of panic the conviction seems furthermore to have spread that if only Serena were out of the way Rome would be saved, on the ground that she was going to betray the City to Alaric, for no one else presumably would have any interest in doing so.[157] This is particularly interesting, since when Alaric did in fact finally take Rome in 410, it was by treachery. Unfortunately the Senate shared these opinions;[158] it is by no means impossible, however, that with the cynical practicality often inseparable from Roman hardheadedness some senators may have been willing to condemn Serena in order to quiet the turmoil among the people. At any rate it was resolved by "the whole Senate" that Serena be put to death. But this was a very delicate matter; in the confusion and panic there was no time for a regular trial, nothing but lynch law (it might be dignified by the metaphoric label of "act of attainder") was available; the Emperor was cut off by the Goths in distant Ravenna and could not be communicated with. And the dispositions of Honorius, as we have seen, indicated that he had no intention of executing Serena, who was furthermore the niece and foster

---

155 Olympiod. Frag. 6 (IV, 59); Zos. 5. 38. 1. The latter says only that the Senate suspected Serena of collusion with Alaric, but it is almost more probable that in a hysterical city such suspicions were not confined to the senatorial class; see Burckhardt, *Schweiz. Rundschau*, XXV (1925–26), 487–88; Bury-Gibbon, *Decline and Fall*, III, 309. On the hysteria in Rome compare the rumor circulating near the end of the siege, that it was not Alaric but someone else besieging the City (Zos. 5. 40. 2).

156 Zos. 5. 38. 2; he goes on to say (2–5) that Serena's death was owing to an act of sacrilege against the goddess Rhea; probably for this reason Chastagnol, *Préfecture*, p. 166, connects the allegation with the pagan party; but there were certainly others who were convinced, whoever started the story, for Zos. says "all the Senate"; in the same sense see also L. Ruggini, review of Sirago, *Placidia*, *Athenaeum*, XL (1962), 373–91, at 389.

157 Zos. 5. 38. 1, cf. 39. 1.

158 Zos. 5. 38. 1.

daughter of Theodosius the Great, cousin and foster mother of the Emperor himself. Accordingly the Senate was eager to share the responsibility, and found Galla Placidia, member of the imperial family, half sister of the Emperor, and available in Rome, willing to share it. The daughter of Theodosius concurred in the resolution of the Conscript Fathers, and Serena was put to death by strangling or suffocation.[159] It is possible that Placidia did in fact sincerely believe in the treason both of Stilicho and Serena, and was confident that she was acting in an emergency in the best interests of the state. But it is hard to believe that she was convinced the woman who had brought her up was in fact in collusion with Alaric against Rome. The only explanation must be that Placidia was already so prejudiced against Serena, disliked her so cordially, that she could entertain the notion of the reality of her guilt on this occasion and concur in the decree condemning her to death. The death of Serena in this fashion is the fact that attests Placidia's dislike of her

---

159 Olympiod. Frag. 6 (IV, 59); Zos. 5. 38. 1. The latter says, "and it seemed best to [i.e., it was resolved by] both the whole Senate in common and to Placidia, sister of the Emperor by the same father, that she [Serena] be put to death, being the cause of the evils hemming [them] in." Note the care with which the exact relationship of Placidia to Honorius is specified (Sirago, *Placidia*, p. 84, says Zos. "transcribes" the official formula; at least there is probably an echo of it here); this fact lends support to the a priori argument in the text that the senators were wary of laying violent hands on a member of the imperial family without some sort of imperial authorization—which Placidia in some degree supplied in this instance. It is doubtful, however, that a woman, Placidia, was invited to the actual deliberations of the Senate, as some writers have inferred. Rather one must suppose that a committee of the Senate sounded her opinion and received her concurrence, orally or in writing, and with this backing the Senate felt nerved enough to pass the decree against Serena. There is no support in the sources for many statements of modern authors about this incident: Thus A. Dantier, *Les femmes dans la société chrétienne*, I, 241, implies that Placidia took the initiative by "denouncing" Serena. Despite Sievers, *Kaiser*, p. 448, it is difficult to believe in a "common decree" of the Senate and Placidia against Serena, implying that Placidia's act was part of the Senate's decree, or that she voted for it presumably in the Senate. The language of Zos., although being capable of construction in this sense, should not be understood in a manner contrary to Roman usage. Hodgkin, *Invaders*, I: 2, 820, n. 2, says that Thierry attributed the initiative to Placidia, that she appeared before the Senate and denounced Serena, and so on. Sirago, *Placidia*, pp. 84–85, says that the Senate invited Placidia to its sitting—possible, but unlikely, for his arguments are not cogent. Bury, *JRS*, IX (1919), 1, says she "voted" (presumably in the Senate!). R. Latouche, *Les grandes invasions et la crise de l'occident au V^e siècle*, p. 86, says Placidia instigated the destruction of Serena. Nischer-Falkenhof, *Stilicho*, p. 154, on the other hand implies that Placidia was forced to act against Serena [by the Senate?]—"müsste . . . bestätigen." Yet so distinguished a scholar as Lot in F. Lot, C. Pfister, and F. L. Ganshof, *Les destinées de l'Empire en occident de 395 à 888*, p. 33, can speak of the "instigation" of Placidia. In general see the cautious remarks of Ensslin, *RE*, XX: 2 (1950), 1912–13.

quondam guardian and validates the interpretation offered in this chapter to try to explain the growth of this dislike or hate.[160] There is also the possibility that, although morally certain of Serena's innocence, Placidia nevertheless cold-bloodedly seized the occasion to encompass her death; yet we find no other incident in the admittedly scanty information about her life that would substantiate such a hypothesis about her character, and Placidia at least in later life was a devout Christian. It seems better to conclude that probability favors her having acted out of sincere prejudice, which was too willing to give credence to allegations against a person she detested.[161] Of course in fact the execution of Serena did not stop or hinder Alaric's laying siege to the City.[162]

[160] On the probability that Placidia strongly disliked or hated Serena (and possibly Stilicho and Eucherius as well), see A. Thierry, "Aventures de Placidie," *Rev. deux mondes*, 1850, part IV, pp. 863–79, at 867 (although his reckless romanticizing of history renders his conclusions of little value); Lot, *Destinées*, p. 31; Hodgkin, *Invaders*, I: 2, 820–21 and 820, n. 2; esp. Demougeot, *Unité*, p. 429, who tries to explain this hate or dislike along much the same lines attempted in this chapter, although to say that Placidia was of the anti-German party is pure supposition. When one can argue, as Demougeot does, that a young girl has strong personal reasons for dislike or hate, it adds little to conclude that therefore she was an adherent of, or favored, a group which also opposed the person she detested. Much of the difficulty with the detailed analyses of "parties" in Roman history (the very word "party" has ill-advised connotations in any period of that history) is that political groupings are frequently seen as sharing a common ideology, while quite different personal motives are adequate to explain motivation. American students might remember that parties as we know them are so recent that the United States constitution makes no mention of their existence. The fact alone should suggest caution in reading "party" politics into the history of the distant past.

[161] On the interpretation of this incident, see Sirago, *Placidia*, pp. 86–88; Schild, *Placidia*, pp. 22–23; Nagl, *Placidia*, p. 14; Ensslin, *RE*, XX: 2 (1950), 1912–13.

[162] As Zos. 5. 39. 1 points out, not without irony.

# 3

# ATHAULF

At the time of Stilicho's downfall Alaric and his Goths were still awaiting in Noricum the payment of the subsidy that had been promised them. Part of the anti-Stilicho, anti-German reaction at court had been a massacre throughout the cities of Italy of the families of the barbarian soldiers in the service of Rome. Most of the barbarian soldiers were thus thrown into the arms of Alaric, from whom they might expect vengeance; some, such as the group which sheltered Eucherius for a time, wandered about Italy by themselves, plundering the countryside. Eventually probably most of the barbarian bands joined up with the Goths, although one suspects that some individuals may well have gone to swell the numbers of brigands who frequently subverted public order in the Late Empire. The general breakdown of government and administration occasioned partly by the persecution of Stilicho's followers, but mostly by the Gothic invasion, naturally favored the activities of bandits and brigands. In the midst of all this violence the new "ministry" of Honorius affirmed its Christian orthodoxy by various laws penalizing other religious groups, pagan or heretic Christian.[1] The Goth Sarus, however, despite the orthodox and anti-German posture of the government, remained in its service, largely because he was an enemy of Alaric. The latter was pressing his claim for payment upon the government, promising to retire to Pannonia on receipt of a sum of money smaller than he had demanded before. In its anti-German bigotry the imperial

1 Cf. Demougeot, *Unité*, p. 430.

government foolishly rejected this offer and thus provoked Alaric to march on to Italy; no obstacle was placed in his path, as he by-passed Ravenna where Honorius and his ministers were safe behind the marshes. The eventual objective of the Goths was Rome itself, but on the way they laid waste to the countryside and villages in their path.[2]

Before crossing the Alps into Italy Alaric had ordered Athaulf, his wife's brother, to join him from Pannonia, together with the forces under his command, Huns as well as Goths in no small numbers.[3] Without waiting, however, for his brother-in-law's arrival Alaric pressed on into Italy, whether out of mere impatience or in the realization that his chances for success were best if he struck while the Western government was still relatively disorganized after the fall of Stilicho. There has been much speculation about the precise aims of Alaric in these years. Surely he had no intention of trying to overthrow the Roman Empire; if such an idea had ever entered his mind (which is unlikely), he must have dismissed it at once. How large the bands of Germans who invaded the Empire were it is impossible to say; it is clear, however, that they were relatively small. Even in the decline of its population the Roman Empire numbered many millions of subjects, and even in the distraction of its dissolution in the West it was capable, under competent administration, of assembling military forces, of whatever origins, still quite formidable to the ill-disciplined barbarian bands, which with wives and children, bag and baggage, were whole tribes on the move rather than armies. What the Goths seem to have been seeking was support whether in terms of money, or supplies (principally food), or land. Eventually they received land in Gaul, land at least for the most part probably worked for them by Roman peasants.[4] In return they were supposed to furnish

2 Sirago, *Placidia*, p. 76, n. 3, argues that since Alaric did not march directly to Rome, he thought of going there only after he had been in Italy for some time. This is possible, yet it seems more likely that he had this intent at the back of his mind from the beginning; possibly he hoped that the devastation of other parts of Italy would force the government to yield to his demands; possibly he and his men were temporarily distracted from their ultimate objective by the opportunities for rich plunder on every side.

3 Zos. 5. 37. 1.

4 It is frequently opined that only the great landowners had to accept barbarian "guests"; for the settlement of the Visigoths in 418–19 we do not know; apparently only the great landowners were involved in the case of the Burgundians in 456 (Mar. Avent. *s.a.* 456 [II, 232]; cf. F. Lot, "Du régime de l'hospitalité," *Rev. belge de*

military assistance to Rome. That such an objective, however, was pursued by the Goths without variation is unlikely. They were after all barbarians, accustomed to the bearing and use of arms as a way of life, with all that implies in terms of honor, acquisition of status, temperament, or whim (from the point of view of civilized man, at least), whether for good or for evil. In some respects their relations vis-à-vis the Roman Empire were like those which the barbarians native to the United States would have had to the American government, if that government had not possessed crushing technological superiority to the Indians.

Thus in the last months of the year 408 Alaric and his Goths arrived before the walls of Rome, only shortly after the executions of Eucherius and Serena.[5] Perhaps at this time, perhaps first at some other juncture years before, Alaric apparently announced that supernatural forces of some kind were impelling him to go to Rome and lay it waste.[6] If in fact he did experience a subjective conviction that Destiny intended him to take the City, the assumption that he had had this idea in the back of his mind for some time is strengthened. On the other hand, on this first appearance before the walls of Rome, it is quite likely that he was merely putting pressure on the government of the City and Empire to compel compliance with his demands;[7] yet had an opportunity offered to penetrate the City's defenses, it seems likely enough that

---

*philolog. et d'hist.*, VII [1928], 975–1011, at 989–93); this implies that the peasants of these great landowners continued to work the lands whose usufruct was thus ceded to the barbarians. But although this fact may make it likely that the same was true of the Visigoths, there is no evidence, especially as of 418–19. While in the fourth century the Goths had apparently had an agricultural economy (E. A. Thompson, "The Visigoths in the time of Ulfila," *Nottingham Mediaeval Studies*, V [1961], 3–32 [now with revisions in his *The Visigoths in the Time of Ulfila*, pp. 25–63], at 11–20), it seems likely that such settled habits had tended to disappear in the wild restless time that followed the year 376. On Gothic objectives in 408 and the following years, Seeck, *Gesch.*, V: 1, 394–95.

5 Sirago, *Placidia*, pp. 80–81, suggests that Alaric hoped to get from the Senate the money he had failed to get from the Emperor, that he realized that the interests of Senate and Emperor were not identical; but this presupposes a knowledge on the Goth's part of the subtle tensions of Roman politics which it seems hard to assume. It seems more likely to infer that the barbarian was out to get what he could, money from Senate or Emperor, as the case might be, or plunder, or both; exert enough pressure on the imperial structure at any point, and it ought to yield.

6 Claud. *Bell. Goth.* 501–3, 546–47; Soc. *HE* 7. 10. 10–11; unfortunately the attitude attributed to Alaric by Claudian may be pure rhetoric (take the first and last, last and first letters of 546–47), which in turn fathered the tradition found in Soc.

7 Demougeot, *Unité*, pp. 434, 435.

he would have taken advantage of it. Since the Goths still had neither the skill nor the equipment to besiege a well-walled city, Alaric formed a blockade of the capital.[8] His first attention was engaged to cut off the victualing of Rome; Ostia was seized and Rome was thus shut off from her all-important supply of grain from Africa. The ravages of famine began to be felt almost immediately by the besieged. Presumably among others who in Christian charity attempted to alleviate the wretched lot of the people were Laeta, widowed second wife of the Emperor Gratian, and her mother Tisamene; from the ample resources placed at their disposal by Theodosius the Great they were able to assist no small number.[9] Evidently a considerable part of the population was still pagan, or half-Christian, with a secret fear of the powers of the ancient gods. Indeed it was a common belief among Christians of the time and for centuries to come, not that the gods were mere myths, but malign demons whose undoubted power was used to torment and damn the human race. The pagans, among whom was the Prefect of the City, initiated a campaign to perform proper expiatory sacrifices to the gods. It was said by the pagans that the Pope, Innocent I, was willing to consent to the performance of these rites in private, but balked when he was told that public celebrations were necessary; these ceremonies had of course been forbidden by Theodosius the Great and the prohibition had been renewed by Honorius. The evidence for the presumed acquiescence of the Pope comes from the pagan historian Zosimus.[10] That the gleeful allegation of the pagan polemicist was true is unthinkable. If the fourth century was not an age of freethinkers, the fifth was even less so; the cynical Rome of the Renaissance papacy was many centuries in the future. That the Bishop of Rome should thus risk damning his own soul to hell forever in accordance with the strict injunctions of his religion, not to mention the souls of the participants in such sacrifices, is absolutely beyond belief. The suggestion that there were murmurs of dissatisfaction with the Pope because he sat out the siege of 410 in safety at Ravenna away from

8 The evidence for the first attack on Rome is assembled and discussed in detail by Demougeot, *Unité*, pp. 434–37.

9 Zos. 5. 39. 4.

10 Zos. 5. 41; Soz. *HE* 9. 6. 4 mentions the pagan agitation, but not the partial participation of the Pope; both say that the town of Narnia was alleged to have been saved by such rites.

his flock, and that these criticisms offered opportunities for pagan invention is attractive.[11]

Finally, the Senate, after a haughty threat to Alaric to beware the ancient valor of the Romans in their multitude was laughed at,[12] was able to purchase the release of the City by paying a huge ransom, which was raised in part by melting down all sorts of objects of precious metal, including important works of art. It is hard to avoid the odious comparison with the panic in the City when Hannibal had seemed about to assail it six centuries before; at that time the Senate had calmly met amid the tumult to consider measures for quieting the populace, and posted guards at the gates to prevent wholesale flight.[13] In the course of the Gothic siege or thereafter large numbers of barbarian slaves fled to the Goths—an additional grievous loss to the citizens, since naturally there could be no question of their return. Alaric also demanded a treaty with the Emperor as part of his price, and an embassy from the Senate dutifully departed for Ravenna to obtain this agreement, as well as the imperial confirmation of the other terms. In the meanwhile the Goths granted a truce to the Romans to purchase supplies at markets by certain of the gates; at the same time brigandage in the surrounding open country was firmly repressed by Alaric (end of 408). The King finally withdrew to Etruria, only a menacing short distance from the City; nevertheless Honorius refused to make any concessions. The failure of Olympius, however, to cope with the Goths provoked his downfall, and in the troubled times of the next years the advisers of the Emperor changed with a frequency which betrayed the vacillation of the court between the necessity for concession and the hauteurs of an inflexible resistance.

[11] E. Caspar, *Geschichte des Papsttums von den Anfängen bis zur Höhe der Weltherrschaft*, I, 299–300; V. Schultze, *Geschichte des Untergangs des griechisch-römischen Heidentums*, I, 371; Sirago, *Placidia*, p. 90; E. Demougeot, "À propos des interventions du pape Innocent I$^{er}$ dans la politique séculière," *Rev. hist.*, CCXII (1954), 23–38, at 30–31, with much less than her usual acumen is inclined to accept the story; G. Bardy, "La Papauté de Saint Innocent à Saint Léon le Grand," in *Hist. de l'Église*, ed. A. Fliche and V. Martin, IV, 241–67, at 243, n. 3; cf. also J. Gaudemet, "Société religieuse et monde laïc au bas-empire," *Iura*, X (1959), 86–102, at 91.

[12] Sirago, *Placidia*, p. 91, remarks that if only the nobles had been willing to arm and train their dependents, effective resistance could have been offered to the Goths. But such a procedure would have been dangerous both to the established order and to the public peace; it was for these reasons that such a practice had been forbidden centuries before by the *Lex Iulia de vi publica* (cf. *Dig.* 48. 6).

[13] Livy 22. 54. 8, 55. 3, 8.

Olympius even returned to power for a short time, but his second downfall was final. Even the Germans and those favorable to them at court were able for a time to return to power.

In Gaul the usurper Constantine raised his son Constans from the rank of Caesar to that of Augustus (early 409 or 410);[14] an embassy to Honorius asking for recognition was favorably received, in part because the latter hoped to save the lives of some of his Spanish relatives who had fallen into Constantine's hands; the Emperor was unaware that they had already been executed. The situation in Italy, however, continued to deteriorate. Reinforcements to the Emperor from Dalmatia were cut down or made prisoner by the Goths, who were themselves finally joined by Athaulf and his following. Although the imperial forces gained a victory over Athaulf, they were unable to prevent his juncture with the main Gothic horde. Negotiations of a sort were intermittently carried on with Alaric, but with the control of the Roman government in intermittent flux it proved impossible to arrive at any settlement. Although he might temporarily be forced to make a show of concession, the Emperor, secure in Ravenna, was stubbornly resistant to any settlement that would be agreeable to Alaric. Honorius' basic intransigence was encouraged by various reinforcements he received from time to time; he or his government even found it possible to send a barbarian general named Generidus to reassert Roman control over the provinces to the northeast of Italy—Dalmatia, upper Pannonia, Noricum, and Rhaetia.[15]

Finally wearying of this profitless game in the fall of 409, Alaric again marched on Rome, and by the renewal of the blockade forced the Senate, probably already ill-disposed to the Emperor for his stubbornness for which the City would have to pay,[16] to recognize

14 Stevens, *Athenaeum*, n.s., XXXV (1957), 330 and n. 94, prefers early 410; cf. Demougeot, *Unité*, p. 459.

15 Zos. 5. 45. 5–6, 46. 2–5. Sirago, *Placidia*, p. 97, sees in this northeastern mission an encircling movement to shut Alaric up in Italy without means of reinforcements from the barbarians beyond the frontier. Possibly, but the way to Gaul across the western Alps was presumably still open to the Goths, who might join, or turn against, Constantine. In any case, if the government had thought that this force could hold Alaric in Italy if he wanted to leave, it would more likely have sent it directly against him in Italy. Yet, despite the efforts of Generidus, from this time onward the hold of Rome on the Danube provinces north of Italy became more and more precarious and nominal; cf. Demougeot, *Unité*, pp. 526–28. In some areas her sovereignty became more and more tenuous until it disappeared without any grand climax. The *Life of St. Severinus* by Eugippius shows this process toward its end in the last decades of the fifth century.

16 Cf. Sirago, *Placidia*, pp. 98–99.

a new Emperor, Priscus Attalus, who had been Prefect of Rome. Obviously Alaric hoped to obtain from an emperor of his own creation what he had failed to secure from Honorius; it may be presumed that the career of Constantine in the Gauls had suggested this expedient to him.[17] Unfortunately, although Attalus was willing to make various concessions, he remained a Roman, refusing to sacrifice any real interests of the Empire to the Goths. Thus, previously a pagan,[18] he allowed himself to be baptized into the Arian belief by the Arian bishop of the Goths, a certain Sigesarius.[19] Alaric was appointed Master of Both Branches of the Soldiery, while Athaulf became Count of the Household Horse *(comes domesticorum equitum)*; Alaric, however (and probably Athaulf as well), received a Roman colleague, doubtless to try to keep a check on him.[20] Gothic envoys had assisted at the new Emperor's elevation; his bodyguard was probably composed of Goths.[21] On the other hand, although Alaric was clearly master of Rome for as far as he wished to press the point, Attalus nevertheless balked at sending Gothic forces under his aegis to conquer Africa, where Count Heraclian, loyal to Honorius, cut off the grain supplies for Rome, while at the same time he contributed much-needed revenues to the resources of the government at Ravenna. To hand over the wealthy provinces of Africa to the barbarian was something no conservative Roman official could contemplate. Hence Heraclian was able to repulse the emissaries of the usurper with no difficulty.

In the City of Rome there still resided the princess Galla Placidia, who once again had not fled as many other Romans, high and low, had done during the time that intervened between the two Gothic appearances before the City. As the sister of the legitimate reigning Emperor she was a prize of great value. She was now in the power of Attalus, which is probably to say, in the control of Alaric if he wished to exert his power. And it is possible that the presence of Placidia within reach of Gothic retribution even before she came outright into Alaric's control was a reason for the Ravenna government to be cautious about any attempt to

[17] Demougeot, *Unité*, p. 447.

[18] Philostorg. *HE* 12. 3. Many modern scholars have rightly seen in Attalus' regime a kind of pagan reaction; cf. esp. G. Manganaro, "La reazione pagana a Roma nel 408–409 d. C.," *Giorn. it. fil.*, XIII (1960), 210–24 (without necessarily accepting the dating of the anonymous *Carmen contra paganos* to this time).

[19] Soz. *HE* 9. 9. 1; apparently one bishop sufficed for all the Goths.

[20] Zos. 6. 7. 2; Soz. *HE* 9. 8. 2.

[21] Zos. 6. 7. 1, 3, with Demougeot, *Unité*, p. 449, n. 38.

push the Goth too hard.[22] And when Alaric deposed Attalus, Placidia remained in the former's keeping, in effect a hostage, but treated nevertheless with all respect and with the full honors befitting a princess of the imperial house.[23] What the reaction of the daughter of Theodosius to her effective imprisonment was, we do not know, nor what she thought of the Goths, whenever it was that she actually passed into their keeping. We shall see, however, that she came eventually to be fairly well used to her lot. Cultures classed as barbarian have many disadvantages from the point of view of civilized persons; one of the advantages, however, is frequently a sort of rude chivalry. And if Placidia had been resentful of being kept in the background during the regime of Stilicho, which had endured for most of her girlhood, she may have found the deference of the dreaded Goths not entirely distasteful.

Meanwhile Honorius and his government were in some distress. With the necessity of having competent soldiers had come the rise once again of Germans in high places; to one of these, Allobic, the Emperor had become almost a captive in his own palace and capital. When Allobic caused Eusebius, Provost of the Sacred Bedchamber and a favorite of the Emperor, to be assassinated, Honorius was powerless to avenge his servant. The usurper Constantine entered Italy at the head of an armed force on the excuse

22 So Ensslin, *RE*, XX: 2 (1950), 1913–14, who obviously therefore believes that Placidia was in the hands of the Emperor's enemies by the end of 409, and not merely in 410. Sievers, *Kaiser*, p. 448, thinks Placidia may have come into the hands of Alaric as early as the conclusion of the first blockade of Rome; so also Güldenpenning, *Arcad. u. Theod.*, p. 215. This view is barely possible, but the first evidence of Placidia in Gothic power is on the occasion of the dethronement of Attalus (at least the reference occurs then); hence the reconstruction advanced in the text.

23 Zos. 6. 12. 3 alone tells us that Placidia was in Gothic hands before the final attack on Rome in 410; all other sources which indicate any date at all say that she was taken away with the Goths after the sack of Rome in that year (see below, n. 38). Obviously this conjunction is easy to make: the Goths took Rome; later they had Placidia with them; so they took her with Rome (cf. Ensslin, *RE*, XX: 2 [1950], 1913); and not a few modern authors have neglected this passage of Zos. as well as the logic of the situation itself (if she were not effectively in the hands of Attalus-Alaric from the moment that Attalus was recognized as Emperor, logic would require us to postulate that she was not in Rome at the time and returned later, somehow, to be carried off in 410), to say that the princess became Alaric's captive only after the taking of Rome in 410. Sirago's arguments, *Placidia*, p. 112, n. 5, in favor of 410 are quite unconvincing; in favor of a date before 410, among many others besides Ensslin, see Demougeot, *Unité*, p. 474. Sirago's attempts to explain why Placidia remained at Rome are unsatisfactory: the grave difficulties in which Honorius found himself prevented her leaving Rome previously (why?); she could not leave Rome because she was a person of such great importance (why? although she may have felt it her duty to encourage the Romans by remaining) (cf. Sirago, *Placidia*, pp. 112–13).

that he wished to help fight Alaric; probably in fact he was in a conspiracy with Allobic which boded no good for Honorius. In desperation the latter was seriously thinking of fleeing to the East, when Anthemius, Praetorian Prefect of the Orient and real master for the time being of the Eastern Empire, anti-German that he was, sent some four thousand soldiers to the succor of the Western Emperor. In the euphoria, commensurate with his previous hopelessness, which the reinforcements brought, Honorius caused, or agreed to, the murder of Allobic; significantly, upon the receipt of this news the usurper Constantine[24] found it best to retire at once to Gaul.[25] At the nadir of his fortunes in 410 Honorius had been willing even to recognize Attalus[26] as he had Constantine; now, despite the threatening presence of Attalus with Alaric and the Goths in the plain of the Po, the Emperor's resistance again stiffened in accordance with his real wishes. Attalus, who had haughtily indicated that he would be content to allow Honorius to abdicate, provided the latter were mutilated (we are obviously in a sort of western proto-Byzantine age where mutilation is used as a punishment, and is a fatal defect in an emperor) was ignominiously stripped of his imperial rank and insignia by Alaric, who was disappointed in the failure of his puppet to achieve the goals he wished, and was probably also disillusioned by the latter's courageous opposition to him in so vital a matter as the conquest of Africa by the Goths. Mercifully, however, Attalus was not handed over to the vengeance of Honorius (Attalus' treason of course merited death by all Roman law), but was kept in safety with the Goths. The dethronement of Attalus occurred in a public ceremony at Ariminum (Rimini; summer, 410); Galla Placidia

---

[24] He had assumed the consulship of 409; cf. *IG*, XIV, 2559; A. Degrassi, *I fasti consolari dell' impero romano*, p. 87.

[25] Soz. *HE* 9. 12. 4–6; Olympiod. Frag. 14 (IV, 60). Cf. Demougeot, *Unité*, pp. 455–56; Stevens, *Athenaeum*, n.s., XXXV (1957), 331. Apparently about this time (409–10) the officials of Rome (Constantine's) in Britain and parts of Gaul (Armorica and vicinity) were expelled by the inhabitants who took arms to protect themselves from barbarian inroads. Upon appeal to Honorius for assistance the Emperor could only suspend the *Lex Iulia de vi publica* and make their activities in their own defense legal (Zos. 6. 5. 3–6. 1, 10. 2; cf. Gildas *Excid. Brit.* 18; J. N. L. Myres, "Pelagius and the End of Roman Rule in Britain," *JRS*, L (1960), 21–36, at 33.

[26] Some scholars have believed that Honorius even went so far as to strike coins recognizing the pretensions of Attalus; cf. Cohen, VIII², 206, no. 9, cited by O. Seeck, *s.v.* "Priscus Attalus" (19), *RE*, II (1896), 2177–79, at 2178; L. Schmidt, *Geschichte der deutschen Stämme bis zur Ausgang der Völkerwanderung*, I, 446.

may well have witnessed the edifying spectacle, but the fact is not certain.[27] If Alaric saw the dethronement of Attalus not only as a measure which revoked a move whose uselessness had been demonstrated, but as a means of conciliating the legitimate government,[28] he was quickly disabused of the latter notion. At Ravenna, in his newly found optimism Honorius listened to Sarus, the Gothic enemy of Alaric and all his family; a threat of attack on Sarus by Athaulf drove the former back to service with Honorius, although he had been acting as more or less a free agent in Picenum.[29] Sarus now attacked the Goths, and in rage at this move, which the Emperor condoned, Alaric broke off discussions with the government, quit the Po valley, and for the third time marched south against the devoted City of Rome (beginning of August, 410).

Thus began the third Visigothic siege, actually blockade, of Rome,[30] an event whose outcome, after some eight centuries in which the imperial City had known impunity from foreign foes, created a shock of horror from Bethlehem to Britain.[31] Once again Gothic bravery found itself daunted by the walls of the Emperor Aurelian; the treachery that the Romans had feared in the beginning in 408 now in fact admitted the Goths by the Salarian Gate, 24 August 410, but not before the City had once again felt the bite of famine.[32] Some buildings were burned, notably the

27 Zos. 6. 12. 3 may carry this implication, but the conclusion does not necessarily follow. Presumably, however, Alaric, not a fool, would have made up his mind what to do with Placidia before he demoted Attalus; if so, he certainly would not have left her at Rome or elsewhere, where she might elude him, but would have had her where he could be sure of her safekeeping.

28 It is quite possible that during this summer Alaric, in order to show his potential usefulness and value to the Emperor, had threatened, or even fought, Constantine; cf. Demougeot, *Unité*, p. 459; Stevens, *Athenaeum*, n.s., XXXV (1957), 332.

29 Zos. 6. 13. 2, the concluding passage of Zosimus' history as it has come down to us.

30 A detailed account of this attack on Rome, its fall, and its sack, based on all the available evidence, will be found in Demougeot, *Unité*, pp. 467–78.

31 Britain's reaction is probable, but not attested. On the East, cf. the Westerner, Hieron. *In Ezech*. 1. praef., 3. praef. Rome had been taken by the Gauls in 390 B.C., presumably according to the chronology of M. Terentius Varro, a scholar contemporary with Cicero; Greek historians put the event in 387 B.C.; the event is undoubted and happened about that time, but like all events in the history of the City before the last half of the fourth century B.C. both the exact date and the details are involved in unresolved and probably insoluble obscurity.

32 Cf. Hieron. *Ep*. 127. 12—not a man to spare his rhetoric; cf. 128. 4, where in effect the City is depicted as reduced to ashes; this simply is not true, although there were in fact fires. Saint Augustine in his *Serm. de excid. urbis* depicts the devastation much more emphatically than in his later *Civ. Dei*. Procop. *Bell*. 3 (*Vand*. 1). 2. 14–23 has an incredible Arabian Nights tale about a "fifth column" of Gothic youths who betrayed the City, and then (27) accuses Faltonia Proba, a woman of the highest

Palace of Sallust the historian, which stood in its magnificent gardens near the gate of entry, perhaps the Basilica Aemilia in the Roman Forum, and the Palace of Saint Melania and Pinianus on the Caelian Hill,[33] then one of the most fashionable quarters of Rome. Palaces and temples were plundered, some persons were slain or tortured to reveal their presumed hidden wealth; some virgins and other females were raped, but churches, especially the basilicas of Saints Peter and Paul, were spared and made places of refuge. The Christians later had edifying tales to tell of the piety of the Christian, even although Arian, Goths. Some churches were burnt, Saint Mary in Trastevere, for example.[34] Depending on their particular biases both Christians and pagans exaggerated or minimized the damage done. But in so vast a City not too much harm could be wrought in the brief time that the Goths had at their disposal, for on the third day they left.[35] In three days, however, they had managed to carry off huge amounts of precious booty; some of it more than a century later, apparently, formed part of the treasure of the Visigothic kings of Spain.[36] Yet other booty eluded them—valuables that had been hidden by their owners (or possibly by looters in some cases) who were then prevented by some chance, frequently fatal, we may presume, from reclaiming them; discoveries of such hoards have not been un-

---

rank and wealth, of admitting the Goths in order to spare the Romans the further horrors of the blockade, including cannibalism (other sources mention cannibalism and there is no reason why it should not be true), by having one of the gates opened. The accusation, which several scholars have doubted, smacks too much of the fifth-century search by Romans for a scapegoat for every disaster. Stilicho was the first, but not the last; this narrative will indicate a whole series of such scapegoats. Soz. 9. 9. 4 knows only that the City fell by treachery, without any details; cf. Demougeot, *Unité*, pp. 468–69; Courcelle, *Hist. litt.*, p. 35; L. Duchesne, *Early History of the Christian Church from its Foundation to the End of the Fifth Century*, III, 140–41; A Cartellieri, *Weltgeschichte als Machtgeschichte*, I, 19, finds the story of Proba and her motives quite credible; cf. Seeck, *Gesch.*, V: 1, 413; 2, 600.

[33] Procop. *Bell.* 3 (*Vand.* 1). 2. 24; S. B. Platner and T. Ashby, *A Topographical Dictionary of Ancient Rome, s.v.* "Basilica Aemilia," p. 75; G. Lugli, *Roma antica: Il centro monumentale*, p. 173; *V. greca S. Mel. Iun.* 14 (p. 156, ed. Gorce) = *V. lat.* 14 (*Anal. Boll.*, VIII, 31).

[34] *Lib. pont.* 45. 2.

[35] Oros. 7. 39. 15.

[36] *Gest. Reg. Franc.* 23 (*Rec. des hist. des Gaules et de la France*, II, ed. M. Bouquet, 557). If Procopius is correct in saying that some of the Temple treasures plundered from Jerusalem by Titus were carried off by the Goths (the rest being left for the Vandals in 455) (Procop. *Bell.* 5 [*Goth.* 1]. 12. 42), some of the objects may still have been preserved in Visigothic Toledo; their historical value rather than their intrinsic worth would make their careful retention a strong possibility.

common in the subsequent history of Rome, both before and after
the time of modern archeology.[37] And with their booty the Goths
carried off Galla Placidia, as they turned to the rich Campania and
the south, as yet untouched by their ravages.[38] Most modern
scholars are agreed that the reason behind this speedy departure of
the Goths was that Rome was almost completely without food
after the blockade; very likely the Goths themselves had consumed
not only what the surrounding countryside had to offer by way of
sustenance, but whatever they had found in the warehouses of
Ostia and Portus as well.[39] The unharried lands of the south, on
the other hand, would be likely to provide adequate provender for
the King's people. A Greek historian some decades later asserts that
Alaric also feared the rumored approach of reinforcements from
the Eastern government for the hard-pressed troops of the West.[40]
Thus, still treated with all imperial honor, we may presume, Galla
Placidia was about to begin several years of nomadic wandering
with the Goths.[41] Behind them the inhabitants of the City began to
pull their lives together again; within a few years, with some exceptions, most of the outward damage had been repaired.[42] The
destruction had also been great in the vicinity of Rome; some
owners did not return to their abandoned farms or villas, which
fell into ruin or were taken over by squatters.[43]

[37] Summary in R. Lanciani, *The Destruction of Ancient Rome,* pp. 61–66; cf.
*idem, Wanderings through Ancient Roman Churches,* p. 68.

[38] Oros. 7. 40. 2 (the statement that Placidia was captured by Athaulf is merely
proleptic of future events); Olympiod. Frag. 3 (IV, 58) (the statement that Placidia
was staying in Rome when she was captured on this occasion need not be taken
literally since these excerpts have been revised, doubtless with explanatory notes, by
Photius, see above, n. 23; since she was in Gothic custody before the siege began,
there would be no reason for her to be allowed to enter the City at this time, and
prudential considerations might well dictate the opposite); Hyd. 44 (II, 17); Prosper
1259 (I, 468); Marcell. *s.a.* 410 (II, 70) (the departure of the Goths is put on the sixth
day); Malalas, pp. 349–50 (Bonn), followed by Theophanes, p. 76 (de B), has a curious
farrago of fact and nonsense.

[39] Seeck, *Gesch.,* V: 1, 415; Schmidt, *Gesch.*2, II, 453; Demougeot, *Unité* p. 477; the
last also suggests that Alaric may well have been seized by superstitious terror at his
own daring in profaning the ancient seat of Empire (p. 478).

[40] Soc. *HE* 7. 10. 7–8.

[41] Nagl suggests, *Placidia,* p. 17, that an imperial princess cannot have found these
prolonged wanderings over the lands of the Western Empire other than fatiguing in
contrast to the smooth protocol and luxury of the imperial palaces of Rome and
Constantinople. This may well be true, but Placidia was young and stout; we may
also presume that she found a considerable interest in the months and years to come
in Athaulf, for reasons that will emerge.

[42] Olympiod. Frag. 25 (IV, 62); Oros. 7. 40. 1; Rut. Namat. 1. 95–114.

[43] See the discussion by R. Lanciani, *Wanderings in the Roman Campagna,* pp.
55–56.

During these last years refugees from Rome had scattered all over the Roman world—as far as Bethlehem, where they told their harrowing tales to a thunderstruck Saint Jerome, as near as the islands of the Tyrrhenian Sea, Elba and others off the coast of Italy, and to Africa, where probably they were not treated nearly as badly by Count Heraclian, the assassin or executioner of Stilicho, as Saint Jerome alleges.[44] Almost at once the pagans pointed to the fall of Rome with the triumphant argument that this sort of thing had not happened as long as the Romans had remained true to their ancient gods. In answer to this superficially attractive argument the Bishop of Hippo Regius in Africa (Bône), an ardent teacher and polemicist in behalf of the orthodox faith, Saint Augustine, began to write his *City of God.* While minimizing the agony of the City in 410 at the hands of the Christian Goths and emphasizing various misfortunes that had in fact befallen the Romans during the time of the unquestioned supremacy of the pagan gods, the greatest Latin Church Father expounded a Christian philosophy of history. In his great classic work of declining Rome and rising Faith (which it is iconoclastic but probably true to suggest could profitably have been cut to half its length) Augustine erected upon the basis of some of the points of view of the Bible a great system of history in which the City of This World, that is, human society, struggles with the City of God, mainly good Christians, in a divine plan for humanity extending through all time. For a thousand years Augustine's view was to remain the dominant European concept of history. Orosius, a Spanish protégé of Augustine, attempted to show in his *History Against the Pagans,* a much inferior piece of work, how in fact God's plan had operated in history up to that time; the calamities and catastrophes of pagans to the time of Christ were mercilessly emphasized. This work also for a thousand years remained the standard account of ancient history in the Latin west and was the principal source for the time it covered, used by countless later narratives. How far the pagans of the fifth century were led by these polemics or apologetics to see the light and the truth it would be hard to say, but surely they confirmed the faith of those already persuaded of Christian verity.

The biographer of Galla Placidia would like to know her thoughts on her own vicissitudes as well as on those of Rome and

---

44 Cf. "The Revolt of Heraclian," *CP*, LXI (1966), 236–42, at 237.

the Roman Empire, but her reaction is lost beyond hope of recovery. This much is certain, that she remained a convinced Christian for the whole of her life; it would be rash speculation indeed
to believe that in her fate in 409 and 410 she saw herself as the
chosen instrument of the Lord, although her contemporaries,
especially Orosius,[45] were shortly to claim the workings of the
Divine Hand in her captivity. If Placidia herself came to think so
(and she was human), she probably thus committed the grievous
sin of pride. At least in the months after the fall of Rome she had
ample opportunity, daughter of a Roman emperor that she was, to
observe her captors' plundering the rich lands and towns of the
south, once almost as much a home of ancient Greek civilization
as Greece itself, and to experience every degree of anguish and
humiliation. For the imperial government in its distracted impotence did not, and probably could not, assist whatever amateur
resistance the Goths encountered in the south.

The precise route of the Goths southward is unknown; it is safe
to assume that they took advantage of the magnificent network of
Roman roads whose construction in the course of centuries had
facilitated communication by land through some of the most beautiful and difficult regions of Italy; presumably the Goths fanned
out from these roads in smaller bands to obtain forage and provender for themselves and their animals, as well as fresh water, not
always easily come by in this season of the year in the hot and dusty
south. Although their coming undoubtedly spread terror and panic
before them, walled cities would generally have been impervious
to unskilled barbarian assault; we hear of only a few towns ravaged
by the Goths. Presumably most of their depredations, necessary or
otherwise, were at the expense of the village peasantry and occasional isolated country farmsteads or villas. The barns and store-
houses will still have held much of the spring reaping; the autumn
sowing would follow after the grapes and olives and fruits were
gathered in;[46] aside from the suffocating heat, itself tempered by
the breezes from the sea, it was not a bad time of the year for a

---

[45] 7. 40. 2; cf. Saint Augustine *Ep.* 111. 7, a general statement which asks whether
God may not have had great intentions for the women who fell into the hands of
barbarian captors.

[46] M. Cary, *The Geographic Background of Greek and Roman History*, pp. 17,
20–21.

foraging horde to prey upon the lands of the south.[47] It was not, however, merely to support his people from the unravaged resources of southern Italy that Alaric had turned his way thither. A far more important enterprise, in terms both of wealth and strategy, drew him in that direction—Africa. Apparently he had learned during his experience with Attalus and Heraclian, if not before, of the great wealth of those transmarine provinces, from which the government of Honorius drew so large a portion of its revenue, and whose master could also dictate the fortunes of Rome itself by his control of the sources of the City's victualing, a matter of anxious care to the emperors themselves for centuries. To Africa Alaric would go; his people would live from its wealth and as its master he could press the Emperor even behind the walls and marshes of almost impregnable Ravenna. The route therefore lay southward near the west coast of Italy, through Campania, then Lucania, and finally Bruttium, to Rhegium,[48] the uttermost toe of Italy, with the fertile grain fields of Sicily across the narrow strait and Africa itself beyond. Speed was necessary, for the winter season with its storms was approaching, when the seas would be closed to all but the most intrepid navigators; in winter to try to transport the Goths to Africa would be unthinkable. While Campania was ravaged, however, and some of the wanderers fell ill,[49] Nola was taken and plundered; its Bishop, Saint Paulinus, was taken prisoner,[50] but soon released.[51] Arrived at Rhegium, the Goths gave the city over to the flames, so we are told by an eyewitness watching from across the straits in Sicily,[52] but this must be an exaggeration, for the city was to be used as a base for crossing to Sicily or Africa. A large number of ships was collected, presumably from the coastal towns all around (it seems hardly likely

[47] It is surely an exaggeration to say that Alaric's sole hope for safety for himself and his people lay in his prisoner Placidia (Sirago, *Placidia*, p. 115); in what did he hope when he began this venture and down to 409?

[48] Jord. *Get.* 156–57; cf. *CTh* 11. 28. 7.

[49] Philostorg. *HE* 12. 3.

[50] August. *CD* 1. 10; *cura pro mort. ger.* 16, 19 (*PL*, XL, 606 = *CSEL*, XLI, 652); Fiebiger and Schmidt, *Inschriftensammlung*, no. 245, p. 119; cf. Courcelle, *Hist. litt.*, pp. 40–41; N. K. Chadwick, *Poetry and Letters in Early Christian Gaul*, p. 87.

[51] Alaric may also have taken Beneventum: Musset, *Vagues*, p. 246, citing *CIL*, IX, 1596, but the latter merely commemorates extensive repairs to public buildings there sometime in the fifth century, and there is no certain connection with the Goths.

[52] Rufin. *Prol. in lib. Num. ad Ursac.*, quoted by Valesius, adn. in Euseb. *HE* 6. 38 (p. 300, ed. Cambridge, 1720).

that there was time to build any considerable number) and the Goths prepared to cross the narrow waters, as terrified Sicilians watched from the opposite shore, Christian and pagan alike imploring the succor of heaven; the pagans later claimed that a miraculous statue at Rhegium had warded the barbarians off from Sicily (it was also protection against the fires of Etna).[53] And the winds of heaven did come; the Goths were beginning to embark when a sudden storm, too characteristic of the Mediterranean solstice, blew up, apparently almost without warning, and destroyed or wrecked almost the whole flotilla; large numbers of the Goths perished while those still on shore watched in horror.[54] What Galla Placidia thought of this disaster, which she may well have witnessed, is unknown, but it is very likely that the allegations of the pagans about the virtues of the wonder-working statue came to her ears, for some years later she ordered the manager of her estates in Sicily to destroy the blasphemous thing.[55]

After such a decisive setback Alaric must needs ponder what to do next;[56] for the present, at least, he and his people resumed their weary march, returning northward along the coast of the peninsula. But whatever his plans might have turned out to be, suddenly the King died; this was in the vicinity of the Bruttian town of Consentia (Cosenza). We are told that the course of the nearby little river Busento was diverted by the forced labor of captives; in the river bed thus exposed Alaric was buried with a sizable treasure, the river was returned to its usual bed, and the captives slain that

53 Olympiod. Frag. 15 (IV, 60); Oros. 7. 43. 11–12; cf. B. Pace, *I barbari e i bizantini in Sicilia,* p. 6.

54 Olympiod. Frag. 15 (IV, 60); Oros. 7. 43. 12; Isid. *Hist. Goth.* 18 (II, 275); Paul. Diac. *Rom.* 12. 14; Jord. *Get.* 157. Sirago, *Placidia,* p. 119, imagines that a Roman fleet was about to try to stop the Goths from crossing; he is certainly correct in thinking that the government far preferred having Alaric in Italy to his crossing to Africa. How far the government, then probably already inspired by Constantius, was following masterly Fabian tactics in allowing Alaric and his Goths to wander at will in Italy is doubtful. The situation in Gaul and Spain with barbarians and usurpers seems adequate to explain the government's relative disregard of Alaric's activities.

55 Olympiod. Frag. 15 (IV, 60) merely attests that Asclepius, administrator of the possessions of Constantius and Placidia in Sicily, threw the statue down. This could be mere coincidence, but probability favors what is said in the text.

56 Jord. *Get.* 157; the statement is hardly necessary. M. Torres in *Historia de España,* ed. R. Menéndez Pidal, III, 53, is sure that Alaric had not renounced his plans, but intended to seize a large port such as Naples and there construct ships; of course he died before he could do any of this, and the matter is mere speculation. At least his trusted lieutenant and successor Athaulf shows no sign of sharing such ideas, if Alaric actually had them.

no man might know the King's resting place (end of the year 410).[57] At the least the motive ascribed for the slaying of the captives is improbable; vestiges of such hydraulic engineering could not be hidden. Modern scholars disagee as to the authenticity of the procedure in general.[58]

If Alaric had any surviving children, they must have been girls,[59] for his successor as King of the Visigoths was his wife's brother and his principal lieutenant, Athaulf;[60] quite possibly he too was a member of Alaric's family.[61] A historian partial to the Goths tells us that the new King was both intelligent and handsome; although he was not particularly tall (for a Goth), his figure was graceful and his features regular.[62] As King of the Goths Athaulf must henceforth have come into frequent contact with his illustrious prisoner, Galla Placidia, even if this were not previously true already when during Alaric's lifetime he had been the late King's trusted lieutenant. The proximate sequel will show that neither of the two found the other unpleasing. Placidia's reaction may have been mixed when she thought of the stalwart Goth and the horrors that he and his people had been and were wreaking on Italy and the Roman Empire. As for Athaulf, we have a report of his own statement made a few years later that he once had ardently desired to overthrow the Roman name, which means that originally he had been quite hostile, consciously, to Rome and all she stood for. Whether the contact with the Romans that he had experienced

---

[57] Jord. *Get.* 157–58; Olympiod. Frag. 10 (IV, 59); cf. Procop. *Bell.* 3 (*Vand.* 1). 2. 37. The date is given by Hyd. 45 (II, 17) erroneously as 409, but in the same year as the fall of Rome (410). On this sort of mistake in Hyd. esp. and in the chroniclers in general, see Courtois, *Byzantion,* XXI (1951), 23–54.

[58] The authenticity is defended by Thompson, *Visigoths,* p. 92 and n. 1; rejected by Demougeot, *Unité,* p. 481 and n. 225; citations of previous discussions in both places. If the prisoners were slain, almost certainly this is to be seen as the survival of a pagan custom of sacrificing to or for the dead. At any rate, the site is still unknown to scholarship; a local tradition is said to specify the confluence of the Busento with another local stream, the Crati; see Baedeker's *Southern Italy and Sicily* (12th rev. [Eng.] ed.; Leipzig, 1896), p. 219.

[59] The Visigothic King Theodoric I later claimed to be Alaric's grandson (Ap. Sid. *Carm.* 7. 505), but the claim may have been honorific or an invention to enhance the King's own prestige.

[60] Olympiod. Frag. 10 (IV, 59); Jord. *Get.* 158; cf. the fragmentary passage in Philostorg. *HE* 12. 4; Oros. 7. 43. 2.

[61] Demougeot, *Unité,* p. 434, n. 418; Jord. *Get.* 158 calls him "consanguineo" of Alaric (cf. Oros. 7. 40. 2: "Alarici propinquo"), but this term could possibly be used elastically to refer to the connection by marriage.

[62] Jord. *Get.* 158; on the origins of Jord. see Mommsen's ed. (*MGH: AA,* vol. V: 1), pp. vi–vii.

since 409 was already beginning to change his mind, or whether Placidia was the one who began to alter his views, cannot be known; we do know that his attitude toward Rome would change to a sincere admiration for much that Rome represented, and in the opinion of contemporaries it was Placidia, who, by God's will, was the main instrument in bringing about the change.[63] At any rate, it would seem that Placidia found it worth her while to converse with the barbarian who, if the historian of the Goths is to be believed, was not without his masculine charms.[64]

The first year of the reign of Athaulf (411) is almost completely a blank to us. Apparently the Goths slowly worked their way along the west coast back toward the north, plundering and harrying the native population in order to support themselves. What forces the imperial government could muster were fully occupied in Gaul,[65] and the Goths were left undisturbed by any organized attempt to halt their plundering or threaten their passage. The statement of the historian of the Goths that on this return march the Goths once again plundered Rome is rightfully dismissed as without foundation by the almost unanimous consensus of modern historians;[66] at most it can represent only another fright experienced by the City as the Gothic horde approached and passed by, like a flight of locusts. If Athaulf had still entertained any hopes of reaching Africa at the beginning of his reign, he must have renounced them as he left the southern part of the peninsula behind him. Apparently that part of Italy was plundered under Athaulf much more thoroughly than Alaric had had time for on the southward passage of the Goths.[67] It seems probable that Athaulf, like his predecessor,

[63] Oros. 7. 43. 3–7; on the authenticity of this account which has recently been challenged, see "Galla Placidia and the Law," *CP*, LXIII (1968), 114–21.

[64] Oros. 7. 43. 2, 7, 40. 2, by implication; cf. the article cited in the previous note.

[65] Seeck, *Gesch.*, VI: 1, 42, suggests that Honorius' general Constantius decided first to deal with Constantine in Gaul rather than the Goths in Italy because the former was already weakened by Gerontius' revolt against him; once Gaul was recovered for Honorius its resources could be used against the Goths. One might add that if the bulk of the imperial forces were to be deployed southward this might leave northern Italy open to the attack of the usurper, who would at once threaten the government at Ravenna and be at the back of Constantius' army, pinning him against the Goths; the natural result would be a combined effort of the Goths and the usurper.

[66] Rut. Nam. 1. 39–40; Jord. *Get.* 159; Schmidt, *Gesch.*[2], I, 454; Stein, *Hist.*, I, 262; Lot, *Destinées*, pp. 39–40; Bury, *History*, I, 185; Dannenbauer, *Entstehung*, I, 203; Romano, *Dominazioni*, p. 63.

[67] *CTh* 11. 28. 7, giving four-fifths tax relief to southern Italy (8 May 413 or 412); cf. 7. 13. 20 (8 Feb. 411; on the year, Seeck, *Regesten*, pp. 73, 320) for devastation in Rome and Italy generally.

was hoping to be able to reach an accord with the government. On general grounds it is likely that he entered or tried to enter negotiations with Ravenna, but if so, they were apparently quite fruitless, and any direct evidence for them has vanished from our sources. Naturally, apart from the destiny of the Goths, if any such negotiations occurred they will also have concerned the future of Galla Placidia.[68] In fact, however, Athaulf had very little to offer the Empire in return for some sort of settlement for his people. The ravaging of Italy, the thrice-inflicted blockade of the City, the taking of Rome itself, all of these things had failed to move the imperial government. The possession of the Emperor's sister had not noticeably influenced him to make concessions. Ravaged Italy, on the other hand, would not much longer support Athaulf's people. What more could the King do? If he killed Placidia, on the assumption that such a recourse would not have been so repugnant to him already that he could even contemplate it, the natural result would be not only the loss of the only lever against the government left to him, but make almost any accommodation impossible, at least as long as the house of Theodosius reigned. But quite possibly there was a more effective way to make capital of his power over the princess, one which for quite other reasons might have been by no means displeasing to him.

Certainly as the Goths traversed the already ravaged lands of northern Italy Athaulf had increasing need of coming to an understanding with the Emperor, who must have been perfectly aware of the fact, or at least his advisers must have been.[69] Eventually the

[68] Sirago, *Placidia,* p. 119, goes too far when he holds that Honorius did not attack the Goths or take any step calculated to jeopardize Placidia; the latter had been in the power of Attalus or the Goths since 409 (410, Sirago), and there is no indication that this fact had influenced the policy of Honorius at all. Aside from a more or less disgraceful episode to be recounted later, at the end of his life, there is no reason to suppose that the Emperor was particularly concerned by his half sister's fate (although he was concerned about the lot of his Spanish relatives at the hands of Constantine, as we have seen); it is notorious that the recovery of Placidia did not become a pressing object of the government until policy was controlled by Constantius, who rose to power in 410–11; in 411 even his attention was fixed in Gaul.

[69] E. Barker, "Italy and the West, 410–76," *CMedH,* I (1911), 392–431, at 400; Marcell. *s.a.* 411, 1 (II, 70) notes that Theodosius II celebrated his *decennalia* in 411, while in the same year Honorius commemorated his *vicennalia* at Rome. Although Boyce, *Festal,* p. 44, n. 8, 44–45, takes this literally, yet it seems doubtful that Honorius, given his character, would have dared visit Rome while the Goths were roaming about the peninsula; one suspects rather that the "Romae" of Marcell. means merely "in the West," or is a sort of slip that should not be pressed.

Goths, presumably in the last half of the year 411, reached the Po valley, and there Jordanes, the Gothic historian, tells us Athaulf married Placidia at Forum Livii (Forli).[70] As almost all scholars are agreed, this statement cannot be literally true, as against all the other evidence which, directly or indirectly, affirms that he married her later in Gaul. Athaulf is said to have entered upon the marriage because of the nobility of Placidia's family, as well as for her beauty and purity of morals, "in order that the [barbarian] peoples, when they learned of this union, might be more effectively cowed, as if the [Roman] state had been united to the Goths"; although Honorius was at the end of his resources, we are told, Athaulf left behind him in Italy a grateful emperor who was almost a kinsman.[71] It is easy, as many scholars have concluded, to understand that Jordanes has mistaken an undertaking to marry for a marriage. But by indirection the passage suggests that negotiations had in fact been in progress between the court and Athaulf, and that either an agreement had been reached, or Athaulf had in effect one-sidedly declared that he would marry Placidia and regard himself as an agent of the Empire against the latter's foes (which at this junction meant, in immediate terms, the barbarian supporters of the usurpers in Gaul). It is also worthy of note that, if we take Jordanes at his word, Placidia was not unpleasing to Athaulf, but the primary motive of the King was political: to join himself and his people by a personal bond to the Emperor and the Empire and from this position to bid defiance to the enemies of Rome as her champion. Since, however, Athaulf did not in fact marry Placidia at this time, since Honorius, or those who made decisions for him, did not, as far as we know, now or later approve of Athaulf's marrying Placidia, since the Emperor did not in fact became "almost a kinsman" or "grateful" to Athaulf, there is no real evidence in Jordanes that

---

70 Jord. *Get.* 160; accepting the ancient emendation of "Foro Livi" for the text "Foro Juli."

71 *Ibid.;* Mierow construes the clause directly quoted in the text differently (trans. [Cambridge, 1966], p. 95). He apparently takes the quoted clause as one of result; it seems much more likely that it is one of purpose, paralleling the previous statements ("ob generis nobilitatem," etc., of Placidia) of purpose; certainly there is no hint in the main clause to indicate that the following "ut" introduces a consequential rather than a final clause. It would be otiose of Jord. to state the result in the clause, and then report it again in 161 where he says that the barbarians of Gaul where terrified by the arrival of the Goths.

the Empire made any concessions whatever to the Goths, although
surely the government will have approved their departure from
Italy.[72] But this last result it had obviously obtained, entirely apart
from any question of negotiations, by the simple expedient of
doing nothing, a policy hardly to be described as masterful inaction
in view of the suffering its own subjects were thereby undergoing.
We should, it seems then, infer a one-sided statement or declaration
of position on the part of Athaulf.[73] He found it desirable to leave
Italy to seek a home or sustenance for his people elsewhere; such
an annoucement, or threat, of intention would serve to put a good
appearance on his departure. We may also note that now or shortly
thereafter the future Patrician Constantius was emerging as the
real power behind Honorius' throne, and Constantius was to be
bitterly opposed to a union between Placidia and Athaulf. It would
be only a guess, however, to suggest that negotiations at this time
between King and Emperor had foundered on this intransigence
about a marriage inspired by Constantius, that the negotiations had
been broken off for that reason, and finally that their failure had
inspired Athaulf to make a defiant statement of policy or intention.
Obviously for Athaulf to have made a declaration about marrying
Placidia and thereby becoming the champion of Rome would have
been quite unrealistic, although, as indicated, such a statement
would have had a certain propaganda or face-saving value. In fact,
once in Gaul, Athaulf rallied for a time to the support of the
usurper Jovinus there.[74] Certainly at least, there is nothing in this
account, for what it is worth, to allow us to infer that Athaulf was
hopelessly smitten by the charms of his captive. That may have

[72] On the absence of a treaty with Honorius, affirmed by many scholars, see
Wietersheim-Dahn, *Völkerwanderung*, II, 155–56; M. Torres in Menéndez Pidal,
*España*, III, 54; Schmidt, *Gesch.*2, I, 454; F. Dahn, *Urgeschichte der germanischen
und romanischen Völker*, I, 350 (undecided on the question); Schild, *Placidia*, p. 29;
F. Dahn, *Die Könige der Germanen*, V, 56 (undecided).

[73] If what is argued here is correct, then the ultimate source of Jord. may have
written something like "se copulaturum esse dixit" and this came in Jord. to be
represented by "copulavit."

[74] It is admittedly difficult to see behind an isolated error in an inferior source to
understand the cause of the error. It would certainly be simpler, possible, and perhaps preferable, to dismiss the whole thing as a mere anticipation of the real marriage which occurred later; on this view the statement of Athaulf's purpose to support the Roman Empire against the barbarians is simply another version of his
celebrated speech about his conversion to pro-Romanism from anti-Romanism at
Narbonne (Oros. 7. 43. 4–7).

become true later on, but what evidence we have implies the contrary as of the end of 411.[75]

However these matters stood, that is, whether or not Athaulf had in fact already announced his engagement as a future husband to Placidia and as a present champion of Roman interests, early in the year 412 the Goths crossed the Alps from Italy to Gaul, whose unhappy provinces were still afflicted by the series of disorders and disasters which had begun 31 December 406, with the final barbarian rupture of the Rhine frontier. At least in the early fall of 409[76] Gaul had been rid of most of the barbarians who had plundered her for two and a half years; the Vandals, Sueves, and most of the others had crossed the Pyrenees into Spain where the extension of the power of the usurper Constantine had fatally weakened any possibility of an effective defense of the passes.[77] At about the same time, however, Constantine's general Gerontius had revolted against his master in the name of a puppet whom he raised to the imperial throne in Spain.[78] Constans, son and co-emperor of Constantine, attempted to overthrow Gerontius, but was himself defeated, driven back into Gaul, and finally slain at Vienne (early 411). Gerontius then laid siege to Constantine himself in his capital of Arles. At this juncture an army of Honorius commanded by the loyal Constantius intervened from Italy; the standard of the legitimate Emperor won over most of the soldiers of Gerontius, who had so frequently changed their allegiance in the last years. Gerontius managed to escape to Spain, where he committed suicide, and his Emperor, Maximus, took refuge among the barbarians who were now desolating Spain as they had Gaul. Honorius was now recog-

[75] T. S. Holmes, *The Origin and Development of the Christian Church in Gaul*, p. 310, nevertheless believes Athaulf had "set his heart" on marrying Placidia. M. Manitius, "The Teutonic Migrations," *CMedH*, I (1911), 250–76, at 274, incidentally, thinks that Athaulf "certainly" [!] married Placidia at this time. A. Solari, *Il rinnovamento dell' impero romano*, I, 361, n. 52, followed by Sirago, *Placidia*, pp. 127–29 with 127, n. 3, thinks of an engagement. It must not be forgotten, however, that it is by no means impossible that Jordanes is simply wrong; nevertheless one thinks that something must be at the root of his error about a marriage.

[76] On the problem of the exact date on which the barbarians entered Spain, see F. Martroye, *Genséric*, p. 89, n. 4; C. Courtois, *Les Vandales et l'Afrique*, p. 51 and n. 4. The latter points out that the harvest of devastated Gaul would be inferior; the barbarians looked for more adequate means of sustenance. The precise route followed through the mountains is unknown *(ibid.)*.

[77] Cf. Courcelle, *Hist. litt.*, pp. 66–67.

[78] On the conflicting evidence about the relation between Gerontius and Maximus see Stevens, *Athenaeum*, n.s., XXXV (1957), 343, n. 159.

nized in Tarraconensis (northeastern Spain); the west and south of the peninsula suffered the misrule of the barbarians,[79] who in the future tried to obtain from the Emperor treaties regularizing their settlement of those regions.[80]

The Spaniard Orosius, who himself fled from his homeland, nevertheless tells us, as does Salvian a little later for Gaul, that some of the provincials preferred the rude and simple justice of the barbarians to the sophisticated taxes and oppressions of Rome.[81] The risings of the Bacaudae in Spain later in the fifth century, apparently spread from Gaul, confirm this crude and obvious form of withdrawal from Rome and even, sometimes, from the barbarian regimes which were the Empire's successor states and which, as they established themselves, acquired an interest in maintaining the social order they had inherited.[82] But the ills of the Roman state and society were too deep and the allegiance of men to the old order too far gone to permit the substitution of even a simplified form of it to continue long in the barbarian successor states. The latter too were eventually to be swept away by external foes, or transformed into a quite different society (especially the Franks) which used many pieces of the old, but little or nothing of its superstructure. But this was in the future; in the year 411 it doubtless was not yet apparent to most men even that the badly shaken fabric of the Empire was entering on the age of its final collapse in the West; that the whole order of life as then known would vanish in centuries of confusion, destruction, and creation to come was doubtless inconceivable to almost every inhabitant, Roman or barbarian, in or outside the Empire. Above all, to Galla Placidia, reared according to Roman tradition, daughter of an emperor, successor of a glorious imperial line that stretched for centuries into the past, such a suggestion, if ever made to her, was not something to be taken seriously. In these years she would successfully impress Athaulf with the

79 Hyd. 48 (II, 17–18) describes the sorry state of Spain, suffering violence, pestilence, famine.

80 Oros. 7. 43. 14; the language of this request, at least, as rendered by Orosius, has rightly been suspected by many scholars; cf. Sirago, *Placidia*, p. 210. Apparently the barbarians divided up Spain among themselves, determined to settle there (Hyd. 49 [II, 18]). This decision did not prevent them from fighting among themselves (e.g., Hyd. 71 [II, 20]).

81 Oros. 7. 41. 7, and cf. the whole chapter, whose purpose is polemical: things are not really so bad now in these Christian days as the pagans say; the fact weakens, but does not destroy the authenticity of the cited statement.

82 Hyd. 128, 158 (II, 24, 27).

greatness and irreplaceability of Rome and its law; in all her life as far as we know it, like most of her contemporaries, barbarian and Roman, like most men in every age, she thought and acted as though the world would continue as it had for centuries, with more or fewer changes, desirable or undesirable; experience and history taught that, but not how Rome and all she knew would soon pass away. It was in these last ages that men most frequently and hopefully spoke of eternal Rome. Only among some Christian seers, especially as the collapse continued, would the conclusion emerge that the Empire was actually in process of disappearing;[83] and their opinion was probably reached at least as much by the study of biblical prophecy as by the observation and analysis of the phenomena occurring about them.[84]

Thus we may be sure that Galla Placidia saw no epochal or millennial meaning in the scenes of destruction she had witnessed in Italy and was about to behold in Gaul and Spain. In Gaul, Gerontius having fled, Constantius and his fellow general, the Goth Ulfilas, resumed Gerontius' siege of Constantine in Arles.[85] A relieving force of allied Alemanni and Franks commanded by a general of the usurper was defeated and its commander slain. Constantine was forced to surrender; although Constantius promised the fallen "tyrant" his life, and although the latter had taken the sacred character of priest as further protection,[86] he and his younger son were executed by order of the Emperor, who remembered the

[83] An ancient Christian tradition looked forward with anticipation to the fall of Rome; cf. e.g., Rev. 14: 8 with Commod. (date unknown) *Carm. apolog.* 889–90, 921–23. This tradition tended to disappear after Constantine and the triumph of the Church.

[84] See Salvian *Gub. Dei,* esp. bks. 6 and 7; note 6. 45–46, 98–99, 7. 29, 53. Note also Prosper *ad coniug.* 17–34 (*CSEL,* XXX: 2, 344–45), esp. 31–34 (after a description of the calamities of the invasions):

> Et si concluso superessent tempora saeclo
> aut posset longos mundus habere dies
> nos tamen occasum nostrum observare deceret
> et finem vitae quemque videre suae.

Note the strong tendency to identify Rome with the "world," *mundus, saeclum.* Cf. Hieron. *Ep.* 123.17: "If Rome be lost, where shall we look for help?" In general, see M. Bolwin, *Die christlichen Vorstellungen vom Weltberuf der Roma aeterna bis auf Leo den Grossen.*

[85] Sirago, *Placidia,* p. 147, says that Constantius invested Arles with "una buona flotta," but there seems to be no evidence for the assertion.

[86] Constantine was far from the last fallen emperor to seek the protection of the clergy; apparently, however, he was the first; see Stevens, *Athenaeum,* n.s., XXXV (1957), 345—another characteristic Byzantine trait found in the late West Roman Empire.

fate of his murdered Spanish relatives. Yet the end of Constantine did not restore Roman Gaul to the allegiance of Honorius.[87] The same motives of discontent with the central government's real or fancied neglect of Gaul[88] led some of the magnates of the region to renew Constantine's alliance with various barbarians in or near Gaul. Presumably the barbarians were more desirous of seeing a usurper reign in Gaul than the supposedly stronger sway of the legitimate government restored there; besides they could expect ample rewards from a usurper who would owe his throne to them. Accordingly, Gundahar, King of the Burgundians, and Goar, King of the Alans, gave their support to Jovinus, the Gallic magnate chosen by his fellows as the new Emperor.[89] The Alans had formed part of the great invasion which began 31 December 406; the Burgundians had followed in its wake into Gaul. Support for the new usurper also came from some of the Franks and the Alemanni. The forces thus at the service of Jovinus seemed so threatening that Constantius and Ulfilas deemed it prudent for the moment to retire to the safety of Italy, keeping intact the hardly replaceable army of the legitimate Emperor.[90] If the Goths were going to enter Gaul

---

[87] Most of northwest Gaul was in the hands of the Bacaudae; we do not know whether the Bacaudae of the Alpine passes had been cowed into subjection, but we hear no more of them after Sarus' misadventure, so presumably they had been; large tracts of eastern Gaul had passed into the effective control of various German tribes.

[88] On the alienation of the Gallic magnates, see Stroheker, *Adel*, p. 45; there is no need to see nationalism in this attitude, but it constitutes partial withdrawal of support from the central body of the Empire at a critical time (similar events were to occur again as they had before). That Jovinus saw himself as continuing Roman tradition, let shamefully lapse by the government at Ravenna, is shown by his coins with the legend "RESTITVTOR REIP (ublicae)" minted at Trier and Arles; cf. O. Voetter, *Römische Münzen und Medaillons*, nos. 2783 (pl. 15), 2784.

[89] On Jovinus, see Sundwall, *Studien*, no. 243, pp. 90–91; Stroheker, *Adel*, no. 204, pp. 185–86. For his brother Sebastian, Sundwall, *Studien*, no. 429, p. 131; Stroheker, *Adel*, no. 348, p. 215. Jovinus seems to have met with some recognition in Britain, cf. O. Seeck, *s.v.* "Iovinus" (5), *RE*, IX: 2 (1916), 2012-13, at 2012; at this time the British were grasping at any straw in their quest for aid against the local and German barbarians bedeviling them.

[90] Seeck, *Gesch.*, VI: 1, 49, followed by Stein, *Hist.*, I, 264. On the substitution of Jovinus for Constantine the best ancient source is Frig. *ap.* Greg. Tur. *HF* 2. 9. Sirago, *Placidia*, pp. 151–52, has various speculations about why Constantius returned to Italy from Gaul; the evidence he cites to prove Constantius' presence in Italy is not cogent. The fact is, there is no indication of Constantius' presence in Gaul in 412, so he must have left. Sirago also believes, by implication, that Constantius had to be physically present to control Honorius, particularly to oppose the project of Placidia's marriage to Athaulf; but if the reasoning in the text foregoing is correct, Honorius had not agreed to this proposal in 411, in Constantius' known absence in Gaul. Other scholars have argued in other connections that only a present minister could control Honorius. Yet Constantius was to dominate the court for ten years during long

as champions of Rome and the Emperor, then the Empire could not but profit, for the struggle that would ensue, whichever party won, would remove one enemy and presumably weaken the other. If they joined the Emperor's enemies in Gaul, the juncture would be less dangerous to Constantius' army if it were cautiously held in Italy, and he would avoid the danger of a two-front war in Gaul, or of being forced to the west and south of Gaul, or even Spain, cut off from land communications with Italy, with the ever-present threat of the barbarians in Spain attacking from a third direction as well. Like his successors in the Byzantine Empire in the East for centuries after him, Constantius must save his army by strategy and commit it to battle only when the odds were in his favor. There is no necessity, therefore, for entertaining the possibility that Honorius had recalled the general from Gaul.[91]

Constantius' success in Gaul had confirmed his position at court; his continuing success in meeting crises also continued his power. He became indispensable to the government, which he dominated, far more completely than Stilicho ever had, for the remaining ten years of his life. Indeed, as a Roman he was able to do what Stilicho could never have done. Some months before his untimely death he was to mount the imperial throne itself. Like so many of the able Roman emperors and generals of the previous two centuries, Constantius[92] was an Illyrian, from Naissus (Niš) in the Balkans, in the so-called Roman province of Dacia Mediterranea.[93] Since he had served many campaigns since the reign of Theodosius the Great,[94] in the teens of the fifth century he was certainly of middle age; he presumably belonged to the generation approximately midway between that of Theodosius and that of the latter's daughter. Apparently he was not prepossessing in appearance; in public he tended to keep his eyes fixed on the ground, and the expression of

periods of which he was absent from the Emperor's side. One may assume that as an elementary precaution he, or anyone in his position, would see to it that the Emperor was surrounded by persons devoted to his interest. At least the immediate cause of the downfall of Stilicho had been precisely his effective neglect of such a maxim of policy; but Constantius, if nothing else, had Stilicho's example to profit from; it will shortly emerge that he was likely to have studied the downfall of that minister with consuming interest.

91 As Sirago, *Placidia*, p. 151, suggests, nor is Constantius' behavior "strange."
92 See Sundwall, *Studien*, no. 109, pp. 65–66.
93 Olympiod. Frag. 39 (IV, 66); cf. Oros. 7. 42. 2.
94 Olympiod. Frag. 39 (IV, 66).

his features in repose was sullen; his eyes appeared unusually large, his neck was long, and his head rather flat. On horseback, we are told, he tended to sit forward and bend over the animal's neck; from this position he shot nervous glances hither and yon. The witness to whom we owe this description, and who apparently had seen him once or more on a state occasion, sums up by saying that he looked like the proverbial tyrant.[95] In private, however, with his cronies, he was a hail-fellow-well-met; at dinners and drinking parties he joined heartily in the merriment and was agreeable to all.[96] He enjoyed the freedom, jollity, and camaraderie of this kind of life;[97] in the same manner, and like many a professional soldier, he was free and easy with his money.[98] This combination of private and public traits suggests that he might have been self-conscious of his appearance and felt unduly constrained in the midst of the solemn pomp of the court.[99] He was an orthodox, at least externally pious, Christian,[100] who was interested in the ending of heresy and the restoration of peace to the Church.[101] His career, more than the attestation of an ecclesiastical historian,[102] proves his ability as a general; he worked diligently and hard at his chosen profession of arms.[103] Since he had served under Theodosius, and from 410 onward rose rapidly to be the commander of the West Roman army, it is a safe inference, even in the absence of testimony, that his career had continued and prospered under Stilicho, as well as that under the latter's regime he had held high and responsible military office.

His attachment to Stilicho seems amply proved by his causing the man who had worked the great general's downfall, Olympius, long since out of power and living in obscure retirement, to be arrested and savagely beaten to death with clubs after the amputation of his ears, doubtless on some easily trumped up charge of treason; this act of vengeance must have taken place not long after

---

95 This description in Olympiod. Frag. 23 (IV, 62) has every earmark of a statement made by an observant eyewitness of the man's comportment in public.

96 Olympiod. Frag. 23 (IV, 62).

97 Olympiod. Frag. 34 (IV, 65).

98 Olympiod. Frag. 39 (IV, 66).

99 Cf. Olympiod. Frag. 34 (IV, 65).

100 Cf. Demougeot, *Unité*, pp. 464–65, who notes the favor he enjoyed among Christian writers; cf. Oros. 7. 42. 15, 43. 1; Soz. *HE* 9. 16. 2.

101 Oros. 7. 42. 16, with Seeck, *Gesch.*, V: 2, 599.

102 Soz. *HE* 9. 16. 2.

103 Oros. 7. 42. 15, 43. 1; Jord. *Get.* 164.

the requisite power was in Constantius' hands, probably about 412.[104] It was Heraclian, now Count of Africa, however, who had actually slain Stilicho;[105] there are indications in the scanty sources which may mean that Constantius had begun the necessarily slow process of removing the Count from his vital position in Africa, preparatory to executing vengeance on the instrument of the murder, now that its instigator had been removed.[106] Thus we are to see in Constantius the former adherent of Stilicho, who had lived to take vengeance on his leader's murderers, and a man who would continue the general's policies.[107] Obviously, therefore, he was not anti-German;[108] at the same time he was himself indisputably Roman, and hence not displeasing to those who opposed the Germans. It was one matter, in their minds, to use Germans for the good of the Empire; it was another to put them, like Stilicho, in highest command. Certainly the avenger of Stilicho and the man who finally settled the Goths permanently in the Empire could have been no anti-German in any doctrinaire sense. But he did intend to control all the military force of the Western Empire in fact as well as in theory; contrary to the practice of the Eastern Empire, he retained Stilicho's law which allowed the Master of the Foot in the Presence to appoint the chiefs of the office staff of his principal subordinate commanders.[109] Obviously he continued and strengthened the Western principle, unused in the East, of concentrating supreme military and generally effective command in the hands of

104 Olympiod. Frag. 8 (IV, 59), confirmed by Philostorg. *HE* 12. 1. On the date and interpretation of this event, see *CP*, LXI (1966), 238–39.

105 Zos. 5. 37. 6.

106 *CP*, LXI (1966), 236–37, 239; cf. esp. Oros. 7. 42. 12. The suggestion of E. A. Freeman, *Western Europe in the Fifth Century*, p. 186 and n., that Constantius was in Africa in 412 is quite improbable and to be rejected.

107 So Mazzarino, *Stilicone*, pp. 110, 156–57.

108 As Seeck, *Gesch.*, VI: 1, 39; 2, 391; followed by Stein, *Hist.*, I, 262; and Barker, *CMedH*, I (1911), 402 (cf., but with reservations which may be correct, Demougeot, *Unité*, pp. 464–65); on the evidence of a law of Honorius, *CTh* 14. 10. 4 (12 Dec. 416), forbidding anyone to wear German dress in Rome; but aside from the doubtful implication that every single law enacted during the time Constantius was principal minister represented his will, to argue that even if he did inspire this law he was anti-German would mean by the same logic that the senators of the Republic who legislated *de luxu mulierum* were thereby proved to be antiwoman. Constantius was a Roman; he was proud of the Roman heritage; Rome must remain Roman, but it does not follow that Constantius was opposed to Germans.

109 Demougeot, *Unité*, p. 498, with n. 20, citing *CTh* 1. 7. 3 in comparison with *CTh* 6. 28. 6.

one man; this circumstance was to have the gravest consequences for the decline of the real authority of the Western Emperors. In the East such exalted powers were commonly rendered less dangerous by being held jointly by several generals. The beginning of Constantius' ascendancy at Ravenna probably dates from the downfall of Allobic in the summer of 410.[110] When he received formal appointment to the highest military office, Master of Both Branches of the Soldiery *(Magister utriusque militiae)* is not clear, but he almost certainly had attained that rank by 411, whether to empower him for the campaign against Constantine or to recognize his success therein.[111]

In any event, when Athaulf and his Goths with Galla Placidia entered Gaul, they found the power of Rome, as far as it extended in the unsettled region, exercised by Jovinus, while Constantius presumably waited watchfully behind them across the Alps in Italy.[112] Once in Gaul, whatever may have been his attitude toward Honorius at the end of 411, Athaulf abruptly veered about in his policy. The gross outline of the following events is clear;[113] the motives of the principals involved are not. It seems clear that if Athaulf had any sort of understanding with the government at Ravenna when he left Italy, nothing was done to implement it; if he made some sort of statement about his intentions toward Rome and Placidia, likewise it made no impression; the King's problems,

110 Stein, *Hist.*, I, 262; Stevens, *Athenaeum*, n.s., XXXV (1957), 344 and n. 167 (on 345); he is seen as exercising power with Honorius in 410: Oros. 7. 42. 16. The rapid changes in politics at Ravenna in previous years had compromised most of the past contenders for the Emperor's ear; cf. Sirago, *Placidia*, p. 118.

111 On the position and title, Ensslin, *Klio*, XXIV (1931), 469–70; date 410 or 411, modern discussions cited *CP*, LXI (1966), 241, nn. 13, 14.

112 In 412 Constantius' friend and adherent was at his instigation installed in the important bishopric of Arles, in place of Heros who had been expelled (Prosp. 1247 [I, 466]). This might mean that Constantius was still in Gaul at the beginning of 412 (so perhaps O. Seeck, *s.v.* "Constantius" (9), *RE*, IV [1901], 1099–1102, at 1100); this in turn would mean that he waited until after the Goths had entered Gaul to return to Italy. But the presence of Constantius at Arles is not necessary for his influence to install Patroclus there, and in view of the fact that he took no action against Jovinus it seems better to assume that he returned to Italy after the campaign of 411, in view of the strategic considerations previously discussed in the text. Jovinus certainly controlled Arles during at least part of his reign, for he issued coins there (see above, n. 88). At his elevation he marched on Arles (Ren. Prof. Frig. *ap.* Greg. Tur. *HF* 2. 9), and presumably took it without resistance from Constantius.

113 The best account is Olympiod. Frags. 17, 19 (IV, 61); the Latin chronicles and histories sometimes supplement his brief narrative.

the victualing of his people and the attainment of some sort of understanding with the Empire such as Alaric and he had wanted since 408, were still unsolved. The ex-usurper Attalus, still trailing along with the Gothic host for safety's sake, advised Athaulf to join Jovinus.[114] His advice may have been disinterested; he may still have nourished imperial hopes which he saw or thought he saw the means of satisfying in the troubled political condition of Gaul. At least, as we shall see, he did later for a brief time assume the title of Emperor again; Jovinus evidently found the Goths unwelcome, and censured Attalus for their coming with dark and riddling remarks. Quite possibly Jovinus' rich Gallic backers were displeased at seeing the Goths battening off their property;[115] the other barbarian allies of Jovinus may have resented the addition of another tribe to his forces.[116] Thus the relations between the Goths and the usurper were hardly cordial from the beginning. Then Athaulf's and Alaric's old enemy Sarus arrived to join the usurper from Italy, where he had deserted the service of Honorius in anger over the Emperor's indifference to the murder of Belleridus, a servant of Sarus. Athaulf, learning of his coming, marched to meet him with a large force, unnecessary since Sarus had only a handful of men. After stouthearted resistance Sarus was taken alive, but later put to death. There can be little doubt that Jovinus was ill pleased at this action of Athaulf. In turn the latter was angered when Jovinus associated his brother Sebastian with himself as co-emperor. Why Athaulf was annoyed by this step is nowhere stated by the sources, and we have no way of guessing the reason.[117] But Honorius' loyal Praetorian Prefect of the Gauls, Dardanus, who

114 Many scholars have suggested that the alliance with Jovinus had been entered upon when the Goths were still in Italy. There is no certainty about the chronology, but if this view is correct, then the case for reposing any trust in Jordanes' statement about the "marriage" of Athaulf and Placidia is materially weakened; as previously admitted, to reject the statement is certainly a possible solution.

115 Cf. Sundwall, *Studien*, p. 11; Stroheker, *Adel*, pp. 45–46; there was a great famine in Gaul in 412 or 413 (*Chron. Gall. a. 452* 72 [I, 654]).

116 Jord. *Get.* 161, a confused and patriotically exaggerated passage, speaks of the fear which the Franks and Burgundians felt at the coming of the Goths; the passage may lend some support to the possibility mentioned in the text.

117 Scholars have suggested that Athaulf wanted to be emperor himself (highly improbable); that he wanted Attalus to be made co-emperor, instead, etc. One might suggest that for reasons unknown he had taken a considerable personal dislike to Sebastian.

may have retreated to Spain at the rise of Jovinus,[118] was able to turn Athaulf's resentment to the use of the legitimate Emperor;[119] with this encouragement Athaulf sent ambassadors to Honorius. Now he had a bargaining point, and the Emperor, and presumably Constantius, listened to the King's promise to deliver the heads of Jovinus and Sebastian; unfortunately the precise return the Emperor was supposed to make for these gifts is not specified, but presumably it was satisfactory. The imperial government now had an opportunity to rid itself of two usurpers whom Constantius was unwilling to meet in the open field with his own army. As before, if the Goths should succeed, the Emperor would profit; if they failed the Emperor would also profit from the mutual damage inflicted by two sets of his enemies on each other.

Upon the return of the ambassadors from Italy oaths were exchanged, between Athaulf and Dardanus, probably, at long last confirming a treaty of peace such as the Goths had wanted for years. It seems fairly certain that the government must have promised shipment of food to the Goths; it may well also have promised Aquitaine in Gaul as land the Goths could occupy.[120] Presumably after disposing of Jovinus and his brother the Goths would continue in the future to serve the Empire militarily, as they had in

118 Stein, *Hist.*, I, 264.

119 *Chron. Gall. a. 452* 69 (I, 654). In the admittedly abbreviated fragment of Olympiod. that we have we are given no indication that Athaulf was at all hesitant at entering into a treaty with the Emperor and agreeing to fight his battles, or that the government for its part was backward in entering this treaty. An argument from silence, this fact nevertheless tends to support the idea that no understanding had been reached in 411 in Italy. Again, when the treaty is broken, originally by the Romans, there is no hint in the abbreviated Olympiod. Frag. 20 (IV, 61) that this was the second time in close succession. On the other hand, that Athaulf entered upon this treaty in 413 tends in general to substantiate the statement of his purpose in 411 as reported by Jordanes. And this is not strange, since, aside from Placidia, the Goths were not asking much more in 411 or 413 than they had obtained from Theodosius. In turn, also, the inference that any plan to marry Placidia in 411 was politically motivated is strengthened by Athaulf's willingness to agree to this treaty and give up Placidia; one is quite free of course to speculate on the possibility that he had mental reservations.

120 *Chron. Gall. a. 452* 73 (I, 654), unless this is in fact an anticipation of the settlement of 418–19, as has been suggested. The objections of Ensslin, *RE*, XX: 2 (1950), 1915, to a cession of Aquitaine (or part of it) to the Goths, especially that Constantius would have opposed it, do not apply to a grant from Honorius at this time; for Constantius thought that Placidia would be returned to him by this arrangement. Ensslin is right, however, in refusing to accept Seeck's suggestion (*Gesch.*, VI: 1, 55; 2, 395) that Honorius gave the Goths Aquitaine on the marriage of Placidia to Athaulf. Kornemann, *Grosse Frauen*, p. 332, follows Seeck.

the time of Theodosius the Great. Constantius was active in the negotiation of this treaty, and included in it a provision to which Athaulf agreed, that Placidia be released to her brother.[121] Thus by some time in the first months of 413 at least, Constantius was already much concerned about the fate of Placidia; noteworthy is the fact that Honorius was, by implication at least, much less concerned. In turn this fact supports the view that Placidia in Athaulf's hands in 411 had not been so much a lever for obtaining concessions from the Emperor as has sometimes been thought. It is hard to believe that Constantius could have had any other interest in thus pressing for the princess' release than his desire to marry her. And it is also difficult to see that as a human being, even if we were to assume that from unknown prior association he were passionately in love with her, he would have been able to avoid the reflection that Honorius was childless, unmarried, and unlikely to marry, particularly if the belief concerning the Emperor's impotence were correct. In turn this should mean that Constantius saw that a marriage with Placidia would open an easy way for him to the imperial throne itself. As to what Placidia thought of being thus bandied about as a pawn in a political game, we have no information; later she would be cordially opposed to marrying Constantius; there is no reason to believe that at that later time she had changed her mind. On the other hand, for centuries Roman girls of rank had regularly been used for the furtherance of political purposes with little regard to their own wishes. While the idea of being used as a political link either with Athaulf or Constantius may or may not have been repugnant to her, in view of the practice of the society in which she was bred and brought up, she may well have been able to face such a prospect with resignation. The ancients rarely conceived of a necessary connection between romantic love and marriage. After marriage—the sequel will show that Placidia had great talent for bending her husband to her will, or at least to her point of view.

The treaty thus concluded, Athaulf was able to seize Sebastian and a younger brother named Sallust; the head of the elder was duly sent to Ravenna. Jovinus was besieged in Valence; the Goths took the town and secured his person. Jovinus was executed by Dardanus at Narbonne, and his head too was dispatched to the

---

121 Olympiod. Frag. 20 (IV, 61).

Emperor. Similarly, and typically, Sallust as well as many of the Gallic magnates associated in this treason was put to death (May/June, 413).[122] Athaulf had kept his word.

As usual the pressing need of the Goths was for victualing. Unfortunately it happened, indirectly because of Constantius' own fault, in all probability, that the government of Ravenna was forced to default on its promises of grain. In Africa, Count Heraclian, the murderer of Stilicho, who had deserved so well of the government during the usurpation of Attalus in Rome, although designated consul—still the highest honor in the Emperor's gift—revolted in 413, the very year of his consulship. This rebellion, the motives of which are only darkly alluded to by Orosius, our principal source of information, was very likely provoked by Constantius' execution of Olympius, and by Heraclian's probably correct conclusion that he would be the next to suffer the vengeance of his superior, the Master of the Soldiers. Like all pretenders who controlled Africa, therefore, one of his first overt acts was to refuse to allow the sailing of the grain fleet to Italy in the spring of 413. In these circumstances the government, in great need of grain to supply Rome itself as well as to fill the requirements of its own troops, was unable to carry out its agreement with Athaulf.[123] Instead, a bit later (June?) Heraclian himself, with the grain fleet to show that he controlled the means of Rome's supply, and with only a small armed force, sailed to Italy. There he was handily defeated by a certain Count Marinus; fleeing back to Africa, the rebel was slain at Carthage by the agents of the Emperor. His confiscated property was given Constantius by Honorius, at the former's request, to defray the expenses of his own consulship in 414. The head of Heraclian was displayed together with those of Jovinus and Sebastian at Carthage in order to inspire second thoughts in future would-be tyrants in Africa or elsewhere.[124] In Africa and among the grain ship masters, the usurper's doubtless unwilling accomplices, the servants of the Emperor and

---

122 Ren. Prof. Frig. *ap.* Greg. Tur. *HF* 2. 9; Olympiod. Frag. 19 (IV, 61); Oros. 7. 42. 6; *Chron. Gall. a. 452* 71 (I, 654); Philostorg. *HE* 12. 6; Procop. *Bell.* 3 (*Vand.* 1). 2. 37 (confused); Hyd. 54 (II, 18); Prosp. 1251 (I, 467); Marcell. *s.a.* 412, 1 (II, 71); *Cons. Ital. s.a.* 413 (I, 300); Theophanes, p. 81 (de B). On the date, Seeck, *Gesch.*, VI: 1, 52; 2, 393; *idem, Regesten,* p. 326.

123 For the sources for Heraclian's revolt and this interpretation of the evidence, see *CP*, LXI (1966), 236–42; for the inability to supply Athaulf with grain, Olympiod. Frags. 20, 21 (IV, 61–62); cf. Stein, *Hist.*, I, 265–66.

124 *CP*, LXI (1966), 239, 241, n. 19.

the secret police *(curiosi)* set on foot the usual terrifying investigations to track down every trace of treason, as well as to continue the attempt to stamp out heresy.[125]

With the fall of Heraclian the imperial government was once more in control of the all-important grain supply. But it was too late. In the late spring of 413 the government had failed to deliver the promised grain to Athaulf's people. Nevertheless, prompted we may be sure by Constantius, a request was made that Athaulf deliver Placidia in accordance with his agreement. Quite naturally the King, who had in good faith overthrown the Gallic usurpers and delivered their heads as agreed, declined to perform the one thing left to him to do, and hand over Placidia before the Romans should demonstrate their own good faith by supplying the grain his people needed. Until this was done, despite the urgency of Constantius, Athaulf had no intention of delivering over his sole remaining means of bargaining. The government, probably in good faith, but probably also without specifying exactly when, promised that if only the King would hand over his prisoner the grain would be given in return. Not unnaturally the King replied that he would give up Placidia as soon as the grain was delivered.[126] By summertime, however, when the government was at last presumably in a position to honor its part of the bargain by delivering the grain of Africa, it was too late. In the meantime Athaulf had come to entertain another idea. If Jordanes' account of events in Italy at the end of 411 has any truth behind it, as we have seen, the idea of marrying Placidia himself had already occurred to the King. We know that he had been married before, and had had children by the marriage;[127] we may assume that his first wife had died. Apparently by the summer of 413 the King had decided that, whatever he may have threatened to do in the past, he would now in fact marry Placidia. Hence, although the government was now able to deliver the promised grain to his people, Athaulf deliberately raised the demands he made in order to avoid having to hand the princess over to her own people. And for his part, of course, Constantius was bound that there would be no peace with the Goths, no accommo-

---

125 The Donatists, who held that sacraments administered by an immoral person were invalid; cf. Frend, *Donatist Church*, p. 293, for this persecution.

126 Olympiod. Frags. 20, 21 (IV, 61–62).

127 Olympiod. Frag. 26 (IV, 63); cf. Schmidt, *Gesch.2*, I, 456 and n. 2.

dation, until Placidia were returned to her brother, that is, to her brother's Master of the Soldiers.[128]

Obviously, for Athaulf, politics—at least as a prime consideration—had been left behind. Political expediency demanded that Athaulf surrender Placidia as he had, at least apparently, been willing to do in the spring. On the other hand, one should not forget that he could not be insensible to the political advantages he might well expect to follow from an alliance with the sister of the Emperor.[129] Yet those advantages were problematical and future; the grain was needed by the Goths without delay. Nevertheless the King refused to give up his captive; it is by no means impossible, it is even likely, that he was aware of the ambitions of his adversary Constantius in this respect. It is very difficult for even the most prosaic student of these affairs to avoid the conclusion that in acting so, in opposition to his immediate political interests, Athaulf was motivated by emotional reasoning that had overridden more mundane considerations; not to put too fine a point on it, that he had fallen in love with Galla Placidia. Since we have no real portrait of her,[130] we cannot judge of her physical charms,[131] we cannot be sure that she was beautiful (cf. Pl. I); but beauty, especially on longer acquaintance, emanates from characteristics of mind and personality. The one portrait bust of the famous Cleopatra which has come down to us certainly exhibits no surpassing regularity of feature; yet the charms of that Ptolemaic princess are notorious or proverbial. If in fact we now find Athaulf to be in love with Galla Placidia, whatever his reason might say for or against her, we are entitled to suspect that he had by no means been insusceptible earlier, and that the emotional response he was making to her was of gradual growth, reaching, as it were, vital intensity only in the summer of 413. Probably only a sentimentalist or a romantic nowadays will believe in the reality of love, as opposed to lust, at first

---

[128] Olympiod. Frags. 21, 22 (IV, 62).

[129] It seems very doubtful at least, however, that Nagl, *Placidia*, p. 21, can be right in suggesting that Athaulf ever thought of being promoted through this marriage to such a rank as Caesar (which, except for the usurper Constantine's promotion of his son to that rank, had fallen into desuetude for some time, until it was revived some years after this for the benefit of the future Valentinian III).

[130] See above, Ch. I, n. 33.

[131] Literary testimonials to her beauty, such as Jord. *Get.* 160, may be veracious, or merely conventional; most princesses tend to be accounted beauties, unless they are positively ugly or malformed.

sight, at least among mature persons. Perhaps it would also be unduly romantic or sentimental to conjecture that the prospect or contemplation of separation from the princess had brought Athaulf to the realization that such an outcome must be avoided at almost any cost. However all that may be, there is little doubt that, whatever label we may wish to use, the King of the Goths had fallen under the domination of Placidia's personality.

Athaulf's attitude toward Rome, we are told, was originally one of hostility, but this had changed, and he became desirous of becoming a mainstay of the Roman state; in the process he became convinced of the importance of law and impressed by Roman accomplishments in that direction. A contemporary, and there must have been many like him, saw in this change of heart on the part of the Gothic King the influence mostly of Galla Placidia; indeed, he goes so far, therefore, as to see in the captivity and the marriage of the princess the work of God himself for the good of the Roman state; this then was to be a marriage literally made in Heaven.[132] Such a basic change in outlook is hardly to be thought the work of a moment's chance remark. Surely we should not be wrong in thinking that Athaulf had many long conversations with his imperial captive; that in some subtle manner the glories, history, accomplishment, order, peace, and law of imperial Rome came to be symbolized in some way in the King's mind by the earnest explanations of Galla Placidia, who must have delicately pointed out to him the shortcomings of his Goths as an imperial people, have hinted to him how he and his people might gain their truest glory in Rome's service as supporters of the ancient majesty of the Empire. Galla Placidia never forget who she was—a Roman and the daughter of Theodosius the Great. At least, it is hard to avoid the conclusion that something like this must have happened. And it would be odd indeed if Placidia had had no idea of the impression she was making on the mind and heart of Athaulf. Finally, there is no need, obviously, to credit her with less than average intelligence; she, too, cannot have failed to realize the implications of the fact of her imperial brother's celibacy. Mercifully, she can have had little idea of the long, hard road she would have to travel in person and in spirit before she arrived at the throne of Augustus, Trajan, Constantine, and Theodosius.

132 Oros. 7. 40. 2, 43. 2–7, esp. 7.

Meanwhile, however much Athaulf might enjoy the inspiring conversation of his captive, the problem of the sustenance of his people was still before him, a pressing question which he was refusing to solve in the most obvious way open to him. Apparently in the course of this late spring and summer the Goths had been working their way westward across the breadth of Gaul to the province of Aquitania Secunda (roughly along the Atlantic coast from the valley of the Garonne to, or almost to, the valley of the Loire, and some distance inland from the coast between these rivers). It seems likely that it was this province which the Goths were to receive as a dwelling place from the Emperor by their bargain with him early in 413.[133] The Goths were peaceably received in Bordeaux, the principal city of the province,[134] and in the later fourth century one of the principal cultural centers of the Western Empire. But the grain of Africa came by sea, and the Goths must have access to this sea and the cargo it carried.[135] At the vintage time (August/September) in 413 the Goths entered the city of Narbo Martius (Narbonne) in the province of Narbonensis Prima, apparently without difficulty or violence;[136] almost certainly the imperial government, which was well aware of the dangers for the Empire if the barbarians should ever become able to transport themselves where they willed over the Mediterranean Sea, the principal highway of the Roman world,[137] and which had hardly forgotten the African ambitions of Alaric, had not conceded the Goths any such access to the Mediterranean. Perhaps it was just before they entered Narbo, if they came from Bordeaux, that the Goths also took Tolosa (Toulouse).[138] But not too far to the east of Narbo was situated the city of Marseilles near the mouth of the Rhone, one of the great ports of the Medi-

[133] Paul. Pell. 285–90 (the reference to *hospites;* cf. Seeck, *Gesch.,* VI: 1, 53; W. Capelle, *Die Germanen der Völkerwanderung,* p. 253 and n. 1 [on 554]).

[134] Paul. Pell. 312 (cf. 44).

[135] Cf., e.g., H. Eicke, *Geschichte der westgotischen Könige seit Alarichs Tod,* p. 20; Schmidt, *Gesch.2,* I, 455; so most students.

[136] Hyd. 55 (II, 18); from the fact that there is no indication of any violence in the Gothic entry into Narbonne, Sirago, *Placidia,* p. 160, concludes that Placidia must have brought about its peaceful surrender. There is no evidence whatever to support this view.

[137] *CTh* 9. 40. 24 (419; issued by Theodosius II) on the prohibition (here reaffirmed and strengthened) against teaching barbarians how to build ships.

[138] Rut. Nam. 1. 496; this must have been about this time, if in this year, for the failure of the attempt on Marseilles must, with the wounding of Athaulf, have put a temporary halt to these adventures. Stein, *Hist.,* I, 266, puts the taking of Toulouse in 414 as part of the reaction of the Goths to the pressure put on them by Constantius.

terranean world in most epochs of its history. Athaulf determined on an attempt to seize this great city with its harbor and its shipping. The Goths of course had no means of assaulting a walled city, but Athaulf had hopes of taking it by a trick; perhaps he thought he could persuade the local administration that he had imperial permission to enter the city. If so, however, he was mistaken; some sort of melee occurred, and the King was severely wounded by a weapon thrown by an able soldier named Boniface, a man whose distinguished career, just beginning, would one day bring him to the heights of power in the Empire; Marseilles was full of praises for its hero of the hour, but the King was carried back to the encampment of the Goths.[139] We may presume that Athaulf required some time for his recuperation. During this recovery he stayed at Narbo, enjoying the society of Placidia and of many of the Roman inhabitants of the city, although this attempt on Marseilles, as probably his previous seizure of Narbo itself, must have worsened the bad relations already existing between the Goths and the government of Honorius and Constantius.[140]

One of the members of the upper classes of Narbo later journeyed to Bethlehem and there told Saint Jerome that he had been an intimate friend of Athaulf at Narbo,[141] and he had often heard the King say

that at first he had ardently desired to eradicate the Roman name and to make all the Roman territory an empire of the Goths in fact as well as in name, and that, to use the popular expression, *Gothia* should be what *Romania* had been, and that Athaulf should now become what once Caesar Augustus had been. But when he discovered from long experience that neither were the Goths at all capable of obeying laws because of their unbridled barbarism, nor ought a state to be deprived of laws, without which a state is not a state,[142] he chose to seek for himself at least the glory of restoring and increasing . . . the Roman name

[139] Olympiod. Frag. 21 (IV, 62). In later years Boniface would be a stout ally of Placidia at a time when she would be in sore need of friends. It is not impossible that, as barbarians frequently do, Athaulf admired the ability of the man who had nearly killed him; and communicated this appreciation to Placidia. Unfortunately we do not know whether she was in the "Gothic tents" at this time; she might have been left behind in one of the cities in Gothic control.

[140] Sirago, *Placidia*, p. 159.

[141] Cf. Olympiod. Frag. 24 (IV, 62) for the friendships of Athaulf among noble Romans.

[142] The explanatory clause is added by Orosius.

by the power of the Goths, and to be regarded by posterity as the author of Roman restoration, since he could not be its transformer.[143]

Hence he strove for peace rather than war, especially moved by the counsel and persuasion of Placidia[144] to all works of good government. Hence Orosius, her contemporary, would say that Placidia had become a hostage of the Goths by divine plan for the welfare of the Roman Empire.[145] Others of her contemporaries thus saw in Placidia's union with Athaulf the fulfillment of the prophecy of Daniel, that the "daughter of the King of the South will come to the King of the North to make a treaty with him."[146] It seems probable that the very conceptualization of Athaulf as thus reported owes much to Placidia. The idea of a succession of Empires is a very old one in the ancient Mediterranean world and still older in the ancient Near East. It seems doubtful that a German, not educated in Roman fashion, should have interpreted by himself the potential relations of Rome and the Goths as one of a possible passing of Empire from the former to the latter. But Galla Placidia, a traditionally educated Roman girl, will have been taught to conceive history in these terms. It will have been she who reconceived Athaulf's idea, confided to her, of original hostility to Rome as an ambition to supplant the Roman Empire with a Gothic. She will have restated the matter to him in terms of the succession of empires, and added that if he accomplished such a thing, he would be a Gothic Caesar Augustus. Such an idea could not but be flattering to the Goth, who will have accepted it, made it his own, and thus repeated it. Likewise the idea of Empire, order, law vs. barbarian, disorder, and lawlessness, the idea that the great achievement of Rome was a creation of law for all mankind, these thoughts too were a cliché, a commonplace of educated inhabitants of the Greek and Roman world for long centuries.[147]

143 Oros. 7. 43. 5–7; on the interpretation and authenticity of this statement see *CP*, LXIII (1968), 114–21.

144 She is described as his wife, but surely as the text here has argued in effect she had begun the work of "conversion" before he married her.

145 Oros. 7. 40. 2.

146 Dan. 11:6; Hyd. 57 (II, 18; cf. Isid. *Orig. Goth.* 19 [II, 275]); Philostorg. *HE* 12. 4; with Bury, *Hist.*, I, 197, n. 1.

147 Cf. M. Pavan, *La politica gotica di Teodosio nella pubblicistica del suo tempo*, pp. 15–19. What the vast mass of the subjects of Rome, not members of the ruling class, thought of this vaunted law and order is strikingly illustrated in the play *Querolus*, where "natural" law or that "of nations" is said to be preferred by the

Once again we have the impression of long conversations of Athaulf with other Romans, but above all with Galla Placidia. We shall see later on that as de facto ruler of the West Roman Empire she was to proclaim the same principles. Athaulf, like all German chieftains of the age of the "Great Migrations of Peoples," will from time to time have found it difficult to control his wild, free people, and the ideas thus formulated will have struck him as obvious truths. Perhaps, too, there is yet another consideration here.[148] In the past generation or so the originally relatively undifferentiated society of the Goths, economically speaking, had been undergoing a conjoint economic, social, and political change which had tended to create ever greater distinctions among them. The recent evolution of Gothic kingship, as distinguished from a more amorphous situation where there had been several chiefs whose relation to each other had been much more a matter of relative prowess and prestige than of an institutionalized hierarchy of power, had been a manifestation of this changing situation. The kings and the more sharply differentiated upper classes thus emerging were quite happy to take over, or at least be inspired by, Roman political and social institutions which bolstered their own preferred position among their people.[149] Thus not only Athaulf but many other Gothic leaders too, presumably, must have been quite willing to accept the rationalization of Roman practice offered by dis-

Bacaudae or Armorican secessionists from the Empire; cf. above, Ch. I, n. 44. Note that the Roman deserter to the Huns whom the historian Priscus tried to persuade of the advantages of the Roman law admitted its advantages in the abstract, but affirmed that it was perverted by its administration; he did not return to the Roman fold, preferring like many others in the fifth century the rude justice and relative freedom of life among the barbarians (Prisc. Frag. 8 [IV, 88]). To the government and the ruling classes, of course, such an attitude was treasonable, and therefore merely immoral perversity.

148 On this matter see Thompson, *Visigoths,* pp. 71–74; *idem,* "The Visigoths from Fritigern to Euric," *Historia,* XII (1963), 105–26, at 113; *idem,* "The Settlement of Barbarians in Southern Gaul," *JRS,* XLVI (1956), 65–75 (without necessarily subscribing to the principal thesis of this article, or to the lengths to which Thompson pushes his conclusions).

149 Regularly, and in varying degrees of thoroughness and speed, once established on Roman soil, in most (the Vandals are a leading exception) of the German tribes there tended to be a coalition of the ruling class among the Germans with the ruling class among the Romans, while their kings regularly tried to preserve as much of the local imperial administration as the ignorance and barbarism of their subjects and themselves would permit. These facts have long been known, and are in fact a commonplace of historical studies of the ancient Germans of this age.

tinguished Romans,[150] and by Placidia herself, since, to be trite, men are regularly easily convinced of verities which conduce to their own profit. A Marxist historian would see here the sum and meaning of the whole incident, but it would be foolish not to consider also the emotional effect of Roman greatness upon the minds of these men and their children's children who for a thousand years could not bring themselves to believe that that pinnacle of human greatness and power had forever passed away beyond all hope of resuscitation. To oversimplify greatly, to the point perhaps of real error in both parts of the statement, one might say that just as the Renaissance tried (in vain) to resurrect the culture of ancient Greece and Rome, the Middle Ages kept trying to resurrect the political ghost of the Christian Roman Empire. And in fact the echoes of this might and glory have not yet entirely died away; we still speak of Eternal Rome, the ultimate symbol of political power.

And at Narbo, in January of 414, Athaulf finally consummated his own personal union, which he doubtless hoped would extend to benefit his people as well as himself, with the Roman Empire in the person of Galla Placidia. Apparently Athaulf's suit was decisively furthered by a certain Candidianus, who persuaded the princess that she should consent to the King's proposal. What her objections were has not been recorded. One of them may well have been that Athaulf, almost certainly a Christian, was probably an Arian heretic like most of his people. And we may be sure that the daughter of the orthodox Theodosius was orthodox herself. But she might have been reminded that her own mother, Galla, had (presumably) been tainted with Arianism before her marriage to Theodosius, and that her soul had been saved for orthodoxy through that marriage. Mixed marriages of this sort did exist, although naturally they were frowned on by the Church,[151] as repre-

---

[150] Such as the citizen of Narbonne who is the reporter of Athaulf's sentiments in Oros. 7. 43. 4; or the Ingenius and Candidianus of Olympiod. Frag. 24 (IV, 62). On Roman advisers behind the "grandes idées" of the German kings, see the examples collected by Musset, *Vagues*, p. 240; for examples of romanization of some Visigoths at the end of the fourth century, see Thompson, *Visigoths*, pp. 104–5, 125, 141; for Latin words in Gothic in the fourth century, *ibid.*, p. 39. H. Helbling, *Goten und Wandalen*, pp. 28–29, compares the declaration of Athaulf with the actual policy of Theodoric the Great, King of the Ostrogoths in Italy at the end of the fifth century.

[151] Cf. F. van der Meer, *Augustine the Bishop*, trans. B. Battershaw and G. R. Lamb, p. 103.

senting a peril to the soul of the orthodox spouse. Yet Placidia may have thought that she might convert her husband to her religion as well as to her politics; examples of such wifely piety are known in this age.[152] Perhaps the fact that she did not have the consent of Honorius,[153] the head of her family, weighed less with her, since she must have been aware that a good part of his reluctance was inspired by Constantius. And of course it seems reasonable to think that she, too, may have seen this marriage as a means of transforming the Goths into faithful servants of Rome. Such a hope or expectation could easily counter any objection that she would be uniting herself to a proven enemy of Rome. At any rate, she gave her consent;[154] we may assume that by January Athaulf was well recovered from the wound he had suffered at Marseilles.[155]

The wedding was celebrated in the house of a certain Ingenius, a leading citizen of Narbo, and obviously one of Athaulf's Gallo-Roman friends. Unfortunately we are not told whether there was any religious ceremony in connection with the making of this union.[156] The marriage festivities, however, throughout were entirely Roman. Placidia took her station in a room of Ingenius' house designated as a bridal chamber; she was arrayed as a bride and with the emblems of her imperial rank; Athaulf took his seat beside her. Symbolically, in accordance with his plans and hopes at this time, he was garbed in a Roman general's cloak, the *paludamentum*,[157] with the usual accompanying Roman accouter-

152 One thinks of Clovis, the Frankish king, whose conversion was at least partly engineered by his wife.

153 The assertion of Seeck, *Gesch.*, VI: 1, 54 (cf. *idem*, *RE*, VIII: 2 [1913], 2789; Hodgkin, *Invaders*, I: 2, 831), that Placidia had received Honorius' consent through Candidianus rests on not a shred of evidence; cf. Ensslin, *RE*, XX: 2 (1950), 1914. Candidianus could have been a Roman who saw in the marriage the possibility of reconciliation between the Goths and Rome, and Placidia may well have agreed.

154 She may have been in love with the handsome Gothic King, but there is no way of knowing. Tillemont, *Empereurs*, V, 630, points out that Placidia was maltreated by Sigeric in 415 because of Athaulf, the murderer of his brother; this might imply that she was thought to be attached emotionally to the King.

155 We should like to believe, with Sirago, *Placidia*, p. 160, that Placidia was much affected by Athaulf's wound.

156 Hodgkin, *Invaders*, I: 2, 831–32, suggests that the Arian Gothic Bishop Sigesarius may have presided; this is a possibility, but one hesitates to think of Placidia's marriage occurring under Arian auspices. On the interest of the Church in Christian marriage, see Tertull. *Uxor.* 2. 8; cf. *CTh* 3. 7. 3 (Constantinople, 428) with Godefroy's comments *ad loc.*, for marriage customs of the Christian Empire.

157 *Chlanis*: cf. Liddell-Scott-Jones, *s.vv.* χλαμύς 3; χλανίς 2; Harpers', *s.vv. chlamys, paludamentum*. It was quite appropriate for him to wear Roman military dress; he would hardly don the cloak of a common soldier.

ments. Together with other wedding gifts the King presented his bride with fifty handsome youths,[158] dressed in silken clothing, and each carrying two large salvers, one piled with gold, the other with precious stones; these treasures of course were part of the plunder of Rome. Obviously Athaulf was trying to imitate imperial magnificence, the largess of an emperor. That the recollection of the source of this wealth must have struck a jarring note amid the festivities is not untypical of the process whereby an individual becomes only partially acculturated to another civilization, for commonly among barbarians booty constitutes a most honorable gift; for that matter, it had among the Romans themselves. Attalus, the ex-pretender, was among those who sang the traditional bridal songs, the *epithalamia*. The occasion was one of great gaiety with salutations from Roman and barbarian alike.[159]

But if Athaulf thought that by presenting the Emperor and Constantius with the fait accompli of his marriage with Placidia he would wring recognition, albeit grudging, of his claims, he was quite mistaken.[160] He was now the brother-in-law of Honorius, true, but it must have been quite easy for Constantius to persuade the latter that Athaulf's act, putting out of bounds the return of the princess, was a direct affront to the imperial majesty. It was quite true that the King had solemnly promised nearly a year before to give up Placidia; now, in defiance of that promise, he had married her. We do not know whether the government thereupon revoked its permission for the Goths to settle in Aquitaine, but it is quite possible that it did; at any rate the Romans, or Constantius, soon commenced to take hostile measures against the Goths. It seems not impossible that Athaulf may have anticipated this hostile reaction, but have expected that in time his marriage even so might have given him and his people the secure place in the Empire they wanted; if there had been enough time, it is quite possible that he would have been right, that despite the ill will of Constantius accommodation such as was eventually arranged with his successor Wallia would have been given him, and on a basis more secure

---

[158] Captured slaves? Surely not captured Roman citizens?

[159] Olympiod. Frag. 24 (IV, 62).

[160] Dahn, *Könige*, V, 59, even suggests that Athaulf aimed in effect at becoming a new Stilicho, supported, however, by his Goths in a way that Stilicho never had been; cf. Stein, *Hist.*, I, 347.

because of this marriage.[161] Naturally, at the time, apart from Constantius, there were Romans who looked upon Placidia's marriage with Athaulf as a disgrace;[162] certainly it is understandable that there were aspects of the marriage which could easily lend themselves to unfavorable comment by tradition-minded Romans. We may suspect that the pride of some Goths as well might have been offended by this marriage.[163]

Accordingly, although Athaulf was sincerely desirous of peace,[164] he once again sought to bring pressure to bear on Constantius and Honorius: once again he elevated Attalus to the purple, a usurpation even more precarious than before, for the Goths were almost the sole support of his regime,[165] although it is not impossible that some of the magnates who had supported the other recent usurpers in Gaul were in favor of another "tyrant."[166] It is possible that Athaulf had been toying with the idea of putting Attalus up as a puppet emperor when he first entered negotiations with Jovinus, and that Attalus had been willing to fall in with the idea. However that may be, now once more on a throne of sorts he proceeded to appoint great ministers of state, phantoms since they had little or nothing to administer;[167] it seems a reasonable conjecture that, like Alaric before him, Athaulf received the title of Master of the Soldiery.[168]

This creation of a new emperor did prod the government into taking new action; undoubtedly Athaulf would have been willing to put down the puppet he had set up if the government had been willing to make such a concession as fulfilling the treaty of 413 and recognizing his marriage with Placidia. But Constantius was un-

---

161 Cf. Seeck, *Gesch.*, VI: 1, 54 (speaking of the year 413 before the marriage).

162 *Narr. de impp. domus Val. et Theod.* 6 (I, 630); written in the early 420's by an admirer of Theodosius II; cf. Mommsen, *ibid.*, p. 617; Bury, *Hist.*, I, 211, n. 1.

163 Cf. Dantier, *Femmes*, I, 246.

164 Paul. Pell. 303–4.

165 Prosp. 1254 (I, 467); Paul. Pell. 297–301; Olympiod. Frag. 13 (IV, 60); Oros. 7. 42. 9; it might have been at this juncture that Attalus as emperor granted the Goths Aquitaine. The *Chron. Gall. a. 452* 73 (I, 654) so dates the grant; but since the Goths peacefully entered Bordeaux in 413, it seems better to transfer the grant (assuming it is not merely an anticipation of 418) to 413; see Schmidt, *Gesch.*[2], I, 457, and above, nn. 120, 133. Displacements of an entry by a year or so in these chronicles are not uncommon; cf. Courtois, *Byzantion*, XXI (1951), 23–54.

166 The suggestion is Sundwall's, *Studien*, pp. 11–12.

167 Paul. Pell. 293–96.

168 Freeman, *Western Europe*, p. 204, n.

ready to make any concessions.[169] We are ill informed concerning the whereabouts of the general during the period immediately preceding this time, whether he was in Gaul or in Italy. In any event he now established his headquarters at the imperial sub-capital of Arles and started to take measures against the Goths with his usual energy. He was still unwilling to risk his precious troops against the foe in the open field. Instead, presumably utilizing what few ships remained from the great imperial fleets of an earlier day and commandeering what others he could,[170] he placed the port of Narbonne under strait blockade,[171] and thus deprived the Goths of all commerce with the outside world, particularly in grain.[172] The results were quite gratifying from Constantius' point of view; the Goths were forced to move; they could not live off the land which had been devastated so many times in the near past, both by the barbarians of 407–9 and by the armies of the usurpers and their foes, the soldiers loyal to Honorius. Hence Athaulf was compelled to decide to follow the example of the Vandals and the others before him and cross the Pyrenees into Spain.[173] Before they left,

169 Philostorg. *HE* 12. 4.

170 On the decline of the war fleets of the Empire in late imperial times, and the reversion to the old Republican procedure of putting together fleets ad hoc for a naval expedition, see C. Courtois, "Les politiques navales de l'empire romain," *Rev. hist.*, CLXXXVI (1939), 17–47, 225–59; G. Gigli, "La flotta e la difesa del basso impero," *Mem. della Accad. N. Lincei*, Cl. scienz. mor. stor. fil., ser. VIII, I (1946), 3–43, at 9. D. Kienast, *Untersuchungen zu den Kriegsflotten der römischen Kaiserzeit*, pp. 124–57, argues that the fourth century saw the continuation of the Roman war-fleets, but (with exceptions) the West in the fifth century had lost its fleets (p. 156 and n. 93). His arguments, esp. for the fifth century in the West, are unconvincing.

171 Oros. 7. 43. 1.

172 Thompson, *Visigoths*, pp. 19–20; *idem*, *JRS*, XLVI (1956), 65–75, at 67, n. 17; is at loss to discover what these articles of commerce were. Surely the main thing was grain, or food in general (as well as a variety of other articles), paid for from the Goths' rich store of booty, for they could not even try to till the fields as long as their relations with the Empire were unsettled, for they were subject to attack at any time. Ruggini, *Athenaeum*, XL (1962), 383–84 tends to minimize this cutting off of provisions as a factor compelling the Goths, since control of the sea and victualing were already in Roman hands. But the Romans had no regular war fleet and the profit motive would have led traders to deal with the Goth despite imperial prohibitions. Hence the naval blockade must have been physical as well as "on paper," and an effective cause in making the Goths' further stay in Aquitaine and Narbonensis impossible.

173 Oros. 7. 43. 1; Hyd. 60 (II, 19); Prosp. 1256 (I, 467); Jord. *Get.* 163 has a more patriotic version: the Vandals (and Alans), fearing their ancient enemies the Goths, had fled Gaul to Spain. In commiseration of the lot of the Spaniards, Athaulf determined to follow them. Sirago, *Placidia*, p. 164, thinks that by diplomatic ultimatums Constantius forced Athaulf to agree to go to Spain. This is stretching the language of Orosius too far; Spain is in the direction of Africa; the decision was Athaulf's.

however, the infuriated Goths plundered the Roman towns they had occupied. Bordeaux thus suffered and nearby Bazas was attacked. In the latter place a large body of Alans, who with their king had joined themselves to the Goths, now went over to the Roman side, and for a time it seemed that war would break out between the Goths and the Alans. At Bordeaux some of the Goths chivalrously tried to protect the Roman "hosts" upon whom they had been quartered. But at Bazas a kind of social revolution broke out in the midst of the general disorder, with the slaves joining some freeborn youths to plunder and slay the upper classes.[174] Presumably more or less similar scenes were enacted in other cities and towns occupied by the Goths. There is no reason to believe that Athaulf had changed his philo-Roman attitude again; it is quite probable that he could not control the excesses of his people, who in any event had to equip themselves as best they could for another long and difficult migration. Winter was apparently approaching and the passage of the Pyrenees would be harsh indeed.

Unfortunately for himself, even the potential usefulness of Attalus was at an end. Making him Emperor to force Honorius to agreement had proved futile when countered by the blockade of Constantius. In fact, even to keep him with the Goths in the future would be an impediment to the peace that Athaulf so urgently wanted; his presence in the Gothic camp would be a perpetual suggestion of ill faith in any future negotiations with the imperial government, which could hardly fail to see in him a potential pawn to be played yet another time against Honorius. With ruthless, not to say callous, logic, therefore, Athaulf expelled him from the Gothic camp. At least the King had the grace not to hand him over to Constantius or Honorius directly. Some time later, apparently when he was trying in a ship to escape to some haven beyond the sea, he was captured and taken to Constantius. When Honorius made a triumphal entry into Rome in 416, Attalus was made to walk before the Emperor's chariot to the imperial tribunal. The "tyrant" was dragged before the imperial throne, two fingers of his right hand were chopped off, and he was sent into exile on the island of Lipara for the rest of his life, being given a modest allowance to defray his living costs. This "victory" was

---

174 Paul. Pell. 285–90, 328–98.

commemorated even in the Eastern Empire, but the relatively slight punishment shows the government's contempt.[175]

In Spain the Goths established themselves at Barcelona;[176] there is no record that their occupation of the city or of the nearby parts of the peninsula was opposed either by the Romans or by the barbarians already established in Spain. The area around Barcelona had apparently enjoyed the direct rule of the imperial government until the arrival of the Goths. At Barcelona Galla Placidia bore Athaulf a son to whom the King gave the name Theodosius; this was a father's natural right, but there can be little doubt that the name represented both the philo-Roman ideas of Athaulf and the influence of the child's mother. In any event, the name confirms the retention by the King of the pro-Roman ideas he had enunciated at Narbo.[177] It has frequently been suggested by modern scholars that the name Theodosius means yet more—that Athaulf (and Placidia presumably) foresaw a future in which this son would reign as Emperor, and presumably also as King of the Visigoths, supported by his own people in both positions. If Athaulf did in fact conceive such an idea or hope, it is by no means improbable that the possibility may have occurred to him even before he married Placidia.[178] Perhaps such a project was feasible; the Emperor Theodosius II, reigning in the East, was the son of Arcadius and Eudoxia, herself the daughter of a Frank named Bauto, although one suspects her mother was Roman.[179] If one believes that if the accession of this child had come to pass the West Roman Empire might have been saved, one must necessarily also subscribe to the theory that great events in history depend on accident rather than on deep-rooted causes, a type of etiology likely to be repugnant to most students of history today. At the very least, however, the child's name witnesses not only the general philo-Roman aspirations of

[175] Oros. 7. 42. 9; Olympiod. Frag. 13 (IV, 60); *Chron. Pasch.*, p. 573 (Bonn); Prosp. 1256, 1263 (I, 467, 468); Philostorg. *HE* 12. 5; Marcell. *s.a.* 412, 2 (II, 71). There is some disagreement about exactly what parts of his hand were severed. Philostorg. *HE* 12. 4 says that the Goths officially surrendered Attalus in 416 at the time Placidia was returned; this must be wrong, cf. Freeman, *Western Europe*, p. 217 and n. For the date of the "triumph" over Attalus, see Seeck, *Gesch.*, VI: 2, 396 *ad* 60. 5.

[176] Jord. *Get.* 163; cf. Oros. 7. 43. 8; Olympiod. Frag. 26 (IV, 63).

[177] Olympiod. Frag. 26 (IV, 62–63).

[178] Nagl, *Placidia*, p. 24; Lot, *Destinées*, p. 44; *idem, Les invasions germaniques*, p. 84; Courcelle, *Hist. litt.*, p. 69; K. A. Schöndorf, *Die Geschichtstheologie des Orosius*, p. 59; Barker, *CMedH*, I (1911), 403.

[179] Cf. Bury, *Hist.*, I, 108.

Athaulf and Placidia, but also the wish to arrive at a settlement with Honorius; Constantius, however, still remained steadfast in his opposition.[180] It is quite possible that the child's birth was the occasion for another diplomatic attempt to persuade the Emperor to recognize the Goths.[181] But all aspirations depending upon the infant were rendered vain by his death not long after his birth. His little body was placed in a silver coffin, which, amid the great grief of his parents, was deposited in a chapel or oratory near Barcelona.[182] Years later it was to be exhumed by Galla Placidia's loving care and in great pomp reinterred in the imperial mausoleum of the Western branch of the Theodosian house at the side of Saint Peter's in Rome. The burial and reburial of the child in these Christian surroundings give reason to believe that he had been baptized as an infant; such baptism was then as now administered to infants in peril of death.[183] Thus too was fulfilled the prophecy of Daniel that the seed of the union of the King of the North and the daughter of the King of the South should not survive.[184] And thus Galla Placidia, who was never to forget it, lost her firstborn child.

But the King of the North himself did not long survive his son. Athaulf had taken into his service a man named Dubius or Euervulf, who had been a servant of a Gothic chieftain slain by Athaulf (the chieftain or king thus slain is commonly thought by modern scholars to have been Sarus). Possibly some joking remarks made by the King about the man's small stature were the immediate cause of his loosing the murderous vengeance he had long been planning. Like all barbarians he went armed, and drawing his sword he mortally wounded the King in the groin while the latter was engaged in looking to his horses in their stable, and relaxing in

180 Olympiod. Frag. 26 (IV, 63); cf. Ensslin, *RE,* XX: 2 (1950), 1915.

181 Cf. Olympiod. Frag. 26 (IV, 63) and Oros. 7. 43. 8: "cumque eidem paci petendae atque offerendae studiosissime insisteret," Athaulf was slain.

182 Olympiod. Frag. 26 (IV, 63).

183 Tillemont, *Empereurs,* V, 629. For such a purpose it made no difference in the view of orthodox Christianity whether the person who baptized him were Arian or not, for heretical baptism was accepted as valid, if performed with good intention, by the orthodox Church. For Church rules on baptism in the fifth century, see J. Gaudemet, *L'église dans l'empire romain (IVe–Ve siècles),* Histoire du droit et des institutions de l'église en occident, ed. G. Le Bras, III (Paris, n.d.), pp. 64–65.

184 Schild, *Placidia,* p. 37; Daniel 11:6 (Theodotion; Vulgate); cf. Hyd. 57 (II, 18); Isid. *Hist. Goth.* 19 (II, 275).

the familiar conversation of his friends and attendants.[185] As he lay dying, Athaulf's last thought, apparently, was for the welfare of Placidia and of his people; he instructed his brother (the man's name is not transmitted to us) to return her to the Romans and win their friendship if possible. Obviously he clearly realized that his retention of Placidia and his marrying her had been the principal obstacle to a peace with the Romans. Then he died (late summer, August? 415).[186] Thus Galla Placidia, who had married when she was in about her twenty-sixth year, a late age for Roman brides, was left a widow after only a little more than a year and a half of marriage. It seems impossible to decide whether she loved Athaulf; it seems, however, that if there ever was a man she loved it was he. Whether she loved him or not, she was to have ample reason in the next few days to regret his sudden death.

[185] Olympiod. Frag. 26 (IV, 63); Oros. 7. 43. 8; Philostorg. *HE* 12. 4; Hyd. 60 (II, 19); Jord. *Get.* 163; Prosp. 1257 (I, 467). For his being engaged in familiar conversation see Hyd.; Barker, *CMedH*, I (1911), 403, n. 1, may well be right, however, when he thinks that the text may merely be a corruption of a reference to the stables. Seeck, *Gesch.*, VI: 1, 58; 2, 395–96, suggests that Dubius may well be the Latin name of a Goth called Euervulf by his own people; such double nomenclature was not uncommon. Hodgkin, *Invaders*, I: 2, 834, n. 1, doubts the identification of the fallen chieftain with Sarus on the ground that Olympiodorus, who was well acquainted with the career of Sarus, would have said so if it were indeed he; on the other hand, we do not have Olympiodorus' work in fact, but a fragment in epitome.

[186] The news of his death reached Constantinople (where it was the cause of great rejoicing) 24 Sept. (*Chron. Pasch.*, I, 572 [Bonn]). Hence most scholars have suggested August as the month of Athaulf's death, allowing four to six weeks for the news to reach the East. Ensslin, *RE*, XX: 2 (1950), 1916, thinks it better merely to specify summer, on the ground that the news was probably longer on its journey than scholars had thought in the past.

# 4

# CONSTANTIUS

Superficially the murder of Athaulf appeared to have been a simple act of vengeance on the part of Dubius-Euervulf to satisfy a private animosity further stimulated by the King's ridicule of the man's short stature. Yet the man who succeeded Athaulf was Sigeric (or Singeric), the brother of the King's mortal enemy, Sarus, whom Athaulf had slain. It is quite tempting to suppose with many modern students that Sigeric had conspired with Dubius to bring about Athaulf's death, whether or not the assassin's former master had been Sarus; obviously both men detested Athaulf. That a conspiracy should have been formed between them, that Sigeric should have aspired to the chieftaincy of the Goths even before Athaulf's death and have worked to bring about the King's murder, seems quite natural. The instructions the dying King had given his brother clearly indicate that he expected the latter to succeed him. Yet, instead, Sigeric became king by virtue of his intrigues and power rather than by legal right, one source tells us; another, that Athaulf was slain by the contrivance of his own people, "it is said."[1] Certainly a principal motive behind Sigeric's usurpation was hatred as well as lust for power. In the major question of Gothic policy, the problem of the relations the Goths should have or try to have with Rome, there was no change. The brother of Sarus who had frequently been a servant of the imperial government (and had perished when about to offer his

1 Olympiod. Frag. 26 (IV, 63); Oros. 7. 43. 8.

services to a Roman usurper) not surprisingly held fast to Athaulf's policy of peace with Rome. But the hatred which animated Sigeric did not stop with the death of Athaulf. Despite the attempts of the Arian bishop Sigesarius to save them, the children of Athaulf's first wife were seized and slain; the Most Noble Galla Placidia, the late King's second wife, was perhaps saved from death by Sigeric's wish for peace with Rome; nevertheless he made her walk on foot in front of his horse, along with other Roman prisoners, out of spite against Athaulf.[2] It was the nadir of the princess' fortunes.

Happily, however, from her point of view, Sigeric was to reign only a week; her tormentor was murdered by his own people after only seven days. The man who succeeded him was a certain Wallia, who was responsible for Sigeric's murder and perhaps for the death of others who shared his own ambitions.[3] The fact that Athaulf had become a philo-Roman in the nature of human affairs implies that there were those who were still opposed to a pro-Roman policy and viewed the late King's attempts to promote peace and friendship with the Roman government with aversion.[4] At the beginning Wallia's policy was necessarily anti-Roman; it was on this understanding that he had been elected king.[5] Placidia, however, was

<hr/>

[2] Olympiod. Frag. 26 (IV, 63).

[3] Oros. 7. 43. 9–10; Olympiod. Frag. 26 (IV, 63); Jord. *Get.* 163; Prosp. 1257 (I, 468); *Lat. Regg. Visig.* 8–10 (III, 465); Isid. *Hist. Goth.* 20 (II, 276).

[4] Oros. 7. 43. 8 indeed implies strongly that Athaulf was slain because of his policy of seeking friendship with Rome. As indicated in the text, other motives seem adequate to explain the murder, but it is by no means impossible that Sigeric despite his own inclinations may have been willing to seek allies among the anti-Roman group, until he had achieved his purpose of killing Athaulf and succeeding him. Then Sigeric's own death would have been brought about by the alienation of the anti-Roman group after he had seized power, as well as by the presumptive personal ambitions of Wallia (and others?) who were also ambitious to succeed to Athaulf's position. It is not certain how profoundly anti-Roman Wallia was; although at the beginning of his reign he eschewed a pro-Roman policy, he made no desperate attempt to avoid it as soon as he found that hostility to Rome would not answer to the situation in which the Goths found themselves. At least the foregoing conjectures do not represent any impossibility, and they take into account the evidence we do have, especially that of the Spaniard Orosius and the Egyptian, but well-informed, Olympiodorus. Some modern scholars opt for the tradition of personal vendetta, others for anti-Roman conspiracy, others for a combination of the two in some such fashion as expounded here. See Dahn, *Urgeschichte*, I, 354; Thompson, *Historia*, XII (1963), 115, n. 43; Suerbaum, *Staatsbegriff*, p. 222 and n. 7; G. Kaufmann, "Ueber das Foederatverhältniss des tolosanischen Reichs zu Rom," *Forschungen zur deutschen Geschichte*, VI (1866), 433–76, at 436; Freeman, p. 219, n.; Lot, *Destinées*, p. 45; Bury, *Hist.*, I, 199.

[5] Oros. 7, 43. 10.

restored to the position she had so long held, of honorable captivity among the Goths,[6] presumably with the same respect paid to her rank as the sister of the Emperor as before, perhaps now also respected as the consort of a Gothic king. Once again, however, she had to resume her weary wanderings with the Goths, for Wallia again took up the old plan of crossing to Africa, to find a home there.[7] But again the attempt failed. Once again the Goths came to a southern promontory of Europe at the season of the storms of autumn. Arrived at the strait of Gades (Cadiz), some twelve thousand embarked on ships they had doubtless seized along the coast, but once more the winds of Heaven destroyed the ships and the men in the narrow passage. It may well have occurred to the Goths, as Orosius intimates, that it was not God's will that they cross to Africa. Yet the everlasting problem of victualing remained—how to support a people on the move in an already devastated peninsula, despite the hostility of the government which still controlled the food and riches of Africa. And there was another danger. As far as we know, Constantius was still at Arles in Gaul, keeping a close watch on Gothic activities. Whether or not the Vandals, Sueves, and other barbarians of Spain had already reached an understanding with the Empire,[8] if the Empire should join any sizeable number of those barbarians in an attack on the Goths from two directions at once, the position of the latter would be perilous indeed,[9] especially after the loss of the warriors who had perished in the Strait of Gibralter. Since the Goths could not leave the dead end that Spain had become for them by sea, they must retrace their steps northward and try to escape the trap in which they found themselves by fighting their way again into Gaul. But after another long march, probably with well-tightened belts, an attempt to traverse the Pyrenees into Gaul was repulsed by Constantius.[10]

---

6 *Ibid.* 12.

7 Is it possible to infer that this plan had been pressed on Athaulf, but that he had refused to lead his people south, hoping for an accommodation with Rome instead? Oros. 7. 43. 11.

8 Oros. 7. 43. 14, with due regard for the exaggeration of his language; cf. J. Straub, "Christliche Geschichtspolitik in der Krisis des römischen Reiches," *Historia,* I (1950), 52–81, at 76.

9 Kaufmann, *Gesch.,* I, 337–38.

10 *Chron. Gall. a. 452* 78 (I, 656); on the passage see Barker, *CMedH,* I (1911), 404, n. 1, who would put this attempt before the southern march; rather, it seems better to put it after the attempt to use that much more desirable exit had failed. Cf. Jord. *Get.* 164; Ensslin, *RE,* XX: 2 (1950), 1916.

Perhaps it was at this time that the Goths were reduced to buying food from the Vandals at famine prices; the Vandals ridiculed the desperation of their ancient enemies.[11] Even the most stubborn foes of Rome must have realized that at least in their present circumstances the Goths could do nothing else than try to reach an accommodation with the Empire.

And since Placidia was now no longer married to Athaulf, there was no reason why her surrender might not be used as an important concession to attain peace and food. If the historian of the Goths is to be trusted, after the death of Athaulf Honorius had promised Constantius that he should have Placidia to wife, if she could be gotten out of Gothic captivity.[12] The Emperor's approval of the indispensable general was further signified about this time by the conferral upon him of the exalted distinction of Patrician.[13] Since both parties, Wallia and Constantius, now wanted peace, the conclusion of a treaty was relatively easily arrived at. A certain Euplutius, an *agens in rebus* (that is, a member of what is often called the secret police of the Empire; its members were used on many kinds of delicate and confidential missions by the government), acted as Constantius' emissary in dealing with the Goths; the parleys took place somewhere in or near the Pyrenees.[14] The Visigoths were awarded six hundred thousand measures of grain and entered the service of the Empire as *foederati* (literally, allies). Placidia was handed over to Euplutius, and doubtless conducted by him to the man who intended to become her husband (early in 416).[15] Apparently in consideration of this agreement the Goths

11 Olympiod. Frag. 29 (IV, 64).

12 Jord. *Get.* 164 (cf. Prosp. 1259 [I, 468]); this may be a mere deduction from what actually happened later, but it is quite likely in itself, except that Jord. represents Honorius as taking the initiative in order to free Placidia from her captivity. Since he seems to have been little disturbed by his sister's situation in the past, we are fairly safe in assuming that the initiative belonged to Constantius, as we know from Olympiod. Frag. 20 (IV, 61) it did in 413.

13 *CTh* 15. 14. 14 (1 March 416) addresses Constantius with this title; cf. Seeck, *RE,* IV (1901), 1101. Ensslin, *Klio,* XXIV (1931), 472–74, against Seeck, holds that the Patriciate was Constantius' reward for the treaty with Wallia in 416.

14 On Euplutius see Sundwall, *Studien,* no. 155, p. 74.

15 Olympiod. Frag. 31 (IV, 64); Oros. 7. 43. 12–13; Philostorg. *HE* 12. 4; Jord. *Get.* 165; Hyd. 60 (II, 19); Prosp. 1259 (I, 468); Cassiod. *Chron.* 1194 (II, 155); Marcell. *s.a.* 414, 2 (II, 71). Philostorg. says it was at this time the Goths handed over the pretender Attalus, but the Western evidence is against him (although he is partly accepted by Stein, *Hist.,* I, 267); see above, Ch. III, n. 175. On the date see Ensslin, *Klio,* XXIV (1931), 473.

commenced to attack the other barbarians in Spain; now with the Emperor's approval and the support of his food they were eager to revenge themselves on their fellows who had ridiculed their weakness only a short time before.[16] In the almost continuous warfare of the next years the Siling Vandals were nearly annihilated; their remnant joined the Asding Vandals, who henceforth may be called the Vandals, without qualification. We may be sure that the Empire watched these proceedings with great satisfaction; war among the various barbarian tribes could not fail to redound to the profit of Rome. In her great days Rome had followed a policy of *divide et impera,* using her allies and associates to pluck her chestnuts from the fire as often as possible. Now, in the last generations of the existence of the Western Empire, the game took on the character of a desperate struggle for survival, as Rome no longer had the resources or the armies to send in to redress the balance, should it incline against her. The success of her generals and statesmen henceforward was to be determined largely by the degree of agility they attained in following this policy. As previous events have demonstrated, Constantius was a consummate master at the game, and hence indispensable.

As usual, we would be happy to know the reaction of Galla Placidia to these events, now that after seven years, during which she had become for a time a wife and mother, she was returned to her loving brother—and to Constantius. As usual, there is no information; we must be content with some general considerations. We shall see that she did not wish at all to marry Constantius; his attentions, therefore, must have been obnoxious for some reason: his person, her recollection of what she likely regarded as his persecution of her and Athaulf, or whatever. It is not impossible she regretted the Goths; when she returned to her own people she brought with her a considerable number of them who had become devoted to her interests.[17] The fact may attest the attraction of Rome for the barbarians as well as the feuds among the Goths; it is also probable evidence that Placidia could inspire devotion; perhaps, more, that a mere woman she possessed qualities of leadership. Nevertheless, even as the widow of Athaulf her position among the Goths must have been uncertain and insecure (who

16 Oros. 7. 43. 15.
17 Olympiod. Frag. 40 (IV, 66).

knew when another Sigeric might succeed to the throne?). She would have been a strange product of settled civilization, if she had not contrasted even her most honored position among the Goths in their wanderings with the amenities and luxuries of civilized life at the imperial court among Romans of the highest rank, wealth, and culture. Certainly she was devoted to Rome and all it stood for in the minds, if not of all men, at least in those of the educated, ruling classes. In an extant letter, written not long before her death years later, she would refer to the greatness of the City, worthy of reverence in all things, since it was the mistress of all lands.[18]

The Emperor Honorius seems to have spent most of the years 416 and 417 at Ravenna, save for a brief journey to Rome to celebrate his "triumph" over Attalus in the spring of 416, and to promise his assistance to the Romans in promoting the recovery of the City.[19] Presumably Galla Placidia journeyed from the Pyrenees to Arles, where we may guess she had a stiff interview with Constantius, and thence to Ravenna, which was to be her principal residence for the remainder of her life. After the lapse of some eight years she again beheld her brother Honorius. It is likely that Constantius remained for the time being in Gaul, whose affairs he was busily arranging in these years; he was certainly in Ravenna by the end of the year. Perhaps he crossed to Italy to join the court in the autumn of 416. For whether or not he had had a promise from Honorius earlier, as Jordanes says, he meant to become Placidia's second husband. Placidia stoutly and repeatedly refused the Patrician's attentions; the latter became convinced that the members of her household were strengthening this resolve of hers; the suspicion made Constantius quite angry. And it is likely that he was justified in his suspicions. The Goths in Placidia's following, if no one else, are apt to have entertained extreme dislike for Constantius, for his blockade of 414, used to force the Goths out of Gaul, with all the suffering which it must have entailed, must have been vividly remembered and resented.[20] It seems likely

---

[18] *Ap. Epp. Leon. Magn.* 56 (*PL*, LIV, 861–62).

[19] Seeck, *Regesten*, pp. 332, 334; Philostorg. *HE* 12. 5; cf. Oros. 7. 40. 1; probably *CIL*, VI, 1191, 1193, 1195, dating from the next few years.

[20] Olympiod. Frags. 34, 40 (IV, 65, 66); cf. Nagl, *Placidia*, p. 29 (but there is no justification for her assumption that Placidia tried to foment a revolt among her Gothic followers); Sirago, *Placidia*, p. 200.

that Placidia's aversion sprang from causes similar to theirs; Constantius had been responsible for the thwarting of the pro-Roman plans of Athaulf, plans which he had undoubtedly conceived under the guidance, or as a result of the guidance, of his wife. And Constantius was ugly to look at, and had unpleasing mannerisms, at least in public (and his private virtues, best seen in the midst of a carouse with his boon companions, are unlikely to have commended him to Placidia). Her refusal might also have been dictated, or rationalized, by reluctance to contract a second marriage, tolerated, but hardly praised, by the Church of the time. And of course the daughter of Theodosius, the former consort of a valiant king of the Visigoths, might well have thought the parvenu Patrician unworthy of becoming her husband and thus opening a way for himself to the imperial throne.[21] The woman in Placidia may also have objected purely and simply to being handed about like a lay object. For Honorius could not afford to alienate his able general and minister; there is no evidence on the point, but we cannot doubt in view of the sequel that pressure came from the Emperor to urge compliance with the wishes of Constantius. It was customary in this age for the emperors of East and West to nominate one consul each. For 417, however, presumably with the acquiescence of the government of Theodosius II, Honorius designated himself as consul for the eleventh time and Constantius for the second.

Before the end of the year 416, apparently, Honorius signified to Placidia in the strongest terms that she must marry Constantius. If Placidia might have withstood the wishes of her brother, she must yield to the command of the Emperor. Hence on 1 January 417, the day on which Honorius and Constantius entered upon their joint consulship, the Emperor took his sister by the hand and much against her will gave her to Constantius. Thereupon (whether the same day, or at least not many days later) the wedding was celebrated with great magnificence.[22] It is very likely, as we

21 On the possibilities for Placidia's motives, see Ensslin, *RE*, XX: 2 (1950), 1916–17; Schild, *Placidia*, pp. 39–40; Güldenpenning, *Arcad. und Theod.*, pp. 238–39; Kornemann, *Grosse Frauen*, p. 333; Sirago, *Placidia*, p. 199 and n. 3; Burckhardt, *Schweiz. Rundschau*, XXV (1925–26), 485.

22 Olympiod. Frag. 34 (IV, 65); Sirago, *Placidia*, p. 201, seems right in understanding by a close reading of this passage that although Placidia was unwilling, she

have seen, that Constantius' principal motive in wishing to marry the Emperor's sister was his ambition; it is by no means impossible, however, that he had also been influenced by the personal charms of Placidia. However that may be, two facts have been preserved which attest that she exercised much the same degree of influence over her second husband as over her first.[23] Before Constantius' marriage, we are told, he was careless of money, but after Placidia became his wife he grew quite parsimonious.[24] A change in attitude toward money is not unknown when men in quite different circumstances marry. Yet one suspects that something more lay behind this change in the attitude of Constantius. He now had a wife, but it is difficult to believe that his finances would be strained to support her. She had possessed an estate of her own since childhood; some of the properties belonging to this estate were situated in the Western Empire, in Sicily, for example.[25] In all probability Placidia was a very wealthy woman in her own right. But politics in most times requires extensive amounts of money. We have seen that Constantius had been involved in politics for some years. Yet he had not become rich; he had had to ask for the confiscated estates of Heraclian to support the expenses of his first consulship.[26] But living at court was expensive; a Patrician married to the Emperor's sister must display a certain state; intrigues, inseparable

---

was not surprised at the events of 1 Jan. In turn, it follows that the Emperor must have used his full authority to compel her unwilling consent in the days and weeks preceding. Cf. also Soz. *HE* 9. 16. 2; Prosp. 1259 (I, 468; cf. 496); Hyd. 62 (II, 19); Cassiod. *Chron.* 1194 (II, 155). Sirago, *Placidia,* p. 201, also thinks that this public action of the Emperor, delivering her to Constantius, was to persuade Placidia's Gothic followers that the marriage was not her wish. This is possible; if Placidia had political ambitions, she would have to accomplish them with the assistance of a husband and children, for it was problematical whether she could work through the Emperor merely as his sister. And if she were to marry, it would have to be Constantius or no one; no one else was politically feasible, nor, if she managed somehow to avoid marrying the Patrician, was it to be imagined that he would have tolerated her marrying another man for the second time. Unfortunately, however, this is only logic, and in matters of this sort human beings are prone to act from illogic; the evidence we have consistently depicts her as unwilling to marry Constantius. Placidia had allowed herself to be persuaded to marry Athaulf; she had to be forced to marry Constantius; it would be an easy inference that she found Athaulf at least attractive.

23 So Nagl, *Placidia,* p. 31, writing with particular reference to Libanius the magician; and Bury-Gibbon, *Decline and Fall,* III, 394.

24 Olympiod. Frag. 39 (IV, 66); cf. above, Ch. III, n. 98.

25 Olympiod. Frag. 15 (IV, 60).

26 *Ibid.* 23 (IV, 62).

from the court of an absolute monarch, required money. Above all, both Constantius and Placidia headed extensive households with numbers of barbarian followers or guards to support.[27] A not insignificant part of the expenses of these households was constituted by the upkeep of the *bucellarii* attached to them.[28] One concludes that Galla Placidia may well have instructed her husband in the uses of money in politics. And when Constantius became Emperor he would discover that even when the resources of the Emperor, whether personal or imperial, were added to the public revenues the sum would hardly suffice to meet the needs of the government.[29]

In 421 a certain Libanius, a magician and thaumaturge, put in an appearance at Ravenna and declared that he could act against the barbarians without using soldiers. He was ready to give a demonstration of his powers, and apparently Constantius was sorely tempted to avail himself of the man's services. Such magical arts, of course, were believed to be quite possible through the agency of the devils who masqueraded as pagan gods; clearly therefore Christians ought not under any circumstances to resort to any such magical practices. Placidia coldly informed her husband that she would separate from or divorce him if he did not put to death a man whom she regarded as in league with Satan. And the man was in fact executed at her wish. The incident shows both that Placidia was a pious Christian who believed in the reality of black magic, and that she cared so little for her husband after some years of marriage that she could use this kind of threat to compel him to yield to her wishes.[30] Her resolute opposition to all things pagan is also shown by the destruction, almost certainly by her order after her return to Italy, of the wonder-working statue at Rhegium which the pagans claimed had been responsible for Alaric's failure to cross to Sicily.[31] About this time, perhaps precisely in 421, Ursus,

[27] *Ibid.* 40 (IV, 66).

[28] *Ibid.* 7 (IV, 59); Seeck, *RE*, III (1899), 934–39.

[29] Cf. the plaintive statement of Galla Placidia in 431: *CTh* 11. 1. 36.

[30] Olympiod. Frag. 38 (IV, 66); cf. E. A. Thompson, "Olympiodorus of Thebes," *CQ*, XXXVIII (1944), 43–52, at 43; Schild, *Placidia*, pp. 42–43; Sirago, *Placidia*, p. 204, thinks that the threat of divorce was probably also used on other occasions. Quite possibly, but it must have been Placidia's ultimate threat, which she would presumably have had enough intelligence to use sparingly.

[31] See above, Ch. III, n. 55.

a steward of the imperial estates in Africa, presumably with the encouragement of both Placidia and Constantius, not only undertook the suppression of the Manichaean heresy in Africa, but completely destroyed the great temple of "the Heavenly Goddess" (*Dea Caelestis,* Tanit in Punic) at Carthage.[32]

Whatever may have been the shortcomings of Constantius as a man, whatever his ambitions for power, legitimate or illegitimate, he certainly possessed some of the traits of sound statesmanship. These are best exhibited in his Gallic policy. Italy of course was the natural core of the Roman Empire; when it was in danger troops would be drawn from other provinces to defend it. This had happened in Stilicho's day; the successful entry of the Goths into Italy had occurred during a period of disorganization and crisis in the government and before Constantius came to power. But after the Goths left Italy, as far as we can follow the movements of Constantius, he regularly kept his army interposed between Gaul with its turbulent barbarians and Italy. He had not let even the rebellion of Heraclian and the latter's descent on Italy deflect his attention from this objective; fortunately a small force commanded by a general of lesser rank had been sufficient to dispose of the rebel. Next in importance to Italy, however, came the provinces of Africa, vital as the source of provisionment of the City itself, and in their relative wealth an important economic mainstay of the government. It was therefore characteristic, and dictated by sound policy, that pretenders or emperors who held Italy regularly attempted to extend their sway to Africa. It was thus also a sound instinct that in the fourth and fifth centuries regularly joined Africa to Italy in a single prefecture. The importance of that transmarine region is also shown by the government's attempts to keep the Goths away from the sea. Africa could hardly be said to be peaceful; the religious and social disorders of the fourth century still continued in the fifth, while the desert tribes beyond the contracted frontiers of the Late Empire were always troublesome, and from time to time could constitute a serious menace. But in the second decade of the fifth century the government of Honorius and Constantius, with the able assistance

32 *Lib. de promiss.* 3. 44 (pp. 576–79, ed. R. Braun [Paris, 1964]); August. *Haeres.* 46 (*PL*, XLII, 36); Possid. *V. August.* 16; Sundwall, *Studien*, no. 481, p. 141.

of such polemicists as Saint Augustine, was making considerable headway against the heretics and the Circumcellions.[33] For the rest, Africa suffered from the chronic disorders of the declining state and society of the fifth century.

But next to Africa the most important region of the West was Gaul, the keystone of the entire far western prefecture, properly named "of the Gauls," although including Britain and Spain (and the far west of North Africa). From Gaul as a base, if it were held securely, Roman power could be reasserted in Spain and in Britain, especially if one assumes that motives other than pride dictated the extension of Roman power to that island, which even in the great days of the Principate had hardly been worth the cost to Rome of administration and protection.[34] Emperors or usurpers who ruled Gaul ordinarily found little difficulty in extending their power to Britain and Spain. Usurpers based originally in Britain had commonly attempted to extend their power to Gaul as soon as possible. The career of the "tyrant" Constantine is a perfect illustration of these principles. But not all Gaul was equally valuable to Rome. If she could not hold it all, then she must at least try to control the southern part. Stilicho thus, while not by any means abandoning northern Gaul, had transferred the seat of the prefecture from northern Trier to southern Arles. Again history shows that this was sound policy. Through the Middle Ages and even till today the institutions and even the language of the Midi betray a far more Roman stamp than do those of the north. The south of France is Mediterranean, in a sense Italian, in vegetation, in soil, in architecture, to this moment. The Romans called their world "the circle of the lands," that is, about the Mediterranean. Southern Gaul is part of that circle. There is reason to believe that in the fifth century, with the ravages of barbarian inroads in the north of Gaul, both by land and sea (the Saxons), much of the country was falling waste and creating a partial vacuum which the Franks would in some degree refill, where German-descended customs would pre-

33 The statement in the text is cautiously worded, for the entire question of the real significance (apart from the purely abstract and theological) of Donatism and its relation to the Circumcellions, to presumed African "nationalism" and social revolt, is a perplexed problem on which there is no consensus among students at the present time.

34 Cf. App. *Praef.* 5.

vail in the Middle Ages, rather than Roman-descended institutions.

This was the fundamental situation of Gaul as it appeared to the rulers of a declining Empire based upon Italy, as Constantius tried to restore Roman order and rule there, and reduce the near-anarchy which had begun to prevail with the great invasion at the end of 406. The political ties which bound Gaul to Italy must be tightened as far as possible; the self-consciousness of the Gallic magnates as a group separate from the aristocracy of Italy must be counteracted. Constantius had begun efforts in that direction even before Gaul had been pacified. One of the principal preoccupations of the later Roman emperors was to check or control the rapacity or ambition of their own officials. The relatively elaborate system of secret police, of spies and counterspies, as well as many other devices, some of which have been mentioned in the opening chapter of this account, was directed to this end. Bishops of the Church admirably filled such a role. As early as the reign of the first Christian Emperor, Constantine, they had come to be recognized as supplementary judges.[35] Thus was begun a development which, by joining the powers conceded the bishop by the government to the natural respect for him which arose from his spiritual authority over his flock, would eventually culminate in an extensive secularization of the episcopate in many parts of Europe during many centuries of the Middle Ages, when kings and other potentates would make bishops their principal assistants in administering their realms. That day was still in the future, but events in the Roman Empire in the fourth and fifth centuries helped prepare the way for it. Under such circumstances even the more pious medieval rulers would frequently prefer administrative ability to sanctity or piety as a prerequisite for episcopal office. In 412 the Bishop of Arles, Heros by name, a man of great reputation for piety, was expelled from office by his own people. The influence of Constantius was successful in installing as his successor a certain Patroclus, a close associate of the general, and a man ambitious to extend his authority. When we are told that Patroclus practiced simony, the selling of church offices, we hear a complaint to be voiced by purists against secular bishops countless times in the

[35] Cf., e.g., *CTh* 1. 27. 1–2; in general, cf. R. Rémondon, *La crise de l'empire romain de Marc-Aurèle à Anastase*, p. 224.

following centuries.[36] Constantius was a pious, orthodox Christian according to most of the standards of his time, although he could be tempted to fall from grace if the reward were great enough, as the affair of Libanius shows.[37] That he should have appointed a man whose character cannot have been unknown to him to such a post must mean that he was acting from secular motives. Arles was the imperial subcapital of Gaul;[38] its bishop must naturally be a man of great importance and power. It is difficult to avoid the conclusion that Constantius wanted to be sure that this power were actively exercised in the interest of the Empire in Gaul, as a tie to bind the Gallic provinces to Rome. But Arles was only one church diocese; the interests of Rome would be even better served if the power of such a bishop were to be extended more widely still. Emperors had not been slow to grasp such ideas; in the third century the pagan Emperor Aurelian, invited to adjudicate a schism in the church of Antioch, is said to have pronounced that he recognized as Bishop of Antioch him who was in agreement with the Bishop of Rome. And the principal objective of Aurelian's reign had been to restore imperial unity after the divisiveness and separatism of the third century.

In March, 417, there acceded to the See of Peter in Rome a new Bishop, named Zosimus. Four days after his elevation he decreed that the Bishop of Arles, despite certain earlier, contrary decisions of the Church, was rightful metropolitan of the three provinces of Narbonensis Prima and Secunda as well as Viennensis (Arles had previously been metropolitan see only of part of Viennensis). Apparently at this juncture Patroclus himself was in Rome; whether he conceived the idea of his own aggrandizement, or whether it

[36] Prosp. 1247 (I, 466); *Chron. Gall. a. 452* 74 (I, 654). There is no evidence, but it has been suggested by many modern scholars that Heros may have been compromised by association with the usurper Constantine who had ruled at Arles during Heros' episcopate, even that it may have been Heros who at the end ordained Constantine a priest in the latter's desperate and futile attempt to avoid punishment for his treason; cf. L. Duchesne, *Fastes épiscopaux de l'ancienne Gaule,* I, 2d ed., 96–97.

[37] Constantius was probably the ultimate source of new antipagan measures, esp. against priests, cult-practices, and property of the pagan gods (*CTh* 16. 10. 20 [415]); he may also have been (if his wife was not) the source of legislation against the Jews, commanding their immediate dismissal from the military, and their future exclusion from the imperial civil service (*CTh* 16. 8. 24 [418]).

[38] A fragmentary inscription of the Arlésiens may commemorate the gratitude of the city to Constantius for favors; cf. J. Carcopino, "Choses et gens du pays d'Arles," *Rev. du Lyonnais,* 1922, no. 6, pp. 47–70, at 48–56.

was suggested by Constantius, it was probably Patroclus who invented a plausible myth to justify this new grandeur.[39] It was said that the first Gallic church had been founded at Arles by Saint Trophimus, sent out as a missionary from Rome. Obviously, therefore, the successor of Saint Trophimus at Arles should "historically" be the premier prelate of Gaul. This story had the advantage of affirming the primacy of Rome over Arles as it affirmed the primacy of Arles over Gaul. And, apart from the convenient legend, this grant to Arles of recognition of its rights came from the Bishop of Rome.[40] Thus ancient "precedent" and contemporary ecclesiastical ambition both served to emphasize the unity of the Church, and therefore of the Empire, under Rome. And many scholars, not without reason, have been unable to avoid the strong suspicion that the elevation of Zosimus did not occur without the exercise of some influence on Constantius' part, although Zosimus may also have been the preferred candidate of his predecessor, Innocent I.[41] If Zosimus was Constantius' choice, this time he had mistaken his man. Such papal intervention in the affairs of a distant see was going far beyond the custom of the time; the primacy of Arles thus decreed created a bone of contention in the Gallic church for decades. Zosimus' successor Boniface partly revoked the concession to Arles; the matter was not finally ended until the middle of the century when Pope St. Leo the Great managed to restore Arles approximately to its previous jurisdiction. But Zosimus possessed a peculiar talent for making wrong

[39] Suggested by E.-C. Babut, *Le concile de Turin*, p. 33, n. 1.

[40] J. Haller, *Das Papsttum: Idee und Wirklichkeit*, I, 2d ed., 107, seems to forget this aspect of the matter when he suggests that Innocent I may well have turned down Patroclus' suggestions, since such importance for Arles would limit the influence of Rome in Gaul. If Innocent did in fact turn down the project of Patroclus, it may have been that he was simply an honest man. J. Zeller, "Das Concilium der Septem provinciae in Arelate," *Westdeutsche Zeitschr. für Gesch. u. Kunst*, XXIV (1905), 1–19, at 7, suggests that when Honorius (Constantius?) in his decree concerning the Council of the Seven Provinces of 418 (see below, n. 45) refers to Arles as a *metropolis*, he is in effect recognizing its new ecclesiastical status; the suggestion is attractive, but it is doubtful that a political document would thus use ecclesiastical terms, and whether or not Arles were a secular *metropolis*, the magniloquent bombast of the legal language of the fifth century was capable of calling it so merely honorifically.

[41] The secondary literature is large; cf. e.g., F. X. Seppelt, *Der Aufstieg des Papsttums von den Anfängen bis zum Ausgang des sechsten Jahrhunderts*, 2d ed., p. 145; Babut, *Concile*, pp. 86–123; Sirago, *Placidia*, pp. 155, 219; L. Duchesne, *Hist.*, III, 161; P. Batiffol, *Le siège apostolique (359–451)*, 3d ed., pp. 214–15; Demougeot, *Rev. hist.*, CCXII (1954), 37; idem, *Unité*, p. 554.

decisions, and an arrogance in trying to enforce them that failed of its purpose and only diminished his prestige and that of the papacy. His attempt to interfere in the internal affairs of the African church met with a humiliating rebuff, and his recognition of the Pelagian heresy (denial of the doctrine of original sin) was too much for the imperial government itself, which condemned Pelagius;[42] and Zosimus was forced to reverse himself. But what is of particular interest is that Galla Placidia agreed with her husband about the usefulness of Patroclus, for when she assumed the effective government of the Western Empire in the name of her son in 425 she conferred upon Patroclus the important, and power-making, duty of searching out heretical bishops.[43] The legislation of her son, Valentinian III, would further assert the primacy of Rome in the Church, and she herself would uphold the influence of the Bishop of Rome even in the eastern church, because the latter was the successor of Peter and held the power of the keys, and also because that Bishop ruled the Church in the City which was the mistress of all lands.[44] And she would directly interfere in the disputed election of Zosimus' successor. Traditionally the Romans had considered religion a matter of government concern; Galla Placidia was the heir of this Roman tradition, which in its later development was to reach its height in the Eastern Empire in the fifth and following centuries. There the emperors would interfere even in matters of church dogma.

One of the devices of the Roman Empire for linking the provinces with the central government and for acting as a check on provincial administration was the use of councils in the provinces.

---

[42] Mansi, IV, 444 = *PL*, XLVIII, 379. Innocent I had condemned Pelagius, cf., e.g., Demougeot, *Rev. hist.*, CCXII (1954), 37. For some conjectures concerning the issuance of the imperial decree, see Sirago, *Placidia*, p. 224 and n. 2 (the identification of Palladius [a not uncommon name] as the *Praef. praet. Italiae* is uncertain; cf. Sundwall, *Studien*, no. 340 and nos. 339, 341, 342, pp. 113–14). African bishops exhorted the government against Zosimus' recognition of Pelagianism, and B. J. Kidd, *A History of the Church to A. D. 461*, III, 111, speculates they may also have worked on the piety of Galla Placidia. We have a letter from Constantius, wrongly called *Imperator*, to Volusianus, *Praef. urb.*, ordering or reiterating the edict of expulsion of the Pelagians from Rome, together with Volusianus' executory edict (*PL*, XLVIII, 404–9). A. Chastagnol, "Le sénateur Volusien et la conversion d'une famille de l'aristocratie romaine au bas-empire," *RÉA*, LVIII (1956), 241–53, at 241–45, would date these documents to the fall of 418 and postulate renewed Pelagian activity in Rome since the command of the Emperor (April, 418). In any case this is a fairly clear example of Constantius' activity as co-regent in fact (in traditional terms, using his *auctoritas*), before he actually became Augustus.

[43] *CSirm.* 6.

[44] *Ep. ap. epp. Leon. Magn.* 56 (*PL*, LIV, 859–62).

The provincial councils of the Early Empire, chosen locally in the provinces concerned, had served in pagan days as vehicles for the propagation of emperor-worship as well as a means of transmitting compliments or grievances of the provincials, or rather the upper classes of the provincials, to Rome. There is some disagreement among scholars today about the degree of effectiveness shown by this institution in providing a real check upon provincial maladministration; however that may be, the imperial government was convinced of the institution's usefulness as a link with the provinces. Thus the councils had survived the revisions of the Late Empire, although with changes in their makeup, and in the Late Empire diocesan councils, or councils for groups of the smaller provinces of that time, had come into being. About 403 the then Prefect of the Gauls had created a council for seven of the provinces of southern Gaul, to meet at Arles. The troublous times that followed had caused the council to lapse. In 418, however, there can be no doubt at the suggestion of Constantius, Honorius directed the then Prefect of the Gauls to reinstate this council.[45] While it seems probable that one of the purposes of Constantius was to assist the reunion of the sympathies of the southern Gallic magnates with Rome, it is quite likely that his attempt failed, and even had an opposite effect: the council may well have served in some degree at least to institutionalize the separate self-consciousness ("withdrawal," if one likes) of the Gallic magnates.[46] Undoubtedly it was also at the suggestion of Constantius that in 416 the Emperor addressed to him a constitution granting amnesty to all who to save their lives had been compelled to commit various crimes during the recent disturbances in Gaul and elsewhere. Litigation or prosecution against such persons was estopped by the Emperor's order, except that misappropriated property clearly proven to belong to the plaintiff in an action must be returned.[47] There can be little doubt that in an age of venal courts and legal oppression such an

[45] The Emperor's order is printed in *MGH: Epp.*, III, 13–15; by E. Carette, *Les assemblées provinciales de la Gaule romaine*, pp. 460–63; by G. Haenel, *Corpus legum ab imperatoribus romanis ante Justinianum latarum*, p. 238. On provincial councils in the Late Empire, esp. this one, see J. A. O. Larsen, *Representative Government in Greek and Roman History*, pp. 145–57; *idem*, "The Position of Provincial Assemblies in the Government and Society of the Late Roman Empire," *CP*, XXIX (1934), 209–20; Zeller, *Westdeutsche Zeitsch. für Gesch. u. Kunst*, XXIV (1905), esp. 8, 10; Carette, *ibid.*, 242–43, 248–49.

[46] Cf. Ruggini, *Athenaeum,* XL (1962), 384–85.

[47] *CTh* 15. 14. 14.

amnesty was an act of enlightened statesmanship. In that age, how-ever, it is a question how far such remedial legislation could be enforced against the magnates and the bureaucracy. Further to ease the plight of Gaul Constantius granted remission of taxes, always a welcome and popular measure among the beneficiaries.[48] The year 417 marked the reassessment of landed property for tax purposes, which was performed every fifteen years; the government seems to have taken special pains on this occasion to promote equity in the functioning of the process.[49]

Even before taking these administrative measures Constantius had naturally attended to the pacification of Gaul. The Bur-gundian allies of Jovinus, who had probably been granted territory along the Rhine to occupy as *foederati,* were confirmed in their settlement by Constantius in 413.[50] It is also likely that the Alemanni, likewise supporters of Jovinus, were somehow induced by Constantius to go back home across the Rhine.[51] About 415 or 416 Roman authority appears to have been restored in Armorica by Exuperantius, probably a lieutenant of Constantius;[52] this revolt had either been connected with or identical with a revolt of the peasants, Bacaudae.[53] Constantius may even have been able to re-

[48] Ap. Sid. *Carm.* 7. 207–14; the poet credits the future Emperor Avitus, then a young man, with persuading Constantius to take this step.

[49] Seeck, *Regesten,* p. 334 (laws of 14 May); cf. Stein, *Hist.,* I, 270.

[50] Prosp. 1250 (I, 467). The discussion of the precise whereabouts of the original Burgundian settlement has provoked a lengthy and inconclusive discussion. E.g., Stein, "Die Organisation der weströmischen Grenzverteidigung im V. Jahrhundert und das Burgunderreich am Rhein," *Römisch-Germanische Kommission,* XVIII Bericht (1928), 92–114, at 99; Schmidt, *Gesch.*2, I, 155; but cf. the wise restraint of F. L. Ganshof, "Notes critiques sur la patrie des Nibelungen," *Rev. belge de philolog. et d'hist.,* XIV (1935), 195–211, at 200–209. It must be admitted that the choice be-tween the *Nibelungenlied* and a doubtful passage in a Greek historian does not inspire much confidence either way. On *foederati,* cf. Dahn, *Könige,* XI, 13–14.

[51] Schmidt, *Gesch.*2, II: 2, 53.

[52] Rut. Nam. 1. 213–16; the date depends on the dating of this poem about which scholars disagree. 415 seems to be the date most recently suggested: I. Lana, *Rutilio Namaziano,* pp. 11–60. Whether this is the end of the revolt of the Armoricans going back about ten years, or whether it represents the end of a fresh revolt is also dis-puted; cf. Stevens, *Athenaeum,* n.s., XXXV (1957), 340; Jones, *Roman Empire,* I, 187; Stein, *Hist.,* I, 268.

[53] Sievers, *Studien,* pp. 449, 469, interprets *Anthol. Lat.* II: 2, 893 (= *CIL,* V, 7781), to show Constantius' activities on the Loire, but cf. Buecheler *ad loc.* Seeck, *RE,* IV (1901), 1101, suggests that Constantius may have visited Spain in 416, for Hyd. 62a (II, 19) notes that a chief of the Vandals was captured by a trick and sent to Honorius. But unfortunately Hyd. does not specify the author of the trick, and since this is a period of Visigothic activities against the Vandals in Spain, the guess that the Visigoths were responsible seems more possible.

store some measure of control over a part of Britain; if so, however, the reestablished connection soon fell into abeyance, for by 429, when we next have some relatively good evidence about the state of the island, there is not the slightest hint of the presence of any of the apparatus of the central government.[54] Constantius also brought the Visigoths back to Gaul. The motive for this act, although nowhere stated, seems clear enough in the light of the traditional conduct of Roman foreign policy. Since the Goths had annihilated the Siling Vandals and most of the Alans that had crossed to Spain, it was much to be feared that the Asding Vandals might suffer the same fate; the Sueves were a relatively weak tribe which might also, it could well be feared, succumb to a determined Gothic attack. Such successes[55] would render the Goths much too powerful for the peace of the Empire. Now more than ever, when the barbarians were established on the soil of the progressively enfeebled Western Empire, its continued safety must depend on its ability to prevent any one barbarian group from becoming too strong, so that by holding the balance of power the imperial government could play off one group against another.[56] What is less clear is why the Goths should have agreed to this arrangement; very possibly it was because they at last obtained from the Empire a settled, permanent home of their own where they were to be quartered (the legal device derived from previous Roman precedents for the billeting of soldiers on civilian proprieters) on relatively generous terms as "guests" (*hospites*), although it is not certain just what proportion of the properties of the Roman landholders was made over to the Goths at the beginning of this regime. Presumably similar arrangements had been made for the Burgundians in 413. The territory affected included the province of Aquitania Secunda, together with some adjacent parts of Novempopulana and Narbonensis Prima with its city of Toulouse, which became the principal seat of the Visigothic kings. This agreement may also have been in effect the resumption of the

---

54 Collingwood and Myres, *Roman Britain,* pp. 295–301; E. Demougeot, "Les invasions germaniques et la rupture des relations entre la Bretagne et la Gaule," *Le Moyen Âge,* LXVIII (1962), 1–50, at 34–36, 41; D. A. White, *Litus Saxonicum,* p. 54. Here too the literature of scholarly debate is enormous.

55 Cf. Hyd. 63 (II, 19); Oros. 7. 43. 15.

56 Perhaps Constantius also concluded a *foedus* with the Sueves at this time, as Stein, *Hist.,* I, 267, suggests on the basis of Hyd. 71, 74 (II, 20).

arrangement of 413 with Athaulf, if in fact that earlier agreement had given the Visigoths Aquitania Secunda.[57] This treaty was concluded with Wallia, who led his people back to Gaul at the end of 418; Wallia, however, died shortly thereafter and was succeeded by Theodoric I, who was to reign until his death in 451.[58] One may also note that the terms of this settlement, like the presumptive one of 413, also kept the Goths away from the sea. Possibly Galla Placidia saw in this achievement of her second husband the frui-

---

[57] See above, Ch. III, nn. 120, 133.

[58] Prosp. 1271 (I, 469); Hyd. 69–70 (II, 19); Stein, *Hist.*, I, 268. Cf. *inter al.* J. M. Wallace-Hadrill, "Gothia and Romania," *Bull. John Rylands Library*, XLIV (1961–62), 213–37, at 218–21; Lot, *Destinées*, pp. 48–49; Eicke, *Könige*, p. 33; A. Loyen, "Les débuts du royaume wisigoth de Toulouse," *RÉL*, XII (1934), 406–15, at 409–10; A Dopsch, *The Economic and Social Foundations of European Civilization*, p. 97. Several scholars have seen a motive of the Empire in the desire to keep down Saxon piracy: Wallace-Hadrill, *Bull. John Rylands Library*, XLIV (1961–62), 216–17 (detailed discussion); F. Lot, *La Gaule: Les fondements ethniques, sociaux et politiques de la nation française*, p. 473; É. Griffe, *La Gaule chrétienne à l'époque romaine*, II: 1, 19–20. There has been some discussion among scholars as to how long the treaty lasted; that is, how long the Goths remained *foederati* technically (in fact they regularly acted as an independent power almost from the beginning), and when they came to regard themselves as legally independent of the Empire. Schmidt, *Gesch.2*, I, 461–62, 464, held that de jure independence from the Gothic point of view came as early as 425. A. Loyen, "Traité de fédération imposé aux Wisigoths par l'empire," *RÉL*, XII (1934), 31 (cf. *ibid.*, 406–15), followed by E. Sestan, *Stato e nazione nell' alto medioevo*, p. 109 and n. 1, is surely right in holding that it was King Euric (466–84) who asserted his full legal sovereignty. This of course was from the Gothic viewpoint, not the Roman. Rome seldom formally abdicated her sovereignty over any land she had ever ruled, despite modern statements to the contrary, notably in the case of the Vandals in 442 (see below, Ch. VII, n. 53). E. A. Thompson, *JRS*, XLVI (1956), 70–71, suggests that the settlement of the Visigoths, and indeed of other barbarians, notably the Burgundians, in Gaul was to create barbarian landholders with vested property interests as a protection against social uprisings such as that of the Bacaudae. This is quite possible, although hardly a sole or principal motive of Constantius (see the reserves of Wallace-Hadrill, *Bull. John Rylands Library*, XLIV [1961–62], 214–16). Many scholars have evolved elaborate theories about pro-German Roman generals, notably Constantius and Aëtius, who presumably actively wished to promote the settlement of Germans in the Empire in armed groups. This view seems doubtful, at best; such a policy was a grudging *faute-de-mieux;* it seems much more likely that such generals would have been willing to eliminate or expel the Germans if they could have inflicted such a fate on all of them. Since they could not, unlike fanatical anti-Germans, they followed the policy of "balance of power" among the tribes as the best thing the enfeebled Empire could accomplish under the circumstances. This must have been the underlying motive of Constantius; it is *possible* he also saw the barbarians as a tool to use against social rebellion as well as against each other. Finally, a query: Is it possible to suggest that in the peace with the Goths in 416 Constantius may have held out the possibility or eventuality of a return to Aquitaine as a Gothic home when the Goths had earned the "gratitude" of Rome in Spain? Naturally, it would be the imperial government which would decide, as it did in 418, and for quite different motives, when that time of reward had arrived. Cf. Philostorg. *HE* 12. 4. *fin.*

tion, in part at least, of the hopes of her first.[59] The majority of the provincials concerned, however, presumably with the sympathy of their fellows elsewhere, are likely to have seen in the treaty the confirmation of their resentment at the policy of the government of Italy.[60] For the future, since to reestablish the Rhine frontier was beyond the strength of the Empire, Constantius thus followed the policy, or hopes, of Stilicho that barbarian *foederati* would provide the imperial defense that the imperial armies no longer could, and established military commands in the interior of Gaul, Spain, and perhaps Britain, to coordinate defense efforts that had once been concentrated along the frontiers.[61]

All in all the work of the Patrician in Gaul was a notable achievement in view of the relatively slender resources with which he had to make do. For the moment something approaching peace descended upon the Western Empire, despite the presence of the barbarians within the frontiers and the continuing difficulties from such trouble spots as the northeast Gallic frontier, where the Franks were restive and in these years attacked Trier.[62] But compared to southern Gaul, northern Gaul, if necessary, could be regarded as expendable, at least until the Golden Age, whose arrival imperial panegyrists were always celebrating, should in fact return. The pacification and reorganization which Constantius had achieved in Gaul was the sort of thing that the greater emperors of Rome had done in the past. By 418 or 419 the Patrician had in fact become co-regent of the Western Empire. The lucky accident of the survival of detailed evidence concerning the disputed election of Pope Zosimus' successor confirms this estimate of the position of Constantius; in very interesting fashion it also shows that his wife

59 Cf. Sirago, *Placidia,* p. 213.

60 Stroheker, *Adel,* pp. 47–48. It seems unlikely there was any conflict between the policy of settling the Goths in Aquitaine and the establishment of the council of south Gallic provinces, both in 418 (as Kaufmann, *Forsch. zur deutschen Gesch.,* VI [1866], 440 and n. 3, thinks). Rome (Constantius) undoubtedly expected that even those provinces occupied by the Goths would continue to be administered in civil matters by Roman officials (in fact, this ceased to be true almost at once; necessarily, for real power was in the hands of the Gothic kings, and Roman officialdom was almost at once reduced to a shadow). There was no theoretical reason, however, why occupied provinces should not participate in the assembly. Cf. Bury, *Hist.,* I, 208.

61 Stein, *Hist.,* I, 269, with nn.; *idem, Röm.-Germ. Komm.,* XVIII Bericht (1928), 96.

62 Greg. Tur. *HF* 2. 9; Salvian *Gub. Dei* 6. 39, 75, 82; different dates in Seeck, *Gesch.,* VI: 1, 52; and Stein, *Hist.,* I, 268.

had no reluctance about interfering herself in important questions of the government of the Church and the Empire.

Zosimus had proved unsatisfactory both as pope and as an instrument of state policy. In his own church at Rome there was an active opposition to him; in a letter written 3 October 418 he complains of opponents who bring accusations against him before the Emperor.[63] His brief recognition of Pelagianism before the government compelled him to retract must have been a shock to Constantius, for, entirely apart from religious considerations, Pelagianism's emphasis on individual consciences could easily lead to a liberty of action which the regimented Empire could only interpret as license.[64] Naturally, however, the unfavorable response of the government to a recognition of Pelagianism had no bearing on its desire to have a bishop of Rome obedient to its wishes, as Zosimus apparently had been in the matter of Patroclus. Fortunately for Zosimus himself and for the Church, the Pope died 26 December 418. That his death should have been followed by a bitterly disputed election is itself evidence of the division and rancor he had imported into the Church.[65]

At the moment of Zosimus' death the City Prefect, chief imperial functionary in Rome, was Aurelius Anicius Symmachus,[66] who had entered office only two days before. Symmachus immediately took steps to ensure the maintenance of public order, for the succession to the Roman See had frequently produced tumults in the past (as it also would in the future). The funeral of Zosimus took place at Saint Laurence-outside-the-Walls. During the obsequies partisans of the archdeacon Eulalius occupied the Lateran basilica, and the latter himself with many deacons and a few priests of the Roman church, accompanied by a crowd of the laity, proceeded thither. The clergy present elected him bishop, and the

63 *Ep.* 14 (*PL*, XX, 679); cf. Caspar, *Geschichte,* I, 360; Babut, *Concile,* p. 31, n. 1.

64 Cf. J. N. L. Myres, *JRS,* L (1960), 21–36, who probably, however, carries the idea too far; crticism by W. Liebeschuetz, "Did the Pelagian Movement Have Social Aims?" *Historia,* XII (1963), 227–41; in general, see also Sirago, *Placidia,* p. 224.

65 See additional note at end of chapter, page 167.

66 Sundwall, *Studien,* no. 456. p. 137; cf. Seeck's ed. of the orator Symmachus, *MGH: AA,* VI: 1, xl, liii. The prefect Symmachus is usually thought to have been a pagan who handled this Christian quarrel with dispassionate equity, but Chastagnol, *Préfecture,* p. 175, argues that he was quite possibly a Christian (how would Chastagnol interpret Symmachus' statement [32. 3] that he could not go to the Lateran Basilica, "ne quis mihi aemulus faceret religionis invidiam"?).

people signified its assent by acclamation. The new Pope and his party then remained at the church until Sunday, 29 December, for the formal consecration which customarily took place on a Sunday. But there were many who opposed this election and maintained that Eulalius had previously agreed that the election should take place in the church of Theodora. There on Saturday, the day after Eulalius had been elected, a majority of the priests of the church elected Boniface, previously a councillor of Innocent, Zosimus' predecessor. Symmachus warned both parties to keep the peace. When Boniface's adherents tried to negotiate with Eulalius in the Lateran, they were rebuffed. Both men, therefore, were consecrated on the Sunday, Eulalius in the Lateran Basilica, Boniface in Saint Marcellus in the Campus Martius. The same day Symmachus directed a report to the Emperor concerning these doings; in it he plainly indicated that Eulalius, elected first and in due order, was in the right. On 3 January 419 Honorius answered, recognizing Eulalius as rightful Bishop of Rome and pardoning the adherents of Boniface provided the latter left Rome. On 6 January Eulalius celebrated the Feast of the Epiphany at Saint Peter's, while Boniface and his friends had retired to Saint Paul's-outside-the Walls. Symmachus asked Boniface to abandon the procession he had planned and present himself at the offices of the urban prefecture. Boniface, however, refused to obey and handed the Prefect's messenger over to the people, who beat the poor man up. But when the procession marched on the City it was halted at the Ostian Gate, not without a scuffle. Boniface was seized by the Prefect's police and conveyed to a lodging outside the walls, where he remained under the surveillance of the Prefect's agents. Calm descended upon Rome for the time being.

But the partisans of Boniface did not intend the matter to rest there. A petition of Roman priests was dispatched to the Emperor at Ravenna; the election of Eulalius was accused of irregularities and the Prefect of having made a false report, while the argument was advanced that Boniface had been duly and properly elected and the Emperor was asked to hear the arguments of both sides in Ravenna. On 15 January, to the humiliation of Symmachus, the Emperor suspended his previous order and cited the two parties to judgment before him at Ravenna together with other Italian bishops who were to hear the case with him on 8 February. In response the Prefect urgently protested his impartiality and asked permission to be present at this hearing. Whether this request of Symmachus was granted or not is unknown; at any rate at the hearing the matter was merely deferred for the consideration of an Italian synod, which in turn advised the Emperor to submit the matter to a still larger synod; the Emperor agreed and summoned this second synod to meet at Spoleto on 13 June. Meanwhile both Boniface and Eulalius were commanded to stay out of Rome; since Easter was approaching the Bishop of Spoleto was asked to go to the City in order to celebrate the indispensable rites of the greatest of all Christian holy days.

Galla Placidia and Constantius favored the cause of Eulalius, who after all had been elected first, and in due form. (The exact detailed niceties of the procedure for electing popes have only gradually been evolved during the many centuries of the existence of the papacy, in answer usually to various specific emergencies and difficulties that have arisen from time to time; in the fifth century the procedure was still quite indefinite and both parties could thus with right claim proper election and consecration.) Eulalius could presumably be expected to assist in the maintenance of imperial cohesion through the influence of the Church, but, one might hope, with more tact and caution and hence more success than his predecessor, and above all without being seduced by doctrinal improprieties. Unlike her brother and possibly her husband, Placidia was unmoved by the arguments advanced by the priestly petition in favor of Boniface. The Emperor wrote to the bishops of Africa (and perhaps to others as well) commanding their attendance at the Synod of Spoleto. The advice of the African bishops had been invaluable in safeguarding the Church from the dangers of the Pelagian heresy; their judgment should also be weighty in adjudicating this vexed question according to the rules of the Church and good doctrine. But this did not suffice for Galla Placidia; although she admits that the letter of "the Lord August Emperor, my brother," should suffice, she also writes (20 March 419) to ask the bishops of Africa, including Saint Augustine and especially Aurelius, Bishop of Carthage and Metropolitan of Africa, to attend the synod at Spoleto in order, in effect, that vice should not triumph over virtue in the leadership of the church of Rome.

With a commonplace pious courtesy which hardly goes beyond conventional religiosity she also avers her great desire to receive the blessings of these bishops.[67] At the same time she also wrote a separate but similar letter to Saint Paulinus of Nola; she may well have become personally acquainted with him at the time when the Goths ravaged Nola in 410 during her captivity among them; it is also quite possible that she had been in correspondence with Saint Paulinus as well as some of the other bishops before this.[68] But what is particularly interesting is that these letters constitute first-hand evidence that Placidia was interested in politics, both secular and ecclesiastical. After nearly two thousand years of the history of the Church we see here two distinct categories, as did Christ ("render unto Caesar"), but it may well be doubted that most Roman Christians as yet ordinarily perceived much difference; certainly emperors who from time to time interfered in nearly every aspect of religious life did not honor the distinction in practice. But in the ancient pagan world secular and religious had been merely two aspects of human affairs which the state as the organization of society felt competent to manage. Obviously Placidia had an intense interest in politics; thus these letters lend confirmation to the idea of her political influence upon Athaulf and Constantius. The letters also attest by implication her consciousness of the importance of her position as the sister of the Emperor. She felt no

[67] Note that in neither the letter of Honorius (26) nor those of Placidia is there the slightest reference to any matter of doctrine, Pelagian or other; the sole matter discussed is the solution of the problem of the disputed election; yet 9 June 419 Honorius found it necessary or desirable to write to Aurelius and Augustine to tell them to caution the bishops against Pelagianism (*Ep. ap. Epp. Augustin.* 201). Especially in Placidia's letter, outspoken as it is in its condemnation of the man she disapproves, one would expect at least a general reference to a problem of true doctrine, if one were in fact involved, and especially if the bishops are being asked in effect to confirm their anti-Pelagian sentiments so recently expressed. The references to morality, or moral way of life, are hardly more than conventional when applied to a bishop, or the reverse when applied to his rival. There is nothing in any of these three letters to warrant belief in any thoroughgoing religious experience on the part of Placidia. She is sincerely convinced of the validity of Christianity, of course; she dutifully and sincerely goes through the forms which she has no difficulty in interpreting as congruent to her own wishes for the government of state and church, but of real religious "conversion" (not in the sense, of course, of from paganism to Christianity—there is no question of her Christian sincerity) to the inner experiences of the Christian faith there is no sign.

[68] Sirago, *Placidia*, p. 229. Indeed the reference to the "(martyr's) crown" (25. 2) in the letter to Paulinus may be a passing reference to his difficulties with the Goths.

qualms or hesitations about concerning herself actively, and not merely by influencing her male relatives, in affairs of state. Hence the letters also imply that she was politically ambitious and aggressive, and thus confirm the implications of many of her activities since she was a girl, as has been seen in the previous narrative. Here, too, of course she was following a Roman tradition of the interference of women in politics that goes back centuries to the old Republic. The typical character of this tradition is confirmed even by old-fashioned moralists who scoffed at and censured the impotence of female ambition.[69]

Easter Sunday in 419 fell on 30 March, but on 18 March Eulalius boldly reentered Rome (this of course was before Placidia wrote her letters two days later, but she was in ignorance of her candidate's disobedience of the Emperor's command when she wrote from Ravenna on the twentieth). Since, it seems, the powerful Constantius[70] was in favor of the claims of Eulalius, in an apologetic tone Symmachus wrote the Patrician (23 March), informing him what had happened and anxiously inquiring for instructions about how to deal with this flouting of the Emperor's order. Constantius replied sharply (26 March) that the Emperor's new commands of the same date must be obeyed without delay. This new imperial letter ordained that Eulalius must depart from Rome under pain of the severest penalties. Constantius, of course, could not acquiesce in open defiance of the government; it is quite possible that this act of Eulalius led him to reverse his previous favorable opinion of the latter. Symmachus himself was beginning to have second thoughts about the merits of a man who bade defiance to both Prefect and Emperor. Meanwhile riots were breaking out in the streets of Rome between the opposing factions; Symmachus himself on one occasion came near being manhandled. Eulalius refused to leave, despite the pressing urgency of the Prefect, and on Holy Saturday, 29 March, forcibly occupied the Lateran Basilica once more, obviously in order to be able to celebrate Easter there the next day. This act on the part of a man whose cause he had favored at such cost to his own pride and prestige was too much for the

69 In general, see the convenient collection of materials by J. P. V. D. Balsdon, *Roman Women: Their History and Habits, passim.*

70 By 420 his power was being recognized in effect on public monuments in terms usually reserved for emperors (cf. below, n. 77).

patience of Symmachus. Apart from anything else, the imperial order that Easter was to be celebrated by the Bishop of Spoleto was quite clear and must be obeyed. The police occupied the Lateran; Eulalius was arrested and conducted under guard to a house outside the walls, and on Easter Sunday Achilleus of Spoleto celebrated the feast at the altar of the Lateran church. Both Constantius and Honorius, as well, probably, as Placidia, in view of her respect for law, had had more than enough of Eulalius, and on 3 April the Emperor recognized Boniface (I) as rightful Pope. The prospective Council of Spoleto was canceled. Finally, in July of 419 or 420, Honorius wrote a sharp letter[71] to Boniface in which he congratulated him on his accession by God's will, but then flatly ordained that if in the future two rival candidates were elected to the Roman See, neither should retain the office, but a new election would be held to choose a third person. Although the affair had given Symmachus great anxiety, and the tone of some of the communications he had received from Ravenna had been coldly polite or even threatening, the Prefect came off quite well in the end, for he was continued in his high office until 420; obviously he had lost the confidence of neither Honorius nor Constantius.[72] For his part Symmachus erected an inscription in honor of Constantius, probably on the base of a statue.[73]

From these proceedings it is clear not only that in effect Constantius was co-regent of the Empire, but that Galla Placidia also evidently found it quite appropriate that she too should take an active part, at the highest level of the determination of policy, in the governance of the Empire. Indeed, her position had been consolidated by the birth of children to Constantius, particularly by the birth of a son whose imperial claims, in view of the childlessness of Honorius, could not be ignored. In the last months of 417 or in 418 she bore a daughter whom she named Justa Grata Honoria; the first two names were after her two maternal aunts, the third obviously in honor of the reigning Emperor, the child's half uncle. The name Justa also carried a reminder of Placidia's maternal grandmother, Justina, and Grata of her half uncle the

---

71 In response to Boniface's request (*Ep.* 7 [*PL*, XX, 765–67]) for guarantees against further disturbances in future papal elections.

72 Chastagnol, *Préfecture*, p. 175.

73 *ILS*, 801.

Emperior Gratian. Commonly the girl would be called simply
Honoria.[74] Then at Ravenna on 2 July 419, she bore a son whom
she named Flavius Placidus Valentinianus.[75] Flavius is probably
the commonest name of the Late Empire; its popularity dates from
Flavius Constantinus the Great. The child's father was Flavius
Constantius, but the fact is relatively insignificant since the name
was so common; the Emperor Theodosius II, for example, also bore
the name. Placidus, of course, was in honor of the boy's mother, and
probably also in honor of the unknown person from whom she had
herself received the name. But the name by which the boy was
commonly known, Valentinian, of course commemorated Placidia's maternal uncle and grandfather, both emperors. The name
Honoria was a wise choice for obvious reasons; the name Theodosius had been pre-empted by Placidia's firstborn. It may be significant that Placidia was emphasizing her imperial ancestry on
her mother's side in conferring several of these names; we know
that shortly after this time the Eastern branch of her family, to
which she was connected through her father, showed that it did not
favor the aspirations of her husband and presumably the hopes of
her children by that father as well. Possibly this coldness had
already begun to make itself felt by the time of the births of her
children. Then, too, there was the old quarrel between Placidia's
mother, Galla, and Arcadius, whose children constituted the Eastern branch. In a sense, therefore, by thus naming her children
Galla Placidia was advertising the fact that she had imperial claims
on both sides of her family (unlike her father's other descendants)
and that these claims were inherited by her children. This might not
have been the primary intention behind the giving of these names,
but the fact remains and it is hard to believe that it was mere coincidence. If there was any doubt about Placidia's ambitions for

74 Olympiod. Frag. 34 (IV, 65); the full name in *ILS*, 818. 1. Honoria was born
before Valentinian (2 July 419), hence her birth must fall in the interval indicated;
cf. Bury, *JRS*, IX (1919), 1.

75 Olympiod. Frags. 34, 46 (IV, 65, 68); Ren. Prof. Frig. *ap.* Greg. Tur. *HF* 2. 8;
Philostorg. *HE* 12. 12; Prosp. 1267 (I, 469); Hyd. 72, 162 (II, 20, 27); *Chron. Gall. a.
511* 569 (I, 657); Marcell. *s.a.* 419, 1 (II, 74); Agnell. 42; Theophanes, p. 83 (de B);
Joh. Ant. Frags. 197, 201. 5 (IV, 613, 615). The date could be 3 July. For the interpretation of the conflicting evidence concerning day and year, see Tillemont, *Empereurs*,
V, 643, 822, n. 45; C. Bugiani, *Storia di Ezio, Generale dell' impero sotto Valentiniano III*, p. 53, n. 1; Seeck, *Gesch.*, VI: 1, 64; 2, 399; W. Ensslin, *s.v.* "Valentinianus"
(4), *RE*, VIIA: 2 (1948), 2232–59, at 2232.

her children, especially her son, this was shortly removed. Sometime before February, 421, she bullied her brother into conferring upon his infant nephew the imperial title of *nobilissimus puer*, "most noble boy"; we have remarked in the case of Placidia herself that this title was conferred on imperial children who had not yet received a higher dignity. We are told that Placidia "forced" her brother to take this step; if this is to be taken with any degree of literalness (and there is a certain degree of hostility to Placidia in some of the sources), anyone acquainted with the methods of women will have little doubt of the nagging pressure Placidia brought to bear.[76] The Most Noble Valentinian was not recognized as heir to the throne by the conferral of this title, but his claims had been advanced a long step in that direction. Galla Placidia could not possibly be emperor in her own right, but she was determined that her son one day would rule.

Meanwhile, of course, Placidia herself still had no higher rank than her son now held; she was still only "most noble," as she had been for many years, ever since her father, presumably, had given her the title when she was not much older than Valentinian was now. But this, too, could be rectified. She could not be emperor, but she could be an Augusta, the highest rank a woman could hold in the Roman Empire, treated with almost the same social deference and almost the same forms of etiquette and protocol as the emperor himself. In 420 Flavius Constantius held the consulship for the third time, an honor in this age almost unheard of for a subject, even one so closely connected with the imperial family; his colleague in the East was the Emperor Theodosius II for the ninth time. And like Stilicho before him Constantius by this time was already being given credit for achievements in terms that ordinarily were reserved only for emperors.[77] And then, on 8 February 421, Honorius conferred the rank of Augustus on the Patrician Con-

---

[76] Olympiod. Frag. 34 (IV, 65); Philostorg. *HE* 12. 12; the order of events narrated by Olympiod. shows that this title was conferred before Constantius was raised to the throne (8 Feb. 421). If Delbrueck, *Kaiserporträts*, pp. 211–14, fig. 73, pl. III. 1, is correct in identifying the so-called Romulus Sardonyx in the Hermitage at Leningrad as depicting the investiture of Valentinian, the chronology is confirmed, for the figure identified as Constantius on that gem does not yet wear the imperial diadem; cf. Ensslin, *RE*, XX: 2 (1950), 1917; *ibid.*, VIIA: 2 (1948), 2232–33; Sirago, *Placidia*, p. 203 and n. 1.

[77] Straub, *Nouvelle Clio*, IV (1952), 106–7, commenting on *ILS*, 801.

stantius, thus associating him with himself on the throne. Again we are told that Honorius took this step "almost unwillingly"; once again we may imagine the pressure of Placidia and probably of Constantius, but in this matter much more serious issues of course were involved. Honorius was doubtless jealous of his preeminent minister, but he also had the wit to perceive that he could not reign without Constantius; he may even have been brought to see, grudgingly, that simple justice demanded that he recognize his great servant as his colleague in law as the latter already was in fact. And we can have little doubt that this had long been Constantius' secret aspiration, at least since he had first conceived the plan of marrying Placidia. Sometime thereafter her husband and brother jointly conferred on Galla Placidia what we may be sure was the much coveted title of Augusta; we may perhaps further conjecture, since she was human, in the light of her conduct in 419 in the Boniface-Eulalius schism, that she considered the promotion to be her simple due.[78]

As a matter of fact Constantius had reason to regret the imperial elevation which he had long planned to obtain. As Emperor he was surrounded on all sides and at all times by the suffocating court ceremonial of the Late Empire. Protocol prescribed the comings and goings of an emperor by elaborate ritual; the amusements and parties of earlier years with his boon companions were now become almost impossible; an audience with the Sacred Presence of an emperor was not called a Silence for nothing. Presumably his friends now fell on their knees in his presence and spoke only when the Divine Mouth addressed them directly. Quite likely the heavily embroidered and bejeweled robes of an emperor made it actually physically difficult to stride about. To the Empire one almost had

---

[78] Olympiod. Frag. 34 (IV, 65); Prosp. 1273 (I, 469); Hyd. 75 (II, 20); *Chron. Gall. a. 452* 88 (I, 656); Philostorg. *HE* 12. 12; Soz. *HE* 9. 16. 2; Theophanes, p. 84 (de B). There are coins as well as inscriptions attesting the reign of Constantius; cf. Voetter, *Münzen,* no. 2776 (with pl. 15); A. Voirol, "Münzdokumente der Galla Placidia und ihres Sohnes Valentinian und Versuch einer Chronologie der Münzprägung unter Theodosius II. (408–450)," *Verhandlungen der Naturforschenden Gesellschaft in Basel,* LVI: 2 (1945), 431–45, at 440, n. 1, is surely wrong in interpreting the coin in Cohen, VIII, 196, 13, to mean that Placidia became Augusta in 420, i.e., before her husband reached the purple. On the date of Constantius' elevation and death, see Tillemont, *Empereurs,* V, 822–23, n. 46; Courtois, *Byzantion,* XXI (1951), 28–29. It is difficult in the light of Olympiod. to see why Seeck, *Gesch.,* VI: 1, 65, believes that Honorius was so overjoyed at the birth of Valentinian that he made his brother-in-law consul in 420 and Emperor in 421. See pl. VIA.

to be born; the conduct proper to an emperor had been exhibited, for example, by Constantius II when he visited Rome in 357: at his entry into the City, although a short man, he bowed his head when he went under an arch in order to permit his greatness to pass; otherwise he looked straight ahead, turning neither to left nor right; when the wheel of his chariot jolted, he remained completely impassive, not permitting the slightest reaction to appear upon his countenance; he was never observed to spit, or wipe his face, or rub his nose, or move his head. This was affectation, our informant remarks, but it also required great patience.[79] But then, Constantius II had been born to the position he held; Constantius III had not been.[80]

Yet these were merely petty, personal annoyances, however wearing they might be. Much more important was the fact that the Eastern government refused to recognize his accession. His elevation had been communicated in due form to Theodosius II (and the latter's sister Pulcheria, who played a large part in the determination of policy at this time). As was also the custom, portraits of the new Western Augustus were also sent to the East, where they, or duplicates, were to be set up in places of vantage throughout the Eastern Empire. For, although in fact one emperor ruled in the East and another in the West, the theory or fiction was still kept up that the Empire was a unity ruled by an imperial college; all laws and edicts of one emperor were also issued in the name of the other or others, and all official reports to any emperor were in wording addressed to all of them. Yet the East refused to recognize Constantius or accept his portraits.[81] Official documents of the West, however, formally recognized three reigning Augusti.[82] The reasons for this hostility are not far to seek. As the policy of Theodosius II a few years later would demonstrate quite clearly, the Emperor of the East, perhaps thinking of emulating his grandfather and namesake the great Theodosius, had ambitions, quite unrealistic, to rule the whole Roman Empire; Constantius and Placidia were not the

[79] Am. Marc. 16. 10. 9–11.

[80] Olympiod. Frag. 34 (IV, 65).

[81] *Ibid.;* Philostorg. *HE* 12. 12. On the imperial portraits see H. Kruse, *Studien zur offiziellen Geltung des Kaiserbildes im römischen Reiche,* Stud. zur Gesch. u. Kult. des Alt., vol. XIX: 3, p. 28.

[82] E.g., *ILS,* 809.

only ones to make political plans based on the childlessness of Honorius. Obviously the Eastern plans would come to nought if Honorius were to have an associate who did himself in fact have an heir. It further seems likely that the Eastern government also did not recognize the new titles either of Valentinian or of Galla Placidia.[83] Since the fourth century the jurisdiction of the Pope over the church of Illyricum, a jurisdiction operated through the Bishop of Thessalonica as vicar, had been generally acknowledged. In 419 Pope Boniface translated the Bishop of Patras to the See of Corinth. The Patriarch of Constantinople, attempting to assert his control over Illyricum, objected to this papal action and was upheld by Theodosius. In 420 Honorius wrote on the Pope's behalf to his nephew of Constantinople. Nevertheless, by a law of 14 July 421, Theodosius affirmed the rights of the Patriarch of Constantinople in Illyricum, undoubtedly influenced by the hostility he felt toward the Western Court. Finally, however, after Constantius' death he yielded and recognized the rights of the Pope.[84] This refractory attitude of the Eastern government angered Constantius profoundly; its policy, unless changed, could cause grave difficulties in the future, especially if either he or Honorius should die in the next few years. We are told that Constantius had some presentiment of his own death through a dream that prophesied that he would reign less than seven months. If he did in fact experience such a dream, it might well mean that he had been worried about the state of his health. Our two Eastern sources for these matters tell us that he was even making warlike preparations against the Eastern government at the time of his death in this same year 421, on 2 September, of pleurisy.[85] Thus once again Galla Placidia was left

[83] This view is *communis opinio* among scholars; Seeck, *Regesten*, p. 26; *idem*, *Gesch.*, VI: 2, 399, followed by Palanque, *RÉA*, XLVI (1944), 290, thinks that the Eastern government did not recognize the third consulship of Constantius, still nominally a subject, in 420, and did not proclaim it in its dominions. This is merely a surmise of Seeck (cf. *Regesten*) and is contradicted by Degrassi, *Fasti*, p. 88, who holds that Constantius' consulship was in fact published in the East, although late in the year; unfortunately he does not cite evidence.

[84] Boniface *Epp.* 5, 13, 14, 15 (*PL*, XX, 761, 774–79); Haenel, p. 240 (= *PL*, XX, 769–70); *CTh* 16. 2. 45 = *CJ* 11. 21); Haenel p. 240 (= *PL*, XX, 770–71); Batiffol, p. 256; Bardy, *Histoire de l'Église,* ed. Fliche and Martin, IV, 256, n. 3; T. Jalland, *The Life and Times of St. Leo the Great,* p. 10; L. Duchesne, *The Churches Separated from Rome,* pp. 166–67, 179.

[85] Olympiod. Frag. 34 (IV, 65); Philostorg. *HE* 12. 12; cf. Theophanes, p. 84 (de B); Prosp. 1276 (I, 469); Hyd. 76 (II, 20); Soz. *HE* 9. 16. 2; Seeck, *Gesch.*, VI: 2, 399–400.

a widow, this time with two small children. It is quite likely that she had mourned Athaulf. There seems no reason to believe that she mourned Constantius, whom she had threatened with divorce also in this same year in order to have her way with him. Nevertheless, she would soon have to regret the death of her second husband too.

### ADDITIONAL NOTE ON THE BONIFACE-EULALIAN SCHISM

It was by no means a division on ideology or principle such as one of pro-Pelagianism vs. anti-Pelagianism. Zosimus had been tactless, arrogant, and stupid; the fact seems sufficient in itself to explain the bitter animosity surrounding him. It is an error, because contrary to the observed facts of human nature, to assume tacitly that all quarrels among men of importance are owing to differences of principle. The only source of any significance for the schism between Boniface and Eulalius is *Coll. Avell.* 14–37 (such a statement as *Lib. pont.* 44. 2 contributes nothing). For recent narratives see Bardy, *Hist. de l'Église,* ed. Fliche and Martin, IV, 252–53; Chastagnol, *Préfecture,* pp. 172–77; Sirago, *Placidia,* pp. 225–30. In *Coll. Avell. Epp.* 25, 27, 28, are attributed to Honorius. Long ago W. Meyer, ". . . epistulae imperatorum ex collectione . . . Avellana . . . editae," [*Göttingen Universität:*] *Index Scholarum,* Winter, 1888–89, pp. 3–41, at 10, showed that the reference to "domni germani mei Augusti principis" (27. 2, 28. 3) fits the mode of address or reference used in these letters neither by Constantius nor Honorius (referring to the other), but only a reference of Galla Placidia to Honorius. The argument is valid despite Seeck's view, *Regesten,* p. 340, that the author was Constantius. But the sentiments and wording of 25 are so similar to those of 27 and 28 that it too must also have been written by Galla Placidia (cf. Ensslin, *RE,* XX: 2 [1950], 1918; Sirago, *Placidia,* p. 229, n. 1; Caspar, *Geschichte,* I, 363, n. 4). It is quite obvious to the reader of these three letters that their writer is taking vehement sides against one candidate and for the other. It is commonly held that the candidate favored by Placidia was Boniface (so Sirago, *Placidia,* pp. 228–29; apparently Chastagnol, *Préfecture,* p. 175; Ensslin, *RE* XX: 2 [1950], 1918). Certainty is impossible, but a fairly good case can be made out that she favored Eulalius and opposed Boniface: (*a*) According to the original view of the Urban Prefect Symmachus and of Honorius (and presumably of the latter's government in general) Eulalius is the Pope in office (15. 3, 16. 7); later Honorius withdrew his recognition of Eulalius, but did not extend it to Boniface (18. 2–3); this was still the official attitude of the government when Placidia wrote these letters; yet she regards the man she favors as Pope, attacked by someone who is not (the election of Eulalius occurred the day before that of Boniface); it is unlikely that she would thus openly reverse the judgment of her brother the Emperor by referring to Boniface as Pope. One must use some circumspection in managing even a sovereign like Honorius. (*b*) We have seen that she favored Patroclus, as did Constantius; yet Boniface was opposed to the pretensions of Patroclus, which he partly quashed, but only after Constantius was dead (Bonif. *Ep.* 12, *PL,* XX, 772 [9 Feb. 422]) and at a time when Placidia was engaged in an almost life and death struggle (which she lost) against elements opposed to her at court. (*c*) Many of the ideas expressed in Placidia's letters echo those in the letters of Symmachus and of Honorius when the latter was in favor of Eulalius, e.g.: Placidia 25. 1 *per vim* (said of disapproved candidate's election); cf. 15. 2 (Honorius writing of Boniface's struggle against Eulalius) *vim perpessi.* Placidia 25. 1, 27. 1 *certamen* against the incumbent; cf. 16. 2 (Symmachus of Boniface) *certaminis.* Placidia of disapproved candidate, 25. 1 *contra haec apostolicae institutionis bona,* and 27. 1 *quae respuit divinae religionis sacrosancta praeceptio;* cf. 14. 7 (Symmachus of Boniface) *contra reverentiam venerandae legis* and 15. 1 (Honorius of Eulalius) *regula catholicae . . . disciplinae.*

Note that the documents indicate no use of force on the part of Eulalius before the time Placidia wrote these letters (or before she had time to learn of it), although Boniface had used force, or his partisans had, before the time of writing. (*d*) When Eulalius finally entered the City contrary to the Emperor's orders, Symmachus wrote in an apologetic tone to Constantius excusing himself (29) and the latter replied (30) that the will of the Emperor (31) is to be obeyed concerning the withdrawal of Eulalius. This looks as though, even if it does not necessarily follow, since Symmachus knew of Constantius' vast real power, there might be some possibility of temporizing in obeying the imperial command that Eulalius depart forthwith. In turn, this would imply that Symmachus thought Constantius (and by implication Placidia) was friendly to the cause of Eulalius. (*e*) Why did Eulalius thus flagrantly disobey the Emperor's command? Because he thought Constantius (and Placidia) was on his side? (Possible, but not cogent, for this act could have been the result of his desperation; knowing or thinking that his cause was likely to be lost, he hoped to present the government with a fait accompli.) (*f*) It is argued that Eulalius was in favor of Pelagianism (presumably opposed by Placidia as well as Constantius), but there is no evidence of this fact (it is merely a conjecture from the fact that Boniface was anti-Pelagian; cf. Sirago, *Placidia*, p. 227). Zosimus had reversed his recognition of Pelagianism; hence the argument that Placidia (with Constantius) was opposed to the assumedly pro-Pelagian Eulalius fails by lack of any evidence. Accordingly, in the text the narrative is here presented as though Constantius and Placidia were in favor of Eulalius, until he put himself beyond the pale by disobeying the Emperor's direct order. No Roman administration could countenance such disobedience on the part of a subject. To pardon such, in Roman eyes, would lead directly to the breakdown of all civilized order. Compare what is said in the previous and subsequent chapters about Placidia's attitude toward the law.

# 5

# THE EMPEROR OF
# THE EAST

The death of Constantius put Galla Placidia in a much less favorable position, however much she had previously ventured to talk of divorcing him. In her attempts, not unsuccessful, as we have seen, to manipulate or use pressure on the Emperor to make him do what she desired, she had had behind her the power of her husband, who was obviously devoted to her, and whose support had been the principal prop of Honorius' government for a decade. Now she must depend almost solely on her own wits to maintain her position of influence and secure the succession of her son. She was to discover that her wits were not enough, without the effective power base that her husband had created, to remain victorious amid the intrigues which preoccupied the court of Ravenna. Her main resource must be whatever affection the Emperor bore her; and the affection of the Emperor was a poor thing at best, as the fate of Stilicho and his family had shown, and as Honorius' complaisance toward her own captivity among the Goths, except when he was under the influence of Constantius, had demonstrated even more conclusively in her own case. Furthermore, the Emperor could not have failed to be aware of the disapproval which his Eastern relatives had evinced toward Constantius, and by implication Galla Placidia and her children. Still, even the sluggish Honorius was a human being; we may strongly suspect that, not without reason, he was without a friend at his own court. Further, it seems likely, although quite beyond proof or disproof, that so energetic and ambitious a person as Galla Placidia must have

169

felt a considerable, although doubtless well disguised, contempt for her imperial half brother.

Placidia, however, did have some allies. Not least of these was what more or less amounted to a small private army, the Goths who had accompanied her home in 416, as well as the *bucellarii* of Constantius. Of great future importance at least as an ally was the soldier Boniface, who had wounded Athaulf years before at Marseilles; we will perhaps not be far wrong if we conjecture that he had been an adherent of Constantius, and perhaps had been well spoken of by an Athaulf who could appreciate the mettle of a valiant foe.[1] Placidia also put great confidence in certain members of her own entourage on whom she evidently felt she could rely implicitly; besides her old nurse Elpidia and Leontius, the administrator of her business and legal affairs *(curator)*, a certain Spadousa is mentioned. If Spadousa is indeed identical with Padusia, the wife of the general Felix who later became Master of the Soldiery, we may perhaps number the general among her supporters at this time.[2] Her principal enemy was another general, named Castinus, who may have been a native of the province of Scythia[3] (at the mouth of the Danube). At some time in the years immediately before this he had been sent by Constantius against the Franks with the rank of Count of the Domestics; we do not know how well he succeeded.[4] The events of the next few years would reveal that it was his ambition to play the part of a Stilicho or a Constantius; that is, that he wished to be the power behind the throne.[5] Such an ambition, however, must necessarily bring him into conflict with Galla Placidia, who intended to act that part herself, at least as long as her son was a child. Besides, if Castinus attained such a position, he might wish,

---

1 Olympiod. Frag. 40 (IV, 66). J. L. M. de Lepper, *De Rebus Gestis Bonifatii Comitis Africae et Magistri Militum*, p. 30, argues on rather thin grounds that Boniface at this time might have been a commander of the imperial guards known as *scholares*.

2 Olympiod. Frag. 40 (IV, 66); cf. *ILS* 1293; Prosp. 1303 (I, 473); on the identity of Spadousa and Padusia, see Hansen, *De vita Aetii* (Diss.; Dorpat, 1840), p. 26, n. 46 (I have been unable to see this book; cf. Sirago, *Placidia*, p. 236); Ensslin, *RE*, XX: 2 (1950), 1919–20; Güldenpenning, *Arcad. und Theod.*, pp. 254–55 with 254, n. 4a. Lepper, *De Rebus Gestis*, p. 53, n. 1, however, regards the identification as quite arbitrary.

3 Lepper, *De Rebus Gestis*, p. 31, n. 3, suggests that the reference to "the Scythian" in Ps.-Bon. *Ep.* 10 (*PL*, XXXIII, 1097) is to the Goth Sigisvult who clashed with Boniface later; in the context this seems unlikely.

4 Ren. Prof. Frig. *ap.* Greg. Tur. *HF* 2. 9.

5 Cf. Hodgkin, *Invaders*, I: 2, 893.

like Constantius, to become emperor himself; that would probably be fatal to the claims of Valentinian. We are surely right in inferring that there were probably other adherents of Placidia, and almost certainly supporters of Castinus, as well as yet others who had ambitions like his, or who merely wished to procure whatever advancement they could from the intrigues connected with this power struggle.

Apparently an opening move by Placidia's enemies was the bringing forward of allegations that Constantius had seized the possessions of various persons unjustly; petitions asking for justice on this account came into Ravenna from all sides. But Placidia was able to persuade her brother that the complaints were misconceived, and the attack failed.[6] Seeking further to bind the Emperor to herself, Placidia showered all sorts of tender affection upon him; at first Honorius gladly returned these signs of affection. Apparently the fact that brother and sister frequently kissed each other on the mouth gave rise to scandal at court, that these caresses were the sign of something shameful.[7] Obviously such "evidence" will support a charge of incest only in the minds of the prurient; in the publicity which necessarily attends the sexual crimes of princes, had there been more than this kissing, the fact would surely have been known. It is possible, however, that a modern psychologist might find a secret spring of Honorius' behavior: if he was in fact impotent, he might find it particularly relaxing to caress his sister, precisely because such affection, according to all law and religion, must be without ulterior motive or sexual demands upon him. His sister

---

[6] Olympiod. Frag. 39 (IV, 66); Olympiod. or his source for these matters is prejudiced against Placidia; according to the historian the petitioners were in the right. However that may be, unless Constantius were an oppressive tyrant, for which there is no other evidence, the multitude of the petitions almost certainly represents an attack on Placidia.

[7] Olympiod. Frag. 40 (IV, 66); cf. Balsdon, *Roman Women*, p. 130. Note again the hostility of Olympiod. to Placidia. This is the sole imputation against the chastity of the princess during her entire life. One may note in passing that in his foreword to C. D. Gordon, *The Age of Attila*, p. x, A. E. R. Boak refers to the "much-married Galla Placidia." The precise meaning of this allegation is uncertain, for she was married only twice, and there is no evidence to indicate that she was excessively devoted to either husband. After Constantius' death, when she was about thirty-three, she lived for the remaining twenty-nine years of her life as a widow without the slightest taint of suspicion save this present report. The psychological possibility put forward in the text to account for Honorius' behavior was approved as a possibility, by my former colleague, Ilza Veith, M. D., a historian of medicine and psychology, in a conversation several years ago.

might well be regarded as a "safe" object of affection by an impotent man. Nevertheless, although the affection of the Emperor might ward off overt attack, as in the matter of the financial complaints, it was quite another thing, without Constantius to back her up, to use that affection for the ends of positive policy. Thus the effective partial revocation of the preeminent position of Bishop Patroclus in Gaul by Pope Boniface in 422[8] probably also marks a defeat for Placidia. The allegation of impropriety on the part of Placidia and Honorius in our source very probably represents insinuations made at the time to Honorius, if not to Placidia. The enemies of the Augusta would obviously use any possible instrument to drive a wedge between brother and sister.

The news of the death of Constantius seems to have had an unsettling effect on the barbarian tribes dwelling in or adjacent to the Empire. The Vandals in particular seem to have attacked possessions of the Empire in Spain; in fact there had been hostilities between the forces of the Empire and the Vandals in 419.[9] In any event a major expedition was sent against the latter in 422,[10] under the command of Castinus, now raised to the rank of Master of the Soldiery. If we assume that by 422 Placidia had come to realize that Castinus was her enemy, then this appointment, too, represented a defeat for her. Boniface, Placidia's ally, was assigned to this expedition in a subordinate command; the Goths sent auxiliary forces to support the Roman army, presumably in accordance with the treaty of 418. Castinus, however, if our source can be believed, by his haughty and inept exercise of command came to quarrel bitterly with Boniface. We may assume that the quarrels of the court were thus transplanted to the camp.[11] At any rate, Boniface came to believe that it would be unworthy, or even dangerous, to continue

---

8 Bonif. *Ep.* 12 (*PL*, XX, 772–74).

9 Hyd. 74 (II, 20); the connection with Constantius' death is made by Seeck, *Gesch.*, VI: 1, 65, who also connects the restiveness of the Franks, requiring the expedition of Castinus against them, to the same cause.

10 Prosper puts the expedition in this year; Hydatius in 421, but as Lepper, *De Rebus Gestis*, p. 29, points out, the chronicle of Hyd. is running about a year behind at this point; cf. Courtois, *Vandales*, p. 55 and n. 4. Sirago, *Placidia*, p. 234, opts for 421. It seems easier, however, to understand the history of the expedition as falling after Constantius' death rather than before. Since the Vandals had clashed with Roman forces in 419, it is possible that the expedition had been in preparation before 422.

11 Cf. Ps. Bon. *Ep.* 10 (*PL*, XXXIII, 1097); Ps. Augustin. *Ep.* 11 (*ibid.*, 1097–98); on the details offered by this doubtful source, see Lepper, *De Rebus Gestis*, pp. 31–34.

on the expedition with Castinus; it is not clear whether he thought the danger would proceed from the ineptitude or the malignancy of the general. Hence, without permission, he abruptly left the expedition even before Castinus set out from Italy, and hastened first to Portus (at the Tiber mouth) and then, abandoning his appointment at court, to Africa, where he had been serving some years before; here he began, originally without legal right, to build up a power base for himself and perhaps for Placidia.[12] In Baetica (Southern Spain) Castinus at first experienced considerable success against the Vandals, whom he seems to have managed to put under a blockade; the barbarians were so hard pressed by the shortages caused by this blockade that there was reasonable hope that they would surrender. Unfortunately the general was soon at bitter odds with the Gothic auxiliaries in his army; they betrayed him in some unspecified fashion; he was defeated and fled to Tarraco (Tarragona).[13] This failure of Castinus must have weakened his position at court for the time being. At any rate Galla Placidia scored in the game by regularizing Boniface's position in Africa; he was promoted Count of Africa, that is, supreme military commander and the most powerful Roman official in the diocese. Given the importance of Africa to the Western Empire, this constituted a considerable victory for Placidia.[14] In this same year the former Spanish usurper Maximus, who had fled for refuge to the barbarians after the downfall of his master Gerontius a decade before, fell into the

[12] Cf. Freeman, *Western Europe,* pp. 315–16.

[13] Prosp. 1278 (I, 469); Hyd. 77, 78 (II, 20); Salvian *Gub. Dei* 7. 45–46; perhaps *Chron. Gall. a. 452* 107 (I, 658; *s.a.* 431) (if L. Schmidt, *Geschichte der Wandalen,* 2d ed., p. 26, n. 5, is right in transferring the entry to this event). Boniface *tribunus* in Africa in 417: August. *Ep.* 220. 7, with Lepper, *De Rebus Gestis,* p. 28. In general on Boniface, see Sundwall, *Studien,* no. 70, pp. 57–58. P. Romanelli, *Storia delle province romane dell' Africa,* p. 637, n. 2, thinks that Boniface was already in Spain when he broke with Castinus and fled to Africa; thus Romanelli cannot understand why Boniface went via Portus. The difficulty is removed by the interpretation in the text; cf. O. Seeck, *s.v.* "Bonifatius" (1), *RE,* III (1899), 698–99, at 698.

[14] In 423 Boniface held the position, Olympiod. Frag. 40 (IV, 66); in 423 Placidia's fortunes had declined so radically that it is impossible to conceive such an appointment for her adherent then; 422, after the news of Castinus' defeat had arrived at Ravenna, seems almost certainly right. Boniface's second marriage, with an ex-Arian heretic, must also fall somewhere about this time; Lepper, *De Rebus Gestis,* pp. 34–36; H.-J. Diesner, "Die Laufbahn des Comes Africae Bonifatius und seine Beziehungen zu Augustin," in *Kirche und Staat im spätrömischen Reich,* pp. 100–126, at 105–6, 107; *idem,* "Die Lage der nordafrikanischen Bevölkerung im Zeitpunkt der Vandaleninvasion," *ibid.,* 27–39 (= *Historia,* XI [1962], 97–111), at 136 and n. 57; Courtois, *Vandales,* p. 156, n. 3.

hands of the government, perhaps in connection with Castinus' otherwise abortive expedition. At any rate Honorius was able to exhibit his captive at the celebration of his *tricennalia,* or thirtieth year of rule; thereafter Maximus was put to death.[15]

But if Placidia could use the defeat of Castinus to counteract his influence and that of his faction, the circumstance that she not only had old ties with the Visigoths but had a large number of them, and probably other Germans as well, about her at Ravenna was an argument that could be worked against her by blaming the defeat of Castinus on the teachery of his Gothic auxiliaries. That Castinus and his adherents won this battle of charge and countercharge is made clear by the fact that he retained his position.[16] The vicissitudes of the power struggle are clearly evidenced by the rapid succession of different persons in the principal offices of state in 422–23.[17] Violence and riots between the partisans of Placidia and those of her foe broke out in the streets of Ravenna; the opponents of the Augusta were successful in persuading the Emperor, already disturbed by the disaster in Spain, which was blamed on the Visigoths, that Placidia was in league with the Goths.[18] Honorius had shown himself ill-disposed to the barbarians at the time of Stilicho's downfall and during the years immediately following; and his sister, without his permission, had married the King of the Goths; in the streets of Ravenna Goths were fighting with Romans. It has probably been too easy for modern historians[19] to see in this

---

15 *Chron. Gall. a. 452* 89 (I, 656); Marcell. *s.a.* 422, 2 (II, 75).

16 Castinus' retention of his rank and power is directly attested if O. Seeck's emendation (*s.v.* "Castinus" (2), *RE,* III [1899], 1761–62, at 1762; cf. Sundwall, *Studien,* no. 87, p. 61) of *Crispino* to *Castino* in the address of *CTh* 2. 23. 1 (25 Feb. 423) be right.

17 See the lists of Praetorian Prefects in Sundwall, *Studien,* p. 22, and of Counts of the Private Estate, p. 28; with evidence from the addressees of laws in Seeck, *Regesten,* pp. 346, 348; cf. Palanque, *Préfecture,* p. 99; Lepper, *De Rebus Gestis,* p. 32; Sirago, *Placidia,* p. 239; Stein, *Hist.,* I, 275.

18 Olympiod. Frag. 40 (IV, 66). The nexus of the argument specified in the text is nowhere attested, but something very much like this must have happened; it is inconceivable that the arguments insinuated to the Emperor did not revolve in large part about the Goths. Olympiod. says that Spadousa, Elpidia, and Leontius directly incited Placidia against the Emperor. They may have done so by various belittling and derogatory remarks, which would have been repeated to Honorius; but almost certainly the struggle for power was between Placidia and her foes for the control of the Emperor's mind and government. It was to the interest of her enemies to embroil her with her brother; it was to her interest, and that of her followers, to retain his approval, for this was the only real power they had.

19 E.g., Solari, *Rinnovamento,* I, 285, 293; Sirago, *Placidia,* p. 236.

struggle (and in others) the clash of "pro-German" versus Roman or "traditionalist" party. Yet it is difficult to see how Placidia, former Queen of the Goths, with her German *bucellarii* could be regarded as anti-German.[20] Certainly she could hardly be described as antidynastic; her whole aim was to procure the succession of her son Valentinian, and this end she could achieve only on dynastic grounds. It is probably a mistake to interpret Roman politics (like modern) as proceeding to any great extent according to issues of ideology or principle.[21] Many Romans were certainly opposed to the Germans and their influence, but in politics ordinarily such attitudes were used rather than followed. The aim almost always was to secure personal power and ascendancy in the government, over the mind of the emperor as once over the deliberations and elections of the assemblies of the people in the Republic. Thus the same person could do things which could be interpreted as anti-German, at other times as pro-German. Constantius had acted as an "anti-German" toward the Goths until he won Placidia; thereafter he followed a policy of settling the Goths (and other Germans) in the Empire, a policy which has frequently been analyzed as pro-German. The point is that his policy did not follow any principle opposed to or favoring Germans, but was purely ad hoc, to establish his personal power and attain his personal ambitions by marrying Placidia; in degree as patriotism and a care for the welfare of the state motivated a person such as Constantius, his personal ambitions were accommodated to the good of the state; presumably this last could be said of most politicians in most times and places.

On this occasion Placidia was accused of conspiring against the Emperor, of entering into conspiracy with the enemies of Rome, presumably the Goths—that is, of committing treason. Honorius, with the evidence in the streets before him and the suspicion of the

[20] Later on Aëtius is depicted as "pro-German," and thereby Placidia must be "anti-German."

[21] This has been demonstrated most recently by C. Meier, *Res Publica Amissa*, pp. 7–23, for the late Republic; there is no reason to believe that fundamental conceptions of politics had changed under the Empire. The letters of Pliny and Symmachus (on the latter see J. A. McGeachy, *Quintus Aurelius Symmachus and the Senatorial Aristocracy of the West, passim*, esp. pp. 87–128) are almost as full of the establishment of personal connections (*necessitudines*) and personal prestige (*auctoritas* and *existimatio*) as are those of Cicero. The unfortunately relatively rare analyses of the workings of practical politics under the Empire (such as those anent the problem of the succession to Hadrian, or the intrigues under Commodus) show no qualitative difference with respect to the politics of the late Republic.

Visigoths in Spain continually insinuated in his ears, was apparently convinced. He was certainly not the first Roman emperor to conceive the darkest suspicions against his close relatives, even a sister. Galla Placidia was exiled from court; whether Constantinople or Rome were specified as the place of her banishment is uncertain. At any rate she went with her children first to Rome and then to her relatives in the East.[22] Possibly after a short stay at Rome Placidia felt unsafe from the further machinations of her enemies (who in their turn would be uneasy lest she return to favor, and hence would continue to intrigue against her), and then took the decision to seek sanctuary in the East (probably early 423). It is uncertain whether she was deprived of her rank of Augusta by Honorius (and Valentinian of his title as "most noble");[23] certainly, however, in the East, as she well knew, these titles were not recognized, and she could hardly expect a cordial welcome from her nephew Theodosius II and her nieces, especially Pulcheria, who possessed the same sort of importance in the government and influence in the affairs of State as Placidia herself had had in the West. The revenues of at least her Western estates seem to have been cut off by Honorius; at any rate she found contributions from Boniface a necessary supplement to the income she presumably still continued to derive from her Eastern properties.[24] Boniface in Africa occupied too strategic a position for his and Placidia's enemies at court to dare move against him as yet. Thus in the East Placidia was able to maintain the state of a personage of high rank, and probably to continue to support a considerable number of her dependents and *bucellarii,* who would presumably have no future at Ravenna without her, and who therefore for the most part may well have accompanied her to the East. One may also suspect that Honorius' health may already have been visibly declining. If he should die in the near future, Placidia and her children, without any political base of importance, might well fear even for their lives. Certainly Valentinian would not be allowed to succeed his

---

22 Olympiod. Frag. 40 (IV, 66); Prosp. 1280 (I, 470); *Chron. Gall. a. 452* 90 (I, 658); *Chron. Gall. a. 511* 577 (I, 659); Cassiod. *Chron.* 1205 (II, 155). Prosper puts this event in 423, probably correctly.

23 Cf. Ensslin, *RE,* XX: 2 (1950), 1920.

24 Olympiod. Frag. 40 (IV, 66). Nagl. *Placidia,* p. 41, thinks that Boniface merely sent Placidia the rents of her own estates; possibly, but these rents would presumably be limited to those from estates in Africa only.

uncle. Distasteful and problematical as it might seem, therefore, any future political ambitions which Placidia might still cherish would depend upon her hostile and grudging relatives in the East, even although she must have been aware of, or divined, the ambition of Theodosius II to succeed his uncle in the West. Yet it is not impossible—there is not a shred of evidence unfortunately—that Placidia was acute enough to realize that such an ambition was fantastic in the present state of Western politics and the growing discord of sentiment between the two parts of the Empire. If so, she may have sailed East with a little hope to comfort her, for if Theodosius could not rule the West, there remained herself and Valentinian, the sole surviving male relative of the Eastern Emperor, even although Theodosius was a young, recently married man, and might have male issue.

So in the early spring of 423 Galla Placidia and her children set sail for the East, for Constantinople, a city where she had been reared as a child, but which she had not seen since she was six years old.[25] The voyage itself, however, was not without mishap; the ship on which Placidia and her children were traveling was overtaken by one of the great storms which plague the Mediterranean in both spring and fall. The ship seems to have been in danger of foundering, but Placidia called upon the intervention of Saint John the Evangelist, promising to erect a church in his honor if he would save her and her children from the peril of the sea. The tempest did in fact abate and the ship rode out the storm safely. Some years later, honoring her vow, Placidia erected Ravenna's Church of Saint John the Evangelist to commemorate the mercy shown to Valentinian, Honoria, and herself.[26] Thus the

[25] Philostorg. *HE* 12. 13; Procop. *Bell.* 3 (*Vand.* 1). 3. 5; see also the citations in n. 22 above.

[26] *ILS*, 818; Agnell. 42; *Ded. Eccl. S. Ioh. Ev.*, Muratori, *Scr. Rer. Ital.*, I: 2, 567–68. The latter source connects the storm and the vow with Placidia's homeward trip; this is unlikely, since she apparently returned home by land. Ensslin, *RE*, XX: 2 (1950), 1920, is too confident in rejecting the homeward trip, since she could, as other scholars have believed, have traveled part of the way by sea. Eastward voyage: A. Thierry, "Aëtius et Bonifacius," *Rev. deux mondes*, 1851, part III, pp. 276–310, at 284; Schild, *Placidia*, p. 45 and n. 1; Sirago, *Placidia*, p. 238 and n. 1; for the homeward voyage argue Nagl, *Placidia*, p. 36; Bury, *Hist.*, I, 262, n. 5; *idem*, *JRS*, IX (1919), 3. On the church itself, see below, Ch. VII, nn. 86–87. There seems to have been no particular reason for Placidia to have asked the intercession of Saint John; he had been a fisherman, but so had others among the apostles. Presumably we must argue a previously existing special devotion to the Evangelist, for whatever reason.

three refugees from the West with their following arrived to what must have been a cold welcome from Theodosius (see a coin of his, Pl. VIB) and his sisters; certainly the Eastern Emperor did not recognize his aunt as Augusta or his cousin as Most Noble.[27] Presumably, however, Placidia herself was recognized as Most Noble, since the title had originally been conferred, in all probability, by Theodosius the Great. Presumably also Placidia was allowed to take up her residence in the palace which belonged to her in Constantinople. Otherwise, she could do nothing but more or less meekly accept the policy of the Emperor of the East.

Pulcheria and her sisters had imparted a tone of almost monastic piety to the Eastern court, in part from natural inclination, in part from a desire to avoid political difficulties in the imperial succession by avoiding marriage in Christian chastity. In all probability Galla Placidia joined her nieces in their pious exercises, since an eastern church historian commends her devotion to religion and the churches.[28] It must have been particularly galling to Placidia to rank below her niece Pulcheria, who had been created Augusta in 414, as well as below Theodosius' wife, Aelia Eudocia, who after the birth of a daughter, Licinia Eudoxia, had also been elevated to the coveted rank at the beginning of 423. Thus passed the remainder of the spring and summer of 423. But on 27 August 423, Honorius, not yet thirty-nine, died peacefully of dropsy, like his father, in his palace at Ravenna; perhaps the most inglorious reign in the history of the Roman Empire was concluded.[29] The imperial corpse was conveyed to Rome and buried in the Theodosian mausoleum by Saint Peter's;[30] intelligence that the Western throne had thus fallen vacant was of course officially communicated to the Eastern court.[31] By his uncle's death Theodosius II technically and legally became sole ruler of the whole Roman Empire; he could not be sure, however, whether his claims would be recognized in

---

27 Olympiod. Frag. 46 (IV, 68); Marcell. *s.a.* 424, 1 (II, 76).

28 Soz. *HE* 9. 16. 2, with Seeck, *Gesch.*, VI: 1, 297.

29 Olympiod. Frag. 41 (IV, 67) (27 Aug.); Soc. *HE* 7. 22. 21 (15 Aug.); Philostorg. *HE* 12. 13; *Chron. Gall. a. 452* 91 (I, 658); Marcell. *s.a.* 423, 5 (II, 76); *Cons. Const. s.a.* 423, 1 (I, 246); Theophanes, p. 84 (de B) (at Rome, 15 Aug.); Paul. Diac. *Rom.* 13. 7 (at Rome). Ravenna is probably the place of his death rather than Rome, because a law was issued there on 6 Aug. 423; cf. Seeck, *Regesten*, p. 348.

30 Paul. Diac. *Rom.* 13. 7; Raynaldus, in Muratori, II, 573C (a very late source); cf. Armellini, *Chiese*, II, 934; Lanciani, *Pagan and Christian*, p. 201; J. Toynbee and J. W. Perkins, *The Shrine of St. Peter*, p. 11.

31 Olympiod. Frag. 41 (IV, 67); Theophanes, p. 84 (de B).

the West. Accordingly he tried for some time to keep the news secret; apparently, however, rumors about it circulated in Constantinople, which the government tried to silence by various statements of one kind or another. Meanwhile, to be ready for any eventuality, troops were secretly sent to occupy the city of Salona in Dalmatia,[32] important as a forward base for any westward expedition and also valuable as a listening post for news of Western developments.[33] For the present, however, Theodosius' apprehensions about his recognition in the West proved unfounded; for some months he reigned in theory as undisputed master of the entire Mediterranean world[34]—for the last time in history the lands of that inner sea were (technically) politically unified during these months. Apparently Theodosius reached an understanding with Castinus whereby the latter would act in effect as his vicegerent in the West; Castinus as well as the Easterner Victor were designated as consuls for the year 424 by Theodosius.[35] As sole Augustus Theodosius was pleased to legislate for the whole Empire, West as well as East.[36] Obviously Theodosius had no intention of recognizing the claims of Valentinian; it must also have been particularly vexatious and humiliating to Galla Placidia to witness

[32] Soc. *HE* 7. 23. 1–2. Seeck, *Gesch.*, VI: 2, 407, points out that at the time of Honorius' death (which he puts on 15 Aug.) Theodosius was in Pisidia (8–9 Aug. *CTh* 16. 5. 61, 12. 3. 2); hence his sister (or wife) must have acted without him; but he could have returned to Constantinople by the time the news of Honorius' death reached the capital.

[33] Cf. Procop. *Bell.* 5 (*Goth.* 1) 5. 2, 11, 7. 2, 26, etc.; J. Rougé, *Recherches sur l'organisation du commerce maritime en Méditerranée sous l'empire romain*, p. 135 and n. 2; the question of the history of the allegiance of Salona, to East or West, in the fifth century is complex; see J. Jung, *Roemer und Romanen in den Donaulaendern* (2d ed.; Innsbruck, 1887), p. 186, n. 2; as of 414–15 it had apparently been in Eastern control.

[34] Hyd. 82 (II, 20); cf. Prosp. 1283 (I, 470); Cassiod. *Chron.* 1207 (II, 155); *ILS*, 1283 (the language "tertio praefecto urbi utriusque inperii iudicii sublimitato" may indicate appointment as Prefect of Rome by Theodosius II; cf. Palanque, *RÉA*, XLVI [1944], 290, n. 3).

[35] Which implies necessarily that an understanding had been reached with Castinus. On Castinus' designation as consul by Theodosius, see Seeck, *Regesten*, p. 349, accepted by Stein, *Hist.*, I, 565, n. 152; rejected or disregarded by Degrassi, *Fasti*, p. 88. Seeck's case rests essentially on the names of the two consuls, Castinus and Victor, written by the Eastern Marcell. s.a. 424 (II, 76) and the Eastern *Chron. Pasch.*, p. 580 (Bonn); for the law of 26 April (*CTh* 1. 8. 2 = *CJ* 1. 30. 1) mentions only Victor. Yet Theodosius, claiming to rule both parts of the Empire, must have named both consuls for 424; hence he must have named Castinus. Had he named someone else, the Eastern sources would have named that man instead of Castinus. In general, see also Ensslin, *Klio*, XXIV (1931), 474–75.

[36] *CTh* 11. 20. 5 *init.*

her nephew's accommodation with her bitter enemy Castinus. It is possible that the secrecy with which the news of Honorius' death was treated by the Eastern government might have been intended, in part, to make firmly clear to Placidia that she could have nothing to expect for her son in the present situation, and to forestall any untoward measure she might be tempted to take.[37] In any event, however, the attitude of Theodosius at this juncture was fully congruent with the policy followed by his government for several years previously. The reaction of Boniface in Africa to this situation is unknown, but, controlling the grain supply of Rome as he did, it is quite possible that he began to exercise pressure on the Western government, and therefore on Theodosius, by preventing the sailing of the grain ships to Italy.[38]

It is perhaps barely possible that, had Theodosius acted decisively by going at once to Italy and consolidating his position there, he might for some time have been able to rule the West in fact,[39] but the experience of the past century and more had clearly shown that even when the Western Empire was in a stronger position than it was now, when its frontiers had been relatively intact, it was no longer feasible to rule the whole vast Empire from one center. Moreover, the two halves of the Empire had been steadily drifting apart for some time, as the division of the imperial position itself shows, and as the increasingly separate economic, political, and cultural developments of the two parts of the Empire demonstrate.[40] In any event, before the end of 423 a new usurper, John, a civil servant who had previously been *primicerius notariorum* ("first on the list of the corps of notaries") was proclaimed Emperor at Rome.[41] The immediate cause of John's elevation re-

37 Cf. Ensslin, *RE*, XX: 2 (1950), 1921.

38 Cf. Stein, *Hist.*, I, 282; Seeck, *Gesch.*, VI: 1, 90.

39 So Seeck, *Gesch.*, VI: 1, 89, followed by Voirol, *Verhandlungen der Naturforschende Gesellschaft in Basel*, LVI: 2 (1945), 441; R. Paribeni, *Da Diocleziano alla caduta dell' impero d'occidente*, p. 256.

40 Demougeot's book *Unité* seeks to demonstrate, with considerable success, that the crucial period for the separation of the two parts was the fifteen years 395–410. But this evolution or devolution had begun earlier, and was to continue for centuries into the Middle Ages. Among many discussions, see Dannenbauer, *Entstehung*, I, 206–7.

41 Ren. Prof. Frig. *ap.* Greg. Tur. *HF* 2. 8; Olympiod. Frag. 41 (IV, 67); Joh. Ant. Frag. 195 (IV, 612); Philostorg. *HE* 12. 13; Prosp. 1282 (I, 470); Marcell. *s.a.* 424, 3 (II, 76); Soc. *HE* 7. 23. 3.

mains obscure;[42] evidently Castinus, who was the moving force behind this coup d'etat, had become dissatisfied with the arrangement he had made with Theodosius.[43] Why the general had changed his mind we can only conjecture; he must have been aware, however, that Placidia and her son had found a safe reception at the Eastern court, if not one as honorable as Placidia could have wished. He had had ample experience of her ability at intrigues at the court of Honorius; if the persuasive intrigues which he, undoubtedly correctly, will have surmised she was conducting at Constantinople were to succeed at any time, she would have created for herself the power base she had lacked before, and Castinus' own power and possibly even his life would be in the gravest jeopardy. After all, nothing that Theodosius had so far done need amount to anything more than a wish to preserve his

---

[42] Many modern historians have spoken about the pro-German faction, or the antidynastic faction, or that of Stilicho [!]; but all of this goes beyond the evidence, and cf. what was said above (n. 21) concerning ideological issues in Roman politics. Stein, *Hist.*, 1, 282 (basing himself on the statement of Procop. *Bell.* 3 [*Vand.* 1]. 3. 5 that court functionaries were responsible for John's elevation), thinks that they were afraid of losing their jobs by the abolition of the Western court. But it is far from certain that this was so; presumably all of the court functions would continue despite the absence of an emperor, except those devoted exclusively to his personal service, in order to carry on the government. Besides, the expression surely indicates primarily the supporters of Castinus, himself a "court functionary"; everything goes to show that Castinus and therefore his supporters were dominant at court from the last months of the reign of Honorius onward. We should thus deduce the actions of Castinus as the essential prime mover in the elevation of John even without the explicit testimony of Prosp. 1282 (I, 470). In any event, it is inconceivable that the civilian bureaucrats would have dared to elevate one of their number without the support of the soldiery (cf. R. Cessi, *"Regnum" ed "Imperium" in Italia*, I, 33, n. 1, deleting reference to the "barbarian alliance"). Malalas, p. 350 (Bonn) (a passage badly jumbled even by the standards of that commonly confused author), attributes John's elevation to the Senate of Rome; on the error of this view, see Lécrivain, *Sénat*, pp. 140–41; Baynes, *JRS*, XII (1922), 221–22; Lepper, *De Rebus Gestis*, pp. 41–42, however, accents the initiative of the Senate; add to the evidence *ILS*, 1283, which at least shows that Anicius Glabrio Faustus, one of the most important leaders of the Senate, had certainly not incurred the displeasure either of Theodosius or Galla Placidia, as his subsequent career amply demonstrates. On the chronology of John's elevation, see Seeck, *Gesch.*, VI: 2, 408.

[43] The supposition of Stein that Castinus had some tergiversations before lending his support to John (*Hist.*, I, 282–83) is unlikely (see previous note), and is based on his acceptance of the dating of the Eastern law of 26 April by Castinus. But Castinus' name is not attested; Victor's name appears alone, cf. above, n. 35. Hence there is no reason to believe that the Eastern government did not revoke his consulate shortly after the beginning of 424 when news of John's usurpation (with Castinus' support) reached Constantinople, and in turn to think, therefore, that Castinus was not behind the "tyrant" from the beginning.

own freedom of action with respect to the West.[44] Perhaps we might also guess that Castinus was not entirely without statesmanship and had come to see the impossibility of administering the Western Empire in its precarious state according to the dictates of a supreme formulator of policy situated some weeks' journey to the east. One did not have to be particularly astute to perceive this fact; the history of the Empire since Diocletian had amply demonstrated it. A question, however, whose answer seems vain even to conjecture is why Castinus did not ascend the throne himself, but preferred to be kingmaker instead.

The intelligence of this usurpation in the West, arriving at Constantinople presumably early in 424, jolted Theodosius, Pulcheria, and their advisers from their complacent and unrealistic dreams of universal dominion.[45] The West must have a separate emperor of its own; the only question was whether this sovereign should be a member of the house of Theodosius the Great or not. And to that question there could be only one answer. The hopes of Placidia were finally realized; the forces of the East once again as in the reign of her revered father should restore order and legitimacy to the West.[46] The Emperor had made up his mind before the arrival of the embassy which John sent to request recognition from the man who he hoped would be pleased to regard himself as his senior colleague. The ambassadors were treated with contumely and sent to various separate places of confinement near the Sea of Marmora.[47] They were, after all, as adherents of the "tyrant," guilty of high treason. Placidia was again recognized as Augusta (and her son as Most Noble); her husband's imperial rank was also recognized at long last.[48] Once again on state occasions Placidia assumed

44 Cf. Güldenpenning, *Arcad. und Theod.*, p. 257.

45 It is not impossible that the dogged support Boniface gave to Placidia may have contributed to the end of the project of ruling the whole Empire from Constantinople; so Seeck, *Gesch.*, VI: 1, 89, followed with greater emphasis by Lepper, *De Rebus Gestis*, pp. 42–43.

46 On the legitimacy of Valentinian's claim, and its value in the West in the minds of men, see Merobaud. *Carm.* 1. 9, with the commentary of F. M. Clover, "An Historical Commentary on and Translation of Flavius Merobaudes" (Unpublished diss.; Chicago, 1963), *ad loc.*, pp. 9, 40.

47 Philostorg. *HE* 12. 13; Soc. *HE* 7. 23. 3–4; Ren. Prof. Frig. *ap.* Greg. Tur. *HF* 2. 8 says the envoys returned to John, reporting their maltreatment. Perhaps some returned or escaped from arrest in the East.

48 Olympiod. Frag. 46 (IV, 68); Marcell. *s.a.* 424, 1 (II, 76). Coins like those of Eudocia were struck in her honor as Aelia Placidia Augusta; cf. J. F. W. De Salis, "The Coins of the Two Eudoxias, Eudocia, Placidia, and Honoria, and of Theo-

the jewel-encrusted purple robe of imperial majesty and the pearl-adorned diadem; once again men humbled themselves to the dust as she passed by.[49] We may be sure that she was convinced that God had granted her most fervid prayer for herself and her son.

Presumably during the summer of 424, extensive preparations for war were set on foot in the Eastern Empire; an expeditionary force must be gotten together and a fleet assembled, since part of the thrust toward the West was to be by sea. The Alan Ardaburius, together with his son Aspar, was put in command of the expedition. Apparently, as for the Western expeditions of the Emperor's grandfather against Maximus and Eugenius, Thessalonica was designated principal rear base of operations. And thither the Augusta Galla Placidia repaired with Valentinian and Honoria to accompany the expedition, probably in the summer of 424.[50] And on 23 October 424, a high court functionary, Helion, the Master of the Offices, in the name of the August Emperor conferred upon the child Valentinian the secondary imperial rank of Caesar.[51] Valentinian's promotion was given the widest possible publicity through the principal means of propaganda available to the Roman government: the mint of Constantinople issued a large number of coins depicting Valentinian standing as Caesar in due subordination to the seated Theodosius, and with the legend SALVS REIPVBLICAE, "Well-being of the State," to declare the purpose of the new crea-

---

dosius II., Marcian, and Leo I., struck in Italy," *Num. Chronicle*, n.s., VII (1867), 203–15, at 211. The imperial rank of Constantius was posthumously recognized by the inclusion of his name in Western laws of 421 as accepted in the *Theodosian Code*; cf. *CTh* 3. 16. 2; T. Mommsen, ed. of *CTh*, p. ccxcvii; Bury, *Hist.*, I, 222 and n. 5. In turn this fact probably implies that Placidia was recognized as Augusta (and Valentinian as *Nobilissimus*) as of the reign of her husband; thus these titles were not conferred again, but recognized as existing; in turn the further implication may follow that Honorius had not formally stripped Placidia and her son of their imperial titles before they were sent into exile.

49 On the costume of an Augusta, see Delbrueck, *Consulardiptychen*, p. 58; V. Schultze, *Konstantinopel (324–450)*, p. 213.

50 To speak of an "exile" of Placidia and Valentinian to Thessalonica as does Seeck, *Gesch.*, VI: 1, 91, referring to the period when they were in the Emperor's disfavor, is groundless; so Ensslin, *RE*, XX: 2 (1950), 1921. While Theodosius hoped to rule the West himself, prudence would have dictated that he keep Placidia under his eye at Constantinople, where any undesirable activities on her part could more easily be detected and suppressed.

51 Philostorg. *HE* 12. 13; Theophanes, pp. 84–85 (de B); Nic. Call. *HE* 14. 7 (*PG*, CXLVI, 1076); Prosp. 1286 (I, 470); Hyd. 84 (II, 20–21; wrongly put at Constantinople); Marcell. *s.a.* 424, 2 (II, 76); cf. *ILS*, 803; on the date, Seeck, *Regesten*, p. 351; *idem*, *Gesch.*, VI: 2, 409.

tion.[52] It goes almost without saying that the real government of the West was to be committed to the charge of Galla Placidia until Valentinian should come of age.[53] The title of Caesar, which since the second century had regularly been used to designate the heir to the throne had fallen into desuetude (except for the case of the son of the usurper Constantine in Gaul, and that hardly constituted an applicable precedent for the legitimate Emperor). It is easy to see, however, why Theodosius revived it for Valentinian, instead of making him an Augustus outright as had been the more recent practice for imperial children destined for the throne. If the military expedition to the West should fail, on the assumption that Valentinian would survive such a failure, he would be back on Theodosius' hands. It would be most awkward to have a full Augustus about, for whom provision would have to be made. Cannily, therefore, Theodosius, or his advisers, conferred only the lower rank until the issue in the West should be settled.

We may assume that the recognition of Placidia and her son and the latter's elevation to the rank of Caesar (and prospectively of Augustus) had been preceded or accompanied by some hard bargaining between Placidia and her nephew. Placidia was aware that, essentially, she had been driven from the West the year before because she had not had a sufficient power base; she must establish such a power base for the future, or her tenure of power, especially until her son came of age, might well prove short. Restoration of her son and herself to rule in the West would not suffice unless there was some surety that the Eastern Emperor would protect her position, in the ultimate analysis at least, against the continued intrigues of her enemies, present or future. She therefore sought to bind Theodosius and the resources of the East more closely to herself and her son than their existing relationship did. She proposed,[54] therefore, that when the parties had reached a suitable age, her son Valentinian should marry his half second cousin, Eudoxia, the infant daughter, and then sole child (in fact, there

---

52 O. Ulrich-Bansa "Le ultime monete della zecca di Aquileia romana," *Aquileia nostra*, XVIII (1947), 3–12, at 9; Voirol, *Verhandlungen der Naturforschende Gesellschaft in Basel*, LVI: 2 (1945), 434–35.

53 Soc. *HE* 7. 24. 3.

54 I am assuming that the initiative in arranging the marriage of Valentinian and Eudoxia came from Placidia, on the ground that she and her son benefitted the more from the project.

were to be no more children born to Theodosius, or at least none that survived, but this fact of course was unknown at the time), of her nephew. Probably the suggestion was not unattractive to the Eastern government;[55] such a marriage would mean that the Emperor's daughter would eventually be an Augusta and imperial consort in the West, and thus occupy a more exalted position than she would presumably hold in the East during the reign of a hypothetical younger brother. The Eastern government, however, with considerable justice, considered that it was doing much for Placidia and her son, and it could not have been blind to the fact that, particularly if this marriage took place, it was in effect guaranteeing the position of Placidia and Valentinian for the future as well as the present. In return, therefore, Placidia had to promise that the long-standing claims of the Eastern court to eastern Illyricum (i.e., roughly that part of the Balkan peninsula which included Greece and the lands directly to the north thereof, leaving to the West mostly what is now Yugoslavia and the land to the south and west of the great bend of the Danube, then called Pannonia) should be formally recognized by the Western government of Placidia. This legal recognition of the right of the East to eastern Illyricum was probably to be effective only upon the actual marriage of Valentinian and Eudoxia.[56] Toward the end of 424 Theodosius designated himself as consul for the eleventh time, for 425, with

[55] Güldenpenning, *Arcad. und Theod.*, p. 259, suggests that Eudocia was in favor of the marriage in order to see her daughter on the Western throne; this is quite possible, but without attestation aside from general considerations such as underly much of the reasoning in the text here.

[56] Cassiod. *Var.* 11. 1. 9; cf. Jord. *Rom.* 329 (all Illyricum ceded, as indeed Cassiod. implies); Marcell. *s.a.* 424, 2 (II, 76). The language of Cassiodorus indicates that the cession of Illyricum was in return for the acquisition of Eudoxia as a daughter-in-law. This may, of course, be an oversimplification; but if it is not, it implies that this legal transfer did not take effect (the East of course had in fact long ruled Eastern Illyricum) until the marriage was celebrated (as Jord. states). Otherwise, in view of the fact that the marriage could not take place for many years, there would be no effective *quid pro quo* in respect of Eudoxia. Whether Western Illyricum in fact, or Eastern Illyricum in law, was meant by this transfer has been much debated by scholars, but the arguments of E. Stein, "Der Verzicht der Galla Placidia auf die Präfektur Illyricum," *Wiener Studien*, XXXVI (1914), 344–47; cf. *idem*, *RhM*, LXXIV (1925), 354–58; showing that Western Illyricum was in the actual possession of the Western government (apart from barbarians) after 437 (the actual date of the marriage) seem decisive. Cf. Alföldi, *Untergang*, II, 93, n. 1; Demougeot, *Unité*, p. 502 and n. 39; J. Zeiller, *Les origines chrétiennes dans les provinces danubiennes de l'empire romain*, p. 6 and nn. 1 and 2; Lot, *Destinées*, p. 53, believes Western Illyricum was meant, and that the provision was secret. It is unclear, however, why Lot thinks the provision was secret.

Valentinian Caesar, consul for the first time, as his colleague. Similarly, in the West John appointed himself consul for 425, although he seems not to have named a Western colleague, even when he became certain of Theodosius' hostility.[57]

In Italy John, although harassed by all sorts of difficulties, seems to have shown himself an able ruler; writing in the sixth century, the Greek historian Procopius[58] praises his mildness, intelligence, and general ability. In religious matters his reign marked a departure from the policy of the house of Theodosius; all Christian sects appear to have been tolerated—surely a statesmanlike measure; not quite so clear is the judgment to be passed on his placing of the clergy under the jurisdiction of the secular tribunals instead of their bishops.[59] In most ages the modern historian would rightly adjudge such a rule quite justified; but in the declining Empire of the fifth century the privileged position of the clergy was, as previously remarked, a means of attaching them to the government and therefore to the imperial system in the hope that their influence would help to counteract the forces of division and disloyalty, or "withdrawal," and that they would serve as a healthy corrective and restraint upon the corrupt bureaucracy and judicial system of the age.[60] John's control of Gaul was insecure, although he minted coins at Arles,[61] and apparently at Trier;[62] his Praetorian Prefect of the Gauls was slain at Arles by an uprising of the soldiery which John was unable to punish.[63] In 425 the Goths attacked Arles;[64] it has been suggested that they used the excuse of their adherence

---

[57] Degrassi, *Fasti*, p. 89.

[58] *Bell.* 3 (*Vand.* 1). 3. 6; this may, however, come from the same anti-Placidia strain in Eastern historiography which we have seen appearing in Olympiodorus, who also implies (Frag. 41 [IV, 67]) that John was popular.

[59] *CSirm.* 6; *CTh* 16. 2. 46–47.

[60] Stein, *Hist.*, I, 283, however, who does not ordinarily exhibit the anticlerical prejudices of Seeck, apparently favors this secularizing measure of John.

[61] P. V. Hill, J. P. C. Kent, and R. A. G. Carson, *Late Roman Bronze Coinage*, pp. 54, 57.

[62] Palanque, add. n. 160 *ap.* Stein, *Hist.*, I, 565, citing an article I have been unable to see; cf. Stroheker, *Adel*, p. 50, n. 35.

[63] Prosp. 1285 (I, 470); *Chron. Gall. a. 452* 97 (I, 658). It is a bit forced to see in Prosp.'s remark that this murder was unavenged by John an indication that the soldiers were acting against an anti-John prefect; if this were so, it would presumably be superfluous to comment that he did not avenge the deed; cf. Freeman, *Western Europe*, p. 273; Sirago, *Placidia*, p. 271.

[64] Prosp. 1290 (I, 471); Isid. *Goth.* 23 (II, 277).

to the cause of Galla Placidia thus to break their treaty.[65] Certainly they did not retire when she had won the day; a Roman army had to drive them off. Of course in Africa Boniface was also hostile;[66] undoubtedly he held back the grain fleet for Rome, and that was, as always, a source of grave concern to the government holding the City.[67] The German general Sigisvult was sent against Boniface, but without success. This diversion of troops across the sea was to help bring about John's own undoing, for it left him shorthanded when the expedition from the East arrived.[68] In any event, in 425 Boniface found it prudent to wall the city of Carthage against future attempts to dislodge him.[69] John had originally hoped, of course, that Theodosius would recognize his claims, and like all usurpers in his position he had "recognized" the legitimate Emperor; in Theodosius' name as well as his own he issued coins at Ravenna.[70] When John learned, however, how Theodosius had treated his embassy, he realized that he could expect only war from the East, and sent one of his younger, but promising, adherents, a certain Aëtius, to solicit the aid of the Huns. Aëtius was John's *cura palatii* (a relatively modest position connected with the oversight of the maintenance of the imperial residences); when a boy, however, Aëtius had been a hostage among both the Goths and the Huns, and had important friends among the latter. This connection with the Huns thus first brought Aëtius to importance; it was to support him in the forefront of events for nearly a quarter of a century. To emphasize Aëtius' claims on the friendship of the

[65] Cf. Dahn, *Könige*, V, 73; W. Seston, "Verfall des römischen Reiches im Westen: Die Völkerwanderung," in *Propyläen Weltgeschichte,* ed. by G. Mann and A. Heuss, IV, 487–603, at 562; it is doubtful that the Goths of this time would really go to war for their former Queen, as Voirol, *Verhandlungen der Naturforschenden Gesellschaft in Basel,* LVI: 2 (1945), 442, suggests. Schmidt, *Gesch.*2, I, 463, seems correct in seeing this attack by the Goths as merely an attempt to extend their own power.

[66] Olympiod. Frag. 40 (IV, 66).

[67] During at least part of his reign John controlled Rome, for he issued coins there; cf. Hill, Kent, and Carson, *Bronze,* pp. 43, 63.

[68] Prosp. 1286 (I, 470); *Chron. Gall. a. 452* 96 (I, 658; Schmidt, *Wandalen,* p. 57, transfers this expedition of Sigisvult to 428; Romanelli, *Storia,* p. 638 and n. 3, agrees [as do other scholars], although he puts it in 427. This is quite arbitrary; there is no reason why Sigisvult could not have led expeditions to Africa on two different occasions; see Lepper, *De Rebus Gestis,* p. 43); Diesner, *Kirche und Staat,* p. 107; Olympiod. Frag. 40 (IV, 66).

[69] *Chron. Gall. a. 452* 98 (I, 658).

[70] Hill, Kent, and Carson, *Bronze,* p. 43.

Huns, he took with him a large sum of gold to buy their assistance (early 425?). John's plan was that, while he offered frontal resistance to the Eastern troops, the Huns should fall on their rear.[71]

Early in 425 the army of the East left Thessalonica for the West; its first move was to recapture Salona, which seems to have been seized again by the troops of the West.[72] Aspar, with the general Candidianus, who may be the man who years before had advised Placidia to marry Athaulf,[73] penetrated Italy by land as far as Aquileia, which was taken by surprise. With this contingent journeyed Placidia and her children. With other troops Ardaburius attempted to cross by sea directly to Italy; again an equinoctial storm of the Adriatic disrupted plans; the fleet was wrecked, and although the general managed to escape with his life to the coast of Italy, he fell into the hands of partisans of John there. Perhaps in the hope of gaining time and preventing a full-scale attack of Aspar's army upon his small forces until the Huns arrived, John treated his captive with great kindness; perhaps he also hoped that by such lenient treatment the way would be opened to reach some sort of accommodation with the East short of the issue of battle. Naturally the capture of Ardaburius caused consternation in his son's headquarters in Aquileia and at the court in Constantinople when the news reached there, especially since Theodosius and his generals must have had some sort of information about Aëtius' efforts to recruit Hunnish assistance. Ardaburius, however, was wily enough to utilize the relative freedom in which he was left to win over the garrison of Ravenna. A secret message was smuggled out to Aspar to attack the city; the latter's troops advanced and were shown by a shepherd a secret path through the marshes that protected the place far better than its walls. The Christians whom John's religious policies had alienated were sure that God had once again shown his interest in the welfare of the faith by sending an angel in the guise of the shepherd; in fact, the event probably attests the continued drying up of the open water and morasses

71 Ren. Prof. Frig. *ap.* Greg. Tur. *HF* 2. 8.

72 On the military vicissitudes of Salona see, however, Ensslin, *RE*, XX: 2 (1950), 1922; it seems unlikely that Aëtius passed through Salona on his way to the Huns, cf. Sirago, *Placidia*, p. 250, n. 2; for the version followed in the text, Seeck, *Gesch.*, VI: 2, 409.

73 Sievers, *Kaiser*, p. 439, cf. 452; Güldenpenning, *Arcad. und Theod.*, p. 259; O. Seeck, *s.v.* "Candidianus" (3), *RE*, III (1899), 1472–73; *idem, Gesch.*, VI: 1, 93; Sundwall, *Studien,* no. 80, p. 60.

about Ravenna. The soldiers of the "tyrant," thanks to Ardaburius' intrigues, admitted the foe, and John, after only a brief scuffle, thus fell into the hands of his enemies through treachery.[74] In accordance with the indiscipline of the times the victorious soldiery proceeded to loot the city, although it now belonged to Placidia and Valentinian.[75]

The news of John's downfall reached the Emperor at Constantinople while he and his subjects were regaling themselves with the spectacles of the Hippodrome. Thereupon Theodosius and his people, abandoning their diversions, proceeded to the church (Saint Sophia?) to offer their gratitude and praise to God for his mercy.[76] The unfortunate John meanwhile had been hurried to Aquileia; there in medieval Byzantine fashion his hand was first cut off; he was paraded on an ass in the circus or Hippodrome to the jeers of the populace, and after suffering various other indignities and insults he was decapitated (about June or July, 425).[77] Such had not been the fate of rebels against the ancient emperors; such men had commonly been merely put to death, sometimes after private torture to ferret out their accomplices, without making a public display of their torments. A large number of them anticipated such a fate by committing suicide; this escape of course was forbidden to Christians. The capture of John came just in time; the reinforcements from the Huns, led by Aëtius arrived in Italy only three days after the usurper's death. There followed some skirmishing between the forces of Aspar and the Huns, but the presence of the latter was useless now, and Placidia soon arrived at an agreement with Aëtius: the Huns were paid off and sent home after an exchange of hostages, but with the rank of Count Aëtius obtained a high military command in Gaul to deal with the

---

74 Philostorg. *HE* 12. 13; Soc. *HE* 7. 23. 4–11; Hyd. 84 (II, 21); Prosp. 1286, 1288 (I, 470); Procop. *Bell.* 3 (*Vand.* 1). 3. 8; Olympiod. Frag. 46 (IV, 68); Joh. Ant. Frag. 195 (IV, 612–13); Nic. Call. *HE* 14. 7 (*PG*, CXLVI, 1077); Marcell. *s.a.* 425, 1 (II, 76).

75 *Chron. Gall. a. 452* 99 (I, 658); cf. G. Wurm, *De Rebus Gestis Aetii*, p. 18. One may note that Theophanes, p. 103 (de B), has an entirely different and unhistorical account of the end of John's "tyranny."

76 Soc. *HE* 7. 23. 12–15. It is possible that the "Golden," or triumphal Gate of Constantinople was erected by Theodosius II to commemorate this occasion, rather than by his grandfather; cf. Bury, *Hist.*, I, 71, n. 4.

77 Olympiod. Frag. 46 (IV, 68); Philostorg. *HE* 12. 13; Hyd. 84 (II, 21); Prosp. 1288 (I, 470); Procop. *Bell.* 3 (*Vand.* 1). 3. 9; Marcell. *s.a.* 425, 1 (II, 76); Nic. Call. *HE* 14. 7 (*PG*, CXLVI, 1077). On the date see Ensslin, *RE*, XX: 2 (1950), 1922; Bury, *Hist.*, I, 224, n. 1.

Visigoths attacking Arles.[78] That a subject should thus presume to treat with his sovereign as Aëtius had done must have profoundly angered the pride of Placidia; for the present she could only acquiesce and wait for a day of reckoning, when Aëtius should no longer be protected by his Hunnish friends. Seven years later she was wrongly to conclude that that day of reckoning had come; unfortunately her sentiments were communicated to her son. In his time the day for ridding the dynasty of the general did come, but in destroying him Valentinian was to set in train a series of events which would lead directly to his own murder and to the final collapse of the West Roman Empire within less than a generation. Needless to say, in 425 these events were totally unforeseen and unforeseeable by anyone. John, however, had had a supporter, or creator, far more prominent than Aëtius, a supporter who was not protected by the friendship of the Huns. This, of course, was Castinus, Placidia's old enemy, of whose acts during the usurper's reign we hear absolutely nothing. Castinus was driven into exile, or had already fled, since this fate was mild indeed considering the man's past history and his present guilt of high treason; a doubtful source says that he found refuge in the Christian magnanimity of another old foe, Count Boniface of Africa.[79] After this time, we hear no more of him.

According to the ancient custom of Rome the winning of a victory in the field merited the title of *Imperator,* which the victorious general received from his troops on the field of battle; under the Empire, of course, when the title came to signify not merely "Victorious General," but "Emperor," such imperial acclamations were reserved for the emperors alone, who had in the first centuries of the Empire sedulously recorded the number of such "imperial salutations" among their titles. Their first such salutation had signified their *dies imperii,* their "Day of Empire," the day of their accession to the throne. The armies of the Late Empire had preserved this right to make emperors, and at some time in 425, one

---

[78] Philostorg. *HE* 12. 14; Prosp. 1288 (I, 471); *Chron. Gall. a. 452* 100 (I, 658); Nic. Call. *HE* 14. 7 (*PG*, CXLVI, 1080); T. Mommsen, "Aetius," in *Gesammelte Schriften,* IV, 531–60 (= *Hermes,* XXXVI [1901], 516–47), at 534. That the Hunnish forces brought to Italy at this time amounted to 60,000 men is impossible; cf. Thompson, *Attila,* p. 49. Perhaps it was on this occasion that Aëtius' son Carpilio went as hostage to the Huns (if he had not been sent to them when his father originally went to ask their assistance); cf. Prisc. Frag. 8 (IV, 81).

[79] Prosp. 1288 (I, 471); Ps.-Bon. *Ep.* 10 (*PL,* XXXIII, 1097).

thinks of the immediate aftermath of the victory over John, the troops of Valentinian Caesar enthusiastically hailed him (Imperator) Augustus;[80] presumably it was the army of the East which thus saluted Valentinian and asserted its right to make emperors. Nevertheless, Placidia, although doubtless gratified by this imperial salutation of her son, which in effect gave him a sort of independent right to supreme authority, preferred to await formal investiture by Theodosius. It would be better for Valentinian to receive his power from his senior colleague in the East than to acknowledge once again the more or less indiscriminate right of the soldiers to create an emperor. She may have recalled the refusal of her maternal grandfather, Valentinian I, to yield at once to the demands of his soldiers that he name a colleague in the Empire. In any event, it clearly would not do to antagonize Theodosius, whom Placidia must necessarily regard as the ultimate support of her son's throne. Her refusal to accept the troops' acclamation is shown by the minting of coins at Aquileia on which Valentinian is represented as Caesar alongside Theodosius as Augustus; other coins were issued for the Empress herself as Augusta, but with the name Galla Placidia, instead of the preferred Eastern form, Aelia Placidia a small gesture of independence, perhaps, on the part of Placidia.[81] By law and custom of the Empire legislation was the prerogative of an Augustus only; yet on 9 July 425, Placidia issued an imperial constitution from Aquileia revoking the antiepiscopal and tolerating acts of the "tyrant" in the name of Theodosius Augustus and Valentinian Caesar;[82] the variety of the addressees in the provisions preserved in the Theodosian Code indicates that it

[80] One version of Prosp. 1289 (I, 471).

[81] De Salis, *Num. Chron.*, n.s., VII (1867), 211–12; Ulrich-Bansa, *Aquileia nostra,* XVIII (1947), 10–11; Boyce, *Festal,* pp. 64–65; the mint of Aquileia was closed soon thereafter and its workers and dies transferred to Rome: *ibid.;* O. Ulrich-Bansa, *Moneta Mediolanensis (352–498),* p. 270, n. 5. The mint at Ravenna, common seat of the court, continued to function.

[82] *CSirm.* 6; cf. *CTh* 16. 2. 46, 47. 16. 5. 62, 63, 64. There is some controversy over the history of episcopal jurisdiction; Constantine had given broad judicial power to bishops, but these had been narrowed in the course of the fourth century. Placidia retained the situation as it had prevailed under Honorius and Arcadius (*CTh* 16. 11. 1; *CJ* 1. 4. 7); this apparently means that bishops had exclusive jurisdiction over religious matters, but could in other matters act only as arbitrators *inter volentes.* So Gaudemet, *L'église,* pp. 230–36; cf. K. Voigt, *Staat und Kirche von Konstantin dem Grossen bis zum Ende der Karolingerzeit,* p. 21 and n. 16; F. Martroye, "Saint Augustin et la compétence de la juridiction ecclésiastique au Ve siècle," *Mém. de la Soc. Nat. des Antiquaires de France,* LXX (1911), 1–78, at 69–73.

was probably addressed to all high functionaries of state. Probably even before the victory over John, Placidia had been making, or confirming, a long series of appointments to major offices. It would be unsafe to conclude that she had dared take the imperial prerogative of legislation on herself, whether in reliance on the imperial salutation of her son or not. More likely she had been conceded beforehand by Theodosius the power to issue whatever laws were necessary to return matters to normal after the downfall of John. The acceptance of the law in the *Theodosian Code,* together with the specification there of both Theodosius and Valentinian Caesar as issuing it, probably at least attests that its promulgation was not in disaccord with the wishes of the Emperor of the East.[83]

From Aquileia Placidia, her son, and their court removed first to Ravenna, and then, with a view to Valentinian's final elevation to the rank of Augustus in the ancient capital, to Rome.[84] Perhaps Placidia, thinking of the various circumstances under which on other occasions she had entered or left the City, meditated upon the mutability of human fortune as the Imperial Advent procession advanced along the Flaminian Way, through the Flaminian Gate, along the Via Lata, doubtless with the full splendor and pomp of such ceremonies, to the Roman Forum and the Palace of the Caesars. The Ever August Emperor Theodosius had intended to come in person to Rome in order to invest Valentinian. Having journeyed as far as Thessalonica, however, he fell ill and was compelled to return to Constantinople; thus it turned out that in his entire life he was never to behold the imperial City in whose name he ruled the East. On this occasion his pride as kingmaker and senior Augustus had to be gratified vicariously. The same Helion, the Master of the Offices, perhaps raised for the performance of this very function to the exalted rank of Patrician, was dispatched in his stead to invest the new Western Augustus. Hence, doubtless according to plan, on 23 October 425, exactly one year after Helion had elevated Valentinian to be Caesar, he conferred upon the six-

---

[83] To see in this act an open defiance of Theodosius II, as does Seeck, *Gesch.,* VI: 1, 96; 2, 410 (cf. Palanque, *RÉA,* XLVI [1944], 290–91), is most improbable in view of Placidia's necessary reliance on friendly relations with the East as an ultimate sanction to support her position in the West; it becomes especially unlikely in view of the presence of Eastern troops and generals in Italy and presumably at Aquileia itself.

[84] Olympiod. Frag. 46 (IV, 68).

year-old boy the imperial diadem and all the appurtenances of supreme power. We may be sure, although details are lacking in the sources, that the ceremony occurred in the presence of Galla Placidia Augusta, of the highest dignitaries of the state, and of the Roman senate, and that the solemnity of the occasion was climaxed by appropriate thanksgivings to God; corresponding ceremonies were held in Constantinople.[85] Coins were minted at Rome to commemorate the event and the Victory of the Augusti;[86] according to tradition, following his accession Valentinian entered upon the consulate for 426 (with Theodosius, for the twelfth time, as his colleague) on 1 January, at Rome.[87] In all this Galla Placidia had not forgotten her elder child, her daughter Justa Grata Honoria; not long after her brother's accession as Augustus, he was made to confer on her the rank of Augusta, as coins issued in her name show.[88]

Obviously Valentinian III was Emperor of Rome for one reason only—his membership in the imperial family. Several years later, when he was a man grown, a court poet would refer to his accession with the words, "Victory returned the world to whom Nature gave it."[89] Contemporary coins showed the legitimacy of Valentinian's accession by depicting his investiture by the Divine Hand coming from Heaven.[90] And later still, when Valentinian as well as his mother was dead, their family in exile, and strangers ruling in Constantinople, in a panegyric delivered in honor of another emperor yet another court poet would ill-naturedly declare that through all his life this legitimacy constituted Valentinian's sole

[85] Soc. *HE* 7. 24. 4–5, 25. 23 (the westward start of Theodosius' journey is confirmed by *CTh* 6. 10. 4, 22. 8, of 22 Sept., 425); Olympiod. Frags. 1, 34 (IV, 58, 65); Philostorg. *HE* 12. 13, 13a; Hyd. 85 (II, 21); Marcell. *s.a.* 425, 2 (II, 76; erroneously at Ravenna); Jord. *Rom.* 328 (erroneously at Ravenna); *Chron. Pasch.*, I, 580 (Bonn); *Chron. Gall. a. 452* 101 (I, 658); Malalas 14, p. 356 (Bonn); Theophanes, p. 85 (de B). On the patriciate of Helion, see G. B. Picotti, "Il 'Patricius' nell' ultima età imperiale e nei primi regni barbarici d'Italia," *Archivio stor. ital.*, 7th ser., IX (1928), 3–80, at 45 and n. 2; Jones, *Roman Empire*, I, 179. There has been some question as to the date; see Güldenpenning, *Arcad. und Theod.*, p. 262 and n. 41.

[86] Ulrich-Bansa, *Moneta*, p. 229; Cohen, *Description*, VIII, 213, no. 24.

[87] Degrassi, *Fasti*, p. 89; the presence of the Emperor is attested at Rome as late as 24 Feb. 426; by 6 March, however, he had gone to Ravenna; Seeck, *Regesten*, p. 352.

[88] Ulrich-Bansa, *Moneta*, p. 227, n. 19; p. 234, n. 38; Bury, *JRS*, IX (1919), 4–5; *idem, Hist.*, I, 224.

[89] Merobaud. *Carm.* 1. 9.

[90] Cf., e.g., Cohen, *Description*, VIII, 213, no. 24.

claim to the throne.[91] Even under the early emperors, despite the Republican traditions with which the Empire had begun, there had been a strong tendency to form dynasties, from the first Emperor Augustus onward. Every emperor who had a son or close male relative to succeed him left the throne to him. In all probability only a few aristocrats, vainly harkening back to the traditions of the Republic, or philosophical theorists dreaming of philosopher kings, objected. Vespasian (Emperor, 69–79) had roundly declared that his sons or no one would succeed him.[92] The Emperor Diocletian's attempt to set up an artificial, nonhereditary system of succession (he had no sons) was foiled in large part by the hereditary ambitions of Constantine the Great, son of Diocletian's junior colleague Constantius I, since the ambitions of Constantine seemed perfectly natural and right to Constantius' army. In the fourth and fifth centuries the dynastic principle triumphed; dynasties lasted as long as there were male heirs to continue them, and the multiplicity of related emperors assured the downfall of such usurpers as did in fact overthrow or slay a reigning member of the family. Thus Honorius, without talent or even ordinary competence, survived a long series of usurpers; Valentinian III, boy and man, overshadowed by his generals, was to keep the throne until two Germans murdered him in vengeance for the death of Aëtius.[93]

Thus Galla Placidia, at long last, attained her ambition and at least theoretically arrived at the summit of human power.[94] As in the case of her brother Honorius as a child, the Roman law did not recognize a regency, largely because of the old fiction that the emperor was an extraordinary Republican magistrate, whose position could theoretically be conferred on anyone, or abolished entirely, at any time. Obviously the idea of a regency (which would imply some legal claim on power other than personal ability) was totally incompatible with such a view. Yet in fact, of course, the

91 Ap. Sid. *Carm.* 7. 532–43.

92 A great deal of nonsense has been written by modern scholars about theories of imperial succession in the Early Empire. It was even in accord with Roman tradition that a man's son was expected to succeed to his father's position in the state. The very fact that emperors without sons in the second century adopted sons to succeed them attests the importance of the hereditary principle, especially given the strict Roman feelings about adoption.

93 See C. E. Stevens, *Sidonius Apollinaris and His Age,* p. 21 and n. 4; Stein, *Hist.,* I, 317; on the triumph of the dynastic principle.

94 *Chron. Gall. a. 452* 103 (I, 658); this entry appears under the year 428, but surely belongs under 425.

dynastic principle implied an entirely different situation from that envisaged by the law. Placidia's position was one of the facts of politics rather than of constitutional law, and it was in this sense that Theodosius had conferred in effect a sort of political *tutela* (a term of private law meaning guardianship) upon her.[95] Valentinian III, although a child, may have had to validate all imperial decrees by his own signature,[96] but there can be little doubt that the placing of that signature was dictated by the child's mother. We have seen Placidia involved in politics for years before this time; there can be little doubt that she had hoped for this accession of power, as a Gallic chronicle states.[97] Yet it is almost as certain that in large part her ambitions were ultimately directed to the welfare and good of her son; surely it is easy for any mother to identify her interests with those of her child. Two generations after Placidia's death a Roman courtier of Amalasuntha, daughter of the Ostrogothic King Theodoric the Great, in order the better to praise his patroness, denigrates Galla Placidia by comparison. Yet even in these circumstances Cassiodorus admits that Placidia was zealous for (the welfare of) her son;[98] such evidence from a hostile source carries considerable weight. But many a fond mother, while consciously willing her son's best interests, has nevertheless "spoiled" him, and in the process unmanned him. And in fact this is the traditional picture of the relations of Galla Placidia and Valentinian, as depicted, for example, by Gibbon, the impressiveness of whose literary genius lesser historians have found it difficult to resist: after remarks about Placidia reminiscent of a satirist's strictures on the impotence of female ambition, Gibbon continues, "The mother of Valentinian was jealous of the power, which she was incapable of exercising; she reigned twenty-five years, in the name of her son; and the character of that unworthy emperor gradually countenanced the suspicion that Placidia had enervated

---

95 Soc. *HE* 7. 24. 3; *ILS*, 802 (with the word *tutela*) = *Anth. Lat.*, II: 1, 288. The inscription is quite fragmentary but the word *tutela* does appear (line 3) in connection with Valentinian III and must refer, in view of the passage in Soc., to Placidia rather than Theodosius (line 4). Mazzarino, *Stilicone*, p. 111, n. 2, is quite exercised over the word *tutela* here, but there is no reason to believe that it embodies any legal, as opposed to political, considerations. On the relationship of politics and law in the matter, see T. Mommsen, "Stilicho und Alarich," *Gesammelte Schriften*, IV, 516–30 (= *Hermes*, XXXVIII [1903], 101–15), at 516, n. 2 (on 517).

96 Cf. Seeck, *Regesten*, p. 5.

97 See above, n. 94.

98 Cassiod. *Var.* 11. 1.9.

his youth by a dissolute education and studiously diverted his attention from every manly and honourable pursuit."[99]

The principle source of this condemnation of the Empress is a statement made by the Eastern historian Procopius,[100] who writes that Placidia, presumably with deliberation, reared her son to be wicked, effeminate, superstitious, and sexually dissolute. Apparently the poet Apollinaris Sidonius, who lived in the middle and latter part of the fifth century, and who composed versified panegyrics on three of the ephemeral successors of Valentinian III, confirms this verdict on that Prince, by his scathing animadversions on Valentinian's moral character and general incapability as emperor. Yet, when not writing with interest to vilify Valentinian, Sidonius can praise him in a startling manner.[101] And hardly anyone nowadays will accept as literally true the story that Valentinian provoked his own murder by the rape of the wife of the man who became his short-lived successor—Petronius Maximus[102]—although this seems to be the only specific sexual crime alleged against him.[103] In fact, one of this century's most distinguished and knowledgeable historians of the Later Roman Empire has thrown grave doubts upon the usual verdict of ineptitude passed upon Valentinian III.[104] There can be little doubt, in view of the undoubted piety of Galla Placidia, that the Empress was careful to give her son a good Christian education.[105] If one does not necessarily accept the traditional view that Valentinian's childhood was prolonged throughout his entire life, the question at once emerges whether Placidia did in fact rule the West Roman Empire for her son after he had reached a man's estate. Certainly as of 425 he was of no age to rule, and certainly his mother ruled for him; while not denying

99 Bury-Gibbon, *Decline and Fall*, III, 398; similar verdict by Hodgkin, *Invaders*, I: 2, 851, 871 (although Hodgkin refuses to countenance the suggestion that she deliberately corrupted her own son to preserve her power; cf. p. 885); Schild, *Placidia*, pp. 54, 68, etc.

100 *Bell.* 3 (*Vand.* 1). 3. 10–11.

101 "Aëtius and Majorian," *CP*, LIX (1964), 23–29, at 26–27, with nn.; to the favorable reference to Valentinian cited in the article (p. 29, n. 26: *Carm.* 9. 300) add *Carm.* 23. 214, 423.

102 Procop. *Bell.* 3 (*Vand.* 1). 4. 16–24.

103 It forms the subject matter of Beaumont and Fletcher's Elizabethan tragedy *Valentinian*.

104 Stein, *Hist.*, I, 337–42 (this does not necessarily signify the acceptance by the present author of the entire theory expounded by Stein in this connection; cf. *CP*, LIX [1964], 25; Carl Shuler, *CP*, LVI [1961], 207).

105 Ensslin, *RE*, XX: 2 (1950), 1927.

that he might have had some effect upon his government before the time of his marriage (437), we will be fairly safe in ascribing "his" acts before that date, when he was eighteen years old, to his mother's will.[106] For the present it will be convenient to postpone to a later occasion any attempt to solve the delicate problem, difficult as our sources become progressively scantier while the fifth century proceeds, of the political relationship between Placidia and Valentinian after the latter had become a man. For the present (425), and for the next twelve years, Galla Placidia was the real Emperor of Western Rome; this de facto, if not de jure, ascendancy of women at times in the imperial government is itself partially a proto-Byzantine characteristic which was to appear again and again in the thousand-year medieval history of the Eastern, or Byzantine, Empire.

There is a strain in both the Eastern and the Western tradition concerning the Empress of undoubted hostility to her, as well as to her son Valentinian. The existence of this hostile tradition does not by itself prove or disprove its authenticity, although we have seen that Cassiodorus, a hostile writer, in effect specifically refutes a serious charge against her. In the East this hostility in part probably goes back to the disfavor shown her after her marriage to Constantius until the decision of Theodosius to install her and her son in the West. In all likelihood, however, the main cause of this hostility in the tradition to the last Western members of the house of Theodosius the Great proceeds from certain general ideas that the ancients had about the nature of history and human motives combined with other ideas that were commonplace in the fifth century. For the most part the ancient Greeks and Romans had even less of an adequate grasp of motive and cause in both individual and collective instances than we do. Or, their understanding of the laws of psychology and society was even more inadequate than our own. For them historical causation was both personal and moral; morals may be less fashionable today as a standard from which to infer causation than they were in the not distant past, but people in general to this day tend to see personalities as the cause of contemporary historical phenomena. The ancients usually had little conception of impersonal causes acting more or less uncon-

---

106 So Sirago, *Placidia*, p. 255.

sciously in the minds and attitudes and wishes of vast numbers of men. Thus, for example, the ambitions of Caesar and Augustus were regarded as the principal reason for the downfall of the Roman Republic and its replacement by the Empire. For the most part the ancients did not make the attempt that modern scholars do to understand why it was that the ambition of those two men could be carried to realization in the particular circumstances of society in which they found themselves. Insofar as ancient thinkers did try to look beyond the "morality" of these two men, it was mainly to reprehend the general immorality of their time in contrast to the virtue of earlier and better periods. Since historical causation was conceived as mainly personal, it followed that causation occurred in terms of the personality and moral character of individuals; further, in the usual analysis of the ancients, these individual traits were ordinarily fixed and unvarying from childhood onward.[107] In addition, whether or not they grasped the real import of their misfortunes, the Romans were appalled by the disasters which befell the Western Empire in the fifth century. According to their lights, individuals must be responsible, so they sought to blame their troubles in large part on scapegoats. Thus Stilicho was declared the real cause of Alaric's capture of Rome; Count Boniface was supposed to have invited the Vandals into Africa and was thus responsible for the loss of that important diocese; the Empress Eudoxia invited Geiseric to intervene in her aid in 455, and thus became answerable for the Vandal sack of Rome in that year, and so on. In the last half of the fifth century the Western Empire rapidly crumbled, from 454/55 to 476. Before 454, when Valentinian III murdered Aëtius (we may urgently note here that, whatever the moral connotations of that deed, they are properly distinct from the *raison d'état* which undoubtedly moved the Emperor to his bloody work),[108] much of the Western Empire had been held together in one way or another. Hence, in a real sense to the ancients, Valentinian was responsible for the downfall of the Western Empire; obviously, therefore, his character must have been thoroughly depraved. But since the ancients had also been for centuries of the belief that education was of major importance in fixing character, then Galla Placidia must therefore,

---

107 Cf., e.g., the analysis of the Tacitean Tiberius in F. B. Marsh, *The Reign of Tiberius* (New York, 1959), pp. 12, 14.
108 Cf. *CP*, LIX (1964), 25.

indirectly, share some of the opprobrium for her son's misdeeds, and for the collapse which had followed upon her regime.[109] Accordingly the modern student of the Empress' tenure of power and that of her son should try to form his own judgments without allowing himself to be too much influenced by the opinions of the ancients, whose verdict was almost certainly determined largely by general principles which are no longer regarded as valid.

In 425, then, Galla Placidia became the de facto successor of Augustus and Trajan, Constantine and Theodosius. The problems which she faced, however, were naturally different from those of previous reigns, although some of the difficulties had originated as recently as the reign of her brother Honorius. In general, she had to face the problems of a declining state, society, and economy, of the waning of culture and education; the decline of initiative, the "withdrawal" in one area or another of allegiance to the traditional patterns of the Greek and Roman world on the part of large groups of her subjects; the increasing inertia and the decreasing competence of an unwieldy bureaucracy, probably too expensive for the strained and ever smaller resources of the falling Empire, and certainly technologically and numerically inadequate to perform the tasks of regimentation and regulation which the government tried to lay upon it, capable therefore only of tyrannizing over and alienating the masses it tried to govern or exploit; these problems have been discussed in the first chapter of this account and touched upon thereafter. It is also worth while pointing out again that it is very doubtful that Placidia grasped her situation in these terms. Like the historians who would more or less inadequately chronicle the events of her regime, she undoubtedly, since she like them was a product of the mental climate of her time, saw things in a much simpler light in terms of individual ambitions and moral successes or failures, with little or no sense of the real causes which had been working for centuries to bring about the downfall of a system whose achievements she had learned from childhood to remember and revere—what moderns have often been pleased to allude to as the glory of Greece and the grandeur of Rome.

Relatively easy to grasp, because symptomatic and superficial,

---

[109] Again see Cassiod. *Var.* 11. 1. 9, where the connection between Placidia and the difficulties of the Western Empire is directly drawn, how correctly the reader may be better able to judge from the narrative that follows.

was the decline of the imperial power itself. In the first instance this was obviously caused by the growth of the power of the great generals in the West at the expense of the power of the emperor. Despite all of the administrative skill of the Romans they had never been able to solve permanently the problem of controlling the force of the state since the last century of the Republic (law hardly enters into the problem, which is one of naked power where mere law is powerless). In the late Republic the incompetence and self-seeking of the oligarchs who controlled the state had partially dissolved the largely unconscious extralegal bonds which in any state bind the governed to obedience to the governors. In those circumstances it had been possible for the great generals in their selfish greed for power to divert the self-seeking loyalty of their men from the legally constituted authority in the state, represented in fact by the oligarchs' organ the Senate, to subserve the generals' own ambitions. The Senate had never been able to regain its former control over the minds and attitudes of Roman citizens; the only solution to avert perpetual civil war as a means for obtaining or retaining political power had been the conferring of all power upon the most successful of the generals; that man created for himself the position we know as that of emperor, and although there existed other bases, legal and extralegal, for his power, it was no accident that the title by which he came to be best known was *Imperator,* Emperor, that is, victorious general. Yet since so much of the emperor's power rested ultimately on the control of the armed forces of the state, he was continually haunted by the possibility of other men's attempts to seize what he held, if ever his grip on the loyalty or self-interest of the armies should sufficiently relax. Thus the peace and order of even the early Empire had been shattered from time to time by successful or unsuccessful military coups.

After the third century, when such military usurpations had reproduced once again the near-chaos of the late Republic, Diocletian and Constantine had been successful, as we have noted, in restoring order and in reducing the frequency of military revolts to roughly the same level of frequency as in the Early Empire. A principal factor in the success of those Emperors and the men who followed them on the throne had been the strong growth of the hereditary or dynastic principle. In the fourth century the Emperors had regularly acted as de facto as well as de jure commanders-in-chief of the imperial armies, taking the field at the head of their "comrade troops" in campaigns both foreign and domestic. But in the fifth century emperors like Honorius remained in the seclusion of their palaces while their generals led the armies in their names. In the East supreme military power beneath the emperor had been cleverly divided among several simultaneously serving Masters of the Soldiery, who functioned as checks upon each other; thus the unwarlike Arcadius and Theodosius II never fell under the domination of a powerful general to the extent that their contemporaries in the West did, although Ardaburius and Aspar came dangerously close to winning such a position for themselves, and there were some other near misses. But in the West Stilicho had, as it were, institutionalized the control of the state's forces in the hands of one man under the nominal control of the emperor (Arbogast's relationship to Valentinian II in a sense constituted some sort of precedent for Stilicho); while Honorius continued to sleep on the Western throne, as some historians have unkindly put it, and when he was succeeded, after the brief interlude of John, by a child, the way was open for the continuation of a circumstance to which men's minds had become more or less habituated.

The feeling for legitimacy protected the emperor's Sacred Person, but his incompetence (Honorius) or nonage (Valentinian III) rendered attempts to seize the reality although not the appearance of supreme power in nominal subjection to the emperor quite feasible. After the downfall of the Theodosian house and legitimacy in the West by the death of Valentinian III, a barbarian Master of the Soldiers, Count and Patrician, debarred in his case from mounting the throne not by legitimacy but by his being German, would manipulate, with varying degrees of mastery, a succession of phantoms or puppets on the throne. Anti-Germanism was strong enough in the West to prevent the accession of a German emperor of Rome, but otherwise in the fifth century West it was merely one element or factor in the realities of politics.[110] But the situation just sketched produced in the last century of the Western

110 It is also true that in the reign of Valentinian III only a few Germans reached the highest military commands (Stein, *Hist.*, I, 317, 575, n. 1), but this is hardly an indication that ideological pro- or anti-Germanism was a primary issue over which men fought and intrigued at court or elsewhere.

Empire curious analogies to what had prevailed in the last century of the Republic. Then the great generals had struggled for control of the state through a Senate whose still great prestige was no longer great enough to enable it to rule for itself; now the generals struggled to gain control of the Emperor, whose prestige was great, but no longer sufficient to control the troops. There can be no doubt that Galla Placidia was perfectly aware of the danger to the imperial power, which the generals threatened to reduce to magnificent impotence. During the first eight years of her "regency" she was to struggle to prevent this military overshadowing of her child Emperor, and not without success. But by 433 Aëtius triumphed, thanks to his Huns, and what Placidia had feared became fact. There is not wanting evidence that she and her son were not content to let Aëtius' triumph run its course, but were continually on the lookout to rid themselves of what they considered an overbearing incubus, and yet failed. Eventually, when Aëtius no longer had the Huns to help him, Valentinian took the desperate step of murdering the general. Unfortunately a few months later he himself was murdered by two Germans to avenge Aëtius—Germans who had no appreciation of the emperor's legitimate inviolability. It is also quite possible that the assassins were stimulated to perform their act of private vengeance by an aristocrat whose ambitions, if not his stupidity, blinded him to the importance of the emperor's legitimacy for the precarious stability of the declining state.[111]

One could also say that Galla Placidia failed partly because she was a woman; she could not, whatever her bold and defiant spirit, command the armies of Rome in person. She could only try to play off the generals against each other until her son should come of an age to command his own armies like his grandfather; unfortunately by that time Aëtius had proved himself indispensable and unassailable. But the military problem was not only a question of command. The "native Roman" armies in the West had rapidly dwindled since the days of Placidia's father. Despite the theoretical army strength of such a list as the *Notitia Dignitatum* more and

111 On Placidia and the generals, see Seeck, *Gesch.*, VI: 1, 103; Stein, *Hist.*, I, 317; L. M. Hartmann, *Geschichte Italiens im Mittelalter*, I, 39; C. Cecchelli, *s.v.* "Galla Placidia," *Encic. ital.*, XVI, 286–87, at 286; Grosse, *Römische*, pp. 189–90.

more of the troops listed as at the disposition of the high commanders of the armed forces were historical vestiges on paper, where the conservative bureaucracy of the imperial court continued to list them decades after they had ceased to exist. Stilicho's desperate denudation of the garrisons of the frontiers and elsewhere is evidence that this diminution of army strength had commenced when Placidia was still a child.[112] In part this was because the declining finances of the Empire could no longer pay for the armies which the West had once put into the field; in part it was owing to the decline of population in the Empire, in part to the increasingly unwarlike character of the mass of the subjects of the decadent state; it was also due in part to the reluctance of the landowners to supply the drafts of the Empire with numerically or physically adequate recruits, when the manpower shortage and their own interests found the need of hands to exploit their vast properties a matter of greater urgency than the necessities of the state. The soldiers also no longer possessed the discipline which had furnished the renowned valor that had won the victories of the Republic and Early Empire. The famed training which had impelled the legions of the past to construct a fortified camp each night, as a Greek historian of the second century B.C. admiringly reports, had vanished. The Roman soldier was no longer by his training and discipline the superior of the taller barbarians as he had been in the days of Caesar's legions and for centuries thereafter; instead he fought only on fairly equal terms with the barbarians.[113] Indeed, "Roman" troops were more and more of barbarian origin; and more and more were even these substituted by barbarian bands fighting as such in the service of Rome, but under the command of their own chieftains rather than as an integral part of the imperial armies. And the kernel, the most essential part of the latter, there is some reason to believe, came

112 Cf. Grosse, *Römische*, pp. 32–33; Dannenbauer, *Entstehung*, I, 229–33; A. H. M. Jones, "The Decline and Fall of the Roman Empire," *History*, XL (1955), 208–26, at 223; idem, *Roman Empire*, II, 607, 612; Bury-Gibbon, *Decline and Fall*, III, 251; G. Hassebrauk, *Westrom zur Zeit des Aëtius 425–454*, pp. 14–15; Demougeot, *Unité*, pp. 509–15; H. St. L. B. Moss, *The Birth of the Middle Ages 395–814*, p. 21; Lot, *Invasions*, pp. 48–49; idem, *RÉA*, XXXVIII (1936), 312–20; idem, *Destinées*, pp. 19–20; Alföldi, *Untergang*, II, 62; E. von Nischer, in J. Kromayer and G. Veith, *Heerwesen und Kriegführung der Griechen und Römer*, pp. 581–82.

113 See Veget. *Re Mil. passim*, esp. 1. 5, 2. 3; Moss, *Birth*, pp. 19–21.

more and more to be the *bucellarii,* the private troops of generals and other great personages, on which principal reliance could be placed.[114] To deal with these problems Placidia could only hope, not very sanguinely, to enforce the laws of her predecessors on recruitment, and against the avarice of the landholders,[115] and try to raise enough money to hire enough barbarians. Through the vain hope of legislation her son would try to reanimate his subjects at least to self-defense in immediate emergencies.

Obviously the question of the military was compounded by the problem of the landowning nobility or aristocracy. Not only did its members form a potent obstacle to recruitment; in general their power relative to that of the throne was growing. In the Early Empire the emperor, in fact an absolute monarch, had in theory been merely the *princeps,* the first among equals; the fifth century in the West saw this theory approaching reality despite the continued outward maintenance of the externals of imperial pomp and splendor. Basic to this increased power of the nobles was their vast wealth, which has already been noticed. In one aspect the economic history of the Roman Empire may be subsumed as a process whereby the wealthy became fewer and fewer, but those few richer and richer. From the political point of view the dangerous aspect of this phenomenon was the fact that the state, the economic resources at the command of the emperor, was becoming poorer and poorer. Various attempts have been made by modern scholars to estimate the revenues and expenses of the West Roman government in the fifth century; although these attempts disagree among themselves as to detail, one thing is clear and certain; the revenues of the state were rapidly diminishing with the increasing impoverishment of both the human and material resources of the Empire and by the progressive loss of province after province to the collection of taxes, as well as by the frequent devastation of areas still more or less nominally under the control of the imperial government.

At the same time, of course, while the loss of territories entailed the diminution of some of the expenses of the state, the latter, especially its military needs, by no means proportionately de-

114 Grosse, *Römische,* pp. 201, 260–62, 266–67, 269; Demougeot, *Unité,* pp. 22–24.
115 Cf. Jones, *Roman Empire,* I, 201.

creased.[116] On the other hand the private revenues of the great noble landowners were reaching fantastic proportions; a generally credible historian of the fifth century tells us that many such households had annual incomes of four thousand pounds of gold; in the second class were aggregates of property bringing in a thousand or fifteen hundred pounds; these figures do not include the income in kind. Correspondingly huge sums were spent by these nobles in conspicuous consumption of all sorts.[117] One student has estimated that the revenues of a noble of highest wealth in the fifth century approached one tenth of the entire revenue of the state itself.[118] Even if from motives of conservatism or prudence we reduce this fraction to a twentieth, the proportion is staggering. The rate of taxation rose steadily in the Later Roman Empire, and bore hardly upon the population in general;[119] just as surely, if the figures for the incomes of the great Roman nobles are even approximately correct, they were not suffering from the rate. It becomes more evident why the imperial government found it difficult to maintain an adequate army or navy; it could not afford them. This economic disparity, or rather equality, between the government and its great subjects made it necessary to cater to the selfishness of the nobles, who were reluctantly willing to part with portions of their huge incomes only in the greatest emergencies,[120] by removing, or imposing and then hastily removing, tax burdens which the aristocrats felt onerous. So far did their assiduous preser-

[116] For a general statement: Salvian *Gub. Dei* 6. 43 (cf. 1. 11) who speaks of the "calamitas . . . fisci" and the "mendicitas . . . Romani aerarii." On the decline of revenues as between the beginning and middle of the fifth century, Stein, *Hist.*, I, 342–44 and nn.; Sundwall, *Studien*, pp. 154–58, with the criticisms of Bury, *Hist.*, I, 53, n. 3, 253, n. 5; A. Segré, "Essays on Byzantine Economic History, I. The *Annona Civica* and the *Annona Militaris*," *Byzantion*, XVI (1942–43), 393–444, at 435–38; Mac-Mullen, *Soldier*, p. 85, n. 33; Demougeot, *Unité*, pp. 505–7.

[117] Olympiod. Frag. 44 (IV, 67–68). These figures are commonly accepted and quoted by modern historians; yet I must confess certain misgivings on contemplating the amounts of gold involved in view of the decline of the monetary economy and of agriculture, for presumably these colossal fortunes were primarily in land. Yet cf. Tjäder, 1 (= Marini, 73) with L. Ruggini, *Economia e società nell' "Italia Annonaria,"* pp. 558–59. Greg. Tur. *HF* 2. 24 tells us the Gallic noble Ecdicius fed 4,000 in a famine; cf. in general, Sundwall, *Studien*, p. 153.

[118] Stein, *Hist.*, I, 583, n. 116.

[119] A. H. M. Jones, "Over-Taxation and the Decline of the Roman Empire," *Antiquity*, XXXIII (1959), 39–43, estimates a rise from one-tenth to one-fourth or one-third as between the Republic and the Late Empire.

[120] Stein, *Hist.*, I, 342.

vation of the traditions of ancient Rome diverge from their practice in the present.[121]

To have forced these great men to disgorge what our age, for example, would consider only an adequate fraction of their vast wealth for the benefit of the state was in practical terms impossible; the government, for all its relatively large and oppressive bureaucracy, simply did not have the means to do so with equity, with all the surveys and estimates such a procedure would entail. Outright confiscation would have been justly viewed as tyranny and probably have provoked civil war and the government's own overthrow at a time when it needed more than all its energies to cope with the barbarians. No government, no matter how theoretically absolute, could oppose the united resistance of those who constituted the most important class of its subjects economically, and therefore socially, politically, and culturally. But the government could not act thus, even if so radical and illegal a measure had occurred to the Emperor, for the government itself was in the hands of these great aristocrats. While in the East the great offices of the state were ordinarily held by members of the middle classes who had risen by their own talents to positions of authority, in the West those offices had become a virtual monopoly of the great nobles, who administered the state and advised the emperor, commonly in their own interest.[122] In turn, a large part of the reason for this situation was a precipitous decline in the West of the educated middle class from which loyal bureaucrats could be recruited.[123] And one suspects that such persons of this nature as there were tended to be attracted by the relative security and esteem of the Church; since their class found the oppressions of the bureaucracy particularly hateful, such

121 Cf. the remarks of N. D. Fustel de Coulanges, *Histoire des institutions politiques de l'ancienne France*, II, *L'invasion germanique et la fin de l'empire*, 205–6.

122 E. Stein, *Untersuchungen über das Officium der Prätorianerpräfektur seit Diokletian*, pp. 71–73; C. H. Coster, *The Iudicium Quinquevirale*, p. 4; G. Gigli, *La crisi dell' impero romano*, pp. 132–35; C. Dawson, *The Making of Europe*, p. 86; Stroheker, *Adel*, pp. 18, 35; W. G. Sinnigen, *The Officium of the Urban Prefecture during the Later Roman Empire*, p. 83 (an example of the greater powers of a Western minister over his subordinates than that of his Eastern counterpart); Stein, *Hist.*, I, 223; K. F. Stroheker, "Politische Kräfte in der Auflösung des weströmischen Reiches," *Orpheus*, I (1954), 68–75, at 70–71; Jones, *Roman Empire*, I, 177.

123 One compares the situation in medieval Germany where in the absence of an educated middle class to administer the state, the emperors were compelled to use the services of the tribal (stem) dukes, although the power of the latter was dangerous to that of the emperor himself.

men would frequently hesitate to enter it. Before this social and financial situation, a whole nexus of vicious circles, Galla Placidia and later her son were helpless; even had the two of them been gifted with the strength of personality of a Charlemagne or a Napoleon, it is in the highest degree unlikely that they would have been able to reverse so fundamental a tendency of their time, by which the typical qualities of medieval society were already appearing within the still-standing framework of the ancient Empire. Had Placidia solved these interlocking problems, it is hardly too much to say that she would have reversed the decline and fall of the West Roman Empire; it also seems safe to say that no statesman in history to this day would have been equal to the task.[124] The processes of decline had been continuing for centuries by 425; many more centuries would elapse before they would reverse themselves, and then without the planned intervention of any person. The power of the great nobles was a fact, and Placidia must live with it; the choice of Rome for her son's accession is doubtless to be viewed partly as a means to impress and, it might be hoped, to win the loyalty of the great Roman nobles by this gesture made to one of the ancient traditions to which they were attached· that if emperors were made elsewhere than at Rome, they should not be. Presumably another motive was to overawe the same nobles with the concrete evidence of the solidarity between East and West and the actuality of the support she and her son had from the other branch of their family,[125] for the pride of place of these great men was colossal, and their self-identification with the greatness of Rome something they took for granted.[126] Probably in practical politics the only realistic course was to conciliate the great landowners. Such an attempt at conciliation would be one of the earliest acts of Placidia's regime.

Another palliative to which both she and her son would resort, to try to counterbalance both the nobles and the generals as well as promote the cohesion of the Empire, was to ally the state with the Church, finding sorely needed administrative talent there (although already there was a marked tendency for great nobles to become bishops of the Church; as such they were unlikely entirely

124 Cf. W. Goetz, *Ravenna*, p. 18.
125 Cf. Sirago, *Placidia*, p. 254.
126 Stroheker, *Adel*, p. 17, citing Sym. *Ep.* 1. 52; *Or.* 5. 3.

to forget their origins or the interests of their class). Placidia's first legislative act, as noted above, was a measure to conciliate the Church. Significantly, however, in that constitution she continued to show the favor her husband had shown to the "political" Bishop Patroclus, specifically entrusting him with the correction of heretical bishops.[127] In Placidia's time the danger to the state from the power of the Church was beginning to appear, but as yet the state had the upper hand.

Problems of the same nature as these also vexed the Eastern Empire; yet the latter survived for a thousand years, while the imperial structure in the West had totally collapsed a quarter of a century after Placidia's death. The reason may be fairly simple: the West was economically poorer than the East, culture and civilization were less firmly rooted, the population was numerically inferior. The same emergencies, as it were, dissipated perhaps roughly similar amounts of the assets of both halves of the Empire; but the East simply had more of those assets and did not founder.[128] The Western dependency on the East for assistance during crises in the fifth century obviously demonstrates the superiority of the East. Yet naturally the East under a separate government consulted its own interests first, as in its abandonment of the war against the Vandals to deal with the Huns; in turn the West had to make

[127] *CSirm.* 6; cf. Sirago, *Placidia,* pp. 261–63. It is hardly true, however, as Sirago concludes, that the Church remained autonomous under Placidia and Valentinian III; like Placidia and Constantius their son also would interfere in Church affairs. On the coincidence of interests of Church and state, see also Solari, *Rinnovamento,* I, 333–34.

[128] Concise statement by Lynn White, *The Transformation of the Roman World,* pp. 303–4; more details in Bark, pp. 45–66. A. R. Lewis, *Naval Power and Trade in the Mediterranean A.D. 500–1100,* p. 12, suggests that while the Empire remained effectively under one government the wealth of the East could be used to support the West, but regardless of theory when the East came to lead a separate existence the West was left to its own inadequate resources and collapsed. Cf. *Ep. Caes.* 48. 18; Theodosius makes good the exactions of the tyrant Maximus (or Eugenius; cf. Güldenpenning and Ifland, *Theodosius,* p. 165 and n. 22) from the resources of the East. Prisc. Frag. 30 (IV, 104) alludes to the separation of the two parts of the Empire, or rather of the imperial positions, as detrimental to the West. The view of Lot (e.g., *Nouvelles recherches,* pp. 159–79) that the West was not economically inferior to the East is not convincing. One might suggest that at least the unfavorable difference in high military command in the West was the result of a historical accident: the ascendancy of Stilicho; but someone had to rule for Honorius, and the superficial or immediate problems of the Empire were military, so almost certainly it would be a general. To go further and speculate on the situation if Honorius had been a strong emperor would open up an endless and ever-widening and uncontrollable vista of footless speculation about what might have been.

peace with Geiseric (442). The good relations with the East which continued for the remainder of Placidia's life were founded not only upon dynastic reasons but on those of state as well. Apparently, for example, during the first years of her regime Placidia allowed the Eastern government to name both consuls,[129] or acquiesced in the practice. Such a desire to placate the Eastern government may also be evidenced in the continued use in the West of coin types of Eastern origin;[130] the practice also served to remind Westerners of the identity of policies and interests of East and West, and therefore of the ultimate support of the Western government by the East. In turn Eastern coins, at least the major gold issues, duly commemorated Valentinian III.[131] Whatever the external difficulties of the West during the next quarter-century, its internal concord was maintained, in all probability, in large part by the support the dynasty had in the East.[132]

Under Galla Placidia the Western Empire, despite various alarms and some losses, did reasonably well; it may be questioned, however, how far this was the work of the Empress. Certainly Aëtius must receive much of the credit. Yet there were no real departures of policy, no novelties or signs of original statesmanship; the Empress participated actively, and frequently decisively, in forming policy during the dozen years following 425, but one can hardly hold that she decisively altered, or affected, the fate of the Roman state or society.[133] It seems not unfair to conclude that she tried mainly to conserve; to conserve both imperial power and Empire for her son.

[129] Palanque, *RÉA*, XLVI (1944), 288.

[130] Boyce, *Festal*, p. 52, but Western types did begin to appear fairly soon, *ibid.*, p. 67; cf. I. Maull, "Le zecche nell' antica Ravenna," *Felix Ravenna*, LXXXIV (1961), 79–134, at 91.

[131] Hill, Kent, and Carson, *Bronze*, p. 43.

[132] Bury, *Hist.*, I, 240; Güldenpenning, *Arcad. und Theod.*, p. 263.

[133] Hence I would take exception to Sirago's full title: *Galla Placidia e la trasformazione politica dell' occidente.*

# 6

# GALLA PLACIDIA
# AUGUSTA

Galla Placidia could expect, and obtained, the backing of the East as a principal mainstay of her power in the West; yet obviously in the nature of the case, appeal to the resources of the East must be reserved for great emergencies; only the existence of this support in the background could be used as an ordinary instrument of everyday politics as a deterrent against those who might otherwise be tempted to intrigue against the throne itself, such as the undoubtedly strongly suspect Aëtius. Since she herself could not command armies, Placidia must exercise extreme caution in making high military appointments. Accordingly her choice for the post of Master of Both Branches of the Soldiery, the highest command of all, fell upon a certain Flavius Constantius Felix.[1] The only hint we have concerning his antecedents is the possibility that his wife Padusia may be identical with the Spadousa said to have been a close friend and councillor of Placidia during the political struggles at her brother's court after the death of Constantius III.[2] Whether in fact Felix had been an old adherent of Galla Placidia, the almost complete lack of previous information about him in our sources may in itself be significant. Military exploits are a category of information which the records

1 Sirago, *Placidia,* pp. 265 and n. 2, 265–66, says that Felix dominated Placidia during the years 425–30 (but the sole evidence adduced for this belief, Prosp. 1294 [I, 471], refers the "arbitrium" of Felix only to the intrigue against Boniface) and that Felix represented the interests of the Eastern court in Ravenna; there is not a shred of evidence to support this latter contention. See Pl. VII.

2 See above, Ch. V, n. 2.

of the fifth century mention by preference in second place only to ecclesiastical developments. We may hazard the guess that Felix was a politician or courtier (the two terms are largely synonymous for Placidia's day) without any particular military qualifications. If this is so, then it is fairly easy to discern the purpose of the Empress in making this high appointment. She was promoting an astute politician (at least he was given to the intrigues and conspiracies which form so much of the substance of politics at the court of an absolute, or theoretically absolute, monarch), but above all she was trying to find a solution to the problem of the generals. By conferring the all-highest military command under the Emperor himself on a military nonentity she might hope to avoid the overweening power which great military prestige combined with that office created, to the detriment of the imperial authority itself. She had two able generals, Aëtius and Boniface; in this fashion she kept them at one step removed from the throne by interposing a level of authority between them and herself.

In fact Placidia found herself in the difficult position of needing able generals for the defense of the realm, yet dreading a general whose prestige or power should become too great. And in this she followed the ancient, traditional policy of the Roman emperors, who had long before reserved triumphs to themselves and, particularly if they were weak or suspicious, had feared military successes gained by their subjects. From the beginning the emperor had been, and must remain, *the* successful general. Yet unavoidably a woman and a child must be militarily weak.[3] If Placidia expected, however, that Felix would remain her docile and obedient tool, she was apparently soon undeceived. As late as 425 she evidently regarded Patroclus of Arles with the highest favor, but the next year a certain Barnabus hacked the Bishop to death and Felix was believed to be responsible. Indeed, Felix seems to have extended his intrigues, to what end is irrecoverably lost, into the Church, for he also had a certain Titus, Deacon of the Roman church, murdered.[4] Yet one cannot deduce from these clerical murders that Felix belonged to an antichurchly party,[5] for he was

---

[3] Felix' position, *ILS*, 1293, 1298; Hyd. 84 (II, 21; cf. Ensslin, *Klio*, XXIV [1931], 475–76; the reference to his Patriciate belongs in 429). In general: Sundwall, *Studien*, no. 170, pp. 76–77.

[4] Prosp. 1292 (I, 471).

[5] As does Wurm, *De Rebus Gestis*, pp. 22–23.

also closely enough associated with another deacon named Grunitus for the latter to be involved in his downfall in 430.[6] In any event Felix was conventionally pious, and together with his wife Padusia presented a mosaic for the apse of the Lateran Basilica in Rome (not long before his death).[7] The retention of Felix in office after 426, however, may indicate that in a short period of time he had so consolidated his power that Placidia feared to attempt his removal; or she may have refused to believe that he was in fact responsible for the death of Patroclus. On the other hand, in 427 by some means Felix seems to have procured the withdrawal of the Huns from Pannonia (at the great bend of the Danube);[8] since we know almost nothing of the circumstances, it is uncertain whether this success on Felix' part was a move against Aëtius, the friend of the Huns, or not. If it was a move against Aëtius, the Patroclus affair would indicate that Felix was acting primarily in his own interest, although presumably Placidia would not have been unwilling to see the power of Aëtius diminished.

For in the years immediately after 425 Aëtius in Gaul was rapidly building a reputation for success with its resulting prestige in a manner reminding one of Constantius' exploits there the previous decade. Here he commanded at first with the rank of Count; it is uncertain whether as Count of the Domestics or as Count and Master (of the Horse?) for the Gauls.[9] Flavius Aëtius made a great impression both on his contemporaries and on subsequent generations, as the favorable opinion of the historian Renatus Profuturus Frigeridus and the general's versifying panegyrist Merobaudes bear witness. In appearance he was of average stature, but well-formed in a manly way, we are told, and possessed of a quick in-

---

[6] Prosp. 1303 (I, 473).

[7] *ILS*, 1293; titles of Felix indicate the dedication was made in 429 or 430.

[8] Marcell. *s.a.* 427, 1 (II, 76); Jord. *Get.* 166 says the Goths and Romans expelled the Huns, but the participation of the Goths (except possibly for some Gothic mercenaries) is improbable and doubtless pure invention. Felix is regularly held responsible for this evacuation of Pannonia by the Huns, presumably because he conducted military affairs at Ravenna and Aëtius was busy in Gaul. The passage of Marcellinus, especially the statement that the Huns had held Pannonia for fifty years, is the subject of considerable controversy among scholars; cf., e.g., Alföldi, *Untergang*, II, 66, 94; Mazzarino, *Stilicone*, pp. 140–57; Lot, *RÉA*, XXXVIII (1936), 303; Thompson, *Attila*, p. 26; Ensslin, *Philolog. Wochinschrift*, XLVII (1927), 847, 851; F. Altheim, *Geschichte der Hunnen*, IV, 186; etc.

[9] Cf. Ensslin, *Klio*, XXIV (1931), 476–77, with *Ann. ép.*, 1950, no. 30.

telligence. He was an excellent horseman and well versed in the use of bow and spear. Foremost general and accomplished statesman, we may add that he was also a practitioner of unscrupulous *Realpolitik*,[10] and had no hesitation at using the Huns to forward his personal ambition as well as the welfare of the Empire. In 425 he had used the Huns to procure high command as well as pardon for himself, yet perhaps characteristically he had done nothing for Castinus. Frigeridus also tells us that he was not avaricious (like so many of his eminent contemporaries), not given to vice, but untiring in application, courageous, easily enduring injury, hunger, thirst, wakefulness.[11] In the sixth century Procopius is at loss whether he or Boniface should be dubbed "the last of the Romans."[12] He was born about 391,[13] and was thus roughly contemporary with Placidia. He was born in the East, in the city of Durostorum, the son of Gaudentius, a magnate of the adjacent province of Scythia (Rumania south of the Danube mouth).[14] Gaudentius had been a general of Stilicho and had risen to be Master of the Mounted Soldiers,[15] but had been assassinated by the soldiery in Gaul;[16] Aëtius' mother was a noble and wealthy Italian.[17] Aëtius himself was to marry twice; his first wife was the daughter of Carpilio (marriage before 423); she bore him a son also named Carpilio. Presumably she died long before her husband, for he married again; his second wife was a lady of royal Gothic descent who also bore him a son, named Gaudentius after his paternal grandfather.[18] It is quite likely that his second wife was

---

[10] Cf. Hassebrauk, *Westrom*, pp. 5–6.

[11] Ren. Prof. Frig. *ap.* Greg. Tur. *HF* 2. 8, possibly based on Merob. *Pan.* 1. Frag. IB; cf. G. Lizerand, *Aetius*, p. 19, n. 2; Clover, "Merobaudes," pp. 25–26. His portrait may be preserved to us in a diptych in the Museum of Bourges; see Delbrueck, *Consulardiptychen*, no. 37, pp. 158–61; atlas, pl. 37.

[12] *Bell.* 3 (*Vand.* 1). 3. 15.

[13] Seeck, *Gesch.*, VI: 2, 413. Bugiani, *Storia*, p. 34 and n. 4, puts his birth a bit later, in 395 or 396. On Aëtius in general, see Sundwall, *Studien*, no. 5, pp. 40–42.

[14] Jord. *Get.* 176; Ren. Prof. Frig. *ap.* Greg. Tur. *HF* 2. 8; cf. Lizerand, *Aetius*, p. 15.

[15] Ren. Prof. Frig. *ap.* Greg. Tur. *HF* 2. 8.

[16] *Chron. Gall. a. 452* 100 (I, 658); Merobaud. *Pan.* 2. 112–15.

[17] Frig. *ap.* Greg. Tur. *HF* 2. 8.

[18] For the evidence and its interpretation, see A. Loyen, *Recherches historiques sur les panégyriques de Sidoine Apollinaire*, p. 67 and n. 1; Lizerand, *Aetius*, p. 18, n. 2; Wurm, *De Rebus Gestis*, pp. 56–57; Bugiani, *Storia*, pp. 138–39; Clover, "Merobaudes," pp. 22–23.

none other than Pelagia, the second wife and widow of his enemy
Boniface.[19] In his boyhood or youth Aëtius was a hostage for three
years among the Goths, and then again among the Huns; at least
among the former he learned the military exercises for whose
mastery he was renowned in later life;[20] among the latter people
he formed the friendships which were to be so profitable for his
career through most of his life. At home as a boy Aëtius, like many
sons of eminent fathers, became either a tribune and notary or a
functionary of the Praetorian Prefect.[21] Under John he served in a
supervising capacity in the maintenance of the imperial palaces;
but after a short while he was sent to the Huns to obtain help, with
the results we have seen. In Gaul, in accordance with his commission, he relieved the siege of Arles by the Visigoths and forced
them to return to the lands assigned them in Aquitaine. In 428 he
compelled the Ripuarian Franks to relinquish territory they had
seized on the left bank of the Rhine.[22] Thereafter he also defeated
a coalition of the barbarian Juthungi with rebellious (peasant
class?) provincials in the province of Noricum (north of Italy—
430–31).[23] It seems quite likely that these as well as subsequent
military victories of Aëtius were won with the aid of Hunnish
auxiliaries, perhaps some of those he had led into Italy in 425 and
who remained attached to him instead of returning to their home
like their fellows.[24]

In the secular Diocese of Africa Boniface continued as the head
of the military establishment and the principal official of the land,
as before with the title of Count of Africa. There he had performed
meritorious service against the incursions of the desert tribes; but
he seems to have fallen away from orthodoxy after he married
Pelagia, a former Arian. It is quite possible that Boniface was

19 Joh. Ant. Frag. 201. 3 (IV, 615). He may also have had a daughter by one of his
marriages, since *Add. Prosp. Haun. ad* 455 (I, 303) qualifies Thraustila, assassin of
Valentinian III, as the son-in-law of Aëtius.

20 Frig. *ap.* Greg. Tur. *HF* 2. 8; Merobaud. *Carm.* 4. 42–46; *Pan.* 2. 127–43; Zos.
5. 36. 1.

21 Frig. *ap.* Greg. Tur. *HF* 2. 8, with the comment of Stein, *Prätorianerpräfektur,*
p. 5, n. 1; Demougeot, *Unité,* p. 130, n. 70; A. Degrassi, "L'iscrizione in onore di Aezio
e l' 'Atrium Libertatis,'" *Bullettino della Comm. Archeolog. Comm. di Roma,*
LXXII (1946–48), 33–44, at 34, n. 10.

22 Possibly on this occasion, to oppose the Franks, Aëtius recalled the last Roman
troops from Britain; cf. Demougeot, *Moyen Age,* LXVIII (1962), 38.

23 On Noricum, see Dahn, *Urgeschichte,* II, 411–12; Loyen, *Recherches,* pp. 43–44,
on Ap. Sid. *Carm.* 7. 233–37.

24 Cf. Lizerand, *Aetius,* p. 23.

disappointed in not being rewarded for his loyalty to Placidia by being named to a higher command.[25] Although his position in Africa was already among the most influential and powerful in the Western Empire, Placidia could have granted him the title of Master of the Soldiers in Africa; there was precedent in her father's promoting Gildo to that rank a generation before; instead merely the title of Count of the Domestic Troops was conferred upon him.[26] The fact that the Empress did not recognize his sterling services by the grant of a higher title may mean that she was as scandalized by his toleration toward the Arians and by other moral lapses as was Saint Augustine.[27] Something like this is needed to explain her willingness to listen to the accusations of a court cabal against the commander of Africa.

It had been common practice for Roman emperors early in their reigns to promise moderation and justice and frequently special privileges to senators. Galla Placidia also attempted to conciliate the Senate, or rather its members, in this ancient fashion. On 1 January 426 Valentinian III had entered upon the consulship at Rome; his doing so was in itself a gracious gesture to the Senate, as had been his remaining in the City since his elevation by Helion. On 3 January an imperial constitution was directed to the Senate in his name; probably it was read in his presence in the Senate house by one of the great officers of state, very likely the Theodosius, "first on the list of the notaries," who is stated to have performed this function on 24 February. If the Emperor was indeed present, that fact too was undoubtedly meant to be taken as a sign of his recognition of the importance and greatness of the venerable body which Cineas, ambassador of King Pyrrhus of Epirus, had long centuries before likened to an assembly of kings. The compilers of imperial legislation have preserved to us some of the statements made in the imperial oration on this occasion. Presumably Placidia began with a general statement that the rights of senators would be respected; this was traditional, even although her predecessors commonly modified the principle in practice as

---

[25] Diesner, *Kirche und Staat,* p. 112; Ensslin, *RE,* XX: 2 (1950), 1922; L. Schmidt, "Bonifatius und der Uebergang der Wandalen nach Afrika," *Hist. Vierteljahrschrift,* II (1899), 449–62, at 455. In 425 or 426 Boniface may well have put in a personal appearance at court; cf. Diesner, *Kirche und Staat,* p. 107, n. 27.

[26] August. *Ep.* 220. 7.

[27] *Ep.* 220. 4; cf. Lot, *Destinées,* p. 54.

expediency dictated, and some of them can hardly have meant what they said when they said it; but as politicians they were well aware that men are ruled by words.[28] Malicious prosecutors and informers were denounced (this too was traditional). Slaves were to be strictly under the control of their masters (of obvious interest to men of great wealth). Senators were to be sued only in their proper court, that of the City Prefect. Tenants of imperial estates shall not have special privileges, but "they must obey the laws by which even princes are constrained." Provincial governors were not to impose compulsory services or contributions (*munera*) on senators.[29]

On 24 February, by another edict read to the Senate by Theodosius, Placidia was graciously pleased to remit to the Senate part of the *aurum oblaticium,* a gift of gold made by the senators to the Emperor at New Year; another part was presented to their beloved City of Rome itself.[30] We should probably also see in a law of 30 March, at least partly, another measure aimed at placating the senators: *coloni* (peasants attached to the soil; the great nobles had thousands of them) were not to be allowed to enter the imperial service (thus escaping their masters) even at the lowest levels. The law further provided that freedmen were also excluded from the service of the state or emperor, although sons of freedmen might fill lower positions; detestation of upstart freedmen was also a traditional prejudice of the Roman aristocracy.[31] In a law of 25 February 429, Placidia in effect confirmed the right of great landholders to collect taxes from their own lands, a practice that had been evolving in the fourth century.[32] This practice was not dissimilar to that permitted by the so-called grants of *immunitas* in Merovingian Gaul in the Early Middle Ages, which allowed the landholders concerned to collect taxes and administer justice on their lands—one of the precedents leading to feudalism in subsequent centuries. Thus Placidia undoubtedly hoped to ingratiate herself with the senators from the beginning. She had by no means,

28 There is no explicit evidence of such a general statement, but it was traditional, and is probably implied in the extant portions of the imperial oration on this occasion.

29 *CTh* 10. 10. 33 (cf. 2. 1. 4), 26. 2; repeated in address to Bassus, Praetorian Prefect of Italy, on 6 March, from Ravenna: 10. 26. 1; *CJ* 12. 1. 14.

30 *CTh* 6. 2. 25 (cf. 7. 24. 1); Ensslin is probably right in thinking, *RE*, VIIA: 2 (1948), 2235, that *CJ* 12. 3. 1 (regulation of precedence) was probably not part of this law, but issued by Theodosius II.

31 *CTh* 4. 10. 3; *CJ* 11. 48. 18 (the law also treated of purely technical matters, *CJ* 5. 4. 21).

32 *CTh* 11. 1. 34; cf. Courtois, *Vandales*, p. 133; M. Gelzer, *Studien zur byzantinischen Verwaltung Ägyptens*, p. 89.

however, forgotten the Church, which both piety and policy urged her to conciliate. A law of 7 April 426 placed heavy disabilities on the rights of apostates from Christianity with regard to wills and bequests; on the other hand, Jewish or Samaritan converts to Christianity might not be disinherited by their parents or grandparents.[33] It may be worth noting that on 30 January 426 Placidia issued a law dealing with the technicalities of inheritance in which she laid heavy emphasis on the rights of mothers to succeed to the estate of a child.[34] Perhaps the Empress is revealing her own strong convictions on the importance of mothers.

There can be no doubt of her real interest in the law in general and her active participation in the process of legislation. On 7 November 426, from Ravenna she issued an imperial constitution; this law treated the technicalities of inheritance further and at length, but it also laid down two rules of general interest. The first of these was the famous, some students would wrongly say infamous, "Law of Citations." This statute named certain jurisconsults of the classical age of Roman law as canonical and prescribed to judges the method to be followed in accepting their opinions as law in court. Where the opinions of these great lawyers differed, the opinion of the majority was to prevail; if, however, the opinions were evenly divided between two opposing groups, then the opinion followed by Papinian (*fl.* A.D. 200) was to prevail. Only if Papinian's authority were not available to break the tie was the judge himself allowed to decide between the two opinions held by an equal number of jurisconsults on either side.[35] Obviously this was an entirely mechanical, unsubtle, gross, unscientific method of determining the law in any given case. To condemn it, however, is to forget the historical situation in which it was promulgated. The fifth century, even in the East, was a period of decline of legal

---

33 *CTh* 16. 7. 7, 8. 28.
34 *CTh* 5. 1. 7.
35 *CTh* 1. 4. 3; there is much discussion among historians of the Roman law whether some of the additional provisions of this section, not mentioned in the text above, are later interpolations, but they need not concern us here. On the law, see, e.g., H. J. Wolff, *Roman Law: An Historical Introduction*, pp. 159–61; Seeck, *Gesch.*, VI: 1, 170, could not resist a sneer at the "juristische Verständnislosigkeit" of a woman; F. Wieacker, *Recht und Gesellschaft in der Spätantike*, pp. 35, 88–108, points out in effect that some of the laws in *CTh* are imprecise and difficult to understand because their framers were more interested in bombastic rhetoric than in law; W. W. Buckland, *A Text-Book of Roman Law from Augustus to Justinian*, 2d ed., p. 33; F. Schulz, *History of Roman Legal Science*, pp. 281–82; Jörs, *s.v.* "Citiergesetz," *RE*, III: 2 (1899), 2608–12.

studies; that decline was even more pronounced in the West, where what higher education still remained tended to be engrossed entirely by rhetorical and literary studies.[36] The age was also one of venal and corrupt judges and judges' staffs. In fact Galla Placidia was exhibiting no mean instinct of statesmanship; she was trying to render the administration of the law as foolproof as she could in opposition to the growing ignorance and ubiquitous corruption and injustice of the times. As early as Constantine the Great's reign, a century before, the emperors had been trying to find some easy rule to guide lawyers and the courts through the vast, scattered, and almost impenetrable thickets of the opinions of the jurisconsults, supposititious opinions, and the commentaries upon commentaries on the books of the great lawyers.[37] Galla Placidia was also trying to find a solution to this dilemma; in fact, however, the problem would not be solved until the compilation of the *Digest* of the opinions of the great jurisconsults in the next century as part of the work of codification of the Eastern Emperor Justinian, itself made possible only by the revival of legal studies in the East in the sixth century.

Most of the later emperors of Rome strove in vain but manfully, according to their lights, to procure some sort of equity and justice for their subjects. Emperors sometimes gave legal relief to special cases (in a manner roughly corresponding, perhaps, to the workings of private bills in the English Parliament or the American Congress); they also issued legislation of general import. One of the abuses against which in their preserved legislation the late emperors repeatedly thundered, in vain, was the illegal use of special legal remedies as precedents applying in other cases. In this same constitution Placidia also tried, not very successfully, to distinguish between general and special laws, with the usual fulminations against those who maliciously confounded the two.[38] The fact that Galla Placidia thus addressed herself to basic questions of the legal administration of the Empire so soon after her attainment of supreme power attests her previous interest in the law and her belief in its importance. In turn this lends no inconsiderable confirmation to the view that the opinions about the importance of

---

[36] On the decline of legal studies, see Am. Marc. 30. 4. 14–17; *NTh* 1. *praef.* and 1.
[37] Cf. *CTh* 1. 4. 1–2.
[38] *CJ* 1. 14. 2–3; cf. Jones, *Roman Empire,* I, 472; for the other, technical, passages of this constitution see the complete list of citations in Seeck, *Regesten,* p. 352.

law expressed by Athaulf at Narbonne were in fact derived from Placidia. Note also her statement in the programmatic imperial oration of 3 January 426 that emperors themselves are bound by the law. In another *obiter dictum* in a statute of 11 June 429 she remarks, "that the Emperor profess himself bound by the laws is a sentiment worthy of the ruler's majesty; so much is Our power (*auctoritas*) dependent on the power of the law (*iuris*); and indeed that the imperial office be subject to the laws is more important than the imperial power (itself). And by the pronouncement of the present decree We point to what We do not allow to be permitted to Ourself."[39] This law deals with imperial estates, and in accordance with the foregoing principle she declares, "For We frankly define by this edict that the possession of property leased in perpetuity cannot be transferred even if the Emperor himself should give it to another, whether of his own accord or upon petition."[40] In a law of 25 February 429, regulating the collection of taxes in Africa, she permits appeals from the representatives of the imperial domains to the court of the Proconsul of Africa, "for We do not disdain that the law be common to Us and to private persons, if the reverence for Our Majesty is preserved."[41] There can be little doubt that this is the authentic voice of Galla Placidia speaking here, rather than that of a minister, for there were two theories about the relation of the emperor to the law in the Late Empire. The one, of Hellenistic origin, held that the emperor was above the law, that he was himself living law, and it was this view which eventually triumphed. The other, going back to the Rome of the Republic and Early Empire, held that the emperor was bound by the law. Since these two different theories were available, we may be sure that the principle that the emperor was inferior to the law would not be promulgated by an official without direct reference to the Empress. Of course in ordinary fact, theory apart, emperors legislated much as they pleased according to the circumstances and their inclinations.[42]

The constitutions of the emperors (laws or decrees) were ob-

[39] *CJ* 1. 14. 4.
[40] *CJ* 11. 71. 5. 1.
[41] *CTh* 11. 30. 68; citations to other passages of the law in Seeck, *Regesten*, p. 354.
[42] On the question of the attitude of Placidia to the law and its importance, see *CP*, LXIII (1968), 114–21, where the two theories about the relation of emperor and law are also discussed. To the references on the two theories in n. 29 of that article, add, now, Dvornik, *Political Philosophy*, II, 659–66.

viously the most important source of law of all; yet these were mostly scattered about the governmental offices of the whole Empire. There was no single official collection of them, and two private collections made in the reign of Diocletian (284–305) only partially supplied the lack. In 429 Theodosius II appointed a commission to collect the imperial constitutions since the days of Diocletian's successor Constantine the Great. After various vicissitudes the *Theodosian Code* was completed and officially promulgated in the East, and subsequently in the West in 438. What is particularly interesting in this connection, however, is that a very high proportion of the constitutions embodied in the *Code* must have come from the archives of Italy and Africa (most of the other provinces of the West were in too distracted a condition to make legal scholarship feasible, and many of their archives must have been destroyed in the convulsions of the recent past);[43] in turn, this fact implies with some probability that the government of the West, that is, Galla Placidia, actively cooperated in the compilation of the *Code;* again the fact is evidence for her interest in the law. Mistakes of various kinds, especially in dating for a variety of reasons, are not uncommon in the *Code;* such mistakes, however, are rarely found in the laws of Valentinian III incorporated therein. It follows that Placidia sent a carefully prepared collection of her son's (that is, her own) legislation to Constantinople for the use of the compilers.[44] The rule laid down by Theodosius II, that when two constitutions disagree the later shall prevail,[45] is not dissimilar in general spirit to Placidia's Law of Citations; one is tempted to surmise some mutual influence between the legal projects of the Eastern Emperor and his aunt.

The Empress obviously had high ideals for the administration of Roman justice under Roman law; at the same time, however, she had always to be attentive to the needs of practical politics; always the intrigues of the great generals to attain a position from which they could dominate the throne and Empire necessarily preoccupied a large part of her attention. A conspiracy against the faithful Boniface, who nevertheless was apparently suffering under her displeasure, was to have the most fateful results for the Empire.

---

43 Seeck, *Gesch.,* VI: 1, 175–76; *idem, Regesten,* p. 12; Mommsen, however, thought that some private collection of an African lawyer was used.
44 Seeck, *Regesten,* p. 29.
45 *CTh* 1. 1. 5.

Felix,[46] technically Boniface's military superior,[47] and aware of the Empress' presumptive coldness toward the Count, prevailed upon her to recall the latter from his important post. Although, presumably, in persuading the Empress to take this step, he could point to various recent derelictions of duty by Boniface,[48] we may be sure that his primary purpose was to rid himself of one of his two principal rivals. In any event, Boniface refused to obey the summons,[49] whether or not he had been informed by Felix or some other friend or foe that his recall was intended to work his destruction. It was justly regarded as a cause for fear and trembling

[46] Prosp. 1294 (I, 471) attributes the move against Boniface to Felix; Procop. *Bell.* 3 (*Vand.* 1). 3. 14–21 (followed by later Byzantine writers) attributes the responsibility to Aëtius. Prosper is a Western contemporary; Procopius lived in the next century and is frequently demonstrably wrong about events before his own time. Later Aëtius did become the great adversary of Boniface; in the next century Aëtius' long and successful career still loomed large, while Felix, whose known career extended only from 425 to 430, was largely forgotten. There can be little doubt, therefore, that the author of this intrigue was Felix, not Aëtius. Modern discussions are numerous: for the argument see Ensslin, *RE*, XX: 2 (1950), 1924; *idem, Klio,* XXIV (1931), 478; Freeman, *Western Europe,* p. 326, see also, among most writers, Diesner, *Kirche und Staat,* p. 112; Schmidt, *Wandalen,* pp. 55, 57; *idem, Hist. Vierteljahrschrift,* II (1889), 455–56. Among recent writers, however, who prefer Aëtius, see A. Audollent, *s.v.* "Bonifacius" (7), *Dict. d'hist. et de géographie ecclésiast.,* IX, 924–31, at 928; Nagl, *Placidia,* p. 41. The sources specify either Aëtius or Felix alone; there is not the slightest indication of the conjunction of the one with the other; methodologically, therefore, to combine the two, disregard the sources, and hold that Aëtius and Felix together conspired against Boniface is undesirable. It is possible that the two men did conspire, but almost anything is possible; it is *possible* to assume that one or the other conspired with X or Y, persons now completely forgotten, against Boniface; but one cannot satisfactorily reconstruct history in this fashion. We are bound by what the evidence says or implies, provided there is no reason to reject it. For the theory of the conspiracy of the two against Boniface, see Lepper, *De Rebus Gestis,* pp. 47–53; Solari, *Rinnovamento,* I, 294–95; Sirago, *Placidia,* p. 269; Romanelli, *Storia,* p. 644; R. Gentili, "La rivalità fra Ezio, Felice e Bonifacio e l'invasione dei Vandali in Africa," *Il Mondo Classico,* V (1935), 363–72, at 366; etc. One may also point out that to speak of "imperial," or "pro-German," or "anti-German" ideologies in this connection is based on nothing in the sources (cf., e.g., B. Rubin, *Das Zeitalter Justinians,* I, 33; Cessi, "*Regnum,*" I, 35, n. 1 [on 37]); a pure power struggle between two individuals amply explains the situation. It would be as correct to explain the struggle between Pompey and Crassus primarily on ideological grounds. A nice question arises for the historian concerning the use of Procopius: putting it grossly, may one use his account as it stands by merely substituting the name of Felix for that of Aëtius? Probably not; the account is too pat; it smacks too much of the type of plot incident found in the late ancient novel; in any event, one can hardly trust the details of an account which, ex hypothesi, has mistaken the identity of one of the two protagonists.

[47] *Not. Dig. Oc.* 5. 125, 128 (p. 121 Seeck).

[48] Cf. August. *Ep.* 220. 7.

[49] Probably not to Rome (Procop. *Bell.* 3 [*Vand.* 1]. 3. 17), for as far as we know, Placidia was in residence at Ravenna in the latter part of 426 and in 427 (Seeck, *Regesten,* p. 352), although there are large gaps in our information about her whereabouts.

to face accusations before the emperor.[50] Boniface's contumacy, of course, made him guilty of treason, and Felix sent a military expedition under the command of three generals to Africa (427);[51] this dispatch of an expedition under multiple command is a curiously Byzantine touch, and is explicable, as when it was resorted to by the Eastern emperors, as arising from a desire to check a general by his colleagues. Felix obviously did not want to run the risk of ridding himself of Boniface merely to create another powerful rival in his place. Such considerations in the Later Roman and Byzantine Empire all too frequently interfered with military efficiency over which they were given priority. It seems that the three generals were able to shut Boniface up in some stronghold; but by the treachery of one of the three the other two were slain; then the traitor himself was slain (how is unexplained), and Boniface remained in power.

The next year[52] the government tried again; it sent another force to Africa, this time under the sole command of Count Sigisvult, presumably the same who had previously fought against Boniface in aid of the usurper John, but who must necessarily have made his peace with the government when the usurper fell. Both sides had the assistance of various barbarian forces, such as were always ready to sell their military prowess to any side in any fight.[53] Sigisvult, probably himself a Goth, had a force of Goths with him, and Goths also fought for Boniface.[54] Thus the armies of Rome,

---

[50] Cf. Epict. *Diss.* 2. 19. 17.

[51] The doubts of Gentili, *Mondo Classico*, V (1935), 368, about the triple command are groundless in view of common Byzantine practice only a little later.

[52] On the chronology (Prosper puts the second expedition also in 427), see Schmidt, *Wandalen*, pp. 57–58; H.-J. Diesner, "Zur Datierung der Augustinbriefe 228–231," in *Kirche und Staat im spätrömischen Reich,* pp. 91–93 [= *Forschungen und Forschritte,* XXXV: 6 (1961), 184–85]; idem, "Zur Datierung des Briefes 220 und anderer Spätschriften Augustins," *ibid,* pp. 94–99 [= *Forschungen und Forschritte,* XXXV: 9, 281–83]; Gentili, *Mondo Classico,* V (1935), 365–66.

[53] These "gentibus quae uti navibus nesciebant" have been the subject of much erudite theory-spinning, especially in connection with the Vandal invasion of Africa. One thing seems certain; the Vandals are not meant, for by this time there is no doubt that they did know the use of ships. Prosper, however, seems to mean merely what I have indicated in the text. On the passage see F. M. Clover, "Geiseric the Statesman: A Study of Vandal Foreign Policy" (Unpubl. diss.; Chicago, 1966), pp. 21–30.

[54] Sigisvult's Goths: Possid. *V. S. Augustin.* 17; August. *Coll. Maximin (PL,* XLII, 709–742); Goths with Boniface: see Clover, "Geiseric," pp. 24–30. On the paper strength of Roman armies on this occasion (apart from barbarian auxiliaries) see Courtois, *Vandales,* p. 158, n. 3.

I. Gold framed medallion of Galla Placidia (two sides, enlarged). Courtesy of Cabinet des Médailles, Bibliothèque Nationale, Paris

II. Silver missorium of Theodosius
the Great, with Valentinian II
(to his right) and Arcadius (to his
left). Courtesy of Real Academia
de la Historia, Madrid

III. Two-layer sardonyx cameo
showing the Emperor Honorius and
the Empress Maria, now in Paris.
From Wolfgang Fritz Volbach,
*Early Christian Art* (New York:
Harry N. Abrams, Inc.), 1961.
Reproduced by courtesy of
Hirmer Verlag München

IV. Stilicho: right panel of an ivory diptych in the Cathedral of Monza. From Wolfgang Fritz Volbach, *Early Christian Art* (New York: Harry N. Abrams, Inc.), 1961. Reproduced by courtesy of Hirmer Verlag München

V. Serena and Eucherius: left panel of the diptych shown in
Plate IV. From Wolfgang Fritz Volbach, *Early Christian Art*
(New York: Harry N. Abrams, Inc.), 1961. Reproduced by cour-
tesy of Hirmer Verlag München

(a)

VI. Gold solidus of Constantius III (enlarged). From Wolfgang
Fritz Volbach, *Early Christian Art* (New York: Harry N. Abrams,
Inc.), 1961. Reproduced by courtesy of Hirmer Verlag München

(b)

VI. Solidus of Theodosius II (two sides, enlarged), now in New
York. From Aline Abaecherli Boyce, *Festal and Dated Coins of
the Roman Empire: Four Papers* (New York: The American
Numismatic Society), 1965

VII. Felix as Consul: panel of an ivory diptych, now in Paris. From Wolfgang Fritz Volbach, *Early Christian Art* (New York: Harry N. Abrams, Inc.), 1961. Reproduced by courtesy of Hirmer Verlag München

VIII. Triumphal Arch of Saint
Paul-outside-the Walls, Rome. From
Giovanni E. Meille, *Christ's Likeness
in History and Art* (London: Burns,
Oates & Washbourne, Ltd.), 1924

fighting even her civil wars, were composed in large part of barbarians; such extensive use of barbarians attests the precipitous decline of the Roman military establishment in the fifth century. Apparently Sigisvult did better than his three predecessors and, although he did not decisively defeat Boniface, the latter was hard pressed. At this juncture, however, Placidia had second thoughts.[55] She may have discovered the real nature of Felix' intrigue against Boniface, or have been dismayed by the wasting of the slender resources of the Empire in a civil war against her formerly loyal supporter; it is quite likely that the government had learned that the Moors were taking advantage of the internecine strife in Africa to invade and harry the area.[56] The Empress may also have been alarmed by the relatively active Arianism of Sigisvult, especially in view of the probability that her original displeasure with Boniface was related to his tolerance of Arianism.[57] At any rate, she determined to end the conflict by peaceable means; certainly it would hardly suit her policy to have Africa fall under the domination of Felix, whose power would thereby be tremendously augmented and far more dangerous to her independence if he succeeded in eliminating one of his two competitors. On the other hand, she would have had no desire to eliminate Felix, for it was desirable to have as many leading generals about as possible; it would be easier to maintain her independence of any one of them by playing them off against each other. We may presume that the length and cost of the war, two years without definite victory in sight, as well as the failure of his underlings in Africa, had diminished the prestige of Felix and thus, almost certainly contrary to his wishes, enabled the Empress to make overtures for peace.[58] A high official

[55] That she was responsible for the peace is attested only in the suspect account of Procopius (*Bell.* 3 [*Vand.* 1]. 3. 27–29); his showing that Boniface had friends at court who also worked on the Empress' mind is also inherently probable. The only other possibility for arranging the peace is Felix. Yet it is most unlikely that he would have sought to end a war against a rival which he was gradually winning. We have no information whether Boniface halted the grain ships, or if he was able to shut off the supply to Rome in either 427 or 428; if he did, the resulting distress in Rome could have been an important factor in forming the Empress' decision. That the affair of Masties belongs here, as Sirago, *Placidia*, p. 286, n. *, believes, is unlikely; the matter probably belongs to a much later epoch.

[56] *Cons. Ital.* 548 (I, 300), with Lepper, *De Rebus Gestis*, p. 71.

[57] See H.-J. Diesner, *Der Untergang der römischen Herrschaft in Nordafrika*, p. 43.

[58] According to Procop. *Bell.* 3 (*Vand.* 1). 3. 22–31, and other late authors, Boniface despaired of success and invited the Vandals from Spain to help him. Placidia learned of the intrigue, of Aëtius, and made peace with Boniface, who asked the Vandals to

of the court, Count Darius, was sent by Placidia to Africa to negotiate a truce with Boniface, a mission which he successfully carried out.[59] The truce was followed by a permanent peace between Boniface and the imperial government, which restored him to his rank as Count of Africa.[60] Presumably Sigisvult was recalled, for we hear no more of him in Africa. Certainly, however, this useless civil war gravely weakened the Roman position in Africa, torn as it was in any event by social and religious disunity, the revolts of the Circumcellions and of the Donatist heretics (and the disaffection of other varieties) against the established order.

For in May 429 the Vandals under their King Geiseric crossed from Julia Traducta (Tarifa) in Spain to the opposite coast of the province of Mauretania Tingitana. We have noted the arrival of the Vandals in Spain from Gaul and their subsequent establishment in the south of the peninsula, as well as Castinus' unsuccessful campaign against them. In short order, however, their part of Spain had proved too small for their ambition or their greed for loot, and during the 420's they pillaged the Balearic Isles (obviously they had learned the use of ships), Cartagena, and Seville, and conducted raids across the Strait of Gibralter into Mauretania.[61] Probably we should see these raids into Africa as preparatory to the invasion of that continent, a plan probably considered and formed originally by King Guntharic. In all likelihood the relative

---

withdraw; of course they would not do so; and that is how the Vandals took Africa (a mortal blow to the Western Empire)—through the treason of Boniface, the intrigues of Aëtius, and the credulity of Placidia. Apart from the fact that the chief authority for this view of events is Procopius, in whose account it forms a single whole with the fabulous story of the intrigue of Aëtius against Boniface, there is not the slightest hint (despite the ingenious attempts of some modern scholars to find such a hint) in the contemporary or near-contemporary sources for the fifth century of any such motive for the Vandal invasion of Africa. In addition, the attribution of the loss of Africa to the guilt of Boniface is in accord with the search for scapegoats on which to blame the principal calamities of the fifth century. The main advocate of the rejection of the Boniface invitation story was the late Ludwig Schmidt; see *Hist. Vierteljahrschrift*, II (1889), 449–62; *Wandalen*, pp. 55–59; cf. Lepper, *De Rebus Gestis*, pp. 75–86; Courtois, *Vandales*, pp. 155–57. Many scholars, however, still accept the story; e.g., Romanelli, *Storia*, pp. 640–50; E. A. Thompson, review Lepper, *CR*, LXI (1947), 130; W. Ensslin, review Lepper, *Gnomon*, XVIII (1942), 142.

59 August. *Epp.* 229–31; on Darius in general, see Sundwall, *Studien*, no. 117, p. 68; A. C. Pallu de Lessert, *Fastes des provinces africaines sous la domination romaine*, II, 289, n. 1.

60 Procop. *Bell.* 3 (*Vand.* 1). 3. 29–30, confirmed by Possid. *V. S. Augustin.* 28; cf. Lepper, *De Rebus Gestis*, p. 72.

61 Hyd. 86 (II, 21) puts all of these activities in the year 425—which is not impossible. On the probable chronology, see Clover, "Geiseric," pp. 5–8.

wealth of Africa, the security of an establishment there, and the strategic value of the area relative to the Roman Empire influenced the Vandal monarch, as the same considerations had previously moved the enterprise of the Visigothic Kings Alaric and Wallia. There also can be little doubt that the progress of the civil war in Africa in 427 and 428 must have favorably influenced the Vandal King's decision to undertake the project. How far, on the other hand, the Vandals were informed of the socioeconomic and religious disunity in Africa, as well as how far they exploited these factors after their invasion, is a subject of dispute among scholars, but it seems, at least, that the Vandals did not utilize these dissensions to any large degree.[62] King Guntharic, however, died suddenly in 428; he was succeeded by his half brother Geiseric, who carried out his brother's plan and for the next half-century remained one of the most determined and successful antagonists, and occasionally for his own purposes, friend, of the Roman Empire, both East and West. Geiseric was moved by few scruples, and with intelligence and pertinacity pursued a policy of *Realpolitik* in a way that very few of his fellow barbarian monarchs managed, or even conceived. When the Sueves of Spain apparently sought to take advantage of the necessary preoccupation of the Vandals in crossing to Africa, Geiseric turned upon them savagely and crushed them.[63] Probably by June, 429, the crossing of some eighty thousand persons, men, women, and children, had been completed. The smallness of the Vandal numbers is vivid testimony (along with the small size of most of the other barbarian peoples) to the decay of the Empire in general, and particularly of its military and naval establishment. In the great days of the past Rome had with relatively little difficulty subjected or destroyed much larger peoples and much better disciplined armies.

We know little of the Vandals during roughly the next year, as they slowly, mainly by land it seems, made their way through the much shrunken and relatively poor provinces of the Mauretanias to the heartland of Roman Africa in the east. In the meanwhile Boniface presumably was organizing his defense and trying to raise

---

62 So Musset, *Vagues*, p. 228.

63 The reference in *Chron. Gall. a. 452* 107 (I, 658) to "almost 20,000 killed fighting against the Vandals in Spain" almost certainly (with exaggeration) refers to this conflict and not to a battle with the Romans.

additional troops to meet this new and apparently unexpected threat. Once arrived in the eastern provinces of Africa, Numidia and Africa Proconsularis, Geiseric seems to have tried in vain to take Constantine in Numidia; a move on Carthage itself in the Proconsular province also failed. Turning back, therefore, to the west, the Vandals encountered the Roman forces under Boniface near Hippo Regius (Bône) and won a victory; Boniface threw himself into the city with his army; it was the see of Saint Augustine, who died during the long investment (28 August 430). Behind the walls of Hippo Boniface withstood the Vandals for more than a year. As usual the barbarians had little ability in fighting the siege warfare necessary to take a well-walled city. The seige began in about June, 430, and lasted until the summer (July or August) of 431; the Vandals, daunted by the city's defenses finally had to raise the siege. The next year, however, Hippo fell into their hands with little difficulty, when the Roman army withdrew to Carthage. Deprived of the protection of the troops, most of the native inhabitants fled; Hippo was hardly as thoroughly burned as the sources would have us believe;[64] for the time being it became Geiseric's principal residence.

There can be no doubt that the Empress and her ministers in Ravenna watched the developments in Africa with great anxiety; Africa's importance to the Empire was an obvious and long-accepted datum of imperial policy. Now the event which the imperial government had feared for twenty years was at last a reality; a barbarian tribe was threatening to seize the major support of Empire. The time had manifestly come for Galla Placidia to fall back upon her ultimate recourse, appeal for assistance from the East.[65] It is a fair surmise that the defeat of Boniface near Hippo

[64] See the discussion and references in Clover, "Geiseric," p. 38, n. 3; H. V. M. Dennis, "Another Note on the Vandal Occupation of Hippo Regius," *JRS*, XV (1925), 263–68.

[65] The aid from the East arrived in fall, 431 or spring, 432, so the resolution to send it, and the presumptive request that preceded the resolution of the Eastern government must belong to some prior time, for preparations for a distant campaign to which troops would have to be transported by sea must necessarily be extensive and time-consuming. A period much earlier than summer, 430, for the request for assistance is ruled out, for an appeal in 429 would probably have seen an Eastern army in Africa in 430, for the Eastern government was vitally concerned in this matter, and by 430 it was free of other pressing matters. Besides, Placidia would probably wait to send such a request until she was sure that Boniface was unable to manage with the forces he had. That assurance was likely brought home to her by

and the Vandal siege of the Roman army in that city determined Placidia to ask for aid from her nephew. This help was the more readily granted since the Vandals, once in Carthage—one of the great ports of the Mediterranean—with their demonstrated willingness to take to the sea would be almost as much a danger to the long and exposed coastlines of the Eastern Empire as they were to become to the West. It has been shown that from this time and for the remainder of his reign Theodosius' apparently pusillanimous and vacillating foreign policy was in fact the difficult balancing act of a man trying to fend off both the Huns to the north and the Vandals to the southwest with resources inadequate to perform both tasks.[66] Of course, for the West there was also the more important, or more immediate, problem of the revenues of Africa for the government and its grain for Rome itself. It is probably not coincidental that in a law of 29 April 431 Placidia states that even imperial private income is often assigned to public expenditures, and landholders must rigorously make all payments due to the government.[67] Then in the fall of 431, or by the spring of 432 in any event, after the raising of the siege of Hippo, an Eastern army, commanded again by Theodosius' chief general Aspar and joined by further reinforcements spared from the dominions of the West, appeared in Africa to assist Boniface. Nevertheless these forces combined with those Boniface already had at his disposition were again soundly beaten by Geiseric's men.[68] At the beginning of autumn, 432, however, Boniface was recalled to Italy by Placidia, and this time he had no hesitation in obeying, for the political situation in Italy had profoundly changed during the years since

---

the defeat of Boniface near Hippo and his subsequent siege or blockade in that city. Cf. Seeck, *Gesch.*, VI: 2, 417; I cannot agree with Courtois, *Vandales*, p. 164, that only after the fall of Hippo (summer, 431) did the imperial government decide to send troops to Africa. Hippo did not fall to Vandal attack; no new basic element had entered the situation since the aftermath of the battle preceding the siege. If Geiseric could defeat Boniface in open field and shut him up helpless in a city, something more would have to be done if Roman Africa were to be saved.

[66] E. A. Thompson, "The Foreign Policies of Theodosius II and Marcian," *Hermathena*, LXXVI (1950), 58–75, esp. 60–61.

[67] *CTh* 11. 1. 36; *CJ* 4. 61. 13, 11. 75. 5; cf. Seeck, *Gesch.*, VI: 1, 122; 2, 422. Laws of 25 and 27 Feb. 429, probably already show the financial stringency proceeding from the civil war in Africa, in their regulation of tax collection; see Seeck, *Regesten*, p. 354; cf. Ensslin, *RE*, XX: 2 (1950), 1925. Likewise a law of 15 Feb. 430 (*CTh* 12. 6. 33) on the management of state warehouses probably reflects concern over the grain supply.

[68] Procop. *Bell.* 3 (*Vand.* 1). 3. 34–35.

Felix had set in motion his intrigues against the Count.[69] For the time being Aspar remained in command at Carthage, where he entered upon the consulship, 1 January 434,[70] a distinction either granted to him by Galla Placidia or, if conferred by Theodosius, acquiesced in by her.

While the fighting had been in progress in Africa Aëtius, as we have seen, had gone on from his triumphs in Gaul to further ones north of the Alps in Rhaetia or Noricum. In 432 he defeated some Franks, but failed, through a deputy, at the request of the Spanish provincials to make peace between them and the Sueves. Thereafter the Spanish bishops managed to persuade the King of the Sueves to agree to a peace.[71] This embassy from Spain asking Aëtius for protection rather than the Emperor, that is, the government at Ravenna, testifies to the general's growing power and prestige. In fact, by this time he had succeeded Felix in the chief military command. In 427, whatever she may have thought about the Boniface affair, Placidia nominated Felix consul for 428.[72] In 429 she created him Patrician, quite possibly as a consolation prize to minimize the resentment he must have felt over her reversal of his policy in Africa; it would not be wise for Placidia to endanger the precarious balance of power that, since she now expected conciliation with Boniface, she hoped to be able once again to maintain among the three generals. But Felix, who had accomplished relatively little by way of positive achievements, and who had just been responsible for a ruinous war in Africa by his intrigues, could not be rewarded while the undeniable services of Aëtius, whom Placidia still probably detested (with good reason), were left unrecompensed. Accordingly the elevation of Felix was followed by the promotion of Aëtius to be Master of the Soldiers in Gaul.[73]

69 For the date see Lepper, *De Rebus Gestis,* p. 104.

70 *Dimidium Temporis* 9, ed. Braun, p. 605 = *PL,* LI, 841.

71 Hyd. 96, 98, 100 (II, 22) cf. Schmidt, *Gesch.*2, II: 1, 207–8.

72 Presumably with the concurrence of Theodosius, if it be true that he was in effect naming both consuls at this time.

73 Prosp. 1300 (I, 472; Sirago's belief, *Placidia,* p. 275, n. 2, that this passage implies the collaboration of Aëtius and Felix has no foundation; cf. Ensslin, *Klio,* XXIV [1931], 477); cf. Hyd. 94, 103 *init.* (II, 22); *ILS,* 1293; cf. Degrassi, *Bull. Comm. Archeol. Comm. Roma,* LXXII (1946–48), 35, with nn.; the rank of Aëtius was *magister militum per Gallias* (cf. *Ann. ép.,* 1950, no. 30). Sirago, *Placidia,* p. 284, believes that Felix gave up the Mastery of the Soldiers when it was conferred on Aëtius. This is improbable; it is incredible that Felix would have surrendered power in this fashion for an otherwise empty title; and it is hardly less unbelievable that Placidia would

Yet since Felix was now also Patrician, he clearly still ranked above Aëtius, and their relative positions were maintained. In fact, it is possible that Felix was promoted primarily to make it feasible to promote Aëtius yet keep him subordinate to Felix.

But Aëtius became convinced that Felix was plotting against him;[74] by 429 or 430 Felix' intrigues against Boniface must have become common knowledge. Under the circumstances Aëtius was almost bound to entertain his own suspicions of Felix; by the same token the man who had intrigued against one of his rivals was in fact likely to be moving against the other as well. Thus believing that he was the intended victim, Aëtius resolved to act first. Apparently his agents stirred up disaffection toward Felix among the troops stationed in Ravenna, for, in May 430 Felix was slain on the steps of the Basilica Ursiana, that is, the Cathedral of Ravenna, in a riot of the soldiery. With him perished his wife Padusia and the deacon Grunitus, both of whom Aëtius presumably believed to be involved with the Patrician in the plot against him; perhaps, once again if Padusia and Spadousa are the same person, he believed that the woman was trying to influence the Empress against him.[75] The chagrin and consternation of Galla Placidia at this crime can

have been willing to let her "balance of power" among the generals be destroyed in this fashion. It is also probably contradicted by Joh. Ant. Frag. 201. 3 (IV, 615), who says that Felix shared the power of general with Aëtius; since the main verb ("he slew") is aorist, the aorist participle ("shared") is presumably coincident in time with the main verb; cf. B. L. Gildersleeve, *The Syntax of Classical Greek*, I (New York, 1900), sects, 339, 345.

[74] Prosp. 1303 (I, 473); Joh. Ant. Frag. 201. 3 (IV, 615), who adds that Aëtius thought that this plotting was at the suggestion of Placidia; it is quite possible that Aëtius, who had every reason to believe that the Empress had little liking or trust for him, thought that she was behind the plot. If so, however, he was almost certainly mistaken; once one admits that her political situation must make the Empress try to play off her three generals one against the other, then it would be clearly contrary to her interest to concentrate the power of the remaining two by removing one. By a rather strained interpretation of the Greek one could understand Joh. Ant. to mean that by intimation from Placidia Aëtius learned that Felix was plotting against him; even if this possibility, which seems rather unlikely, is correct, it can hardly be doubted, however, that Placidia had no desire that Aëtius should go as far as he did to protect himself, thus unbalancing her precious equilibrium.

[75] Prosp. 1303 (I, 473); Hyd. 94 (II, 22); Marcell. *s.a.* 430, 2 (II, 77); Agnell. 31 (perhaps from the lost, but important Annals of Ravenna; cf. O. Holder-Egger, "Untersuchungen über einige annalistische Quellen zur Geschichte des fünften und sechsten Jahrhunderts," *Neues Archiv der Gesellschaft für Ältere Deutsche Geschichtskunde*, I [1876], 13–120, 213–368, at 312); Joh. Ant. Frag. 201. 3 (IV, 615; cf. above, n. 73). There is every reason, despite Stein, *Hist.*, I, 321; Kornemann, *Grosse Frauen*, p. 344; to believe that Placidia would not have concurred in Aëtius' plot to assassinate Felix; in general, see Ensslin, *RE*, XX: 2 (1950), 1925.

only be imagined; for the moment, at least, she had lost her independence, and Aëtius had moved a long way toward making his ascendancy absolute. Obviously the situation in Africa in May 430 was such that she could not invoke the assistance of Boniface. In the background, also, was another unpleasant fact: Aëtius' friendship with the Huns in effect gave him a power base outside the Roman Empire such as neither Boniface nor Felix possessed. The possibility that Aëtius might bring in the Huns was enough to stay her hand in making any move against their friend,[76] especially since with intervention from the Huns it might be questionable whether even an appeal to Theodosius might guarantee even her personal security and Valentinian's. The Eastern Empire thought it necessary to buy off Hunnish attacks on its own dominions; Theodosius might be unwilling or unable to interfere in the West against the Huns even to assure or avenge the personal safety of his relatives. For the present, Aëtius had been taught by the example of John and the failure of the rebels against Honorius not to move against the throne itself; nothing must be allowed to force a change in his mind on that subject. One way out of the difficulty would have been to have Aëtius assassinated; presumably it would not have been impossible to instigate some friend of the murdered Felix to do the deed, and thus avoid any odium. It seems difficult to believe that the possibility did not occur to the Empress. If it did, however, she discarded the idea, whether because it seemed impractical, or because her loyalty to the Empire would not allow her to remove the principal military talent she had left for the defense of Europe, or because she felt it repugnant and immoral to stoop to such methods as Aëtius himself had employed. In fact, of course, we have no information about her thoughts and plans; the foregoing analysis, like similar ones in this account, is based on an attempt to understand her situation as it would presumably have appeared to her as a reasonably intelligent person at the time. At least, it is certain, as far as our evidence goes, that for the time being she took no action against Aëtius; in the latter part of 431 she nominated him for the consulship of the next year.

The political and military situation, however, was about to change, or at least seem to change, in a way which would remove the drawbacks to an attempt to remove Aëtius from power. In 431

[76] Cf. Joh. Ant. Frag. 201. 3 (IV, 615), who explicitly credits Aëtius' power to his "alliance" with the barbarians, i.e., the Huns.

and 432 the great Roman noble Nicomachus Flavianus the Younger held the office of Praetorian Prefect of Italy; both he and his father had supported and served under the pagan-tolerating usurper Eugenius in the time of Theodosius the Great; later the younger Flavianus had been admitted again to imperial favor. Now, during the son's Praetorian Prefecture, in behalf of his virtues and abilities, so the Empress stated in a letter to the Senate, the elder Flavianus' memory was rehabilitated and thereby this whole family of important Roman aristocrats with wide connections throughout the rest of the Roman nobility was obviously gratified. It has been suggested that this rehabilitation was undertaken at the initiative of Aëtius, who wished to consolidate his position by alliance with the Roman aristocracy.[77] Perhaps, but it seems more natural, on the basis of *cui bono,* to think that it was Galla Placidia herself who was responsible for this step; before the prepotency of Aëtius she was in desperate search of allies, and hoped to find them in the Roman aristocracy or in elements thereof, even if they still had pagan leanings. On 24 March 432 Placidia issued a law confirming various privileges of imperial bureaucrats;[78] since the imperial bureaucracy in the West was intimately connected with the aristocracy, possibly this measure is to be interpreted as a further move to win the support of the nobility. Likewise the nomination in this same year of the great noble Petronius Maximus to be consul for 433 may be similarly interpreted.[79] The opportunity Galla Placidia was looking for, however, seems to have come from another direction. Sometime around the year 430 the Huns under their King Uptar attacked the Burgundians domiciled around the Main and the Neckar; just before the battle, however, Uptar died, and in the ensuing struggle the Huns were defeated by their recently Christianized foes, who attributed their victory to the favor and power of their new God; a large number of the Hunnish warriors, ten thousand is the figure we are given, perished.[80] Obviously

[77] *ILS,* 2948; in general, see Solari, *Rinnovamento,* I, 303–4, 336; *idem,* "Tolleranza verso il paganesimo nella prima metà del sec. V°," *Philologus,* XCI (1936), 357–60, at 359–60; Stein, *Hist.,* I, 340; Sirago, *Placidia,* pp. 289–90. On Aëtius and the aristocracy, see below, nn. 95–107. See also Sundwall, *Studien,* no. 183, pp. 79–80; Seeck, *Regesten,* pp. 358, 360.

[78] *CTh* 6. 23. 3.

[79] On Maximus, see Sundwall, *Studien,* no. 310, pp. 104–5.

[80] Soc. *HE* 7. 30. 1–6; cf. E. Demougeot, "Attila et les Gaules," *Mém. de la Soc. d'Agriculture, Commerce, Sciences et Arts du Dép. de la Marne,* LXXIII (1958), 7–41, at 10; Thompson, *Attila,* pp. 66–67.

this was a staggering blow to the Huns; it seems difficult to believe that this news did not soon arrive at the court of Ravenna to delight the heart of the Empress. That she thought, by error as it turned out, unfortunately for herself, that the power of the Huns was crippled, if not permanently, at least for the time being, seems the only logical explanation of the fact that in 432 she thought the time had come to move against Aëtius.[81] In that year therefore she appointed Boniface Master of the Soldiery[82] and recalled him to Italy. When the choice narrowed itself to Boniface, her old and faithful supporter, who in the time of her exile to the East had demonstrated his loyalty to her personally by his deeds, or Aëtius, who had supported the usurper John, who had used his friendship with the Huns to compel his original appointment to command in Gaul, and who had stooped to murder to checkmate Felix, there could be little question of her decision. At least there was a strong chance that Boniface would be loyal and not encroach excessively upon her independence of action; even in control of the military forces of the Empire he might well be content to be her servant instead of her master. Then in a few years Valentinian could revert to ancient imperial practice and command his own armies. By 432 Valentinian was a boy of thirteen and able to comprehend his situation; in view of his own later attempt to do just this,[83] there seems little doubt in the light of her own difficulties with her generals that his mother inculcated this aim of his future policy in her son. In Africa what Boniface could do, and that was little, had been done. With Aspar and the forces of the East to hold against Geiseric, Boniface could be summoned to the succor of the dynasty in Italy without thereby inflicting important damage on the cause of the Empire in Africa.

It must have been made plain to Boniface before his return to Italy that he would doubtless have to fight Aëtius in order to hold the power which the Empress intended. Accordingly he came from Africa with a considerable force, including doubtless his presumably numerous *bucellarii*. Placidia conferred upon him, prob-

81 Just as in 454 the death of Attila and the revolt of the subject peoples of the Huns were to convince Valentinian III that it would be safe to rid himself of Aëtius. Like his mother Valentinian miscalculated, but in a different fashion.

82 Prosp. 1310 (I, 473); Ensslin, *Klio*, XXIV (1931), 477–81, argues convincingly that this appointment must have been made even before Boniface returned to Italy, but it seems unlikely it would have been made before Placidia broke openly with Aëtius.

83 Cf. *CP*, LIX (1964), 25.

ably at that time, the additional rank of Patrician, making him
Aëtius' clear superior in rank, as Felix had formerly been.[84] Aëtius,
who had been fighting the Franks,[85] was dismissed from his position, but he refused to accept this deposition. Instead, a few months
later he marched on Italy with troops and probably his own *bucellarii*; a battle was fought between him and Boniface at the fifth
milestone from Ariminum (Rimini). Boniface was victorious in
the fight, but was mortally wounded and died three months later.
He was succeeded in his position by Sebastian, his son-in-law
(presumably the husband of a daughter by his first marriage).[86]
For the time being Aëtius retreated to a fortified dwelling he
possessed on his estates (in Italy, apparently). So powerful a man
as the late commander of Gaul must have had many enemies;
whether it was a sudden attack upon his place of refuge made by
some of these, or by persons acting under orders of Sebastian, who
naturally had reason to fear an attempt of his father-in-law's rival
to regain power, Aëtius became frightened for his life and fled,
first to Rome, and then to Dalmatia and Pannonia and the Huns
where he sought the help of his old friends (spring, 433?).[87] Quite
possibly the fact that Aëtius had not earlier asked assistance from
the Huns confirms the view that their power was believed to have
been severely shaken by the defeat of King Uptar's army.

Fortunately for Aëtius the report of the loss of Hunnish strength
had been greatly exaggerated; from King Rua (or Rugila) he was
able to obtain the promise of assistance to enable him to reclaim
power. In return, in all probability, he promised to cede Roman
territory to the Huns and to send them his son Carpilio as a

[84] Marcell. *s.a.* 435, 2 (II, 79); cf. *idem s.a.* 432, 2 (II, 78; the reference to Aëtius as
Patrician here is an anticipation); Sundwall, *Studien*, no. 70, p. 58. If we can trust the
doubtful account of Procop. *Bell.* 3 (*Vand.* 1). 3. 36, at his interview with Placidia
Boniface was able to remove any lingering doubts she may still have had concerning
his loyalty.

[85] Hyd. 98 (II, 22); cf. above, n. 71. Perhaps by this time, since the death of Felix,
Aëtius had already been (out of necessity) promoted to be Master of (Both Branches
of) the Soldiery.

[86] The fall of Aëtius is probably indicated by the fact that the deputy, Censorius,
whom he had sent to negotiate with the King of the Sueves, reported back not to him
but to the court (Hyd. 100 [II, 22]).

[87] Prosp. 1310 (I, 473–74); Hyd. 99 (II, 22); *Chron. Gall. a. 452* 109, 111 (I, 658);
*Add. Prosp. Haun.* (I, 301); Marcell. *s.a.* 432, 2–3 (II, 78); Joh. Ant. Frag. 201. 3 (IV,
615). The story of Marcell. that Aëtius personally wounded Boniface with a specially
prepared, longer than usual, weapon smacks of the fabulous. One the chronology, see
Lepper, *De Rebus Gestis*, pp. 102–4. If Aëtius' flight to Rome means that he sought
the support of the aristocracy, obviously he did not receive it.

hostage.[88] For their part Placidia and Sebastian tried to obtain reinforcements from the Visigoths. Unfortunately it is unknown whether this help was forthcoming or not,[89] or whether it was necessary for Aëtius actually to fight in order to recover his position; very possibly merely the threat of a Hunnish invasion was sufficient to compel the government to yield. Sebastian was dismissed as Master of the Soldiery and the position was given to Aëtius. The latter's defeated rival found it expedient to flee to the East, then to the Goths, and eventually to Geiseric. In all probability all of this activity was aimed at obtaining assistance against Aëtius; his quest was in vain, however, and Geiseric eventually put him to death. Aëtius was also created Patrician (433 or 434), and the government was forced to cede portions of Pannonia to the Huns. Boniface's old enemy Sigisvult, who had apparently originally attached himself to Felix, is henceforth found associated with Aëtius, rising to be Master of the Soldiers (inferior of course to Aëtius), consul, and eventually Patrician.[90] Galla Placidia had lost the game; her delicate balancing of power among three generals in order to retain independence for herself had failed after eight years. Henceforth Aëtius would remain dominant in the Western Empire for the next twenty years,[91] until after the death of the Empress herself. One should not, however, infer from this fact that he was all-powerful (at least one part of the accord made with the Vandals in 442, for example, must have been made contrary to his wishes), and from time to time the court would attempt to strike

88 Rua died in 434 and was succeeded by the joint rule of Attila and Bleda; if Cassiod. *Var.* 1. 4. 11 is to be taken literally, Carpilio was not delivered as a hostage until after Attila's accession; cf. Altheim, *Hunnen*, IV, 188, n. 10. In the 430's Aëtius sent Attila a Latin secretary to show his friendship with the Hunnish King and also doubtless to keep himself informed of doings at Attila's court; see Prisc. Frag. 8 (IV, 84) with Thompson, *Attila*, pp. 127–28.

89 Schmidt, *Gesch.*2, I, 466.

90 Prosp. 1310 (I, 474); Hyd. 99, 103 (II, 22); *Chron. Gall. a. 452* 112, 113, 115, 116 (I, 658, 660); *Chron. Gall. a. 511* 587, 588 (I, 659); Prisc. Frag. 7 (IV, 76). Exactly what parts of Pannonia were ceded to the Huns is in dispute; see Thompson, *Attila*, p. 64; Altheim, *Attila*, p. 84; Demougeot, *Mém. Soc. d'Agricult. Comm. Sciences et Arts du Dép. Marne*, LXXIII (1958), 10–11. On Carpilio: Thompson, *Attila*, p. 64; Alföldi, *Untergang*, II, 91, n. 1; Sundwall, *Studien*, no. 82, p. 60. On Sebastian's subsequent fate: Hyd. 99, 104, 129, 132, 144 (II, 22–25); Vict. Vit. 1. 19–21; Marcell. *s.a.* 435, 2 (II, 79); cf. Lepper, *De Rebus Gestis*, pp. 109–13; Seeck, *Geschichte*, VI: 2, 419. On Sigisvult: Ensslin, *Klio*, XXIV (1931), 481; Stein, *Hist.*, I, 322; W. Levison, "Bischof Germanus von Auxerre und die Quellen zu seiner Geschichte," *Neues Archiv der Gesellschaft für Ältere Deutsche Geschichtskunde*, XXIX (1904), 95–175, at 132; there is no reason to doubt the statement of the *V. S. Germani* 38 that in the late 440's he was Patrician.

91 Cf. Joh. Ant. Frag. 201. 3 (IV, 615).

at him through his supporters,[92] or try to detach some of those supporters;[93] but in general we may assume that for the next twenty years whenever Aëtius wished to bend the government to do his will he was able to do so. Probably at some time after his return to power the general was able to increase his own personal wealth and broaden his personal power base. For apparently after his return, some time in the 430's, he married Pelagia, the widow of Boniface, who became the mother of his younger son Gaudentius; and with Pelagia he acquired control not only of the wealth of Boniface to add to his own, but probably and more importantly, of Boniface's *bucellarii* or personal troops.[94]

The late E. Stein, one of our century's most distinguished students of the Later Roman Empire, argued that Aëtius formed an alliance with the aristocracy, that the Emperor Valentinian III (and before him his mother Galla Placidia) was helpless before this combination, which weakened the basis of imperial power to the profit of the great landowners and of Aëtius, and that the typical picture of the sloth and indolence of Valentinian III was therefore mistaken or exaggerated, the Emperor could do nothing before this prepotent alliance.[95] This view has come to command general agreement among most scholars who study the fifth century; although its general approach seems right, it should probably be modified in an important respect. It is quite doubtful that the imperial aristocracy of the West as a whole supported Aëtius; rather it seems more likely that he was the leader of an important part of it, but not of the great landowners in a more or less solid bloc. In general, throughout the entire history of ancient Rome, Republic and Empire, one never finds the ruling class united behind one political figure; some will be for him, others will be against him. In other words, the aristocracy is always found politically divided in factions; it would be surprising indeed if for twenty years the aristocracy had been unanimously or nearly unanimously in al-

92 Probably the recall of Merobaudes from Spain in 443: Hyd. 128 (I, 24).

93 Ap. Sid. *Carm.* 5. 116–25 (the father of Majorian); Majorian himself (*CP*, LIX [1964], 23–29); on the opposition of the imperial family to Aëtius, in general: Sirago, *Placidia*, p. 340.

94 Marcell. *s.a.* 432, 3 (II, 78) states that Boniface, dying, recommended his wife to marry Aëtius; Joh. Ant. Frag. 201. 3 (IV, 615) seems to mean that the marriage actually took place. Sirago, *Placidia*, p. 291, n. 1, with some justice doubts the historicity of this advice; yet the tale would have been pointless unless Pelagia had in fact married Aëtius; so Lepper, *De Rebus Gestis*, pp. 113–14; in general, see Diesner, *Kirche und Staat*, p. 115.

95 *Hist.*, I, 337–42.

liance with Aëtius. This is true even though the "class" or socio-economic interests of the aristocracy at any given time were presumably homogeneous, or nearly so. Secondly, most of the favorable notices of Aëtius come from Gaul (Apollinaris Sidonius and Gregory of Tours transmitting the ideas of Renatus Profuturus Frigeridus), when not from his panegyrist Merobaudes, who stood to Aëtius in more or less the same relation as the poet Claudian to Stilicho. The possibility therefore arises that the traditional heart of the aristocracy in Italy might have viewed him differently (without asserting that the aristocracy of either Gaul or Italy reacted to Aëtius as a bloc). Almost certainly the great Italian nobleman, Petronius Maximus, and presumably thereby most of his noble connections, which may have included the Anicii, the greatest of all noble houses, was opposed to him;[96] after Aëtius' death he wanted to succeed to his position of power at court.[97] Various laws of Valentinian III certainly do tend to the increase of the power and prestige of the aristocracy; such laws are taken at face value by Stein[98] as attesting the growth of the power of the aristocracy, doubtless with the assistance of Aëtius. On the other hand, laws to improve the finances of the state, laws addressed to great nobles in high office, and sometimes suggested by them, are interpreted as the working of a Machiavellian policy which allowed the emperor, in effect, to play games, in the secure knowledge that such legislation could not be enforced.[99] It would seem more natural to assume that such laws were suggested by, if not necessarily addressed to, great nobles who still had some political and social conscience as far as the welfare of the state was concerned. It would seem simplistic to believe that every single aristocrat without exception had forgotten every shred of responsibility to the state; or even that a great noble might not, in the usual context of Roman factional politics, wish to use such laws against a particular rival, or group of rivals, that was vulnerable to them.

96 Joh. Ant. Frag. 201. 1 (I, 614); Procop. *Bell.* 3 (*Vand.* 1). 4. 25; on the possible connection with the Anicii, Sundwall, *Studien,* no. 310, p. 104. On Maximus as an opponent of Aëtius, see also A. Gitti, *Ricerche sui rapporti tra i Vandali e l'impero romano,* p. 61; Wes, *Ende,* pp. 128–33.

97 Joh. Ant. Frag. 201. 4 (I, 615).

98 *Hist.,* I, 342.

99 *Ibid.,* 339, note the reference to the law of 24 Jan. 440 (*NVal* 4) addressed to and suggested by Petronius Maximus as Praetorian Prefect; the law suppressed various fiscal privileges abusively obtained.

Stein also believes[100] that Aëtius could have enforced these laws if he had wanted to do so; but then one might inquire why the much more powerful emperors of the previous century had also frequently been unable to enforce their salutary legislation. The answer of course is the corruption and inadequacy of the bureaucracy, with or without the complicity or oppression of the great landowners. In general, however, it is quite likely that Aëtius co-operated with some of the aristocracy to secure the growth of their personal power and the increase of their dependents at the expense of the state; for while the great landowners wanted to increase both their domains and the number of their dependents to work them, Aëtius wanted to increase his personal army (*bucellarii*) by the same or similar illicit means, extending his authority and increasing the number of his personal fighters at the expense of the public authority of the state. Yet certainly the wealth of the great aristocrats and probably their near-monopoly of high office under Valentinian III should not be seen primarily as a result of their collusion with Aëtius; these things can easily be explained without recourse to such a theory.[101] All of the evidence cited to prove Aëtius' interference in the details of the financial administration of the state falls in the period 450–54.[102] This period was inaugurated by the Praetorian Prefecture of Firminus, almost certainly of a great Gallic noble family.[103] At the same time Venantius Opilio was Master of the Offices, and then Urban Prefect, Consul, and Patrician;[104] he too was probably from the great Gallic family of the Venantii.[105] This suggests that Aëtius' intimate control of the finances is related to a time when his Gallic friends had been able to interfere with the monopoly of high Italian office by the Italian aristocracy. Venantius is the first Gallic Urban Prefect since Rutilius Namatianus in the reign of Honorius; in the mean-

---

[100] *Hist.*, I, 340.

[101] I am happy to acknowledge in what follows on this subject my indebtedness to several suggestions and arguments made by Briggs Twyman in a seminar paper written at the University of Chicago in 1966 and entitled "Aëtius and the Aristocracy." It is to be hoped that a version of this rather lengthy paper will eventually be published; what is used here is only a brief résumé of a small part of it. On Stein's thesis, see also Salvatorelli, *Italia*, p. 34.

[102] Joh. Ant. Frag. 201. 2 (IV, 614); *NVal* 33 (31 Jan. 451) (perhaps not relevant); 36 (29 June 452); 1. 3 (14 March 450).

[103] Cf. Stroheker, *Adel*, nos. 154–58, p. 174; no. 112, p. 166.

[104] Sundwall, *Studien*, no. 334, p. 112.

[105] Stroheker, *Adel*, no. 196, pp. 183–84; no. 404, p. 226.

while the urban prefecture had been dominated by Italian aristocrats. Firminus as well as Opilio became Patrician; the last such Gallic example was Dardanus under Honorius.[106] Certainly these facts would seem to indicate some sort of special alliance between Aëtius and the Gallic as opposed to the Italian aristocracy. Apart from Petronius Maximus, note also Caecina Decius Acinatius Albinus, who was a great Italian noble (with undoubtedly extensive connections) and who quarreled bitterly with Aëtius in 440.[107] Accordingly, we may conclude that Aëtius was the ally of a faction of the nobility only, that that faction probably included more Gallic than Italian representatives, and that his control of the civil, or at least financial, administration was probably closer at some times than at others.

Thus Aëtius attained greater power than in the minds of Galla Placidia and her son it was fitting for a subject to possess. In the next years after 433, however, doubtless to the Empress' relief, he was much occupied with the affairs of Gaul, which, if the foregoing discussion is correct, was not only the preferred scene of his military exploits but, with its aristocracy, his major power base inside the Roman Empire. We may assume that Aëtius did not often put in an appearance at the Emperor's court, where we may also assume that appearances were sedulously preserved, but in an atmosphere of freezing chill. The minutely regulated and ceremonious protocol of the court will have helped immeasurably to maintain the external fiction of concord between the Emperor and his too powerful minister. On the other hand it also seems safe to conclude that Aëtius, through his friends and agents at Ravenna and Rome, kept continuously informed of what went on in the entourage of the Empress and her son. His life might depend on such knowledge. The court poet and panegyrist Merobaudes, an adherent of Aëtius,[108] who gives us an occasional glimpse of life

106 Sundwall, *Studien,* no. 116, p. 67; Stroheker, *Adel,* no. 99, pp. 162–63.

107 Sundwall, *Studien,* no. 14, pp. 45–46; esp. Prosp. 1341 (I, 478). The Cassiodori were friendly to Aëtius; cf. Cassiod. *Var.* 1. 4. 11, with Wes, *Ende,* pp. 125–26.

108 We may fairly safely assume that it was Aëtius who caused the dedication of a statue to Merobaudes in the Forum of Trajan with a fulsome inscription in the name of the "Lords of Creation" Theodosius and Placidus Valentinianus in the summer of 435 (*ILS,* 2950). Merobaudes may have delivered a (lost) panegyric on Aëtius' first consulship in 432; cf. *Pan.* 1. Frag. 2A. 2–3 with Clover, "Merobaudes," *ad loc.* (p. 27). He received either the suffect consulship, or the consular ornaments, or the rank of Patrician, in return for these praises; cf. Vollmer *ad loc.* in his ed. in *MGH: AA,* XIV, 9; Clover, "Merobaudes," p. 28.

about the court in these next years, of course offers no hint of the real nature of the relations between his hero and the imperial family, but it is a fair assumption that if Placidia had disliked and distrusted Aëtius before, she now hated him with a cold hate which she doubtless transmitted to her son and which Aëtius' undeniable services to the Empire in Gaul did nothing to assuage. At least he did not try to make himself emperor; he was, however, eventually to conceive the idea of marrying his younger son Gaudentius to Valentinian's daughter, and thus in a sense to plan to succeed to the throne legitimately through his son.[109]

Not long after Aëtius' secure installation in power, the affairs of Gaul required his careful attention. Since they had supported the usurpers Jovinus and Sebastian in 413 the Burgundians had been quiet; suddenly in 435 for reasons unknown they broke out of the reservation Constantius had assigned to them and ravaged the province of Belgica Prima; possibly they were joined by the Alans under their King Goar. At about the same time the Bacaudae or peasant rebels once again rose against the oppression of the Roman political and social order throughout much of Gaul. Now or in the next years the Franks also assailed Roman territory along the Rhine. Aëtius, however, proved equal to the situation; with his Hunnish auxiliaries, or possibly with the assistance of Huns brought in for the purpose from Attila, he attacked the Burgundians. Despite their submission to Aëtius they were destroyed by the Huns, so the sources say. Certainly some of them, however, survived, although the carnage among them was to be the germ of the situation described in the *Nibelungenlied,* which also confused this great havoc with the campaign of Attila in Gaul in 451.[110] The Visigoths, quick to take advantage of the difficulties of the imperial government,[111] in 436 resumed their push toward the Mediter-

---

109 *CP,* LIX (1964), 24.

110 On the controversy over this campaign against the Burgundians, the role of the Huns, and its relation to the campaign of 451, cf., e.g., Demougeot, *Mém. Soc. d'Agricult. Comm. Sciences et Arts Dép. Marne,* LXXIII (1958), 15, with nn.; Kaufmann, *Forschungen zur deutschen Geschichte,* VI (1866), 451, n. 1; Altheim, *Attila,* p. 89; L. Wilser, *Die Germanen: Beiträge zur Völkerkunde,* II, 3d ed.,123–28 (who denies that [Aëtius'] Huns destroyed a large part of the Burgundians in 435/36, and puts the destruction in 451, when the Burgundians were fighting for Aëtius against Attila; he puts the settlement of the Burgundians in Sapaudia not in 443, but after "Chalôns." Much of this is unacceptable.)

111 Cf. Dannenbauer, *Entstehung,* I, 208.

ranean and laid siege to Narbonne. Litorius, a lieutenant of Aëtius, having put down a revolt in Armorica, hastened to the relief of the city and raised the siege (437). About the same time the leader of the Bacaudae was captured and for the time being these rebels ceased to be a threat to Roman rule in Gaul.[112] Litorius continued with the war against the Goths, however, and seemed on the point of taking the Gothic capital of Toulouse, when he was wounded in battle, captured, and killed in captivity (439). He was a pagan, and his taking of the auspices caused the Christians to attribute his death to the vengeance of God. Nevertheless the Visigoths had been so weakened by this war that they gladly accepted the terms which Avitus, Praetorian Prefect of the Gauls (later briefly Emperor), offered them.[113] Although they received some increase of territory, there is no real reason to believe that they were recognized as sovereign or independent of the Empire.[114] For the next decade, at any rate, the Visigoths remained quiescent. For the earlier of these victories Aëtius was rewarded with his second consulship (437), which he held with Sigisvult as his colleague. Evidently Theodosius II had generously allowed the Western government to nominate both consuls for this year; that Aëtius and his lieutenant were thus simultaneously honored of course attests his power. His consulship was perhaps distinguished by the pronouncement of the so-called *First Panegyric* of Merobaudes.[115] Quite obviously the policy of Aëtius cannot be called pro-German or anti-German; his aim was to promote the interests of Rome (or his own welfare) by whatever means or lack of means at his disposal.[116] Unless the Huns who "destroyed" the Burgundians did so without his permission,[117] we may conclude that he had no objection to the annihilation of German tribes if he thought it possible. Apparently also he had no objection to Litorius' attempt to bring the Visigothic kingdom to its knees, or quite possibly "destroy" it; at least there is no evidence that he tried to interfere with what

112 The *V. S. Germani* apparently puts the revolt of the Bacaudae under Tibatto about a decade later; on the difficulties, cf., e.g., Chadwick, *Poetry*, p. 261.

113 In general, Stein, *Hist.*, I, 322–24.

114 Thompson, *Historia*, XII (1963), 122, n. 6.

115 Cf. Vollmer, *MGH: AA*, XIV, 7; but *Pan.* 1 may refer to his third consulship in 446; see Clover, "Merobaudes," p. 25. On Aëtius' *cursus* to this point see *Ann. ép.*, 1950, no. 30.

116 Sirago, *Placidia*, p. 270.

117 *Chron. Gall. a. 452* 118 (I, 660); Prosp. 1322 (I, 475) does not contradict the responsibility of Aëtius.

Litorius was doing. It seems difficult to believe, in view of Rome's centuries-old past policy when she was sufficiently powerful to deal with barbarians as she liked, that any Roman general would not have preferred, if he had the power (the qualification of course is most important), to eradicate German dominion from the soil of the Empire. Whether the Empress was in agreement with such ideas or not we have no way of knowing, even in the case of the Visigoths. In any event the question was academic, for if there was any part of the Empire in which Aëtius in effect usurped the powers of sovereignty, it was of course Gaul.

Presumably Aëtius had a relatively free hand to preoccupy himself with the affairs of Gaul in 435–39 because Africa was at peace and further hostilities from Geiseric were not to be expected.[118] Aspar had remained in command there after Boniface had left;[119] but despite his consulship in 434 he did little against the Vandals. In all probability he returned to the East in the course of that year because of further menaces from the Huns against the Eastern Empire despite the death of King Rua, also in 434, and the accession of the brothers Attila and Bleda.[120] The failure of Boniface against Geiseric had shown that the West could not successfully meet the threat he constituted; victory had also proved impossible with reinforcements from the East; it was probably in recognition of this fact that Placidia had thought herself entitled to recall Boniface in the hope at least of using him against Aëtius. Aspar alone had also accomplished nothing. Now on his departure for the East the garrison of Carthage and its hinterland must have been greatly reduced. Possibly the West could have made another attempt in force to destroy Geiseric or drive him out of Africa (presumably back to Spain where his presence would have been less dangerous), but such a policy would of course gravely hinder Aëtius' activities in Gaul. And since Aëtius' power rested in considerable part on Gaul, there could be no doubt on which side

---

[118] Stein, *Hist.,* I, 322.

[119] Despite the Eastern tradition (e.g., Procop. *Bell.* 3 [*Vand.* 1]. 3. 36) which has him leave Africa at the same time as Boniface; in general, see Clover, "Geiseric," pp. 43–53.

[120] Cf. Thompson, *Attila,* pp. 70–73; for the "usurper" John the Vandal in Theophanes, pp. 97, 103, see Clover, "Geiseric," pp. 46–47. It seems likely that during this period of Aspar's stay in Africa he came to some sort of understanding with Geiseric which led to his future policy of relative neutrality as to the Vandals; see E.-F. Gautier, *Genséric, Roi des Vandales,* pp. 181–83, and the further remarks of Clover, "Geiseric," pp. 43–53.

Aëtius' decisive resolution of the question, Gaul or Africa, would be found. And it was of course true that the Empire still held Carthage and its hinterland, especially the province of Africa Proconsularis, the wealthiest part of the diocese. Accordingly Placidia and Valentinian must resolve to make peace with Geiseric. Early in 435 a high court official named Trygetius was sent to negotiate peace with the Vandal King. The latter undoubtedly wished a breathing spell to confirm the position of his people in Africa before making another attempt on Carthage and its territory, the natural aim of the Vandals, and one which the King had doubtless had in mind since the beginning of the invasion. Agreement, therefore, was reached at Hippo between the King and the imperial ambassador on 11 February 435. By this treaty, as "allies" of the Empire Geiseric and his people were "allowed" to occupy (more or less like the Goths or Burgundians in Gaul) the provinces of Mauretania Sitifensis and Numidia and part of Africa Proconsularis—that is to say, what they effectively controlled at that moment.[121] That this treaty, which Roman pride could view as merely the granting to a group of barbarians of permission to occupy one part of the Empire (Africa) instead of another (Spain), turned out only to have given the Vandals time for the consolidation of their position is no fault of Galla Placidia, or even of Aëtius.

The time was in fact approaching, however, when the Empress, if not able entirely to lay down the burdens of state, could trust some or most of them to her son. In 435 Valentinian III reached his sixteenth birthday and in 437 his eighteenth. By ancient Roman regulation at the age of seventeen a male became subject to military service; at fourteen he was deemed capable of entering on a legal marriage, although he commonly waited until he was older.

---

121 Prosp. 1321 (I, 474); cf. Isid. *Vand.* 74 (II, 297). Procop. *Bell.* 3 (*Vand.* 1). 4. 13 knows only one peace, but in the main his terms are those of the treaty of 442, not that of 435 (despite Schmidt, *Wandalen,* p. 65; cf. Seeck, *Geschichte,* VI: 1, 119, 121; 2, 421); Sirago, *Placidia,* p. 293, is probably wrong when he says that Huniric was handed over as a hostage to the Romans at this time rather than in 442 or immediately thereafter; cf. Merob. *Carm.* 1. 8 with *CP,* LX (1965), 6. Geiseric may have sworn an oath not to attack Roman dominions again (Isid. *Vand.* 74 [II, 297]). On the treaty in general, see Courtois, *Vandales,* pp. 169–72 and 169, n. 7; Clover, "Geiseric," pp. 53–58; Romanelli, *Storia,* p. 656 and n. 1. The nn. of these accounts cite the later ancient sources besides those specified here. That Trygetius was sent by the Empress primarily, and not by Aëtius, is probably to be deduced from his embassy to Attila in 452, at a time when that later embassy was a response of Valentinian to the despair of Aëtius. See Sundwall, *Studien,* no. 474, p. 140; Prosp. 1367 (I, 482).

The position of Aëtius, at least for the time being, was such that there could be no question of Valentinian's taking over actual command of the army, but he could certainly contract the marriage with the only daughter of Theodosius II that the Eastern Emperor had arranged with Placidia when Valentinian had been only a child. Thus the alliance necessary to the stability and safety of the Western branch of the dynasty would be reaffirmed and drawn closer. It is not impossible that, failing to realize the degree of the ever growing separation between East and West, Placidia will also have contemplated, not without satisfaction, the fact that Theodosius had only this one child and no son, and reflected upon the chance that either her son or a grandchild by this marriage might well succeed one day to the throne of the East, thus reversing the speculation with which the Eastern branch of the family had awaited the demise of Honorius.[122]

In 436 the Roman noble Volusianus was sent to Constantinople formally to ask Theodosius and Eudocia for the hand of their daughter Licinia Eudoxia, and to make preliminary arrangements for the marriage itself. Although Volusianus died at Constantinople on 6 January 437, shortly after his conversion to the true faith, in part through the good offices of his niece Saint Melania the Younger, who had journeyed from Jerusalem to see him, the consent of the Emperor and Empress of the East was obtained and Thessalonica was appointed to be the scene of the wedding, as being convenient for both parties. With a delicate sense, however, of the respect due to the senior Augustus, Valentinian later sent word that Theodosius need not trouble himself so much, that he, Valentinian, would come to Constantinople.[123] Accordingly, in the latter part of the summer of 437 Valentinian set out from Ravenna for the East, together with a suite including some of the most distinguished nobles of the West;[124] he made his formal entry into the Eastern capital on 21 October. We are told that he had devised sufficient arrangements for the protection of the West to permit him to undertake this journey,[125] courtly language which

---

122 In actual fact, of course, so far apart had East and West grown that when Theodosius II died Valentinian's technical right of succession or appointment to succession was ignored in the East.

123 *V. (greca) S. Mel. Iun.* 50 (p. 224, ed. Gorce) = *V. (lat.)* 2. 19 *(Anal. Boll.,* VIII [1889], 51); Soc. *HE* 7. 44. 1–2; cf. A. Chastagnol, *RÉA,* LVIII (1956), 253.

124 *Gest. Sen. ad CTh* 2, for Anicius Acilius Glabrio Faustus.

125 Soc. *HE* 7. 44. 3.

thus referred to the military ability of Aëtius and Sigisvult who were currently holding the consulships. More to the point, his mother stayed home to keep an eye on political matters, and of course on the valiant Aëtius himself. On 29 October, doubtless with all the due pomp surrounding the activities of two emperors and an empress, the marriage was formally celebrated.[126] The groom was eighteen years of age; Eudoxia, the bride, born in 422,[127] was fifteen, a not uncommon age for Roman brides. In honor of the occasion a gold solidus was coined by the mint of Constantinople to serve as a medallion, with the legend on the reverse: FELICITER NVBTIIS ("with good fortune, for the marriage"). Theodosius was depicted wearing the diadem, taller than the likewise diademed Valentinian on his left; the two hold an orb symbolizing universal dominion, the union of East and West as well as of Valentinian and Eudoxia, who stands to their right. The medallion was quite likely distributed to the guests who witnessed the ceremony.[128] Another coin honored Eudoxia with the legend, SALVS ORIENTIS FELICITAS OCCIDENTIS ("well-being, or salvation, of the East, good fortune of the West"), again symbolizing through her the union of the two parts of the Empire, especially since Theodosius had no son.[129] At this time there was also consummated, as agreed years before, the transfer by the West to the East of the former's rights to Eastern Illyricum.[130] If the union envisioned by

126 *Ibid.* (the apparent dating to 436 is the result of misinterpreting a "postconsulate"—a common error; cf. Seeck, *Regesten*, p. 66, n. 3); Evag. *HE* 1. 20. 2; *Chron. Pasch.*, p. 582 *(Bonn)*; Prosp. 1328 (I, 475); *Chron. Gall. a. 511* 593 (I, 661); Cassiod. *Chron.* 1229 (II, 156); Merobaud. *Carm.* 1. 10; *Gest. Sen. ad CTh* 2; Marcell. *s.a.* 437 (II, 79); Malalas 14, p. 356 (Bonn); Theophanes, p. 92 (de B).

127 Marcell. *s.a.* 422, 1 (II, 75).

128 O. Ulrich-Bansa, "Note sulle monete dell' Augusta Aelia Licinia Eudoxia," *Numismatica e scienze affini*, I (1935), 25–31, at 27; *idem, Moneta*, p. 224, pl. I, 6; H. Dressel, "Erwerbungen des Königlichen Münzcabinets in den Jahren 1890–1897 (antike Münzen)," *Zeitschrift für Numismatik*, XXI (1898), 210–49, at 247–48 and pl. VII, 15; Voirol, *Verhandlungen der Naturforschenden Gesellschaft in Basel*, LVI: 2 (1945), 435–36.

129 De Salis, *Numismatic Chronicle*, n.s., VII (1867), 206.

130 Cassiod. *Var.* 11. 1. 9; Jord. *Rom.* 329; cf. above, Ch. V, n. 56; for details of what was involved, see Stein, *RhM*, LXXIV (1925), 356–57; Ensslin, *RE*, VIIA: 2 (1948), 2236. In view of this cession, apparently some bishops of the Balkan peninsula, subject to the Metropolitan of Thessalonica as the Pope's vicar, had shown some disposition to interpret the transaction as affecting the ecclesiastical sphere as well. On 18 Dec. 437, Pope Xystus wrote cautionary letters to the Illyrian episcopate and to Proclus, the Bishop of Constantinople, warning all concerned that ecclesiastical procedures in the Balkans should continue unchanged; Xyst. *Epp.* 9, 10 *(PL,* L, 612–18); cf. Batiffol, pp. 405–7.

this marriage had in fact taken place so that the children thereof had actually come to rule over East and West as was contemplated in 437, the effect of this transfer would have been of much less importance.[131]

But the de facto division of the Empire was nevertheless demonstrated during this same nuptial visit of Valentinian to Constantinople. During his stay in the Eastern capital the Western Emperor gave his assent to the promulgation of the *Theodosian Code,* then completed and awaiting publication;[132] by a constitution of 15 February 438,[133] the *Code* was published as law for the dominions of Theodosius, taking effect from 1 January 439. The Eastern Emperor summoned the Western consul for 438, Anicius Acilius Glabrio Faustus, who was present in Constantinople as a member of the entourage of Valentinian, and delivered a copy of the *Code* to him "by his own divine hand." At Rome in December of 438 in a meeting of the Senate held in the house of the consul Glabrio, who was also serving as Praetorian Prefect at the time, and under his presidency the *Code* was promulgated in the West,[134] with all Byzantine pomposity and the rythmical acclamations characteristic of the age.[135] But by the very constitution promulgating the *Code* Theodosius enacted, and Valentinian acquiesced, that Eastern laws should be valid in the West only by cognizance of the Western Emperor, while similarly Western laws had to be officially accepted by the Emperor of the East to obtain validity in that part of the Empire. The stated purpose of this provision was to avoid forgery,[136] but its effect was to accentuate the de facto increasing division of the Empire into what were gradually becoming two different states and societies. As a matter of fact, the legislative separation of the two parts of the Empire, in typical Roman fashion, was

---

[131] Güldenpenning, *Arcad. und Theod.,* pp. 309–10.

[132] *Gest. Sen. ad CTh* 2.

[133] *NTh* 1.

[134] *Gest. Sen. ad CTh* 2, 3, 7; on the question of the exact date in Dec. of the Senate meeting see Pietro de Francisci, "Per la storia del senato romano e della curia nei secoli v e vi," *Rendiconti Pont. Accad. Rom. Archeologia,* ser. 3, XXII (1946–47), 275–317, at 281 and n. 39.

[135] In *Gest. Sen. ad CTh* 5 is listed a series of acclamations, each with a number. Mommsen, *StR,* III, 1019, n. 3, held that the number indicated the number of persons who pronounced it; O. Hirschfeld convincingly argued, however, "Die römische Staatszeitung und die Acclamationen im Senat," *Sitzungsberichte . . . Berlin,* 1905, pp. 930–48, at 939–41, that the number indicated the (to us wearisome and ridiculous) number of times the acclamation was shouted.

[136] *NTh* 1.5–6.

by no means new; this law merely made explicit the de facto legislative isolation of the dominions of each Augustus which had been usual (although with exceptions) in the fourth century and absolute in fact since 395.[137] In the course of time, by a constitution of 1 October 447[138] Theodosius transmitted a number of his laws to Valentinian, who duly promulgated them for his own subjects on 3 June 448.[139] But Valentinian seems never to have sent his own laws to the East.[140] At least, Valentinian in 438 could feel satisfaction at the completion of a legal work in whose furtherance his mother in his name had taken such an active interest; neither he nor she could know, of course, that the principal historical importance of the *Code* would be its effect upon the laws of the new barbarian peoples of Europe rather than upon the Western Empire, whose years were numbered, and its role as almost the sole means of transmitting the Roman law to the Middle Ages until the rediscovery of Justinian's better sixth-century work of codification in the eleventh century. Nevertheless the *Theodosian Code*, with its severe limitations and its overshadowing by Justinian's work, as a vehicle for the transmission of the Roman law plays a part to this day in the rules under which the great majority of the civilized peoples of this planet lives.

After the marriage, perhaps in the hope of finding an atmosphere somewhat freer of the oppressive rigor of imperial protocol than the court of Constantinople, the bride and groom journeyed westward to Thessalonica where they spent the winter.[141] Then in the spring when the "good" season for traveling commenced they fared onward to the West and finally made their triumphant entry into Ravenna.[142] Our sources of course are not of the sort to tell us anything about the relations of Eudoxia with her mother-in-law or her sister-in-law, the Augusta Honoria. It will be seen, however, that the latter may well have felt that life had condemned her to a dull

137 See M. A. de Dominicis, "Il problema dei rapporti burocratico-legislativi tra 'occidente ed oriente' nel basso impero romano alla luce delle inscriptiones e subscriptiones delle costituzioni imperiali," *Istituto Lombardo di Scienze e Lettere, Rendiconti*, Cl. Lett. e Sci. mor. e stor., LXXXVII: 2 (1954), 329–487, esp. conclusions, 470–75.

138 *NTh* 2.

139 *NVal* 26.

140 Ensslin, *RE*, VIIA: 2 (1948), 2236, however, refuses to follow Seeck in drawing this conclusion from the sources.

141 Marcell. *s.a.* 437 (II, 79).

142 Marcell. *s.a.* 438, 3 (II, 79); *Chron. Gall. a. 511* 595 (I, 661).

and impotent backwater; if so, it is quite possible that she was jealous of the imperial consort, her sister-in-law. Eudoxia was to bear her husband two children, both unfortunately girls. The elder, named Eudocia after her maternal grandmother, was born either in 438 or 439; in all probability, as was customary at this time at the birth of the first child to the consort of an emperor, as a reward for the fulfillment of her duty, the rank of Augusta was conferred upon Eudoxia, 6 August 439.[143] The naming of the first daughter after the Empress of the East and the subsequent elevation of Eudoxia to the rank of Augusta undoubtedly pleased the Eastern branch of the family.[144] The second daughter, dutifully named Placidia after her paternal grandmother, was born about 442.[145] Unfortunately, both from the point of view of the dynasty and from that of the Roman Empire, which had to suffer intrigues stimulated by Valentinian's lack of a male heir, the Augusta Eudoxia bore no more children. That Valentinian III thus remained the last male descendant of the ruling house whose legitimacy was a principal element in what stability the Western Empire still possessed was a calamity which beyond doubt accelerated the disappearance of the imperial line in the West after his death; indeed, had he had a male heir, it is quite likely that Petronius Maximus might not have instigated his murder.

The Empress Licinia Eudoxia is still commemorated by a monument in Rome, although most of the thousands of persons who visit it every year are unaware of the fact. The ancient name of the

[143] Agnell. 31 gives the day and month (cf. *Cons. Ital.* 551 [I, 301]); *Chron. Gall. a. 511* 599 (I, 661) remarks, "Eudoxia Ravenna regnum accepit," which must mean her promotion to the rank of Augusta. This datum is listed for the year 438, but the taking of Carthage by Geiseric is dated to the same year by the Chronicle in the same entry; although that event certainly happened in 439; hence Seeck dates her promotion to 6 August 439, *s.v.* "Eudoxia" (2), *RE*, VI (1909), 925–26; Clover, "Geiseric," p. 129, n. 1; cf. *idem,* "Merobaudes," pp. 13–14; more cautiously refuses to decide between 438 and 439. Eudocia could therefore have been born either in 438 or 439; from early November, 437, to August, 438, is nine months. What we know of the rest of Eudocia's life accords with her birth in 438 or 439. She certainly was older than the younger Placidia, on whom see below, n. 145.

[144] Sirago, *Placidia,* pp. 314–15.

[145] Clover, "Merobaudes," pp. 15–18, on the ground that the daughter of Valentinian who married Palladius was Placidia (*CP,* LIX [1964], 27–28) argued that she must have been at least twelve at the time (the minimum age for a girl to marry under the Roman law); hence her birth occurred not later than 442 or 443. Merobaud. *Carm.* 1 celebrates the baptism of Placidia (shortly after her birth, presumably) and in that poem refers to the betrothal of Eudocia to Huniric, which occurred about 442, in connection with the Vandal treaty of that year.

Roman church of San Pietro in Vincoli is Basilica Eudoxiana (Italian Eudossiana); it contains Michelangelo's great statue of Moses, which presumably, rather than the reputed chains of Saint Peter, is the principal attraction that brings visitors to the church nowadays. This shrine on the Esquiline Hill, near the ancient site of the offices of the Urban Prefecture, was built originally in the fourth century and dedicated to all the apostles, it is likely in emulation of the Church of the Holy Apostles in Constantinople. At the expense mainly of Eudoxia during the pontificate of Xystus III[146] the building was handsomely reconstructed and dedicated primarily to Saints Peter and Paul; the new columns of Greek marble were probably taken from nearby ancient buildings, quite possibly the adjacent Baths of Titus and Trajan. The provenance of the chains of Saint Peter in the building is unclear.[147] Presumably such piety, especially in the form of building churches, a favorite occupation of Galla Placidia, made for a bond between the latter and her daughter-in-law.

[146] Probably in connection with the stay of the court in Rome in the winter of 439–40 (cf. Seeck, *RE*, VI [1909], 926; *idem, Regesten*, p. 368), despite the imminence of serious trouble with the Vandals (cf. Ensslin, *RE*, VIIA: 2 [1948], 2239).

[147] Best account in J. P. Kirsch, *Die römischen Titelkirchen im Altertum*, pp. 45–51; Lanciani, *Destruction*, p. 75. The dedicatory inscription is *ILS*, 819.

# 7

# OUR LORD
# JESUS CHRIST

In the year 438 when Valentinian III returned to Ravenna with his bride, his mother reached approximately half a century of life. Of her father's children who survived childhood neither Arcadius nor Honorius had attained any such age; fifty years were a full life in terms of the expectancy of antiquity. For the last thirteen of those years Galla Placidia had administered the West Roman Empire in the midst of the final crisis which was to terminate its existence. In the next century a courtier of another ruling princess would flatter her by writing that Galla Placidia had administered the Empire "slackly";[1] his bias is amply demonstrated by his writing that she had alienated (the whole of) Illyricum in order to gain a daughter-in-law. In the same exaggerating, perhaps willfully misunderstanding way he avers that she also "dissolved the soldiery by excessive peace." We have seen that if there was one area of government where she had little to say it was the military, and that surely quite contrary to her wishes. It is true that the imperial armies precipitously declined during her regime, for causes that in large part were beyond her grasp. It is more than amazing, however, to find any part of her lifetime called a period of "excessive peace." In any event, in late Roman practice a scapegoat must be found for military decline, and if it were not the Empress it must be Aëtius, and that was unthinkable, for Aëtius in the view of later Romans came to be identified as almost the last stalwart support of the Western Em-

---

[1] "Remisse," Cassiod. *Var.* 11. 1. 9.

pire. Hence the guilty person must be Galla Placidia, who had also corrupted and made effeminate her own son. Undoubtedly the political problem which Placidia grasped most easily, for it was obvious and imminent, was that of the great generals, and for that problem she failed to find a solution; it is difficult to see, however, how a woman who could not command the troops herself could possibly have done better.

She had in fact done well for five years until Aëtius murdered Felix; even then she might have retrieved the situation but for the death of Boniface and above all Aëtius' connections with the Huns, which she could not successfully counter even with the presumptive help of her first husband's people the Goths. In the last analysis she could rely upon the legitimacy of the dynasty backed up by her careful preparation and maintenance of alliance with the Eastern Empire, at least to keep the appearance and legal reality of power for her son, until the day should come when Aëtius would stumble, or would become alienated from his Hunnish friends. And she could ally herself and teach her son to ally himself with some elements in the Roman aristocracy in order to avoid falling into total and helpless dependency on Aëtius, and hope by trying to alienate supporters of the general to their side to increase their freedom of action. We shall see that in 442 Valentinian conceived an ingenious plan to try to counteract the influence of Aëtius; whether the inspiration was originally Placidia's or not, there seems little doubt that she heartily concurred in the project. Her piety and good works, shortly to be chronicled, were intended not only to benefit her own immortal soul, but to promote the welfare of the Roman Empire; the belief of that day that God would take care of the Roman Empire, if its rulers looked first of all to pleasing him, even at the apparent expense of attention to the Empire's welfare, was undoubtedly shared by her.[2] This idea too was basically Roman; the dim ancient kings of Rome over a millennium before had had as one of their principal duties the maintenance of good relations with the divine, the *pax deorum*. The divine was now the One True God, but the method of procedure remained, in what was once again, after centuries of doubt, an age of faith. At the same time, like Constantius, Placidia saw

[2] So Pope Celestine writes to Theodosius II, *Ep.* 19 (*PL*, L, 511–12); cf. the language of *NVal* 17. 1 (*init.*).

no contradiction in using the Church to serve the needs of the state and, as her conduct in the schism of Eulalius and Boniface demonstrated, also perceived no reason why the state should not interfere in the affairs of the Church, at least to preserve order, if not to promote other aims of its own. Against such obvious evils of her time as the declining finances of the Empire we have seen Placidia struggling; we have already exculpated her for not being able to halt or reverse the decline and fall of the Roman Empire. Although her appreciation of the value of law, Rome's great contribution to mankind, was more than lip service, she was no great statesman. With limited comprehension of the forces at work dissolving her ancient realm (hardly a justifiable charge against almost any statesman or politician of history), she had done her best both to guard the integrity of the Empire and to secure the accession of her son. One may note that she had not called Boniface from Africa to deal with Aëtius, from fighting for the Empire to fighting for the dynasty, until it was fairly clear that no more could be done in Africa, even although she may have learned of the presumed great disaster of the Huns sometime before she thus set in motion her attempt to overthrow Aëtius.

The presupposition underlying the foregoing discussion is that the growth of Valentinian III to manhood, conveniently symbolized by his marriage and return to Ravenna with his bride, did in fact mark a change in Galla Placidia's role in the government of the Empire. There can be little doubt that the acts of Valentinian as a boy are actually the acts of his mother. A difficult question is the real nature of Valentinian's acts after he became a man and before his mother's death. If Valentinian were the indolent voluptuary, the "half man out of his head" that Apollinaris Sidonius contemptuously calls him in a panegyric delivered to honor one of his successors,[3] it would be easy to continue the history of Galla Placidia by the expedient of attributing imperial policy (as distinct from Aëtius' influence) to her rather than her son. So some of our sources thought; a chronicler, for example, dates the beginning of Valentinian's reign only to his mother's death,[4] and

---

[3] *Carm.* 7. 359; cf. 532–33; 5. 305–6.

[4] *Chron. Gall. a. 511* 612–13 (I, 663); Agnell. 26 says that Valentinian began to reign at the time of the death of Saint Peter Chrysologus; the latter died in 450 (E. Stein, "Beiträge zur Geschichte von Ravenna in spätrömischer und byzantinischer Zeit," *Klio,* XVI [1920], 40–71, at 52); cf. Ensslin, *RE,* XX: 2 (1950), 1927.

many a modern scholar agreed until Stein's vindication of the Emperor, powerless in the grip of Aëtius.[5] Yet Sidonius himself, when he is not writing ex parte can refer to Valentinian as "dear for his pleasing the people," a "prince loyal to his obligations" (or, "pious"), a "just Emperor."[6] Yet could not even a good, just, and affable man be overly responsive to his mother's wishes, if not her puppet? Did Valentinian in fact exercise the imperial power for himself, as far as was possible in his time and circumstances? Some of his laws may indicate (whatever the cause) a piety somewhat less rigorous than his mother's. In 439 a law was promulgated which, according to precedents set by previous emperors, tried to preserve for the use of the remaining curials the property of their colleagues who entered the clergy, while for the future curials were forbidden to enter the Church at all; the reason for this enactment of course was that their property was needed to guarantee the collection of taxes for the state.[7] In 441 various tax immunities of ecclesiastics, as well as of other persons, were revoked, while in 452 (after Placidia's death) slaves, tenant farmers bound to the soil, curials, and members of the compulsory urban trades associations were forbidden to enter the clergy (in order not to lose their taxes or their services) and ecclesiastical jurisdiction was limited.[8] But of course such laws can well be attributed to the pressure of the nobility or Aëtius or both, or merely to a compromise with piety necessitated by the increasing financial difficulties of the Empire, as the revenues rapidly declined, especially after the loss of Africa. Certainly much of Valentinian's legislation was devoted to an ever more desperate search for revenues or their more adequate and efficient collection.

In the most famous and misunderstood of his laws, however, the Emperor Valentinian on 8 July 445 recognizes the pope's supreme jurisdiction over the churches of the West. But it is important not to look at such a grant in the light of the history of the Middle Ages to come, but of the history of Rome that had been. The state acknowledges this authority in the pope, as a matter of fact actually merely rendering more emphatic a decision of the Emperor

<hr />

5 *Hist.*, I, 337–42; Sirago, *Placidia,* most succinctly on p. xii, yet holds that Placidia dominated both Honorius and Valentinian; cf. W. Seston, *Propyläen Weltgeschichte,* IV, 565.

6 *Carm.* 9. 300, 23. 214, 423.

7 See above, Ch. I.

8 Stein, *Hist.,* I, 340, citing *NVal* 3, 10, 35.

Gratian to the same effect in 378. In the Roman tradition the state regulates the procedures of the state religion basically in its own interest, as a means of obtaining unity, or whatever state goal; and the reasons stated in this law are clearly secular, the dignity of the City of Rome and its Bishop, as well as the primacy of Peter. Like his father and mother before him Valentinian intends to use the Church in the service of the state, and in the tradition of the emperors his predecessors, both pagan and Christian. Valentinian is undoubtedly convinced that what the state has granted it can, if necessary, also take away.[9] This imperial command sprang from Pope Leo the Great's eventually successful attempts to suppress the efforts of Hilary, the contemporary Bishop of Arles, to vindicate the privileges once granted Patroclus partly, in all probability, through the efforts of Valentinian's father; the fact is ironic but irrelevant. The principle both men were following was the same, although circumstances dictated precisely opposite means of its application. And this principle was also that of the Empress mother.[10]

One aspect of the relation of Placidia and her son, however, strongly implies that she did not control him merely as a puppet. In 426, after the entry of the child Valentinian on his second consulship, Galla Placidia and the court left Rome after 24 February and arrived at Ravenna before 6 March. Thereafter the Empress remained at Ravenna, as far as we can tell from the places specified for the promulgation of her laws in her son's name, until 438.

---

[9] *NVal* 17 (cf. Leo *Ep.* 10 [*PL*, LIV, 628]), above all with the discussion of W. Ensslin, "Valentinians III. Novellen XVII und XVIII von 445," *Zeitschrift der Savigny-Stiftung*, Rom. Abt., LVII (1937), 367–78, at 374; cf. also Solari, *Rinnovamento*, I, 334; it is quite unhistorical to interpret this constitution in terms of the Middle Ages where the balance between the evanescent state and the Church often inclined in favor of the latter, instead of the Roman past from which it historically sprang, a past in which the religion of the state was considered merely one branch of state activity. Likewise *NVal* 18 (19 June 445) which proscribes the Manichaean heretics, undoubtedly in accordance with the wishes of Pope Leo (cf. *Ep.* 7 [*PL*, LIV, 620]), should not be seen primarily as an instance of the state's subserving the purposes of the Church. Leo had begun his attacks on the Manichees in accordance with long-standing imperial legislation; that he should suggest further measures to the Emperor against them is precisely the sort of thing done by the reports of secular officers in the process of initiating imperial legislation; in general see Ensslin, *ibid.*, 368–74; but cf., with a more traditional interpretation, Haller, *Papsttum*, I, 162.

[10] In 452, after his mother's death and perhaps with the removal of her influence, Valentinian much more narrowly limited the jurisdiction of bishops over the laity than she had done: *NVal* 35; cf. Gaudemet, *Église*, pp. 236–37; Voigt, *Staat und Kirche*, p. 21; Martroye, *Mém. de la Soc. Nat. des Antiquaires de France*, LXX (1911), 73–74.

Naturally, especially since the extant laws are not very numerous, this evidence does not preclude occasional short visits to Rome or other places. In 438 and 439 Valentinian appears in residence at Ravenna, but the first months of 440 were spent at Rome; the court then returned to Ravenna before 4 June 440 and remained there presumably through the first months of 441. In the summer of 442 the presence of Valentinian is attested at Rome and Spoleto; 443 and 444 place him at Rome or Ravenna, but the years 445–47 find him at Rome. The one law extant from 448 is dated from Ravenna as are the two of 449. We know that early in 450 Valentinian and his mother went to Rome. His mother remained there for the last months of her life and the laws attest the Emperor's presence in April and October 450.[11] In view of Placidia's decided preference for Ravenna, where she must have been largely involved in her building activities, especially after 438, these changes of residence show that Valentinian had a mind of his own, at least as to the residence of his court, and that his mind was not his mother's. Entirely apart from her obvious preference for Ravenna, however, there is some evidence that on at least one occasion while the Emperor was at Rome his mother remained at Ravenna (and presumably, therefore, on other occasions as well). In the summer of 445[12] Saint Germanus of Auxerre visited Ravenna in order to obtain pardon for the revolted Armoricans.[13] The account of this

---

[11] Seeck, *Regesten*, even-numbered pp. 352–86. It is a textbook maxim that the emperors of the fifth century regularly ruled from Ravenna; on the contrary, from the later years of Valentinian III onward more and more of their time was spent in the City. As far as we can tell, for the rest of his life, 450–55, Rome remained the usual residence of Valentinian; cf. *ibid.*, even-numbered pages 386–400; admittedly the evidence is scanty, no laws of Valentinian being preserved from 453, for example.

[12] For recent discussions of the date, cf. P. Grosjean, "Notes d'hagiographie celtique," *Analecta Bollandiana*, LXXV (1957), 158–226, at 180–85; E. A. Thompson, "A Chronological Note on St. Germanus of Auxerre," *ibid.*, 135–38. In the past other scholars have opted for 448: Bugiani, p. 155 and n. 4; Duchesne, *Hist.*, III, 412; Schmidt, *Gesch.*2, II: 1, 43; Stroheker, *Adel*, no. 178, p. 178; Chadwick, *Poetry*, p. 250; Lot, *Destinées*, p. 62, n. 30 (between 444 and 450, but probably 448); *idem, Gaule*, p. 482; Holmes, *Church*, p. 471 (death 449). In 448 Valentinian is attested at Ravenna on 3 June; Germanus was probably at Milan on 19 June and died at Ravenna on 31 July, cf. Grosjean, *ibid.* Hence Germanus could have just missed seeing Valentinian. In his recent ed. of the *V. S. Germani* (Paris, 1965), p. 106, R. Borius prefers 448 as the date of Germanus' visit to Ravenna.

[13] Const. *V. S. Germ. Autiss.* 35–45; this account was written about 480; cf. Stroheker, *Adel*, no. 97, p. 162. Ch. 35 should not be taken as implying that Valentinian was at Ravenna at that time. Likewise in ch. 44 the mention that "the Emperor" provided for the expenses of the homeward journey of Germanus' remains and granted permission to use the imperial post *(evectiones)* for the purpose as well as

visit, written to do honor to the saint, makes much of the veneration in which he was held by the Empress and the Bishop of Ravenna, Saint Peter Chrysologus, and recounts with great satisfaction their attentions to Germanus. Since it is incredible that the Emperor, Placidia's son, if present, would have paid no similar attention to the saint, we may conclude that he was not present, for no such attention is recorded. The implication of this account confirms the prima facie deduction from Galla Placidia's regular residence at Ravenna in 425–38 and her preoccupation with her works of piety there, that she did not ordinarily accompany her son when he went to Rome or elsewhere. But if Galla Placidia were in fact running the government of the Roman Empire after 438 as she had before, she must have accompanied the court. Besides, it is a general rule that if one is going to advise or manipulate another person, especially a person who regularly receives advice from many quarters, one had better not get too far away from him.

In fact, Valentinian seems to have had some disposition to free himself from the perhaps rather overpowering personality of his mother. Instead of remaining with her in the former residence of emperors at Ravenna, he constructed a new palace of his own, *ad Laureta* ("By the Laurel Groves"); we are told that he spent much of his time there.[14] This palace was quite possibly decorated with mosaic pictures of the imperial family, pictures which inspired the court poet Merobaudes to flights of more or less poetic fancy in his extant verses.[15] We also happen to be told by Apollinaris Sidonius[16] that Valentinian managed relations with the Eastern Empire himself. We may be sure, however, that Placidia continued to exert

---

imperial attendants for the journey does not necessarily imply that he was present in Ravenna, for undoubtedly his mother felt free to use the facilities of the court or state with or without her son's specific permission. The laws show that if the visit took place in 445 Valentinian could hardly have been at Ravenna, for 8 July found him at Rome where he remained the rest of the year. See Seeck, *Regesten*, pp. 374–76 (all laws from Rome).

14 Agnell. 40; cf. *Excerpt. Vales.* 55. Sirago, *Placidia*, p. 326, may make too much of this when he speaks of a "spirit of rebellion"; many a quite dutiful son, once married, has wished to remove himself from immediate parental supervision. On the other hand, when Sirago conjoins this "spirit of rebellion" with "indolence of character" (cf. Nagl, *Placidia*, p. 37), he seems to go beyond the evidence except for the traditional portrait which is to be disregarded as biased, as we have seen.

15 Merob. *Carm.* 1; cf. *CP*, LX (1965), 4–7.

16 *Carm.* 23. 228–32; if the reference is to a time after his mother's death, at least it implies that the Emperor did not supinely devolve the task on his ministers.

considerable influence with her son; Saint Germanus came to her so that her piety, presumably, would obtain the pardon he wished for the Armoricans. At the end of her life Placidia was able to persuade her son to spare his sister Honoria, although the latter was patently guilty of treason. And the fact that in general her son's policy is a continuation of her own, even after her death, also attests their good relations as well as her continuing influence on him. We know little about the Empress Eudoxia; although there is no evidence to suggest that she domineered over Valentinian as her mother (for a time) and her grandmother had dominated their husbands, yet one source seems to suggest that both she and her mother-in-law were able to influence Valentinian.[17] About 440 or 441 a coin of Ravenna commemorates twenty years of Galla Placidia's tenure of the rank of Augusta, with auguries for the next ten years.[18] We may assume, however, that after his return from the East in 438 Valentinian III presided alone over his Sacred Consistory.[19]

Valentinian was no more able to perform the superhuman task of stemming the decline and fall of the West Roman Empire than his mother had been; like those of his predecessors, his laws which try in vain to halt corruption, to distribute taxes more equably, to provide for the defense of the Empire by its native inhabitants, to divert the greed and oppression of the great landowners, to augment the diminishing revenues of the state[20] constitute a mirror which reflects the chronic ills of a society in dissolution.[21] Not only

[17] Polem. Silv. *Laterc.* 83 (I, 523); cf. Ensslin, *RE*, VIIA: 2 (1948), 2237. Unfortunately the passage states that the Empire was "possessed" by Theodosius and Valentinian with Placidia and Eudoxia, and may merely be a reference to the fact that all four had the title of Augustus, -a. See Dill, p. 164; Ensslin, *RE*, XX: 2 (1950), 1927.

[18] Voetter, *Münzen*, no. 2777, with pl. 15: DN GALLA PLACIDIA PF AVG; VOT XX MVLT XXX.

[19] W. Ensslin, "Valentinian III," in *Menschen die Geschichte machten*, ed. P. R. Rohden and G. Ostrogorsky, I, 223–28, at 225.

[20] The continuing desperate state of the government's finances is shown by such laws as *NVal* 6. 3 (persons of high rank to pay a money commutation for recruits—which they undoubtedly disliked but probably preferred to furnishing recruits themselves from their diminished manpower; 14 July 444) and *NVal* 15 (a sales tax to support the desperate needs of the imperial troops; last months of 444 or first days of 445). The government had need of more gold than it could collect in taxes, so the treasury had to buy it on the open market; see J. P. C. Kent, "Gold Coinage in the Later Roman Empire," in *Essays in Roman Coinage Presented to Harold Mattingly*, ed. R. A. G. Carson and C. H. V. Sutherland, pp. 190–204, at 196–97.

[21] A. Piganiol, "La Gaule au temps d'Attila," in *Saint Germain d'Auxerre et son temps*, pp. 119–33, at 124; Ensslin, *Menschen die Geschichte machten*, pp. 226–27.

was the lion's share of the provinces of the formerly great Prefecture of the Gauls either in the control of barbarians or suffering from their devastations or from the revolts of their disaffected peasants, the Bacaudae,[22] but the richest parts of Africa, still remaining to the Empire and its treasuries, were soon to be lost; the return of the poorer parts would make more for a drain on the revenues than a net gain. Thus Italy, imperfectly recovering from the devastation and capital destruction of 408–11, and shortly to be subjected to Vandal incursions and alarms, was left the almost impossible task of supporting the burden of Empire, a burden necessarily shouldered in the political and social conditions of the time by those least able to bear it. Thus Valentinian like his mother found it necessary to yield to the importunities of the great landowners; at a time of desperate financial straits he finds it politic to forgive all land-tax delinquencies up to 1 September 447 (law of 5 March 450).[23] Yet the Emperor could also concern himself with the administration of law and justice, demonstrating an interest which was part of the Roman tradition, but also an interest in which he was doubtless influenced by the precept and example of his mother. Thus in a law of 13 August 442 he concerns himself with the regulation of the careers, responsibilities, and privileges of lawyers; a year later he legislates for the relief of lawyers who have found it necessary to flee from Africa.[24] His interest in the administration of justice can cause him to admit that he has made a mistake in judging a case and reverse himself.[25] This is the more notable in that the Later Roman emperors, who proudly enact their constitutions as laws "which shall endure forever," were not ordinarily prone in their Sacred Imperial position to admit openly to mistakes.

There was always, however, the question of Aëtius, who from his preeminent position overshadowed the throne itself, even while on public occasions, presumably, he humbly knelt before his sovereign. In the next century Cassiodorus, favorably disposed to the Patrician, writes how Valentinian, "the Lord of the Earth (*rerum*)" followed Aëtius' advice in all things, in view of his own

---

22 Seeck, *Gesch.*, VI: 1, 124.

23 *NVal* 1. 3. 3; cf. Jones, *Roman Empire*, I, 205–6, 365.

24 *NVal* 2. 2–3; cf. Ensslin, *RE*, VIIA: 2 (1948), 2242.

25 *NVal* 8. 1 (9 June 440), revoked by 8. 2 (27 Jan. 441).

wisdom and the Patrician's "glorious labors on behalf of the state,"[26] for if Valentinian presided over a declining society, economy, and culture, he did not witness a marked decline of the theoretical extent of his dominions, except in Africa, largely because of Aëtius. Not only emperors, but even adjacent tribes, obeyed the Patrician's injunctions, says a late Byzantine, presumably copying an early source.[27] Apparently after the destruction of Litorius' Huns at Toulouse by the Goths Attila sent no more auxiliaries to Aëtius,[28] but the presumably continuing friendship of Attila and Aëtius, as well as the undoubted usefulness of the latter to the Empire (we may hope), stayed the Emperor's hand. New honors accrued to the Patrician; in the open area behind the Senate House in Rome a statue was erected in his honor, about 440, or at least after his second consulship in 437. The inscription on its base recorded his titles, his achievements in war, and his military decorations, this last a record uncommonly exhibited since the beginning of the third century.[29] It is probably correct, however, to see in Valentinian's creation of several Patricians as well as Masters of the Soldiery an attempt to diminish the importance of Aëtius.[30] Although he certainly must have visited Gaul from time to time, Aëtius seems to have spent much more of the decade of the 440's[31] in Italy than he had in the 430's. In the winter of 440/41 a boy was born to Aëtius at Rome, his second son, Gaudentius—the first and, as far as we know, only son of his second wife. The poet Merobaudes composed a poem to celebrate the child's first birthday in the winter of 441/42.[32] Both of the child's parents were in the City for this occasion.

A principal reason for the presence of Aëtius in Italy at this time was the renewal of hostilities with the Vandals. On 19 October 439 Geiseric, doubtless noting the involvement of the forces of the West

26 Cassiod. *Var.* 1. 4. 11.

27 Joh. Ant. Frag. 201. 3 (IV, 615).

28 Thompson, *Attila*, p. 125; Demougeot, *Mém. Soc. d'Agricult. Comm. Sciences et Arts Dép. Marne*, LXXIII (1958), 16.

29 Lugli, *Roma antica*, p. 138; A. Bartoli, "Il senato romano in onore di Ezio," *Rendiconti della Pont. Accad. Rom. di Archeologia*, 3. ser., XXII (1946–47), 267–73; Degrassi, *Bullett. Comm. Archeolog. Commun. Roma*, LXXII (1946–48), 33–44; Sirago, *Placidia*, pp. 367–68; *Ann. ép.*, 1950, no. 30.

30 Sirago, *Placidia*, p. 349, n. 2.

31 Levison, *Neues Archiv*, XXIX (1904), 140; in view of various of Aëtius' acts in Gaul in the 440's Sirago, *Placidia*, p. 349, seems to go too far when he says that Aëtius did not leave Italy in that decade.

32 Merobaud. *Carm.* 4, with Clover ("Merobaudes," pp. 21–24) and Vollmer, *ad loc.*

in Gaul, took Carthage by surprise, probably by suborning some sort of treachery in the city. Thus he undoubtedly achieved what had been his purpose since he first crossed to Africa. From this time the orthodox Christian sources depict a savage persecution on the part of the Arian King and his people against the orthodox church and its communicants in Africa. These statements are obviously polemical and ex parte; accordingly modern scholars are divided as to the weight that should be attached to them. But certainly they are hardly without foundation; otherwise it would be difficult to explain the undying aversion of the orthodox to the King and all his works, an aversion that is ultimately responsible for the unpleasant connotations which the term Vandal still bears. In the full expectation that the Western Empire would not spinelessly suffer the loss of its most valuable remaining province, as well as in the well-founded fear that the West would be assisted by the forces of the East which would also consider itself threatened, Geiseric did not passively await attack, but characteristically in 440 opened an offensive against Sicily. There was panic all along the exposed coasts of Italy, which momentarily expected the landing of Vandal soldiers. Valentinian therefore in effect suspended the Julian Law against Public Force and encouraged his subjects to take arms in their own defense.[33] Various measures were also undertaken to provide for the protection and threatened victualing of the City of Rome itself, and its walls were repaired.[34] Recruits were to be levied, while deserters and their fautors were to be arrested; nevertheless no citizen of Rome (the City) was to be compelled to serve except to man the walls; this last constituted a significant retreat from the principle of universal subjection to military service.[35] Some places in Sardinia and Italy were apparently raided in fact.[36] Sicily was an obvious staging area for any attack on Africa, as well as a principal source of Roman grain supply outside Africa itself; Geiseric shrewdly struck where the blow would do most harm.[37] At the end of 440, however, the Vandals withdrew from Sicily and returned to Africa; the forces of both the Eastern

---

[33] *NVal* 9 (24 June 440).

[34] *Ibid.* 5 (3 March 440).

[35] *NVal* 6, 5. 2; cf. Grosse, *Römische,* p. 202 and n. 2; Bury, *Hist.,* I, 39; Jones, *Roman Empire,* II, 619.

[36] Clover, "Geiseric," p. 74, suggests that improvements to the walls of Constantinople undertaken about this time may have been ordered out of fear of the Vandals.

[37] *Ibid.,* pp. 76–77.

and Western Empire were gathering against them; Aëtius was collecting what troops he could, and Theodosius was planning to send a naval expedition. In these circumstances Geiseric had no wish to be cut off from his African base and retired home to wait for further developments.[38] In the spring of 441 an Eastern armada arrived in Sicily; unfortunately, for one reason or another the expedition did little more than make itself a burden to the people of the island. In part this may have been due to restiveness among the Huns, which could have discouraged an Eastern expedition from becoming too involved elsewhere; in large part, however, it may have been owing to the malign influence of Aspar at the East Roman court. There the dominant military figure, Aspar did not want an expedition against the Vandals to succeed where he had failed less than a decade before; such a success would be too damaging to his prestige, and presumably he took steps to insure the expedition's inactivity.[39] And in the spring of 442, in view of attacks on the Eastern Empire by the Huns in Europe and other peoples in Asia, the expedition sailed home. Again the dependence of the West on the resources of the East for any large military undertaking was demonstrated by the fact that Valentinian thought he had no recourse but to open negotiations for peace with the Vandals.

Geiseric demanded and received for himself Byzacena and certain adjoining territories, including part of Numidia. Africa Proconsularis was divided among the Vandal warriors in hereditary allotments. The remaining provinces of North Africa, including territories previously occupied or ravaged by the Vandals, were returned to the Emperor.[40] The Vandal King also agreed to pay tribute each year, and handed over his son Huniric as a hostage to demonstrate his good faith.[41] In connection with this treaty, or shortly thereafter, an agreement was reached between Valentinian and Geiseric that Huniric should be affianced to the Emperor's daughter Eudocia.[42] Thus it is quite understandable that relations between the Vandals and the Western Empire were henceforth so

---

[38] *NVal* 9; cf. Clover, "Geiseric," pp. 79–80.

[39] Clover, "Geiseric," pp. 82–87, following a suggestion of Prof. W. E. Kaegi.

[40] Vict. Vit. 1. 13; cf. Prosp. 1347 (I, 479).

[41] Procop. *Bell.* 3 (*Vand.* 1). 4. 13; it is generally and rightly agreed that Procopius conflated the treaties of 435 and 442, and that these provisions belong to the latter date.

[42] Merobaud. *Carm.* 1. 7–8 (cf. 17–18, with Clover, "Merobaudes," p. 13), with *CP*, LX (1965), 5–7.

good that Huniric was eventually, before his marriage to Eudocia, returned to his father.[43] As a matter of fact, for the rest of Valentinian's life the Vandals did abstain from ravaging the Western Empire.[44] Sometime before 442 Geiseric had reached an understanding with the Visigothic King Theodoric. The latter's daughter, although the Goths and the Vandals were ancient enemies, had been affianced to Huniric; then, whether in view of the superior attractions of an alliance with the imperial house, or before that project was mooted for other reasons unknown, Geiseric suddenly broke off the alliance with the Goths and the engagement (or marriage) by claiming that the girl was trying to poison him; her nose was cut off, her ears clipped, and in this frightful condition she was returned to her father.[45] Geiseric's motives for welcoming this good understanding with the Empire are probably easy to divine. By thus guaranteeing the peace with a marriage alliance he probably concluded that he was effectively confirming his undisturbed possession of Africa without having to fear future attempts of either the Eastern or Western Emperor to dislodge him. Some of the Vandals were restive under his autocratic rule and the peace gave him a free hand to concentrate his attention on removing any check to his power among his own people. The tribute that he agreed to pay according to the treaty probably amounted to a promise to allow the grain supply of Rome to continue to be drawn from Africa; thus, as long as he abode by his agreement, the preoccupation of the Western government on that score would be set at rest. Likewise Valentinian by taking Huniric as hostage and arranging this marriage secured himself from future Vandal attacks, which the weakened Empire, with little or no navy and with what troops it had largely pinned down in Gaul, was in a very poor position to repulse. Presumably the rupture of good relations between the Goths and Vandals was also a source of relief both to Valentinian and to Aëtius.[46] But it is also likely that both parties had ulterior motives. Geiseric might now think of

[43] Procop. *Bell.* 3 (*Vand.* 1). 4. 14. If sect. 15 is taken literally (which is doubtful, for this is probably merely an approximately chronological transition), then Huniric returned home after Placidia's death (450).

[44] Hyd. 131 (II, 24) refers to an attack on a portion of Spain ruled by the Sueves; cf. Clover, "Geiseric," pp. 103–5.

[45] Jord. *Get.* 184; the reason for the savage treatment of the girl seems inexplicable, unless Geiseric perhaps was honestly convinced that she was in fact involved in a plot against him; in general see Schmidt, *Gesch.*2, I, 468–69.

[46] Clover, "Geiseric," p. 110.

himself as a future power behind the throne of the West. Even if
Valentinian were to have a son, that son would be the brother-in-
law of a Vandal king; in this fashion the Vandals might expect to
be able to exert pressure on imperial policy not only to favor themselves directly, but to the disfavor of their antagonists among other
barbarians such as the Goths. And if the Emperor had no son,
although Geiseric was probably knowledgeable enough to realize
that Huniric or Huniric's son could probably not be emperor, yet
any emperor of the house of Valentinian would be a close relative
by marriage, for example, a husband of Valentinian's daughter
Placidia the Younger. In fact, after Valentinian's death it was by
no means accidental that Geiseric favored the accession of Placidia's husband, Olybrius, to the Western throne.[47] But Valentinian had something even more to gain.

In 455 Geiseric was pleased to hold that the treaty of 442 was
dissolved by the deaths of Valentinian and Aëtius who had concluded it.[48] We may be sure that this pronouncement was merely a
legalistic excuse for acts which were really undertaken for quite
different motives, but it is some evidence that Aëtius in 442 was
an important figure in the conclusion of the treaty. Since his principal military interests were in Gaul rather than Africa, and since
any attempt to dislodge Geiseric, successful or unsuccessful, must
weaken his military position in Gaul (and presumably therefore
his alliance with important elements of the Gallic aristocracy), he
must have been quite relieved to have peace arranged with Geiseric
on these terms. Yet it is inconceivable that he could have welcomed
the marriage alliance between Valentinian and Geiseric.[49] For thus
the imperial family had gained powerful support from outside the
Empire, from a source that was beyond Aëtius' control. Eventually
he was to try to nullify this support by betrothing his own son
Gaudentius to the younger Placidia,[50] thus almost certainly insur-
ing the ultimate accession of Gaudentius to the throne; it was also
he, in all probability, who delayed the actual marriage of Huniric

47 Prisc. Frag. 29 (IV, 104).
48 Joh. Ant. Frag. 201. 6 (IV, 615); cf. Gitti, *Rapporti*, p. 72.
49 Despite Solari, *Rinnovamento*, I, 306; *idem*, "Dissidio costituzionale alla morte
di Valentiniano III," *Rendiconto delle sessioni della R. Accad. delle Scienze dell'
Istituto di Bologna*, Cl. sci. mor., ser. 3, X (1936–37), 11–45, at 23; Sirago, *Placidia*,
p. 300.
50 Prosp. 1373 (I, 483); cf. *CP*, LIX (1964), 24.

and Eudocia.[51] In 453 and 454 quarrels over this subject were to play an important role in precipitating Valentinian's murder of the general as the only way to rid himself of this incubus. So shrewd a politician as Aëtius must have understood this situation perfectly in 442. We must conclude, therefore, that this projected marriage was a plan of the imperial family in defiance of Aëtius. True, the Vandals were not nearly so powerful as the Huns, but they constituted some sort of counterbalance to Aëtius. It is easy to believe that Galla Placidia had wished long before this for barbarian auxiliaries of her own to employ against Aëtius; apparently she had tried to use the Goths for this purpose but had failed. She must have approved this project of her son's if she did not suggest it.[52] Nearly three decades before she and Athaulf had hoped that their marriage would bring the Goths to the support of the Empire; now perhaps the same end could be achieved by the marriage of her granddaughter.

It is commonly believed that by the treaty of 442 the Empire recognized Geiseric as an independent sovereign in Africa; almost certainly this is not true;[53] whatever the facts, the pride of the Late Empire did not formally cede territory or sovereignty, but merely allowed lands to be occupied "temporarily" by the barbarians under whatever conditions. In fact, of course, Valentinian must have realized that Africa was lost. Altogether, even with the marriage alliance, the peace was a humiliating one for the Empire. Much more importantly, it was a mortal blow from which the Western Empire was never to recover. Economically the imperial government had lost its most important source of revenue, and fell rapidly into ever greater impotence. While Valentinian lived the facade of Empire remained, but after his death his ephemeral successors came rapidly to rule little more than Italy, and that only in name mostly, since in varying degree they were dominated by their barbarian Masters of the Soldiery. The loss of Africa was beyond doubt the greatest single element in the dismemberment of the Empire, and in view of the importance which Africa had

[51] Gitti, *Rapporti,* pp. 54–61; Clover, "Geiseric," pp. 129–30, who points out that Eudocia was of marriageable age according to Roman notions in 450 and 451, yet the marriage did not take place.

[52] Gitti, *Rapporti,* pp. 52–53, speaking wrongly, however, of the year 446.

[53] See *NVal* 12. 2, 34. 3 (laws trying to relieve the afflicted provincials of Africa); Romanelli, *Storia,* p. 661; Gitti, *Rapporti,* p. 16 and n. 1.

obviously had in the past, it is unlikely that any statesman of the time could have failed to recognize the importance of its loss. The contemporary Eastern Bishop and historian Theodoret wrote that the tragedy of the Vandal conquest might even surpass the ability of Aeschylus and Sophocles to describe.[54] Nevertheless the court poet Merobaudes in a poem written not long after the conclusion of this peace celebrated it as a triumph of the all-highest Emperor, and could describe in the most flattering terms mosaic portraits of the imperial family which included no less a person than Huniric. The poet is inspired to happy thoughts of the concord and affection prevailing in the imperial family and to hint at the aid which the Vandal fleet may be presumed to bring the Empire. Galla Placidia is described as moved by great affection for her son.[55]

At Ravenna, however much she may have been involved in the Vandal marriage alliance, the Empress's thoughts and interests appear to have turned more and more to considerations of religion and the life to come. A contemporary chronicler speaks of Placidia's "blameless life after her conversion."[56] Unfortunately we are not told when this "conversion" took place. In all probability, however, we will not be far wrong if we date it either to about 423 or 438 or sometime in between. In 423 occurred her escape from the peril of the sea by imploring the intercession of Saint John the Evangelist; after 438 there is a strong presumption that she withdrew from the day-to-day conduct of the affairs of state. As the term "conversion" was used in the fifth century, the leading of a more perfect life to please God was understood. Sometimes persons who had professed an attempt to lead a perfect Christian life removed from their families to dwell near monks (or holy women); more often they continued to reside with their families or close by. Above all, they led lives of perfect chastity which for many centuries Christians conceived to be particularly pleasing to God; obviously,

---

54 Theodoret *Ep.* 29 (*PG*, LXXXIII, 1208); cf. Thompson, *Hermathena*, LXXVI (1950), 59.

55 Merobaud. *Carm.* 1; cf. *CP*, LX (1965), 4–7. Merobaudes was a partisan of Aëtius; naturally, however, in public Aëtius must profess himself quite satisfied by the arrangements with the Vandals. See also *Pan.* 2. 27–29. *Contra:* Gitti, *Rapporti*, pp. 23–24. A panegyrist says what is appropriate to say, not necessarily what is true. There is no more reason to accept Merobaudes' implication that Aëtius approves of the marriage than there is to concur in his flattering interpretation of the peace in general.

56 *Chron. Gall. a. 452* 136 (I, 662); cf. Soz. *HE* 9. 16. 2; Oros. 7. 43. 7.

therefore, Placidia could hardly have entered upon such a regime before her second husband's death in 421. If she had entered into a pact of chastity with Constantius after the births of Honoria and Valentinian, as married couples sometimes did, this would have been a notable fact which the historian Olympiodorus would have commemorated, and his episcopal epitomator Photius would have been very likely to extract. Apart from chastity, a "convert" embraced a life of austerity in food and clothing, commonly read holy books, and regularly and frequently attended upon the services of the Church. Thus Placidia thought it incumbent upon her on the occasion of a visit to Rome first of all to pay her respects, or rather to offer her devotion (together with her family), to Saint Peter.[57] Frequently baptism was the occasion of "conversion," but we have no idea when Placidia was baptized.[58] It is quite possible that she was led to embark upon this kind of life by the example of her pious niece in Constantinople, the Augusta Pulcheria. In 450 Placidia writes to the latter and mentions their common devotion to the faith;[59] it is quite possible that she is referring to their common attachment to a semimonastic life, as well as to their shared theological beliefs.

The piety of the Empress, as well as her acceptance of many of the beliefs and practices of the popular religion of her day, can be seen in her welcome to Saint Germanus of Auxerre on the occasion of his visit to Ravenna, probably in 445. Saint Germanus had hoped to avoid the crowds which flocked to greet him by entering the city under the cover of night. But tidings of his coming had preceded the holy man and a watch was kept for his arrival. Even if the sentinels meant were not official guards, we may assume that Placidia had had a part in instituting this watch. Both Placidia and Bishop Peter Chrysologus, with most of official and ecclesiastical Ravenna following their example, eagerly made Germanus welcome. Placidia sent to his quarters a silver dish containing a variety of delicious meatless foods. The saint accepted the gift, distributing

---

57 *Ep. ad Theod. ap. Epp. S. Leon. Magn.* 56 (*PL*, LIV, 859–62, at 859); *Ep. ad Pulch. ibid.* 58 (*ibid.*, 863–66, at 863); hereafter these will be cited merely as *Ep. ad Theod.* and *Ep. ad Pulch.* respectively.

58 On "conversion" in the fifth century, see esp. E. Griffe, "La pratique religieuse en Gaule au Ve siècle: Saeculares et sancti," *Bulletin de littérature ecclésiastique,* LXIII (1962), 241–67, at 253–54; for examples of female conversion, *ibid.*, 264–67. The use of the word in this sense is illustrated and defined in *V. S. Lup. Trecc.* 2.

59 *Ep. ad Pulch.*

the food to those who attended him and the proceeds of the silver salver to the poor. In return he sent the Empress a wooden plate with a barley loaf; Placidia was delighted by this exchange as well as by the charity which her gift had made possible. She had the wooden plate set in gold, and the bread was preserved as a precious relic which worked healing miracles. The adopted son of a court eunuch serving as Provost of the Sacred Bedchamber (to the Empress presumably) was healed by the saint's exorcism after the Empress arranged for the young man to be taken to him. When Germanus fell ill of his mortal illness the Empress went in person to visit him, and provided at his request that his remains should be taken back to Gaul. When he died, Placidia eagerly took possession of his little box with holy relics; in return she provided the vestments for the corpse.[60] She also apparently had a high opinion of another holy man, Saint Barbatianus, about whom almost nothing is known, for together with Saint Peter Chrysologus she arranged for his burial at Ravenna.[61]

While the Empress was thus willing to credit the miracles of God through his saints, living or dead, like a good Christian, as we have seen, she was also unalterably opposed to the practice of black magic, or to pagan miracles.[62] We may take it for granted that she regularly attended the service of God in the various churches of Ravenna. An extant sermon of Peter Chrysologus (Bishop from some time after July 432 until his death on 3 December 450),[63] delivered either on the day of his consecration or at least on an anniversary thereof, mentions the presence of the Augusta Placidia, "mother of the Christian, enduring, and faithful Empire," and compliments her faith, charitable work, and holiness, to the glory of the Holy Trinity. He then goes on to draw a flattering parallel, which another age would regard in the worst of taste, if not outright blasphemous: "she has (thus) merited to procreate, embrace, and possess an August Trinity"; that is, she bore Valentinian III,

60 Constant. *V. S. German. Autiss.* 35, 39, 42–44. Some of the details may be suspect in a work of hagiography, but they reflect the popular religion of the time and there is no reason a priori to reject them, especially since the standard of historicity of this *Life*, written about a generation later, is quite high.

61 Agnell. 51; the *V. S. Barbatiani*, Muratori, II: 1, 195–98, is clearly a work of pious fiction.

62 See above, Ch. IV, n. 30; Ch. III, n. 55.

63 Stein, *Klio*, XVI (1920), 52. Saint Peter Chrysologus was proclaimed a Doctor of the Church by Pope Benedict XIII in 1729; his feast is 4 Dec.

Augustus, married Constantius III, Augustus, and holds the rank of Augusta herself. At the end of the sermon he exhorts his brethren to pray that the devotion of the clergy may be the return of the "pious devotion" of the Christian emperors.[64] The church of Ravenna had indeed good reason to be grateful to Placidia, for entirely apart from her extensive building of churches in the city, it is quite possible that she endowed the service of God in her favorite city with estates in Sicily where she is previously recorded with Constantius as owning properties extensive enough to require a steward.[65] The Empress was a wealthy woman in her own right; her father had granted her valuable estates in the East, when he founded the "household of Placidia" for her,[66] and presumably her Western properties were not limited to Sicily, for, apart from her father, she was the heiress of Constantius and perhaps of Honorius as well. All taken together these properties were sufficiently extensive to require the establishment of a separate bureau of accounts for them in the imperial administration.[67] The existence of a Provost of the Sacred Bedchamber to the Empress, as revealed by the *Life of St. Germanus*[68] presumably implies the existence of a separate imperial household for the Augusta, as one would expect; presumably she would support this household from her own income.[69] The Augusta Honoria had a household of her own,[70] probably set up for her by her mother. Some of the revenues of Placidia may have been diverted to the needs of the state,[71] but much of it must have gone to support the Empress's piety, which she doubtless also conceived as being in the service of the state. Apart from Pope Celestine's declaration to the effect that the real service of the state was the service of God, Placidia wrote to

[64] S. Petr. Chrys. *Serm*. 130 (*PL*, LII, 556–57).

[65] Agnell. 31 with Olympiod. Frag. 15 (IV, 60); the suggestion is Schild's, *Placidia*, p. 65.

[66] These properties eventually passed to her son and then to her grandchildren; cf. Malch. Frag. 13 (IV, 120).

[67] *Not. Dig. Oc*. 15. 9 (p. 159, Seeck); with J. B. Bury, "The Notitia Dignitatum," *JRS*, X (1920), 131–54.

[68] Ch. 39.

[69] On the estates of empresses in general, see His, *Domänen*, pp. 81–82.

[70] Marcell. *s.a.* 434 (II, 79; wrongly dated); Joh. Ant. Frag. 199. 2 (IV, 613).

[71] *CTh* 11. 1. 36 (431); by Galla Placidia, referring, however, to the *patrimonium* of the Emperor, and perhaps only to the *res privata* (but if by *patrimonium* she meant only *res privata* rather than the really private estates of the individual who happened to be emperor, the statement loses much of its force).

Pulcheria[72] that God "has entrusted the world to Our empire to be governed and preserved." Thus according to divine disposition service to God and the Empire amount to the same thing, the traditional Roman view that religion and what we call politics are identical.

Theologically Placidia professes herself devoted to the cause of orthodoxy as guarded by the emperors from Constantine the Great (although the latter was baptized on his deathbed by an Arian bishop as we have noted, orthodox Christians preferred to forget this uncomfortable fact; and several of his successors in the East had had strong Arian leanings);[73] likewise in her extant letters at the time of the schism between Eulalius and Boniface she laid strong emphasis on the desirability or necessity of good moral character on the part of bishops. Yet on the one hand she had not scrupled to marry an Arian Goth (and possibly to allow her first-born son to be baptized by an Arian bishop), and even after her "conversion" presumably to acquiesce in, if not to promote, the marriage of her granddaughter to the son of an Arian heretic and a persecutor of the orthodox. On the other hand, she had also felt no visible compunction at forwarding the ambitions of Patroclus, both before and after her second husband's death, although common report, at least, held his morals to be most questionable.[74] It seems fairly obvious that when the interests of the Roman Empire or of her family were involved (and the two were probably closely related if not indistinct in her mind), Placidia's religious convictions were quite capable of some degree of elasticity. And when she writes to Pulcheria and Theodosius in 450 to promote what she considers orthodoxy as interpreted by the Bishop of Rome, one wonders how much of this zeal is purely religious and how much is owing to Roman pride which sees in the Bishop of the City the supreme head of the whole Church. Naturally Westerners, from Pope Saint Leo the Great (440–61) himself, saw the occupant of the Roman See as head of the Church, or at least its most high-ranking dignitary, partly because of the primacy of Peter, but in large part because the Pope was the Bishop of the imperial City. It would be only human for Placidia, who with her

---

[72] *Ep. ad Pulch. ad fin.*
[73] *Ep. ad Theod.; Ep. ad Pulch.*
[74] *Chron. Gall. a. 452* 74 (I, 654).

son owed so much to the support of Constantinople (support which she could hardly forget had not been originally willingly granted), to find a certain consolation amid the grave difficulties of the West to be able to assert in the name of God and religion the primacy of the elder Rome. After all, it was the *Roman* Empire.

It was also quite human that Placidia's religion should be inconsistent, or even illogical. Of the sincerity of her belief, however, there can be little doubt. She fervently believed in her God; that that God had a strongly Roman tinge is no argument against the assertion; nor is it to be held against her that she accepted some of the crasser beliefs of popular religion. Again, since she was human, she probably fell into the sin of pride and thought of herself as a good Christian, although not a saint. She had every right except for the Christian prohibition of pride to do so, for her contemporaries acclaimed her piety in both East and West. We may be sure that Galla Placidia loved her Lord and tried to do his bidding as she understood it; that her motives were not unmixed merely means that like nearly all his followers she had not attained the perfection of a saint like Francis.

Among the Christian Roman emperors and empresses Galla Placidia Augusta has a distinguished record as a great builder to the glory of God, and deservedly so, for if the casual American or European retains any recollection of the Empress, it is likely to be as a builder of churches. It is an instance of the irony not uncommon in history that the building by which she is best remembered by men who have even the slightest appreciation of art is probably erroneously connected with her name. In the imperial City itself the name of Galla Placidia is still most conspicuously to be seen in the Basilica of Saint Paul-outside-the-Walls. The first half of the pontificate of Pope Saint Leo the Great coincided with the last ten years of the life of Galla Placidia. During that period she apparently contributed heavily to the restoration of Saint Paul's, which had been severely damaged by a thunderbolt. The work in which the devotion of the Empress played a part is still commemorated in the mosaics of the fifth century which adorn the triumphal arch leading into the choir (see Pl. VIII). Beneath the ceiling and next to it a mosaic inscription records the fact that Theodosius the Great began the work of erecting a more imposing church to replace the basilica Constantine the Great had erected over the tomb of the Apostle, and the work thus begun had been continued by Honorius. On the arch itself another mosaic inscription reads, "The pious [or, faithful] mind of Placidia rejoices that the whole beauty of her father's work is resplendent through the zeal of the Pontiff Leo." Between the two inscriptions are mosaics which had been ill restored even before the great fire which gutted much of the church in 1823. Above the center of the arch is a portrait of a bust of Christ, whose head is surrounded by a radiate nimbus. In his left hand he originally held a cross, which has unfortunately been restored merely as a wand of authority. The figure seems in the tradition of the Christos Pantokrator, Christ the Ruler of All, which, regularly with the stern features of the Supreme and Final Judge, was simultaneously to glorify and render awesome the interior of so many Byzantine churches for centuries to come in the Middle Ages. On either side of the head of Christ are two of the symbols of the four evangelists, and beneath them on each side a praying angel and twelve of the twenty-four elders of the Revelation (4 : 4, 10–11), offering their crowns to Him Who sits upon the Throne. Below, one on each side of the springing of the arch, are the two apostles, Saints Peter and Paul.[75] The Roman church now known as Santa Croce in Gerusalemme, but originally as Sancta Hierusalem (Jerusalem) was built not by Constantine the Great, as Christian tradition has it, but by one of his successors; a hall of the Sessorian Palace, former residence of the Empress Saint Helena, mother of Constantine, was utilized for the purpose. The church was supposed to contain a fragment of the true cross which Saint Helena was reputed to have found in Jerusalem. Galla Placidia, acting also in the name of her son and daughter, consecrated mosaics here sometime before the year 438; an inscription now lost recorded the fact: "May the kings of the earth and all peoples, leaders, and all judges of earth praise the name of the Lord. Valentinian, Placidia, and Honoria, Augusti, have paid their vow to the Holy Church Hierusalem." It has been thought that the vow was connected with the saving of Placidia and her children from the sea in 423, but that vow was directed to Saint John the Evangelist, and there is no reason to believe that Placidia with her

---

75 *Coll. Avell.* 3; *Lib. Pont.* 47. 6 (in Duchesne's ed., with I, 240, n. 7). Nagl, *Placidia*, p. 57; Armellini, *Chiese*, II, 1151–52, 1158; Grisar, II, 74; F. W. Deichmann, *Frühchristliche Kirchen in Rom*, pp. 31–34; E. Kirschbaum, *The Tombs of St. Peter and St. Paul*, trans. J. Murray, pp. 185, 187–90, 193–94.

children could not have made another vow on some other occasion, this time in connection with the Church of Jerusalem in Rome.[76] All certain trace of the mosaics has vanished, and the building today has been hideously transformed by successive rebuildings in the course of centuries.[77]

Although Placidia was a confirmed believer in the greatness of Rome, as we have seen, her preferred residence was Ravenna; it must be admitted, however, that it is a little hard to see why. At the present time Ravenna is relatively dry, although the water table is just beneath the surface of the ground, as the puddles of water frequently standing on the floor of San Vitale and the pumping service for the lower floor of the Mausoleum of Theodoric the Great attest. But in antiquity it must have presented a watery appearance such as we now associate with Venice, Amsterdam, or Stockholm. It was surrounded by water with the sea to the east, marshes to the west, arms of the Po to the north and south; part of the river's waters also flowed through the city itself in canals. The Greek geographer Strabo, writing four centuries before Galla Placidia's time, speaks of the tides scouring out these canals and the resultant purity of the air. But in the later fifth century Apollinaris Sidonius talks of the barge poles turning up noisome sediment from the bottom of the canals, and of the midges or mosquitoes which infested the place. At the end of the first century the poet Martial had complained of the difficulties of obtaining potable water, and although shortly afterwards the Emperor Trajan had constructed an aqueduct to bring fresh water to the city—an aqueduct still in use in the early sixth century—nevertheless Sidonius also complains about the lack of good drinking water.[78] It seems quite probable that the progressive drying up of the land because of the deposit of silt carried down by the Po had changed Ravenna's air and water for the worse. In the fifth century the city existed in three parts: Ravenna proper, its bustling port of Classis

[76] Although Agnell. 42 does quote an inscription from Saint John the Evangelist's Church at Ravenna referring to the Temple of Jerusalem.

[77] *ILS*, 817; *Lib. Pont.* 34 (with Duchesne in his ed., I, 196, n. 75); Lanciani, *Churches*, pp. 226–27; Bury, *Hist.*, I, 262, n. 5; Nagl, *Placidia*, pp. 57–58; Armellini, *Chiese*, II, 981, 986, 1282; R. Vielliard, *Recherches sur les origines de la Rome chrétienne*, pp. 59–60; Deichmann, *Kirchen*, pp. 30–31; R. Krautheimer, *et al.*, *Corpus Basilicarum Christianarum Romae* (1937 ff.), I, 168; Ensslin, *RE*, XX: 2 (1950), 1930.

[78] Strab. 5. 213; Mart. *Ep.* 3. 56, 57; Ap. Sid. *Ep.* 1. 5. 5–6, 1. 8. 2–3; *Excerp. Vales.* 71; Procop. *Bell.* 5 (*Goth.* 1). 1. 16–23; Jord. *Get.* (from Cassiod.) 147–51; Cassiod. *Var.* 5. 38. 2.

originally built three miles away by the Emperor Augustus, and a long joint suburb of both, strung out along the road between them. Of this suburb hardly a trace remains today; the rustic solitude which surrounds the Church of Sant' Apollinare in Classe, a solitude broken only by the sound of trucks whizzing by on the main road to Ravenna, is the site of the once great port and Early Empire naval station of Classis.

Like most Roman cities Ravenna had a Capitol; there was also a temple of Apollo, and other shrines were consecrated to various of the ancient gods; presumably these were closed and deserted in the fifth century. Entering Ravenna by the road from Classis one passed through the Porta Vandalaria. Another entry was by the Porta Aurea, or Golden Gate; nearby were an amphitheater and a stadium. Salvian says disgustedly that the obscene performances of the theater were still exhibited in fifth-century Ravenna. In the area surrounding the present Church of Santa Croce were extensive buildings which comprised the imperial complex; modern archeology has discovered some magnificent mosaic flooring of the early fifth century.[79] Stretching from Ravenna northward and around the head of the Adriatic to Istria and Dalmatia were luxurious villas belonging to the rich and the noble, and forming a resort which Cassiodorus in the sixth century compares to Campania.[80] Since the days of Augustus the Prefect of the Imperial Fleet had been an important figure in Ravenna; in the Late Empire he seems to have remained significant in the secular administration of the city, although by the fifth century the war fleet that he commanded existed mainly on paper. Responsible to the Master of the Soldiers in the Presence, besides the Fleet Prefect, there was a Prefect of the "Junior Italic Soldiers," who probably served as police.[81] The statement in a late source that Valentinian III "commanded and decreed" that Ravenna should be head of Italy, second

[79] Salvian *Gub. Dei* 6. 49; R. Farioli, "Ravenna paleocristiana scomparsa," *Felix Ravenna*, LXXXII (1960), 5–96; LXXXIII (1961), 5–88 (to be used with caution, for she ignores the work of Stein, *Klio*, XVI [1920], summary, p. 52, in reconstituting the list of the bishops of Ravenna); Diehl, *Ravenne*, pp. 12, 22; Goetz, *Ravenna*, pp. 8–9; M. Gütschow, "Grabungen in Ravenna," *Gnomon*, III (1927), 126–27, at 126; Hodgkin, *Invaders*, I: 2, 853–54. On the mints of Ravenna, Maull, *Felix Ravenna*, LXXXIV (1961), 80.

[80] *Var.* 12. 22.

[81] Stein, *Klio*, XVI (1920), 59–60, 63, n. 1 (for a discussion of the local administration of Ravenna in general, see 59–71); at least in the time of Cassiodorus (*Var.* 7. 8) there also existed a "Prefect of the Watch" (with responsibility for fires as well?) of the city of Ravenna.

only to Rome,[82] is doubtless a fiction of local pride, but as long as the emperors frequently resided in the city the statement must be true in fact. The presence of the emperor at Ravenna also worked powerfully to enhance the position of its bishop in the ecclesiastical hierarchy, much as had happened above all at Rome, to a lesser extent at Arles and Milan (here of course the powerful personality of Saint Ambrose had been at least as important a factor). In the time of John I (Bishop of Ravenna 396–after 431) Valentinian, that is, very probably Galla Placidia, raised the bishop of Ravenna to the rank of metropolitan (archbishop) over several surrounding dioceses at the expense of Milan or Aquileia.[83]

This city, with its trade and commerce, flourishing even in the Late Empire,[84] distinctively Christian although with pagan survivals, Galla Placidia proceeded to adorn with monumental church buildings. Even though most of these have vanished, her name has been indelibly connected with the city, along with that of Theodoric the Great and Justinian in the next century (and Dante, whose tomb is there, to the irritation of modern Florentines).[85] In accordance with her vow of 423 Placidia constructed in the imperial quarter a church in honor of Saint John the Evangelist. We may assume under the circumstances that the building was erected not long after her accession to power in 425; in any case it must have been built and dedicated before 438. Unfortunately the building which honors the saint in Ravenna today is a twentieth-century learned reconstruction of the Empress's church, which carefully incorporates the rather insignificant surviving fragments of her original structure. In general the modern building can give only a vague idea of the character of the original structure, for the mosaics with which the Empress caused her church to be adorned are completely lost; we can only guess at their original character

---

82 Agnell. 40. Nagl, *Placidia*, p. 58, relates this statement only to the church of Ravenna, but it would seem that Agnellus intended a wider application, since it comes at the end of a chapter in which he has dilated upon Valentinian's favors to the church and to the city as well.

83 Agnell. 40 (with Holder-Egger *ad loc.*); Jalland, *St. Leo*, p. 97 and n. 7; Stein, *Klio*, XVI (1920), 48–52; L. Ruggini, "Ebrei e orientali nell' Italia settentrionale fra il IV e il VI secolo d. Chr.," *Studia et documenta historiae et iuris*, XXV (1959), 186–308, and n. 82 (with additional citations); Ensslin, *RE*, XX: 2 (1950), 1929.

84 In general, Ruggini, *Economia e società*.

85 Many a tourist has come to Ravenna primarily to visit the poet's tomb, and has left impressed rather with the great monuments of the art of the fifth and sixth centuries. But Dante's imperishable monument is not to be found in edifices subject to bombing or reconstruction, or undermining or the vibration of modern traffic.

and quality from descriptions and approximate copies, and from the slightly later mosaics of her so-called Mausoleum. The church was extensively rebuilt in the Middle Ages and again remade in the Baroque style in 1747. There were still some ancient elements to be seen despite these rebuildings at the beginning of the twentieth century. Unfortunately the railroad station of modern Ravenna was constructed nearby and the church was almost completely destroyed by aerial bombs in 1944.

From literary descriptions of the mosaics of the apse and triumphal arch it is possible to gather an approximate idea of their subjects. Apparently there were mosaic pictures of Theodosius II and Eudocia on the right, and on the left Arcadius and his wife Eudoxia the Elder. Somewhere there were also portraits of other Late Roman emperors, presumably those mentioned in the inscriptions. In the vault God was depicted seated on a throne with twelve sealed books; at his side was an inscription by which Galla Placidia Augusta with her son Placidus Valentinianus Augustus and her daughter Justa Grata Honoria Augusta dedicated the church to "the Holy and Most Blessed Apostle John the Evangelist," in accordance with their vow for having been saved from the peril of the sea. Christ was also depicted holding a book on which were written the Latin words, "Blessed are the merciful, for God will have mercy [on them]" (not quite Matt. 5 : 7). Another scene showed God delivering a book to Saint John the Evangelist. A mosaic picture also showed Saint John in the act of saving the Empress and her children from the sea; this was apparently balanced by a scene depicting various symbols of the Book of Revelation. Finally, in the apse above the bishop's throne there was a picture of a bishop, apparently Saint Peter Chrysologus, represented in the act of celebrating mass. An inscription identified the portraits of Placidia's relatives; another read: "Galla Placidia has paid her vow in behalf of herself and all of these." Then were listed "the divine Constantine, the divine Theodosius, the divine Arcadius, the divine Honorius, Theodosius Most Noble Boy"; and in a corresponding series, "the divine Valentinian, the divine Gratian, the divine Constantius, Gratian Most Noble Boy, John Most Noble Boy."[86] Thus Galla Placidia commemorated not only the discharge

---

[86] The inscription is no longer extant and depends upon a copy (*ILS*, 818. 1–6, with Dessau's notes). With Ensslin, *RE*, XX: 2 (1950), 1915, I read *n. p.* for the *nep.* of the copy; almost certainly, also, the second Constantinus should be Constantius.

of her vow to Saint John, but her family as well, and thereby the legitimate claim of herself and her children. Deceased emperors are entitled "divine," a usage which was originally pagan. The Most Noble Gratian and John are almost certainly Placidia's brothers who died in infancy; the Most Noble Theodosius can only be her son by Athaulf. We shall see that there is also even more striking evidence to show that her long lost firstborn child still had a secure place in Galla Placidia's heart. Here with fond and loving pride she places him in her imperial family and gives him the imperial title of Most Noble Boy. But the feature which most clearly indicates that this building and its decorations are to serve the purposes of pride and propaganda as well as piety is the inclusion of the "divine Constantine," that is, Constantine the Great. His granddaughter had been married to Placidia's half uncle Gratian; Christians so reverenced the first Christian Emperor that Galla Placidia thought it most desirable to stress so important, although tenuous, a connection with her family. The veneration continued; the name Constantine was to be that most commonly borne by Byzantine emperors; both Placidia and her nephew Theodosius II agree in their correspondence of 450 that it is necessary to maintain the faith as handed down from Constantine.[87]

The principal church of the imperial quarter of Ravenna was that of the Holy Cross (Santa Croce), which Galla Placidia also either constructed or embellished, to serve in effect as a chapel for the palace. It was filled with works of art and value, mosaics and marbles, honoring "Christ, the Father's Word, the Concord of the

[87] *Ep. ad Theod.*; Theod. to Placidia, *Ep. ap. epp. S. Leon. Magn.* 63 (*PL*, LIV, 877–78); cf. W. Hartke, *Geschichte und Politik im spätantiken Rom*, Klio, Beiheft xlv, p. 80 and nn.; Treitinger, *Oströmische*, pp. 129–33 and nn.; A. Chastagnol, "Le problème de l'histoire auguste: État de la question," *Antiquitas*, 4th ser. *Beiträge zur Historia-Augusta-Forschung*, II (1964), 43–71, at 65; Van Millingen, p. 24. On the Church of Saint John and its mosaic decorations in general, see E. Müntz, "The Lost Mosaics of Ravenna," *AJA*, I (1885), 115–30, at 119–21 (followed in the text); Goetz, pp. 20–22; Farioli, *Felix Ravenna*, LXXXIII (1961), 21, 42, 44–48 (cf. fig. 51, p. 48, with a reconstruction of the whole system of mosaics and inscriptions according to Ricci); Nagl, *Placidia*, pp. 52–54; G. T. Rivoira, *Lombardic Architecture: Its Origin, Development and Derivatives*, I, trans. G. M. Rushforth, 21–26; L. Scevola, "La Basilica di S. Giovanni Evangelista a Ravenna," *Felix Ravenna*, LXXXVII (1963), 5–107, at 42–46. A miniature from a 14th century MS of Rainaldus in the Bibliotheca Classensis, it has been suggested, is copied from, or inspired by, the mosaic showing Saint John saving Placidia and her children; see G. Galassi, *Roma o Bisanzio*, I, 2d ed., 31, fig. 7, with references. On the imperial portraits, see Grabar, *L'empereur*, p. 28. In general see also Agnell. 27, 42; *Ded. Eccl. S. Iohan. Ev.*, Muratori, I: 2, 567.

whole world."[88] This church also has long since vanished, and the building that stands on the site and is known by its name has little other connection with the ancient edifice. The ancient structure was considerably longer than the present one; it extended across what is now a street into the complex of San Vitale and the so-called Mausoleum. The latter was built at some time later than the church,[89] and connected to the church's narthex. In the Middle Ages it was consecrated to Saints Nazarius and Celsus; in the ninth century we first hear of a tradition that it was the Mausoleum of Galla Placidia,[90] and in relatively recent times one of the three sarcophagi in the building was pointed out as hers.[91] On the other hand, the Empress died at Rome and almost certainly was buried there; yet later her body could have been removed to Ravenna, although this seems unlikely. Nevertheless perhaps a majority of scholars at the present time believes that the building was not her tomb.[92] Presumably the antechapel of Santa Croce, as it almost certainly was, was dedicated originally to Saint Laurence, for one of the two most prominent mosaics in the building represents him and his gridiron, the instrument of his martyrdom.[93] The other most prominent mosaic is that of Christ the Good Shepherd. Whatever the original dedication and purpose of the building, its mosaics

[88] Agnell. 41; E. Dyggve, *Ravennatum Palatium Sacrum: La basilica ipetrale per cerimonie*, p. 4, n. 1; G. Bovini, *Il cosiddetto mausoleo di Galla Placidia in Ravenna*, p. 9, n. 1; Farioli, *Felix Ravenna*, LXXXII (1960), 61–62; A. Grabar, *Martyrium: Recherches sur le culte des reliques et l'art chrétien antique*, I, 224; Nagl, *Placidia*, pp. 49–50.

[89] Some archeologists have dated the structure as late as the second half of the fifth century, in which case it can have nothing to do with Galla Placidia. Most scholars, however, date it to the middle of the century or just before.

[90] Agnell. 42, ordinarily not noted for his caution, here cautiously qualifies "ut aiunt multi," which must mean that unanimity of belief on the subject did not exist in his time.

[91] The other two were identified as those of Valentinian III and Constantius III.

[92] See *CP*, LX (1965), 10, n. 32, a small selection from the voluminous literature, to which Bovini's detailed argumentation, *Mausoleo*, pp. 14–18, should at least be added. Most recently of all, see J. Vogt, *Der Niedergang Roms*, p. 586.

[93] Almost as much controversy has raged among scholars on this subject as concerning the question of the original purpose of the building itself; for an introduction, see W. Seston, "Une interprétation nouvelle du Mausolée de Galla Placidia à Ravenna," *Association Guillaume Budé: Congrès de Nice, 24–27 avril, 1935*, pp. 234–35; *idem*, "Le jugement dernier du Mausolée de Galla Placidia à Ravenne," *Cahiers archéologiques*, I (1945), 37–50; answered in favor of Saint Laurence by P. Courcelle, "Le gril de Saint Laurent au Mausolée de Galla Placidia," *ibid.*, III (1948), 29–39. Photographs of the mosaics of the "Mausoleum" are common; cf., e.g., G. Bovini, *Ravenna Mosaics*, pls. 1–5; Hutton, *Ravenna*, p. 179, complains that restoration has injured the original quality of the mosaics.

defy description for their glowing beauty. Outside the structure presents the nondescript brick appearance of the Roman ecclesiastical architecture of its time; inside in the soft light of the modern alabaster windows it is a veritable jewel box of colored mosaics which impress even those most insensitive to art. The building was almost certainly constructed either by Valentinian or Galla Placidia; since the latter built or adorned the church to which this building was originally attached, she is usually awarded the credit. The present writer, however, no archeologist or art historian, with utmost diffidence advances the claims of her son: at Ravenna in the fifth century there existed, probably from the reign of Honorius, a church or chapel dedicated to Saint Laurence.[94] Like most Christian emperors, and doubtless with the enthusiastic approval of his mother, Valentinian III made precious gifts to various churches. He seems, however, to have been particularly devoted to Saint Laurence, for he made impressive gifts to the shrine of that saint in or near Rome, and apparently contributed the ground or a previously existing building for its construction, in the pontificate of Xystus III (432–40), perhaps at the same time that his wife was extending her largess to San Pietro in Vincoli. At Ravenna too he seems to have dedicated a shrine to Saint Laurence.[95] If, then, it is true that Valentinian had a special interest in Saint Laurence, it may well have been he who was responsible for building the "Mausoleum."

The Empress also contributed precious gifts to the Cathedral of Ravenna, the Basilica Ursiana;[96] this building, too, no longer exists and has been replaced by a nondescript modern structure. It is also possible that she contributed to Saint John the Baptist at Ravenna,[97] and if our ninth-century informant can be trusted and there is a kernel of truth in a miraculous story he tells about

[94] Augustin. *Serm.* 322 (*PL*, XXXVIII, 1444); Agnell. 34. 35; Müntz, *AJA*, I (1885), 118.

[95] *Lib. Pont.* 46, with Duchesne in his ed., I, 235, n. 12 (there is some question whether the Roman church in question is San Lorenzo fuori le Mura [more probable], or San Lorenzo in Lucina [in the City]); at Ravenna, *ILS*, 816, although unfortunately the provenance of the inscription is not certain. On the question of San Lorenzo at Rome, see Krautheimer *et al.*, *Corpus*, II, 9; Kirsch, *Titelkirchen*, pp. 82–83; F. Castagnoli *et al.*, *Topografia e urbanistica di Roma*, p. 310. Valentinian also made precious gifts to the great Basilica of Saint Peter in Rome, as well as to that of Saint Paul, *Lib. Pont.* 46. For other gifts, see Ensslin, *RE*, VIIA: 2 (1948), 2239.

[96] Agnell. 27.

[97] Nagl, *Placidia*, p. 55; Goetz, *Ravenna*, p. 22.

Singledia, the niece of the Empress (otherwise unknown, but possibly a relative of Constantius or Athaulf); she eagerly seconded Singledia's building of a shrine to Saint Zacharias, the father of the Baptist,[98] and presented it with a chalice. At Ariminum (Rimini), Ravenna's neighbor to the south, she erected a church for Saint Stephen,[99] also now vanished. Almost the sole secular building she is thought to have constructed was the Portico of Placidia (Porticus Placidiana) at Portus, the port of Rome; this was a colonnade which ran along the north bank of the canal which connected Portus with the sea; it was over two hundred yards in length.[100]

While at Ravenna Galla Placidia devoted herself more and more to her benefactions to the Church and to the service of God, and therefore through him to the ultimate welfare of the Roman Empire, the power of Aëtius became ever more securely rooted, doubtless to the impotent, and ordinarily well-concealed, fury of the Emperor. In Spain successive Masters of the Soldiers (we have noted Valentinian's cheapening of this rank by its frequent grant), presumably partisans of Aëtius, struggled with varying success against the Sueves or the Bacaudae. Among these generals was the poet Merobaudes, no stranger to arms as well as verse, who was recalled after a victory over the Bacaudae in 443 by a cabal at court, probably as interested in striking indirectly at Aëtius as directly at Merobaudes.[101] It is quite likely that Valentinian was ready to fall

---

98 Agnell. 41; Sirago, *Placidia*, p. 261 and n. 2; and Nagl, *Placidia*, pp. 50–51; at least accept a kernel of truth; Hodgkin, *Invaders*, I: 2, 870–71, rejects the whole account and thinks it is a doublet of something that happened in Honorius' time. In general, see Farioli, *Felix Ravenna*, LXXXII (1960), 69; H. Leclercq, *s.v.* "Galla Placidia," *Dict. d'archéol. chrét. et de liturgie*, VI: 1, 248–75, at 252 and n. 4.

99 Agnell. 42; *V. S. Barbat.*, Muratori, II: 1, 198.

100 *ILS*, 805; *CIL*, XIV, 141; R. Meiggs, *Roman Ostia*, p. 169, connects the structure with Galla Placidia; R. A. Lanciani, "Ricerche topografiche sulla città di Porto," *Annali dell' Instituto di Correspondenza Archeologica*, XL (1868), 144–95, at 183, however, had thought of her son, Placidus Valentinianus. The tradition which connects Placidia's building activities with San Lorenzo in Milan seems too late and too tenuous to deserve credence: *V. S. Verani* 12 (*AASS*, Oct., VIII, 468); O. Wulff, *Altchristliche und byzantinische Kunst*, I, 249; A. Calderini, G. Chierici, and C. Cecchelli, *La basilica di S. Lorenzo Maggiore in Milano*, p. 141; A. Calderini, *La zona monumentale di S. Lorenzo in Milano*, pp. 24, 26, 42; E. Arslan, "Milano e Ravenna, due momenti dell' architettura paleocristiana," *Felix Ravenna*, LXXXIV (1961), 5–38, 27 with n. 34 (on p. 37).

101 Hyd. 128 (II, 24). We have noted (above, Ch. VI, n. 96) that Petronius Maximus was an enemy of Aëtius. On 13 March 443 (*NVal* 11) the Emperor ordained that the holder of two consulships should outrank the holder of one plus the Patriciate. Rightly, the law is taken to refer to Maximus (e.g., W. Ensslin, *s.v.* "Maximus" (32),

in with such plans; nevertheless for reasons obscure to us the Eastern Emperor Theodosius conferred upon Merobaudes an exalted title, perhaps that of Patrician;[102] Merobaudes attributes the honor to his praises of Aëtius, and perhaps Theodosius was not well acquainted with the state of intrigues at the Western court. Perhaps he wished Valentinian to pursue a policy in real rather than apparent agreement with his powerful minister.[103] In 443 Aëtius removed the chastened remnants of the Burgundians from their original home on the Rhine to Sapaudia (modern Savoy, more or less) where as *foederati* they shared out the land with Roman proprietors; the arrangements were similar to those made for the Visigoths in 418/19 in Aquitaine. Probably Aëtius thought that in their weakened state the barbarians would help serve in their new home as a counterpoise to the Visigoths, yet not be a danger to the Empire itself.[104] Aëtius could not foresee the future after his death when the Burgundians would expand into the adjacent provinces of the Empire, and one of their chieftains for a brief time would dominate the phantom of Empire in Italy itself. Even before this Aëtius had domiciled some Alans around Valentia in the province of Viennensis, and others under King Goar in the Loire valley near

---

*RE,* XIV: 2 [1930], 2543–45, at 2544); this exaltation of Aëtius' enemy should perhaps together with the recall of Merobaudes this same year be taken as evidence of a cabal against Aëtius, favored by the Emperor taking cautious action against the general.

102 Merobaud. *Pan.* 1. Frag. IIA. 3–7, with Vollmer *ad loc.;* Clover, "Merobaudes," pp. 28–29, laying emphasis on the "nuper" in line 4, perhaps a date about 445.

103 Compare Theodosius' later urging Valentinian to allow Honoria to marry Attila (Joh. Ant. Frag. 199. 2 [IV, 614]), advice which Valentinian utterly rejected. Or the honor may have been awarded through the good offices of Aspar, who was on good terms with Aëtius (Prisc. Frag. 11 [IV, 96]).

104 If Thompson, *JRS,* XLVI (1956), 71–74, is right in seeing this also as a move against the Bacaudae of the region, i.e., against social revolution, it nevertheless seems doubtful that this was Aëtius' prime purpose. A. Coville, *Recherches sur l'histoire de Lyon du Vme siècle au IXme siècle (450–800),* pp. 115–17, however, thinks that it is unlikely that Aëtius would have freely granted so strategic an area to the Burgundians, and on this purely a priori ground thinks that it must be a concession extorted from the Empire. A common suggestion is that the Burgundians were put in Savoy to thwart the Alemanni; this view is rejected by Thompson, and by Lot, *Destinées,* pp. 59–60. In general, see Wallace-Hadrill, *Bull. of the John Rylands Library,* XLIV (1961–62), 216; Demougeot, *Mém. Soc. Agriculture Comm. Sciences et Arts Marne,* LXXIII (1958), 17, n. 61. In view of general considerations about Roman weakness in 440, how much credence should be placed in Merobaud. *Pan.* 2. 5–7, which implies that Rome again (before 446) controls the Rhine frontier (at the expense of the Ripuarian Franks presumably) seems uncertain, despite Stein, *Hist.,* I, 332; Ensslin, *RE,* VIIA: 2 (1948), 2246.

Orleans. The natives revolted against these Alans of the Loire and it was in hopes of obtaining pardon for them that Saint Germanus made his celebrated visit to Ravenna in 445. A revolt of the Bacaudae seems to have been connected with this insurrection; in 448 a Bacaudic chieftain, the physician Eudoxius, fled to the Huns, a strong indication that Attila's friendship with Aëtius not only was cooling, but was known to be. It was also of ominous, paradigmatic importance for the future of the Empire that a member of an educated group, above the peasantry, could become so alienated from Roman society, or in the language previously used in this account, could withdraw from it so far as to make common cause with the lower classes against it.[105] These deeds of Aëtius were signally recognized in 446 when he entered upon his third consulship, an honor which no person not a member or prospective member of the emperor's immediate family had attained for over three centuries, since the spacious days of the Emperor Hadrian, in fact.[106] Merobaudes duly turned out a panegyric in honor of the achievement.[107]

In 446, or in the years immediately following, the Britons appealed for help to Aëtius against the invasions of the Picts, Scots (i.e., from Ireland), and Anglo-Saxons, which, coming from all directions, threatened to overwhelm the island.[108] Thereafter a darkness descends upon the history of the island, a darkness lit only

[105] Compare the social revolution at Bazas in 414 which some elements of the upper classes joined, even though the latter were apparently hotheaded youths; see above, Ch. III, n. 174.

[106] And this instance was Servianus, Hadrian's brother-in-law, whose enmity the Emperor thought to appease by this honor, but whom he was finally forced to execute, although Servianus was a nonagenarian.

[107] *Pan.* 2; one would like to know if he also composed one for the *Vicennalia* and sixth consulship of Valentinian in 445 (444), but no trace of such seems to have come down to us.

[108] Gildas *Excid. Brit.* 20; Gildas says that the request was directed to Aëtius, "thrice consul"; it is usually held that the expression dates the request to 446; nevertheless, since ex-consuls regularly bore in their titles the number of their last consulship, a subsequent year is by no means excluded; cf. P. K. Johnstone, "Vortigern and Aetius—A Re-appraisal," *Antiquity*, XX (1946), 16–20, at 18–19; C. E. Stevens, "Gildas Sapiens," *EHR*, LVI (1941), 353–73, at 360; E. A. Thompson, "Zosimus on the End of Roman Britain," *Antiquity*, XXX (1956), 163–67, at 166–67, argues that the motive of the appeal to Aëtius was the British landowners' fear of social revolution, for they were impressed by Aëtius' successes against the Bacaudae in Gaul. On the problems in general, see, e.g., F. Lot, "De la valeur historique du De excidio et conquestu Britanniae de Gildas," *Medieval Studies in Memory of Gertrude Schoepperle Loomis* (Paris, 1927), pp. 229–64, at 241–42; Demougeot, *Moyen Age*, LXVIII (1962), 46–47 (the literature of scholarly discussion of the end of Roman Britain is enormous).

occasionally to our view by the lurid flames of burning cities and farmsteads and punctuated from time to time by the screams and groans of the dying. One should never lose sight in history by using abstract terms such as "social upheaval," "barbarian invasion," and so on, of the terrible cost in human welfare and happiness of such catastrophes. A recent and excellent account of modern history[109] concludes with a remark to the effect that when one part of the land is sinking, another part is probably rising, or so men think. Possibly this is quite true; certainly the descendants of the Romano-Celts of Britain had a glorious destiny when their descendants joined with the Anglo-Saxons and Normans to form the English, but it is doubtful that even had they known this fact it would have consoled the Roman provincials as they died, quickly and horribly from fire and sword, or slowly and horribly from disease and starvation. To resume the metaphor, philosophy of history is hardly availing to those strangling and choking for breath as the huge waters of the encroaching seas crash down upon the sinking land. Sometimes it is said that Rome ended not with a bang (like Nineveh, for instance), but with a whimper. Nevertheless the human pain which accompanied and followed the fall of the West Roman Empire is beyond even the figures of astronomy to calculate. Every kind of suffering which man is capable of inflicting on his fellows, from wounded pride to loss of livelihood, to witnessing the tortured death agonies of those one loves, became a relatively common experience of life. Individual kindliness and heroism did not die, but they underlined the other things. This is what the Decline and Fall of the Roman Empire meant, even with the birth of new nations and new cultures.

Aëtius cannot have failed to detect with consternation the change in Attila's attitude, both because of his dependence on the Hun's friendship as his ultimate support in power and because as a Roman he must dread the turning of the Huns' enmity against the Western Empire. Attila had become sole monarch of the Huns in 445 when he murdered his brother Bleda.[110] Since by 448 Attila was known, or thought, to be contemplating a reversal of his policy

---

[109] R. R. Palmer, *A History of the Modern World* (2d ed. with J. Colton; New York, 1956), p. 876.

[110] The sources give dates ranging from 444 to 446; on 445 see Thompson, *Attila,* p. 88 and n. 3, following Marcell. *s.a.* 445, 1 (II, 81).

toward the Western Empire, the possibility suggests itself that the policy favoring the Western Empire may have been Bleda's primarily, and Attila, not long after his assumption of sole power began to change this. Attila's principal antagonist had been the Eastern Empire, which he mulcted of successively larger sums of tribute by enforcement of a campaign of terror against its European provinces. Although progressively attenuated, the feeling of imperial unity was by no means yet extinct in the West, and there is indication that in some Western quarters there was dissatisfaction with Aëtius' policy of friendship with the Huns and a belief that the West instead should make common cause with the East against them.[111] Attila began to take a haughty tone with the embassies of Aëtius and Valentinian which came to his court beyond the Danube, and, it seems, deliberately to pick quarrels with the Western Empire. A certain Constantius, a Roman secretary of Attila furnished him by Aëtius, had absconded to Rome with sacred vessels of the church of Sirmium which Attila was pleased to regard as his rightful booty and property. At Rome Constantius pawned them with a goldsmith named Silvanus. Attila insisted under threat of war that the luckless Silvanus be handed over to him as the thief of his property (or as a receiver of stolen goods, presumably) (449). But then he was given an unexpected diplomatic lever to use against the West as the result of an intrigue in the imperial family itself.

Galla Placidia's daughter, Justa Grata Honoria Augusta, was a severely frustrated young woman. In 449 she had reached the age of thirty-one, yet she was forbidden to marry (like Pulcheria and the other sisters of Theodosius II) and devoted to Christian celibacy by command of her brother the Emperor.[112] Especially as the Emperor had no male heirs, almost any man of rank whom Honoria might marry, and it would be inconceivable for her to marry a person of inferior station, must necessarily become a person of the greatest political importance with some claim to the imperial succession, especially since he would be older and hence better established than the future husband of Placidia (Eudocia of course was the betrothed of Huniric). Although by priority as Augusta Honoria possessed a thin theoretical superiority of rank over her

<hr />

111 *Chron. Gall. a. 452* 132 (I, 662), with Thompson, *Attila*, pp. 93–94.

112 Jord. *Get.* 224, *Rom.* 328 (presumably from Cassiod., who ought to have been well informed on the subject).

sister-in-law, her position as merely the sister of the reigning Emperor must necessarily be inferior to that of his consort. Honoria's acts at this time show that she inherited or emulated the political ambition of her mother, but without Placidia's discretion or strong sense of what conduced to the welfare of the dynasty and the Empire. In 449 it was discovered that the administrator of her household and properties, a certain Eugenius, had been secretly visiting her bed; furthermore there was some suspicion that she was conspiring against the Emperor with her paramour.[113] Apart from the conspiracy against the Emperor, the mere fact of having illegitimate sexual relations with a princess of the imperial house constituted *maiestas laesa,* high treason, in accordance with the provisions of the Julian Law on the subject.[114] Therefore Eugenius was executed and Honoria banished[115] to Constantinople, where she might be expected to learn the piety and decorum of a princess as an exile in the monastic-like seclusion of Pulcheria in the Palace of Constantinople (449).[116] But Honoria was not penitent for her sins; she burned with resentment against her brother. Well aware of the wavering relations of the Western court and Attila, and further impressed by the obsequious attitude the Eastern court regularly adopted toward the King of the Huns, she sent to him asking for assistance. Correctly evaluating his cupidity, she also sent him money as well as her ring in token of her good faith, using as her messenger a trusted eunuch of her suite named Hyacinthus. Attila, however, whether out of guile or in accordance with Hunnish custom, chose to regard this approach to him as tantamount to an

113 This is the necessary implication of the statement about the man to whom she was hastily affianced, Herculanus Bassus, that he was "safe," that he would not aspire to the throne or to revolution; by unavoidable implication, therefore, Eugenius had, or would have, conspired (Joh. Ant. Frag. 199. 2 [IV, 613]).

114 Tac. *Ann.* 3. 24; cf. F. S. Lear, *Treason in Roman and Germanic Law,* p. 30.

115 This statement of Marcell. *s.a.* 434 (II, 79) (cf. Jord. *Rom.* 328) is explicitly or implicitly ignored by some modern scholars, but while Marcell. has fallen into error, presumably by mistaking the proper indiction, as to the date, this does not mean that as an Easterner, drawing on Eastern sources, he is in error as to the fact of Honoria's presence in Constantinople. And the exile of the guilty princess is also in accord with the example of the Emperor Augustus, see previous note. Unfortunately the attempt of Sirago, *Placidia,* p. 330, n. 4, to prove this absence of Honoria from Italy by the fact that she unlike the three other Western Augusti did not send a letter to the East in Feb., 450, is an argument from silence, and the silence could also easily be explained by the disgrace in which Honoria languished at the time. It is, however, peculiarly fitting under the circumstances that she should be exiled to the custody of Pulcheria, as indicated in the text.

116 On the chronology, Bury, *JRS,* IX (1919), 10.

offer of marriage. Whether or not he proceeded to ask the hand of Honoria from Theodosius II as the senior member and head of the imperial family, at whose court the princess was in fact in residence, or whether Theodosius, whose court was in continual diplomatic relations with the Huns, heard of Honoria's request and Attila's response more indirectly, the Eastern Emperor (recently proved guilty beyond doubt of having conspired to have Attila assassinated), wanted no more complications in his difficult relations with the Huns. Posthaste, therefore, he handed over the problem to Valentinian by sending his sister and her eunuch back to him;[117] at the same time he wrote to his son-in-law, recommending that the latter accede to Attila's demands and send him Honoria as a bride to take her place in the Hunnish King's already numerous harem (late spring/early summer 450).

The wrath of Valentinian at this latest political coup of his sister, coming as it did so closely upon the heels of her crimes with Eugenius, must have been terrible. Hyacinthus was put to the question under torture; finally his head was struck off. In all justice there could be no doubt that Honoria had conspired now not merely against her brother, but against the Roman Empire; apparently Valentinian determined this time to execute his sister for high treason. There was precedent for an emperor's thus punishing his sister, even of August rank; the Emperor Commodus (180–92) had thus, and with good ground, first banished and then executed his sister Lucilla. During the summer of 450 both the Emperor and his mother were in Rome; Galla Placidia loved all her children devotedly, and while as a good Roman, familiar with the problems of Empire, she cannot have failed to disapprove her daughter's actions in the strongest terms, she managed to procure Honoria's life by repeated entreaties. We may take it for granted that the Empress adjured her son in the name of Our Lord Jesus Christ to heed his injunction to forgive one's enemies; perhaps she also urged him not to follow the example of long-dead pagan monsters. The fact that her entreaties succeeded in this grave case amply attests both her influence with her son as well as its limitations, and also her son's respect and affection for her. Placidia may also have felt some sympathy for her daughter's frustration and ambition in

---

[117] This is nowhere directly attested, but once it be admitted that Honoria was sent to the East, something like this must have happened, in the light of subsequent events.

recollecting her own languishment under the dominion of Stilicho and Serena long before. Honoria, therefore, was merely deprived of her rank as Augusta,[118] and hastily married off to Herculanus Bassus, to whom she may have been betrothed before she was sent to Constantinople. Bassus was a "safe" man who, Valentinian thought, would not aim at the throne or try a coup d'etat. It is quite possible, as many modern scholars think, although it is nowhere directly attested, that Honoria thereafter was kept under close guard; this would have been the only way to make sure that she would not run off to Attila or engage in further treasonable activity against Emperor and Empire. The trustworthy Bassus, however, was eventually rewarded by the consulate of 452. In due course Attila sent an embassy to demand of Valentinian the hand of Honoria and to insist that her imperial rank be restored and she receive no harm. Apparently also he was pleased to interpret (as many of the vulgar of the time did) the rank of Augusta as conferring a real share in the government of the Empire. His ambassadors were answered that it was impossible for him to marry Honoria, since she had been given to another husband, and that in the Roman Empire only men, not women, held the imperial power.[119] During the next years, last in 452, Attila nevertheless was to repeat his demand for the hand of Honoria many times. In 452, therefore, we may assume that she was still alive; her name, however, is conspicuously lacking among those of important persons carried off from Rome by Geiseric in 455. We may presume that by that time she was dead; whether she died naturally, or at the command of the Emperor when he no longer had to dread Attila (d. 453; kingdom in dissolution 454) or his mother's wrath and grief, depends upon an estimate of his character which we do not have evidence adequate to make.[120]

Aëtius must have urged the Emperor not to comply with Attila's demand for the hand of Honoria; he must have been well aware that Attila's marriage project was in large part, perhaps primarily,

---

[118] Since Attila demanded that she be given back the "scepter" (Prisc. Frag. 15 [IV, 98]), which expression Joh. Ant. uses to describe her previous position as Augusta (Frag. 199. 2 [IV, 613]).

[119] Jord. *Get.* 223–24; *Rom.* 328; Joh. Ant. Frag. 199. 2 (IV, 613–14); Marcell. *s.a.* 434 (II, 79); Prisc. Frag. 15 (IV, 98); esp. Bury, *JRS,* IX (1919), 9–11; Ensslin, *RE,* VIIA: 2 (1948), 2248–51.

[120] Cf. Bury, *JRS,* IX (1919), 12; Sirago, *Placidia,* p. 333.

directed against him,[121] for an alliance between Valentinian and Attila would render Aëtius otiose, and the latter could hardly have failed to be aware that the Emperor had no love for him. Fortunately, in view of the experience of his father-in-law in the East with Attila, Valentinian must have been aware that to accept the demands of the Hunnish King would be to put himself in the power of the latter far more than he had ever been in that of Aëtius; as a human being he may also have regarded the prospect of a triumph of his sister over him, as she would triumph by such a marriage, as almost an even worse fate. Accordingly for once he and his overbearing minister were in agreement about the answer to be given Attila's suit. Aëtius, however, was by no means satisfied by the Emperor's agreement on this occasion. In fact, the general must have felt the ground beginning to give way beneath his feet as Attila's attitude became progressively ever more hostile. He could not fail to remember that Placidia had gladly seized the opportunity of a serious defeat of his Hun friends to try to rid herself of him. As it turned out, she had been mistaken in her estimate of the situation, and the friendship and sufficiently undiminished strength of the Huns had restored him to power. Now, however, he could probably sense the masked anticipation with which the Emperor and his mother, whatever might be their fear of the Hun, were watching the growing hostility of Attila, which they must have been aware was directed in considerable part against the general, "Our Aëtius," as the Emperor by official protocol formally referred to him. He also learned to his dismay that the Emperor, after several years during which the Empress Eudoxia had presented him neither with a third daughter nor a doubtless eagerly desired son, was beginning to plan in terms of his not having any more children. In other words, Valentinian was beginning to look for a husband for the younger Placidia, a husband who might eventually succeed him on the throne with the support of his brother-in-law, Huniric the future King of the Vandals and destined spouse of the Emperor's other daughter Eudocia. The candidate was found by the Emperor, or suggested to him by Aëtius' enemies, in a young man named Majorian, whose father the court had tried in vain to turn against Aëtius.[122] Majorian had distin-

121 Cf. Joh. Ant. Frag. 199. 2 (IV, 614).
122 Ap. Sid. *Carm*. 5. 116–25.

guished himself in a subaltern capacity fighting in Gaul against the Franks under Aëtius' own command.[123] Aëtius, once aware of the danger, moved quickly to ward it off by rusticating the young man to his estates (before 451), whence he was to be recalled by Valentinian only after the general's death.[124] Obviously he did not as yet take the Emperor's move as a sufficient threat to himself to have Majorian murdered. Instead, sometime between this time and 454 he moved to consolidate his position while he still had the power or influence to do so by compelling the Emperor to swear to friendship with him and to agree to betroth Placidia to his own younger son Gaudentius.[125] At the same time he probably tried to ensure the Emperor's continued dependence on him by putting off the agreed marriage of Eudocia to Huniric, although the girl was reaching the age of marriage according to Roman standards;[126] it is quite possible that he hoped by this measure to provoke a rupture between the Vandals and Valentinian, and thus end once and for all the potentiality of the Vandals' support for the Emperor.[127]

We may assume that Galla Placidia approved in general of her son's plans to checkmate her old foe Aëtius, and of his perhaps only half-formed intention to betroth her younger granddaughter to Majorian. The latter was in fact destined later to become Emperor, although under circumstances quite different from those planned by Valentinian; in his relatively brief reign as Emperor the young man revealed traits and abilities which in happier days might have numbered him among the abler of the long imperial line. It is quite possible that these talents were already apparent to the discerning eye of Placidia and her son.

In February of 450 Galla Placidia journeyed in the company of her son and daughter-in-law, and presumably of her two grand-

---

123 *Ibid.*, 211–30; cf. Loyen, *Recherches,* pp. 64–68.

124 Ap. Sid. *Carm.* 5. 290–91, 293–94, 203–6; cf. *CP,* LIX (1964), 23–29; W. Ensslin, *s.v.* "Maiorianus," *RE,* XIV: 1 (1930), 584–90, at 584.

125 Prosp. 1373 (I, 483); *CP,* LIX (1964), 23–29.

126 Clover, "Geiseric," pp. 129–30.

127 Prisc. Frag. 15 (IV, 98); Jord. 181, 184–85 (probably from Prisc.); represent Geiseric as urging Attila on to attack the Visigoths, his enemies. Many scholars have accepted this story, although they agree that Attila certainly acted on his own account. Clover, "Geiseric," pp. 112–16, argues plausibly, however, that the initiative in an understanding between Geiseric and Attila belonged to the latter, who wished to diminish as far as possible the number of enemies, actual or potential, in the West, before he moved in the latter direction. This is not to deny, however, that Geiseric was probably in hearty favor of an attack upon the Visigoths, his enemies, whatever might have been his view of an attack on the Western Empire.

daughters, to Rome, where she intended to perform various works of piety. The imperial advent in the City fell on 21 February.[128] The next day was the Feast of Peter's Chair and the imperial party duly proceeded to the Vatican basilica to participate in the festivities; Placidia wrote of the occasion that she was conscious of the interest that the saints in heaven have in earthly matters, and of her corresponding devotion to their cult, especially of course to that of Saint Peter on this day.[129] While the Augusti were in the church, Pope Leo, accompanied by a large group of bishops (he was holding his local council at the time), approached them and requested with many tears and groans (such displays were considered neither unseemly nor unmanly by the ancients) the good offices of the imperial family in the matter of a complicated theological, ecclesiastical, and political struggle which was (as so many times before) convulsing the East. Dioscurus, the bishop of Alexandria, in large part because he wished to triumph over his peer of Constantinople, Bishop Flavian, had engineered a plot whereby the latter, having condemned a certain Eutyches for heresy, was himself accused of heresy. Eutyches was condemned for adherence to the so-called Monophysite heresy, that he professed that Christ had only one (divine) nature after his incarnation. The view that he had two perfect natures, divine and human, the view that was eventually to triumph as Christian orthodoxy, was also the view of Leo and the West in general. Among others, Flavian had appealed to Leo for support, and the latter had energetically advocated Flavian's cause with the Eastern Church and government. Among other things this interference in the church affairs of the East tended to increase the power and authority of the only apostolic see of the West. A council held at Sardica (modern Sofia in Bulgaria) in 343 or 344 had in fact recognized appeals from local councils to the Bishop of Rome; this council was not recognized by the Eastern Church, although it naturally was by the Western Church which evidenced some disposition to confuse its decrees with those of the First Ecumenical Council, at Nicaea in 325, thus attributing far more validity and importance to them. Dioscurus, however, had maneuvered very cleverly; Eutyches was the friend of the eunuch Chry-

---

128 *Ep. Val. ad Theod. ap. Epp. S. Leon. Magn.* 55 (*PL*, LIV, 857); Seeck, *Regesten,* p. 384; cf. *Ep. ad Theod., Ep. ad Pulch.*
129 *Ep. ad Pulch., init.; Ep. ad Theod.* **init.**

saphius, whose influence at this time was all-powerful with Theodosius II. The Empress Eudocia had been driven from the court in disgrace and had found refuge in Jerusalem; the Emperor's sister, Pulcheria, had almost entirely lost the great influence she had previously exercised over Theodosius. Pulcheria was strongly anti-Monophysite in her opinions; perhaps, it has been suggested rather unkindly, primarily because of her hatred of Chrysaphius.[130] Not long before the arrival of Valentinian and his family at Rome Theodosius had confirmed the findings of an Ephesian synod convoked to decide this theological question by an imperial constitution. This council had been intended to be an ecumenical council; instead it has lived in infamy in the history of the Church as the "Robber Council" (*latrocinium*) of Ephesus, largely because Leo the Great so labeled it. Leo's exposition of his (the Western) faith, known as Leo's Tome, which he had sent the council, was not even read. The Pope's tears and groans in February, 450, therefore, were to persuade the imperial family to write to their relatives seconding the Pope's efforts to have a new council called in Italy under his auspices to consider the whole question of Flavian and the faith from the beginning. In the past Honorius had thus interfered in Eastern ecclesiastical disputes, and with considerable success.

The three Augusti agreed to write letters as Leo wanted.[131] The arguments urged in the letters clearly imply that they were suggested by the Pope. The arguments are much the same in each, but the letter of Eudoxia to her father quite closely follows the tenor of her husband's.[132] Galla Placidia's letter lays greater stress on details of Leo's personal intervention with his sovereign, and emphasizes continuity with the faith of Constantine (instead of "ancestors" in general). She refers not merely to the primacy of Peter but to the power of the keys (to bind and loose), as well as to the

---

[130] Cf. P. Goubert, "Le rôle de Sainte Pulchérie et de l'eunuque Chrysaphios," in *Das Konzil von Chalkedon*, ed. A. Grillmeier and H. Bacht, I, 303–21.

[131] The style of the three letters is so different that there can be no doubt that they were actually written by three different persons, almost certainly those to whom they are ascribed, and not merely prepared in the papal chancery, as has sometimes been suggested; so Nagl, *Placidia*, p. 61, against Haller, *Papsttum*, I, 178. One may note that the Latinity of Valentinian seems relatively simple and straightforward (considering the age of bombast in which it was composed), while that of his mother has a tendency to be awkward and involuted.

[132] *Epp. Val. Eud. ap. Epp. S. Leon. Magn.* 55, 57 (*PL*, LIV, 857–60, 861–64).

position of preeminence of the City Rome, his bishopric, and "the mistress of all lands." Unlike her son and daughter-in-law she also wrote to Pulcheria in a less formal fashion; along with arguments similar to those used to persuade Theodosius, she refers to her interest in the cult of the saints; she also speaks of the community of faith between Pulcheria and herself and concludes with a reference to God's having granted the world to be governed and preserved by "Our Empire," or "Our imperial power."[133] The idea of the primacy of Peter and his successors in the Church was emphasized by Leo throughout his entire pontificate; obviously Placidia accepts this view,[134] yet she also emphasizes in effect that the Empire itself is derived from divine authority. Obviously there is room for conflict between these ideas; much of medieval history was to be involved in that conflict, but in true Roman fashion the Empress does not conceive of variance of interest between organized religion and the state. It is unlikely there was in her mind any question that the Pope was the servant of the state, ultimately. Theodosius answered courteously and coldly that he was in fact maintaining the faith of the fathers, and that was the end of the matter; fortunately, therefore, from the point of view of Western orthodoxy, his reign was almost over.[135]

Placidia remained in (or near) Rome with her son and his wife for the next months. It was here that Honoria came from the East and here that her mother was successful in saving her life from her brother's wrath, while the negotiations with Attila continued. One rather wonders at the reason for this prolonged sojourn at Rome. Perhaps one reason was her love for another of her children, the long dead, firstborn son she had had by Athaulf. It is possible that it was on his account that she had originally undertaken the journey from Ravenna. In her church to Saint John the Evangelist she had proudly inserted the name of the Most Noble Theodosius on the roll of the imperial family. But members of the Western branch of the imperial house were interred, as we have remarked, in a round sepulcher at the side of Saint Peter's in Rome. The

---

133 *Ep. ad Theod., Ep. ad Pulch.;* in general, see also Theophanes, p. 101 (de B).

134 *NVal* 17 (8 July 445). *praef.* alludes to it in support of papal jurisdiction over Arles.

135 *Epp. ap. Epp. S. Leon. Magn.* 62–64 (*PL,* LIV, 875–79); the last letter, to Eudoxia, is the most interesting; it is polite and affectionate, but means, "Father says no, and that's that."

small body of her son Theodosius, the Empress decided, must join this imperial company. Many of the beliefs of popular religion were also held by Galla Placidia; the inscriptions and graffiti recently recovered beneath Saint Peter's show the fervent belief of many Christians from very early times of the value of burial close to the Prince of the Apostles. It seems very likely that Placidia shared this view, as presumably did the rest of her family buried close to the sacred precinct. Accordingly, and presumably by the imperial authority needed in such cases according to the Roman law,[136] the body of the little Theodosius was exhumed from its resting place near Barcelona and brought to Rome. There with Pope Leo himself officiating and in the presence of the Empress and of the Roman Senate, with, we may be sure, the appropriate ceremonies of the faith of Christ, the body was laid to rest again, and the son of a German chief slept among the tombs of the Caesars, by the Fisherman, the apostle of Christ. The Emperor Valentinian is not listed among those present; perhaps this is a mere oversight of the chronicler or scribe; perhaps he disapproved of conferring such a signal honor on his half brother. If so, once again he had yielded to his mother's wishes where her other children were concerned. In view of this reburial of her son in the family Mausoleum we may be sure that Placidia intended to be buried there herself, and that another motive for this reburial was her wish to have this long lost child with her as she slept.[137]

For in this same year 450, Galla Placidia was approximately sixty-two years of age. On 28 July 450 the Emperor Theodosius II,

[136] On the law and practice of the transference of corpses in general, see the materials gathered and discussed by E. Gabba and G. Tibiletti, "Una signora di Treviri sepolta a Pavia," *Athenaeum*, XLVIII (1960), 253–62. For an example of a transfer of such a once-buried corpse over an even greater distance, see the case of Cynegius, Praetorian Prefect of the East, whose body was moved from Constantinople to Spain in 388 (*Cons. Const.* 338, 1 [I, 244–45]).

[137] *Reich. Add. Prosp.* 12 (I, 489). The Theodosius involved cannot possibly be the Emperor Theodosius II, who was certainly buried in the Church of the Holy Apostles at Constantinople. No plausible reason for inventing such a burial (of the Emperor) seems to exist; hence the only available Theodosius is this child. The burial is listed in the augmented chronicle under 451 (by error for 450, for Placidia herself died in 450). Unfortunately the insertor of this notice in Prosper's Chronicle may well not be its author; if so, the former quite possibly thought that the notice referred to the Emperor, who died in 450. In that case the reburial could have occurred any time between 440 and 450 (that is, the period when Leo's pontificate coincided with the last decade of Placidia's life). One very slender argument in favor of 450 can be advanced: it helps explain the Empress' sojourn in Rome in 450. For more detailed argumentation see *CP*, LX (1965), 7–8.

her nephew, succumbed to injuries sustained in a riding accident. Presumably the news was received in Italy during August. At Rome on 27 November A.D. 450, Galla Placidia Augusta fell asleep in Our Lord Jesus Christ.[138] The cause of her death is today completely unknown; we may only assume that she had been in relatively good health when she came to Rome from Ravenna in February. Perhaps only after the interval of forty days[139] was she herself buried in the Mausoleum by Saint Peter's.[140] We may be sure that in the presence of her imperial son as well as of the assembled dignitaries of the Roman state and church her interment was celebrated with the full solemnities of holy religion, commending her body to the earth,[141] and her soul to God. Thus like David she slept with her fathers (cf. I Kings 2 : 10).

[138] *Reich. Add. Prosp.* 16 (I, 490); Agnell. 42; Hyd. 148 (II, 26); *Ovet. Add. Prosp.* 9–10 (I, 489); *Chron. Gall. a. 452* 136 (I, 662); Procop. *Bell.* 3 (*Vand.* 1). 4. 15.

[139] Cf. the example of her father Theodosius the Great, above, Ch. II, nn. 70–71; *V. (greca) S. Mel. Iun.* 56 (p. 238, ed. Gorce).

[140] On the question of her burial, see what has just been said about the burial of her son Theodosius, and cf. above, n. 92, on the so-called Mausoleum at Ravenna. The tradition that she was buried at Milan, G. Allegranza, *Spiegazione e riflessioni sopra alcuni sacri monumenti antichi di Milano,* pp. 4–8, 42–44, may be rejected out of hand.

[141] Cf. Possid. *V. S. Augustin.* 31.

# 8

# EPILOGUE:
# THE END OF THE
# DYNASTY

 Thus the Emperor Valentinian was bereft of his mother's experience and sage advice, and perhaps of her restraint. In general, however, one notes little change in imperial policy in the West during the next few years.[1] At the moment of his mother's death undoubtedly the question of the Huns formed the principal preoccupation of Valentinian and his ministers, above all of Aëtius. The latter's uneasy vision of a future when he would no longer be supported by the Huns led him to seek ever more imperiously for reassurance, to banish Majorian, to betroth Gaudentius to the younger Placidia, to bind the Emperor to him by an oath of friendship. But this very insistence, to which for the present the Emperor had no choice but to yield, may very well have done much to transform a deep-seated aversion in Valentinian to an active hatred. Yet the general was still all-powerful, and above all indispensable for dealing with the Hunnish crisis, and Valentinian must still bide his time.

Probably another humiliation felt by the Emperor in the latter part of the year 450 was the total disregard of his legal rights on

1 Sirago, *Placidia*, pp. 325–27, sees a marked deterioration in the character of the Emperor after his mother's death; released from her overbearing and damping presence, he gave himself over to vice, magic, and the free exercise of his libido. But this is drawn from Procopius (Sirago, *Placidia*, p. 336, for example, accepts the tale that Valentinian seduced the wife of Petronius Maximus, a tale which seems a clear invention to explain in the form of salacious folk gossip the murders of Aëtius and Valentinian and the subsequent accession of Maximus). Nor does the tradition in Agnell. 42, cited by Sirago, bear any particular stamp of hostility to Valentinian apart from the implication which makes him responsible for the following debacle of the Empire. Cf. above, Ch. VII, nn. 3–6.

the part of the Eastern government. In the East the imperial family became extinct with the death of Theodosius (his wife still survived in exile in Jerusalem, dying in 460), except for his sister, Pulcheria Augusta, who was fifty-one. In accord with the powerful general Aspar, Pulcheria chose as her husband (thus surrendering the appearance if not the reality of her celibacy in the interests of the state, the continuation of the legitimate dynasty) the soldier Marcian, some years her senior; on 25 August 450 Marcian was proclaimed Emperor. By all purely legal right and precedent with the death of Theodosius Valentinian became sole Emperor and should have the right to name a colleague to rule in the East (as Gratian had named Theodosius I long before), or, quite theoretically, to rule alone over the entire Empire. Theoretically he could also have transferred himself to the East with or without naming a colleague to rule in the West. In truth, of course, such interference of the West in the affairs of the East would no longer be tolerated. But Valentinian was not even nominally consulted in the choice of Marcian, and when the latter sought recognition from the now senior Augustus, Valentinian refused to accept him. This was futile, for the far weaker Western Emperor had absolutely no means of giving his objections any real effect, and before the menace of Attila it was highly impolitic in this manner to alienate his new colleague. Not until the spring of 452 did Valentinian finally officially recognize Marcian, possibly on the insistence of Aëtius. One of Pulcheria's first acts after her brother's death had been to order the execution of the hated Chrysaphius; with Marcian she also at once withdrew the imperial favor from the Monophysites. Anti-Monophysite bishops were installed in sees where Monophysites had ruled; the reputation of Flavian, who had died in the meanwhile, was rehabilitated. Marcian was determined to call a new council to reverse the verdict of Ephesus, and was in continual correspondence with Pope Leo on the subject (despite the attitude of his own sovereign Leo recognized Marcian as Emperor in the East). Marcian insisted that the new council be held in the East; Leo was opposed to this, and therefore changed his mind and urged no council at all. The anti-Monophysite policies of the Eastern government and his own determination of the question would suffice. Nevertheless Marcian did summon the Fourth

Ecumenical Council; it met at Chalcedon. Monophysitism was condemned; but to the dissatisfaction of the Pope, although his views on Flavian and the faith were vindicated, the twenty-eighth canon of the council put the See of Constantinople practically on a plane of equality with Rome. Leo protested, but in vain.

In the meanwhile Attila had continued his diplomatic offensive against the West; he gave his support to one candidate for the kingship of the Ripuarian Franks, and Aëtius and the West supported the other. By this time the Huns were demanding not merely the hand of Honoria, but half of the Western Empire as her dowry. Attila also wrote to the Visigothic King Theodoric offering his alliance against the Empire, while he informed the court of Rome that he intended merely to attack the Visigoths; perhaps, however, he approached the Visigoths only after repeated rebuffs by Aëtius and Valentinian (winter–spring, 450–51). Meanwhile in the East Marcian changed the policy of Theodosius. Quite likely under the influence of Aspar who had played so large a part in his elevation to the throne Marcian determined to bid defiance to the Huns, and refused to pay the tribute promised by his predecessor; on the other hand, in keeping with Aspar's policy of nonhostility to the Vandals, he apparently renounced any project for war with them.[2] Attila's real purpose in turning against the West instead of the East remains obscure. Perhaps he really wanted to supplant Aëtius as the real power in the Western Empire;[3] if in fact Valentinian evinced any desire to exchange King Log for King Stork, his general prevented it.[4] Yet this belief is mostly predicated on a statement in the sources[5] that Attila's first purpose was to overthrow Aëtius, and that statement may very well merely reflect the tradition that Aëtius was the main bulwark of the Western Empire at the time. On the other hand, Attila may merely have thought that his chances of gaining richer booty from largely unprotected Gaul,

---

[2] Accepting in general the arguments of Thompson, *Hermathena*, LXXVI (1950), 58–75, *passim*.

[3] Demougeot, *Mém. Soc. d'Agricult. Comm. Sciences et Arts Marne*, LXXIII (1958), 19–20; Seeck, *Gesch.*, VI: 1, 299–300; A. Alföldi, "Attila," in *Menschen die Geschichte machten*, ed. P. Rohden and G. Ostrogorsky, I, 229–34, at 232–33 (who suggests that in effect Attila wanted to remove Aëtius as the "middle man" in purveying the services of the Huns to the Western Empire); Thompson, *Attila*, pp. 131–32.

[4] Cf. Seeck, *Gesch.*, VI: 1, 304.

[5] Joh. Ant. Frag. 199. 2 (IV, 614) (from Priscus?).

and eventually Italy, were greater than from the systematically plundered European provinces of the Eastern Empire.[6] However that may be, in the early spring of 451, collecting numerous contingents from the German tribes subject to the Huns, Attila commenced his march to the West. Aëtius, of course, without his trusty Huns to serve him had only his own *bucellarii* and the scraps to which the West Roman field army of the time was largely reduced to meet the foe. His task was doubtless rendered the more difficult by the great famine from which Italy had suffered in recent months. The various *foederati*, Burgundians, Alans, and others, who also marched under his command, did not make up the total of effectives to anything near an adequate number to meet the mixed horde Attila was bringing with him. Finally the Visigoth Theodoric was persuaded of the danger that also loomed over his people[7] and joined forces with the Roman army.

The combined forces were able to raise the siege of Orleans (June), and there followed the so-called Battle of Châlons (whose importance in European, not to say world, history has been much exaggerated in the past), fought in what is today Champagne, on the Mauriac Plain or Catalaunian Fields, whose exact situation has been the subject of much inconclusive debate among scholars (20 June? 451). After severe fighting the victory inclined to the Romano-Visigothic forces, for Attila retreated thereafter, but with his forces relatively intact. King Theodoric fell on the field of battle; his son Thorismund was acclaimed King in his stead. We are told that Aëtius persuaded the new King to return home almost at once in order to forestall the ambition of his brothers. If this is so, Aëtius once again was merely following the ancient Roman policy of divide and rule. The Visigoths, who had hardly been friendly to the Empire in the immediate past, might well in the first flush of a victory for which their presence had largely been responsible be tempted to turn upon the Roman army or take other action to the detriment of the Empire. Possibly also by his confidential counsel to the King Aëtius hoped to make a friend who might in the future help to shore up his position at court. Furthermore, the Visigoths would remain a possible threat to the Empire which would, it could be hoped, continue to render the general

6 Schmidt, *Gesch.*2, I, 472.
7 Cf. *ibid.*, 474.

indispensable, while their presence in Gaul and their demonstrated willingness and ability to oppose him might presumably help deter Attila from further ventures in that direction. Once again, by such delicate balancing of forces either potentially or actually hostile to it did the enfeebled Western Empire manage to prolong its existence in the fifth century. As a matter of fact, the new Visigothic King proved to be decidedly anti-Roman in his policy; whether or not he saw through Aëtius' policy in his "friendly" advice, there is no indication that he showed any friendship for the general, but his very hostility to Rome, it is likely, prolonged somewhat the power and life of the general who might continue to be useful or necessary to oppose Gothic ambitions.

Attila, however, had not been decisively defeated. And it was vitally necessary that he make good his check in Gaul immediately, both to maintain his position as undisputed ruler of the united Huns, whose tradition as nomads in the sparse grass steppes of Asia had been to roam in much smaller bands under petty chieftains without obedience to any central Hunnish authority, and to avoid revolts of the subject peoples, mainly Germans, who might become restless at this proof that their Hunnish masters were not invincible, especially since some Germanic peoples had in fact played an important or preponderant role in defeating them. Hence Attila resolved upon an invasion of Italy itself. Here there would be no Goths to assist the imperial army, for while those *foederati* might fight to defend their Gallic homeland, there was no reason for them to bail out the Empire in Italy itself. Attila's attack on Italy in 452, then, followed the soundest principles of strategy. A victory over the Empire here ought to be easy, and such a victory would at once procure any and all of his wishes as far as the Western Empire was concerned, for the imperial government would be powerless to resist him. At this juncture Aëtius, moreover, committed the worst mistake of his political and military career; apparently he did not foresee this move on the part of Attila.[8] The mistake was to cost him dear, but he must have overrated the losses inflicted upon the Huns in Gaul; at least he did not even attend to the garrisoning of the Alpine passes where his small forces might well have served against the foe with results out of

---

[8] Prosp. 1367 (I, 482).

proportion to their size. Once these passes were behind the Huns, however, it is difficult to see what he could have done; Pompey the Great had said, reportedly, centuries before that he could raise legions by stamping his feet. If Pompey was unable to do this in an age when martial virtue had not yet failed in Italy, Aëtius certainly found it impossible in 452. His lack of foresight of course found its critics in Italy,[9] where there were important elements of the most influential classes already in opposition to him.

In 452 Attila traversed the unguarded passes of the Alps and penetrated into the heartland of the Empire itself. The great city of Aquileia was taken and razed; a more or less legendary account holds that inhabitants of the region fleeing to low-lying islands off the delta of the Po founded a community at first called Rialto, but which later became known as Venice. Milan and other cities of the Po valley were taken and pillaged; one hears little of any resistance to the Hun. At Rome the Patrician counseled the Emperor to join him in flight, abandoning Italy and the City to their fate. The Italians, of course, could not view with equanimity the adoption of such a plan; the Senate or the aristocracy pressed upon the Emperor the alternative of trying to open negotiations with the King of the Huns. Valentinian listened to them rather than to his general, whose prestige had never been lower, and sent envoys to treat with Attila. This famous embassy included Avienus, a man of consular rank, and Trygetius, the envoy used by Galla Placidia to conclude the first peace with the Vandals in 435; he had meanwhile been distinguished by tenure of the Praetorian Prefecture, presumably of Italy. But these two were quite thrust in the background by the dominant personality of the third envoy, none other than Pope Leo himself. The embassy was in fact successful in persuading Attila to depart from Italy; this he did in part because he was superstitiously afraid of marching against Rome lest he meet the fate of Alaric who had died shortly after taking the City, partly because his forces were suffering severely from famine in the ravaged land of northern Italy, itself gravely afflicted by the dearth of past years, as well as from disease in the heat of an Italian summer along the watery plains of the Po, with presumably but rudimentary sanitation. Another reason may also have been that Mar-

---

9 *Ibid.* with a caustic reference to his lack of foresight.

cian in the East sent an army to attack the Huns' homeland; this force was commanded by an Eastern general, also named Aëtius, who was rewarded with the consulate in 454.[10] Contemporary tradition, later much emphasized at Rome, also attributed great importance to the presence of the Pope as God's chosen instrument is owerawing Attila; it seems difficult to imagine that the heathen King would have been so thoroughly impressed, had it not been for the other factors mentioned. As it was, Attila retreated with the threat to resume his ravaging Italy with even more vigor if he were not given Honoria and her dowry. Fortunately, however, the Hunnish peril was almost over; in 453 Attila suddenly died; his sons, quarreling over their inheritance, provoked a successful rising of their subject Germans (Battle of the River Nedao, somewhere north of the Danube, 454); thereafter the Huns almost totally disappear from European history.

In turn the death of Attila and the breakup of his Empire were the almost inevitable prelude to the downfall of Aëtius. The latter's failure in 452 even to make the most elementary provision for the defense of Italy and his unaccepted advice to flee had alienated many persons who had heretofore been among his supporters. Even worse, Valentinian's government had managed to extricate itself and Italy from frightful danger without any intervention of the Patrician. Still, the victor of the Mauriac Plain might yet be useful to fend off another Hunnish attack. But the downfall of the Huns removed that condition. Any last possibility that the need of the Patrician's services might be urgent in the near future was seemingly removed when the Gothic King Thorismund was murdered by his two brothers, one of whom succeeded as Theodoric II (453–65), and commenced to follow a much more philo-Roman policy than his late brother or father. Even the Sueves of Spain entered upon a treaty of peace with the Empire in

---

10 Some scholars have argued that the Aëtius concerned was the Western Patrician, and that it was the same Western Aëtius who received a fourth consulate in 454. It is difficult on the face of it to see the Western Aëtius in the East in 452; that it was not the Western Aëtius who received the consulship (for an unparalleled fourth time) is shown by an inscription, J. Vives, *Inscripciones cristianas de la España romana y visigoda* (Barcelona, 1942), no. 191, where an epitaph dated by the consuls of 454 does not give any number for the consulship of the Aëtius concerned, implying that it was his first. Recently Sirago, *Placidia*, p. 363, n. 3, has held that Hyd. 154 (II, 26–27) means that Marcian sent troops which served against the Huns under the Western Aëtius; this contradicts both what Hyd. seems to mean as well as Prosp.'s statement that Aëtius' sole hope was in flight (1367 [I, 482]).

453. It cannot be doubted, however, that the main factor which fatally undermined Aëtius' position at court was his failure in 452, followed by the disappearance of the Hunnish danger. We may be sure that the enemies of Aëtius at court, notably we are told a eunuch named Heraclius who was an imperial chamberlain (*Primicerius Sacri Cubiculi*), and among the Roman aristocracy, especially Petronius Maximus, eagerly invited the Emperor's attention to the changed situation. Probably, however, such intrigues were basically unnecessary; any moderately intelligent person, such as Valentinian surely was at least, could perceive the new circumstances for himself.

But it would not suffice merely to dismiss the Patrician from his offices to compel him to retire; it was presumably doubtful whether the Emperor would be able to enforce such an order; he may well have pondered the experience of his relative and namesake Valentinian II with Arbogast in this respect. Aëtius was the commander-in-chief of the Roman army, which quite likely would rally to his support in resisting such a dismissal; besides he possessed a large number of *bucellarii,* many of whom exhibited the characteristic Germanic virtue of strong loyalty to their war chief. In view of the general's refusal to accept his dismissal at the hands of Placidia twenty years before, it was only reasonable to suppose that since resistance to dismissal was possible, Aëtius would resist. Since the Emperor had no adequate armed force at his disposal whose loyalty to himself he might trust, it would be impossible to arrest Aëtius or even put him on trial with any hope of success. It followed, therefore, that he must be assassinated; it would not be the first or the last time that a Roman emperor had found it convenient to destroy his enemies in this fashion. This course had probably been open to Galla Placidia, especially before Aëtius had become either so indispensable or so well established in military power and victory; yet, as we have seen, she had not taken it, possibly from motives of Christian conscience. But murdering Aëtius presented difficulties too, surrounded as he ordinarily was by his faithful bodyguards. Here Valentinian made a serious tactical mistake (entirely apart from moral considerations); he determined, or allowed himself to be persuaded (so the hostile and prejudiced sources describe his weakness), to slay Aëtius with his own hand. It is quite possible that his personal detestation of the general who prevented his being master in his own house, who had forced him to bind himself by an oath, who had plans to perpetuate his power by forcing the marriage of his son to the Emperor's daughter, blinded Valentinian's judgment to the dangers of such a measure. In view especially of the loyalty of the general's barbarian bodyguard, a loyalty which was personal and took no consideration of Emperor or Empire, it would have been much wiser to procure the murder by the hand of a third person, who could then be sacrificed as a scapegoat if necessary. But as Heraclius and the other eunuch personal attendants upon the Emperor probably pointed out, Aëtius would not be accompanied by his bodyguard when he entered the Sacred Presence to discuss measures of state. The motives of Heraclius and his followers are clear; without resorting to hypotheses concerning the natural spite or viciousness of eunuchs: their power and influence depended upon their relation to the Emperor; the ascendancy of Aëtius in the state therefore reduced their power, venal or otherwise, to very little.

Hence on 21 September 454, when Aëtius presented himself before the Emperor to discuss ways and means of filling the ever empty treasury, Valentinian provoked an angry quarrel with him, accusing him of treason and of ambition for the Empire itself; the reference was undoubtedly to the general's project for the marriage of Gaudentius and Placidia.[11] Thereupon the Emperor drew his sword and, joined by Heraclius, who also carried a weapon under his cloak,[12] cut repeatedly at the general's head, perhaps because it was not protected by armor. Thus perished Aëtius. The Emperor also found it desirable to execute Boëthius, the Praetorian Prefect of Italy and a great friend of Aëtius, and perhaps others as well. Whether this murder of Aëtius was justified or not is a nice moral question. Certainly Aëtius was a traitor who had purchased his

[11] If the accusation of ambition in both East and West as reported by Joh. Ant. Frag. 201. 2 (IV, 614) is correct and not merely rhetoric of the source, then perhaps one should construe some sort of reference to Aëtius' friendship with Aspar, or to the question of the West's recognition of Marcian (cf. W. Ensslin, *s.v.* "Marcianus" (34), *RE*, XIV: 2 [1930], 1514–29, at 1518; *ibid.*, VIIA: 2 [1948], 2251; *idem, Menschen die Geschichte machten*, I, 227).

[12] If Joh. Ant. Frag. 201. 2 (IV, 614) does mean it was a cleaver, the statement is to be construed as a characteristic expression of contempt for a eunuch (and therefore for his master who stooped to such assistance), as though the chamberlain could not arm himself with a proper weapon.

power twenty years before by the use of armed force against his country, armed force purchased by the cession of his country's territory. And for twenty years by his control of that armed force he had dominated the legal government of the state. Several Roman laws existed to condemn such conduct as a capital offense. However that may be, it will shortly emerge that the manner of his death was unwise. Perhaps Placidia could have warned her son by the words of Christ that those who take the sword shall perish with it.[13]

Meanwhile Valentinian acted vigorously. At his command the bodies of the slain were exposed in the Forum as a deterrent to all who might be moved actively to resent the sudden turn of affairs. The Senate was convened and addressed by the Emperor, who listed the charges against Aëtius and his supporters in order to prevent any adverse reaction among the great nobles of that body. Ambassadors were sent to the various barbarian peoples, presumably to inform them that the fall of the minister meant no change in the Empire's relations with them. In all probability Geiseric was reassured that the Emperor intended to honor his commitments to the Vandals, probably especially with regard to the marriage of Huniric and Eudocia, to which Aëtius had been opposed and for whose postponement he had probably been responsible. Geiseric's friendship was signified by his permitting the Catholics of Carthage to elect a bishop.[14] As far as his own government was concerned, Valentinian was determined to be the master in his own house like the emperors of the past; never again would he permit a subject to attain such power as Aëtius. Thus Petronius Maximus' intrigues to be allowed to succeed to the position of Aëtius as Patrician and Master of the Soldiers in the Presence were rebuffed, to the indignation of that great noble, who doubtless ascribed to himself a more important role in persuading the Emperor to the destruction of Aëtius than was actually the case.[15] In

---

13 Cf. Ap. Sid. *Carm.* 5. 310–11. Mommsen, *Gesamm. Schrift.*, IV, 544, regards the execution of Aëtius as quite legal under the laws of the Late Empire.

14 See Stein, *Hist.*, I, 347, with refinements of interpretation by Clover, "Geiseric," pp. 134–36.

15 Joh. Ant. Frag. 201. 4 (IV, 615) presents a garbled version of this transaction. He represents Maximus as seeking the highest office, or the consulate (the Greek could mean either thing), although Maximus had already been consul twice; consul the third time he would have attained eminence equal to that of Aëtius as far as official dignity was concerned. We are then told that, unable to obtain this office, he asked to become Patrician. But this cannot be literally correct, for he had already attained this dignity too (before Dec. 445, *NVal* 19). It is clear that what he was aiming

fact, Valentinian intended to resume the actual control of the armed forces himself; this was a necessary step if he were to avoid imposing another master on himself. To win over the troops and especially the *bucellarii* of Aëtius, who must have comprised a relatively large, and probably the most efficient, part of the troops available to the government, Majorian was recalled to court and given an important military command (probably *Comes domesticorum*).[16] A weakness of Valentinian's position was his lack of a son to succeed him; that circumstance by itself was a temptation to intrigues among the ambitious. Resuming a project that he had doubtless devised earlier, he apparently planned, if Majorian turned out as well as expected, to marry him to Placidia; such a marriage would eventually entail Majorian's association in the Empire, or at least his successsion to Valentinian.[17]

To ingratiate himself with the barbarian bodyguard of Aëtius, the Emperor formed the habit of engaging in military exercises in their company. Two of them, among others, named Optila and Thraustila, he assigned to his personal suite. The keeping of Aëtius' former followers close to his person must have appeared to the Emperor in the light of a calculated risk. He might in fact have won his gamble, had it not been for the ambitions of Petronius Maximus. Highest ranking of the nobles of his day, thwarted of his ambition to be the power behind the throne, he now conceived a plan to murder the Emperor and ascend the throne himself. The history of the Roman Empire is monotonously full of such conspiracies of great nobles; unfortunately for himself and the Roman Empire Maximus lacked the perception to understand fully the role of legitimacy in the Late Empire, not only in maintaining Valentinian on the throne, but in holding the dwindling Empire together. At least he presumably had the wit to perceive that since the last descendant of Theodosius the Great in the East, Pulcheria

---

at was a position of prepotence in the state like that of Aëtius, as Joh. Ant. goes on to state explicitly. The Eastern historian of course also, following the hostile interpretation of Valentinian as an incompetent, docile weakling, attributes the failure of Maximus to the counterpersuasion of Heraclius. But it seems very clear that the purpose was the Emperor's, although Maximus will certainly have found Heraclius an opponent of his ambitions; the latter, having helped to destroy Aëtius, naturally had no desire to allow anyone else similarly to interfere with the potency of his influence with the Emperor.

16 Ap. Sid. *Carm.* 5. 306–8; Prosp. 1357 (I, 483).
17 *CP*, LIX (1964), 24–25.

Augusta, had died in 453, it was likely that no Eastern army would march West to avenge Valentinian. And he was also, whether out of acumen or cowardice, loath to strike the fatal blow himself. Instead he suborned Optila and Thraustila to do the deed for him, urging them to avenge their former master.[18] Thus on 16 March 455, Valentinian engaged in military exercises in the presence of the two would-be assassins, as well as Heraclius. Seizing the opportunity, Optila approached the Emperor and smote him on the temple; as Valentinian turned, probably already mortally wounded, he received a second blow across the face which felled him. In the meantime Thraustila killed Heraclius. Thus perished the last direct male descendant of Theodosius the Great; he was not yet thirty-six years of age.[19] The suddenness of the deed left the other members of the Emperor's suite at loss, especially since they might well expect that other *bucellarii* would turn on them. The two assassins picked up the imperial diadem and, taking Valentinian's horse, hastened to present both to Maximus.

The sudden death of the Emperor at once raised the question who should succeed him. Not all elements of the army and *bucellarii* had been won over to Maximus; some favored a certain Maximian, an associate of Aëtius. The Empress Eudoxia kept her head and urged that the choice fall on Majorian, doubtless in view of her husband's plans for the latter. Presumably he would at once have married Placidia so that his legitimacy would be guaranteed by the connection as well as by the sponsorship of the senior surviving member of the imperial family. Instead, probably by judicious threats as well as bribery, Maximus was able to secure his own accession; he was proclaimed Emperor by the troops pres-

18 On this duty of vengeance see O. Seeck, "Das deutsche Gefolgswesen auf römischen Boden," *Zeitschrift der Savigny-Stiftung*, Germ. Abt., XVII (1896), 97–119, at 118.

19 I have inferred that Valentinian had engaged in military exercises with the *bucellarii* on occasions other than the day of his death, and that Maximus chose to work on the minds of Optila and Thraustila because they were frequently in the presence of the Emperor. Joh. Ant. Frag. 201. 4–5 (IV, 615); Prosp. 1375 (I, 483–84); *Cons. Ital.* 572 (I, 303); Agnell. 42; Hyd. 162 (II, 27); *Add. Prosp. Haun.* 572 (I, 303; Thraustila said to be son-in-law of Aëtius); *Prosp. Chron. add.* 27 (I, 490); Greg. Tur. *HF* 2. 8; Marcell. *s.a.* 455, 1 (II, 86); Vict. Tonn. *s.a.* 455 (II, 186); Evag. *HE* 2. 7; *Chron. Pasch.*, pp. 591–92 (Bonn). I have discarded as quite fictional the story of Procop. *Bell.* 3 (*Vand.* 1). 4. 16–24, 36, about Maximus' vengeance for the seduction of his wife by Valentinian; see above, Ch. V, nn. 102, 103. The story about Maximus' wife is also found in [Joh. Ant.] Frag. 200. 1 (IV, 614), but this fragment is mistakenly attributed; cf. Morosi, *L'invito*, p. 7.

ent at Rome on 17 March 455, the day after the assassination. The
new Emperor was by no means insensible of some aspects of the
claim of legitimacy and the prestige of the Theodosian house. In
all probability it is a fairly safe guess that he caused the body of
the murdered Emperor to be interred with full imperial honors
in the Mausoleum by Saint Peter's.[20] More important, for the same
end, he forced the widowed Empress, much against her will, to
marry him and his son Palladius was likewise joined to the younger
Placidia. Eudocia of course remained engaged to Huniric, for
Maximus would not have been so foolish as to break with her
prospective father-in-law.[21] Geiseric, however, was not to be pla-
cated so easily.

Several of the sources allege that in her grief and resentment at
Maximus' participation in the death of Valentinian and her
detestation of her forced marriage with her husband's murderer
Eudoxia appealed to the Vandal King for help. The tale may be
rejected as basically another example of the Late Roman search
for scapegoats on whom to blame the catastrophes of the Empire,
in this case the Vandal sack of Rome.[22] Declaring that the treaty of
442 had been abrogated by the deaths of Valentinian and Aëtius
(the pure formality of this allegation for propaganda purposes is
shown by the fact that Geiseric had been particularly friendly to
the Empire after Aëtius' death), Geiseric with his fleet and army
set sail for Italy and Rome at the end of May. In large part his
motive certainly was the seizure of the tremendous booty still to
be found in the City; there is also some evidence which can be
interpreted to mean that the Vandal King feared a new rapproche-
ment between the Empire and his old enemies the Goths and as
usual struck first.[23] The Vandals landed at Portus by the Tiber
mouth and proceeded along the Via Portuensis to the sixth mile-

20 There is no (real) evidence for this assertion. Since Maximus did in fact wish
to use the prestige and legitimacy of the imperial family to shore up his own position,
it almost necessarily follows that he must have treated the remains of the late Emperor with all honor. To do so, furthermore, would help exculpate him from complicity in Valentinian's murder in the view of the public. On the burial of Valentinian
see Koethe, *Roem. Mitt.*, XLVI (1931), 11; Wes, *Ende*, pp. 158–59.

21 *CP*, LIX (1964), 27–28.

22 The arguments of Morosi, *L'invito*, still seem quite convincing, despite objections
from several more recent scholars.

23 *Prosp. Auct. ad ed. a.* 455 3–4 (I, 492); *Hyd.* 167 (II, 28); in the light of the
implication of Ap. Sid. *Carm.* 7. 360–62, 543–44; as interpreted by Clover, "Geiseric,"
pp. 156–62.

stone from the City. Rome was thrown into a panic; many of its inhabitants fled. The new Emperor was among the number trying to escape; he was stoned by the populace in the streets of Rome, his body torn limb from limb, and cast into the Tiber (31 May 455). Presumably his son Palladius perished at about the same time. On 2 June Pope Leo met the King at the Porta Portuensis and obtained a promise of no burning, no bloodshed. Thereupon for two weeks at their leisure the Vandals plundered Rome. They took many captives, among them the Empress Eudoxia and her daughters Eudocia and Placidia as well as Aëtius' son Gaudentius. On the 16th the Vandals left the desolate City and sailed back to Carthage vastly the richer. Their depredations had obviously been much more thorough than those of the Visigoths forty-five years before (among other things their booty included the sacred ornaments of the Temple of God that Titus had carried off from the sack of Jerusalem nearly four centuries before, together with the insignia of the Roman emperors);[24] nevertheless the physical fabric of the City still stood in most of its ancient grandeur when the marauders departed. In Gaul the Visigoths and some of the Gallic magnates proceeded to the elevation of a new Emperor, Avitus (455–56); after his short reign, the barbarian Master of the Soldiers, Ricimer, created Majorian Emperor (457–61) under far different circumstances from those Valentinian had intended; Ricimer eventually murdered Majorian, who had attempted to follow policies much like those of the Theodosian house, for showing too much independence of his master.

Meanwhile the three women of Valentinian's family languished at Carthage in the captivity of Geiseric, although they seem to have been treated with honor.[25] At least twice Marcian sent embassies to Carthage to try to secure the release of the imperial captives, but in vain.[26] Instead, Huniric was in fact married to Eudocia as previously arranged; Placidia finally married the great Roman noble Anicius Olybrius, whether after her eventual release, or before then at Carthage under the auspices of Geiseric.[27] To

24 *CJ* 1. 27. 1. 6–7.
25 So Malalas 14, p. 366 (Bonn), a doubtful source.
26 Prisc. Frag. 24 (IV, 101–2). The variant tradition that he succeeded (Evag. *HE* 2. 7; Malalas 14, p. 368 [Bonn]; Niceph. Call. *HE* 15. 11, 12 [*PG*, CXLVII, 37, 40]; etc.) is to be rejected.
27 *CP*, LIX (1964), 28, with n. 30 (p. 29).

Huniric Eudocia bore Hilderic, the next to the last King of the Vandals. Finally in 462 the Eastern Emperor Leo I managed to procure the release of Eudoxia and Placidia, who did not go back to Italy, but proceeded to the East where they were presumably supported by the estates in the Eastern Empire originally granted by Theodosius the Great to Galla Placidia, although some portion of the estate of Valentinian III was conceded by Leo to Geiseric.[28] The Vandal King still cherished hopes of a close working arrangement with the Western Empire, or perhaps its domination, through his marriage alliance with the Theodosian house, and wanted to make Huniric's brother-in-law Olybrius Emperor. The latter did become Emperor of the West, but died shortly after his accession (472). Placidia bore him a daughter named Anicia Juliana, and through her the descendants of Galla Placidia can be traced for some generations among the nobility of the Eastern Empire. In 472, perhaps in euphoria at his presumed success in establishing Olybrius finally on the Western throne, Geiseric relaxed his vigilance over Eudocia, who made good her escape from her detested Arian husband and sought refuge in Jerusalem, where she passed the remainder of her life.[29] Geiseric himself finally expired in 477, a few months after the overthrow of the last phantom West Roman Emperor (Romulus Augustulus) recognized as such by important groups in the West. In the score of years following the murder of Valentinian most of the remaining provinces of the West were rapidly lost. By 476, traditional date for the end of the Western imperial line, the "Empire" ruled little more than Italy, and in Italy effective power was in fact in the hands of the barbarian Master of the Soldiers. The downfall of the legitimate house of Valentinian and Theodosius almost certainly accelerated, although it did not cause, this political disappearance of the Empire in the West.

Such was the fate of the children and grandchildren of Galla Placidia and of the great imperial state of which she was so proud, and whose support she was convinced was in the hand of God. It seems unlikely that she is to be blamed for the murder of her son

---

[28] Hyd. 216 (II, 32); Prisc. Frags. 29–30 (IV, 103–4); Procop. *Bell.* 3 (*Vand.* 1). 5. 6.

[29] Cf. Clover, "Geiseric," p. 206 and n. 2; on the descendants of Galla Placidia, see Du Cange, *Historia*, I, 74; Sievers, *Studien*, pp. 528–29.

less than five years after her own demise. It has been argued above that she hardly corrupted Valentinian, whether voluntarily or involuntarily. Possibly originally she communicated her aversion for Aëtius to her son; on the other hand, the dislike of any self-respecting man, a man who was not an Honorius, for the position in which he found himself, of nominal absolute power yet in fact of subjection to a subject who did not boggle at treason to maintain himself in power, is probably sufficient explanation of Valentinian's murder or execution of Aëtius, a deed which led directly to his own death.

Certainly Galla Placidia in her lifetime had been successful in keeping her family firmly on the throne of the West, especially in the years when she effectively exercised what imperial power had not been usurped by her generals. A perennial question among students of history is whether great men make history, or are themselves produced by historic evolution. Probably both propositions are more or less true. Yet the fifth century saw the emergence of no really great men in or near the Roman Empire. The men whose names loom most prominently during the adult lifetime of Galla Placidia—Attila and Geiseric—were hardly great men in the sense that it can be argued that they basically shaped events. Both had a certain cunning or shrewdness; both were able leaders of men; but both seem to have been produced by the circumstances which molded them. Their careers as they actually occurred were possible only because of the decline of the Roman Empire, and that great historic phenomenon had roots in a complicated interworking of impersonal causes which can hardly be unraveled today. It seems implausible that even one of history's "great men" could have healed the many social diseases afflicting the West Roman Empire; certainly Charlemagne was unable to do so in a not entirely dissimilar situation some centuries later. And Galla Placidia was no "great man"; being what she was, she could only apply old and insufficient remedies to the evils of her time. As a member of a ruling Roman family, called upon to rule herself, she could only apply the standard moral canons and traditional views of her civilization to problems which admitted of neither moral nor traditional solutions. As an heiress of the Roman political tradition in an age when that tradition was passing away, she could only be as she was, a conservative, resisting as far as she could almost all change as evil. The outstanding source of strength of her day, the Christian Church, she could only view as a Christian Roman, that is, as a phenomenon which was essentially identical with the Roman Empire and Roman culture. Since she was not an original thinker in matters religious any more than she was in matters political or social, she was able only to become a pious Christian laywoman according to her own judgment and the judgment of the times. Beyond question, she did not have the religious insight of a saint, or even of a Salvian, who was at least able to rid himself of many of his Roman prejudgments in looking at the world about him. But then, his father had not been an emperor.

In large part it is the romantic possibilities in her adventures with Athaulf that attract the attention of later ages. And here Placidia most nearly approached originality. Antecedents for the idea of using barbarians in the service of Rome can be found in the plans of various Roman statesmen such as Stilicho, whom Placidia cordially disliked, in all probability, and her father Theodosius, whom she almost certainly revered; yet the prime impetus thereto in her mind was undoubtedly her captivity among a barbarian people whose King had probably fallen in love with her. She and Athaulf together, and there seems little doubt that it was she who led the way, conceived of a union of Visigoth and Roman, of civilization and barbarism, as a key to the future welfare of both peoples. Yet even if Athaulf or the little Theodosius had lived, it is doubtful that the prospect which Athaulf so enthusiastically sketched at Narbonne could have come about. Long centuries in a ferment of destruction and rebirth and fusion were to elapse before the union of two cultures which the royal pair had dimly envisioned was to become a reality, and then on terms vastly different from the merely mechanical support of a declining Empire and its tired civilization by the strength of a barbarian. As it was, historical accidents caused the plan to abort at the beginning.

Galla Placidia Augusta was proud, a thoroughgoing Roman; she loved power—this last hardly a sin unless we are to condemn all politicians. She managed fairly well to play a role in politics and government despite the disadvantages of her sex. Except for the death of Serena, a deed for which the exact degree of Placidia's responsibility is uncertain, she had, as far as we know, no great crime upon her conscience; probably none after her "conversion."

She was a chaste wife, a devoted mother to her children; the architectural manifestations of her Christian piety which stamped her name on the city of Ravenna made her an enduring legend among the folk of the district until very recent times.[30] Unlike her half brothers Arcadius and Honorius, she was a worthy child of the most Christian and Roman Emperor Theodosius the Great.

[30] Pasolini, *Ravenna*, pp. 38–41.

# BIBLIOGRAPHY
## of Secondary Works Cited

(N.B.: Not all works cited only once, especially in Chapter 1, are listed again here.)

Alföldi, A. "Attila." In *Menschen die Geschichte machten,* edited by P. Rohden and G. Ostrogorsky. I (Vienna, 1931), 229–34.

———. *Die Kontorniaten.* Budapest, 1942–43.

———. *Der Untergang der Römerherrschaft in Pannonien.* 2 vols. Berlin, 1924–26.

Allegranza, Giuseppe. *Spiegazione e riflessioni sopra alcuni sacri monumenti antichi di Milano.* Milan, 1757.

Altheim, Frànz. *Attila und die Hunnen.* Baden-Baden, 1951.

———. *Geschichte der Hunnen.* Vol. IV. Berlin, 1962.

Armellini, Mariano. *Le chiese di Roma.* 3d ed. 2 vols. Rome, 1942.

Arslan, Edoardo. "Milano e Ravenna, due momenti dell' architettura paleocristiana." *Felix Ravenna* LXXXIV (1961), 5–38.

Audollent, A. *S.v.* "Bonifacius" (7), *Dictionnaire d'histoire et de géographie ecclésiastiques,* IX (Paris, 1937), 924–31.

Avery, William T. "The *Adoratio Purpurae* and the Importance of the Imperial Purple in the Fourth Century of the Christian Era." *Memoirs of the American Academy in Rome* XVII (1940), 66–80.

Babut, E.-Ch. *Le Concile de Turin.* Paris, 1904.

———. "Recherches sur la garde impériale et sur le corps d'officiers de l'armée romaine aux IVe et Ve siècles." *Revue historique* CXIV (1913), 225–60; CXVI (1914), 225–93.

Balsdon, J. P. V. D. *Roman Women: Their History and Habits.* New York, 1963.

Bardy, G. "La papauté de Saint Innocent à Saint Léon le Grand." In *Histoire de l'église,* ed. by A. Fliche and Victor Martin. IV (Paris [?], 1937), 241–67.

Bark, William Carroll. *Origins of the Medieval World.* Garden City, 1960.

Barker, Ernest. "Italy and the West, 410–76." *CMedH* I (1911), 392–431.

Bartoli, Alfonso. "Il senato romano in onore di Ezio." *Rendiconti della Pontificia Accademia Romana di Archeologia,* 3d ser., XXII (1946–47), 267–73.

Batiffol, Pierre. *Le siège apostolique (359–451).* 3d ed. Paris, 1924.

Baynes, Norman H. "A Note on Professor Bury's 'History of the Later Roman Empire.' " *JRS* XII (1922), 207–29.

Boak, A. E. R. *Manpower Shortage and the Fall of the Roman Empire in the West.* Ann Arbor, 1955.

Bolwin, Margarete. *Die christlichen Vorstellungen vom Weltberuf der Roma aeterna bis auf Leo den Grossen.* Excerpt. diss. Münster, 1922.

Bouchard, Léon. *Étude sur l'administration des finances de l'empire romain dans les derniers temps de son existence.* Paris, [1872].

Bovini, Giuseppe. *Il cosiddetto mausoleo di Galla Placidia in Ravenna.* Città del Vaticano, 1950.

———. *Ravenna Mosaics.* Greenwich, Conn., 1956.

Boyce, Aline Abaecherli. *Festal and Dated Coins of the Roman Empire: Four Papers.* New York, 1965.

Brisson, Jean-Paul. *Autonomisme et christianisme dans l'Afrique romain de Septime Sévère à l'invasion vandale.* Paris, 1958.

Brown, P. R. L. "Aspects of the Christianization of the Roman Aristocracy." *JRS* LI (1961), 1–11.

Buckland, W. W. *A Text-Book of Roman Law from Augustus to Justinian.* 2d ed. Cambridge, 1932.

Bugiani, Carlo. *Storia di Ezio, generale dell' impero sotto Valentiniano III.* Florence, 1905.

Burckhardt, Felix. "Galla Placidia." *Schweizerische Rundschau* XXV (1925–26), 409–19, 481–89.

Bury, J. B. *History of the Later Roman Empire.* 2 vols. New York, 1958.

———. "Justa Grata Honoria." *JRS* IX (1919), 1–13.

———. "The Notitia Dignitatum." *JRS* X (1920), 131–54.

Calderini, A.; Chierici, G.; and Cecchelli, C. *La basilica di S. Lorenzo maggiore in Milano.* Milan, 1951 [?].

Calderini, Aristide. *La zona monumentale di S. Lorenzo in Milano.* Milan, 1934.

Cancellieri, Francesco Girolamo. *De secretariis veteris basilicae Vaticanae.* Vol. II. Rome, 1786.

Capelle, Wilhelm. *Die Germanen der Völkerwanderung.* Stuttgart, 1940.

Carcopino, Jérôme, "Choses et gens du pays d'Arles." *Revue du Lyonnaise,* 1922, no. 6, pp. 47–70.

Carette, Ernest. *Les assemblées provinciales de la Gaule romaine.* Paris, 1895.

Cartellieri, Alexander. *Weltgeschichte als Machtgeschichte.* Vol. I. Munich, 1927.

Cary, M. *The Geographic Background of Greek and Roman History.* Oxford, 1949.

Caspar, Erich. *Geschichte des Papsttums von den Anfängen bis zur Höhe der Weltherrschaft.* Vol. I. Tübingen, 1930.

Castagnoli, Ferdinando; Cecchelli, Carlo; Giovannoni, Gustavo; and Zocca, Mario. *Topografia e urbanistica di Roma*. Bologna, 1958.

Cecchelli, Carlo. *S.v.* "Galla Placidia." *Enciclopedia italiana* XVI, 286–87.

Cessi, Roberto. *"Regnum" ed "Imperium" in Italia*. Vol. I. Bologna, 1919 [?].

Chabouillet, Anatole. "Observations sur deux médaillons d'or d'Honorius et de Placidie." *Revue numismatique,* 3d ser., I (1883), 70–91.

Chadwick, Nora K. *Poetry and Letters in Early Christian Gaul*. London, 1955.

Chastagnol, André. *La préfecture urbaine à Rome sous le bas-empire*. Paris, 1960.

―――. "Le problème de l'histoire auguste: État de la question." *Antiquitas,* 4th ser., *Beiträge zur Historia-Augusta-Forschung* II (1964), 43–71.

―――. "Le sénateur Volusien et la conversion d'une famille de l'aristocratie romaine au bas-empire." *RÉA* LVIII (1956), 241–53.

Clover, Frank Metlar. "Geiseric the Statesman: A Study of Vandal Foreign Policy." Doct. diss. Unpublished. Chicago, 1966. Available on microfilm.

―――. "An Historical Commentary on and Translation of Flavius Merobaudes." Master's diss. Unpublished. Chicago, 1963.

Cohen, Henry. *Description historique des monnaies frappées sous l'empire romain communément appelées médailles impériales*. 2d ed. Vol. VIII. Paris, 1892.

Collingwood, R. G., and Myres, J. N. L. *Roman Britain and the English Settlements*. 2d ed. Oxford, 1937.

Costanzi, Vincenzo. "La rivolta di Pavia e la catastrofe di Stilicone." *Bollettino della Società Pavese di Storia Patria* IV (1904), 481–523.

Coster, Charles Henry. *The Iudicium Quinquevirale*. Cambridge, Mass., 1935.

Courcelle, Pierre. "Le gril de Saint Laurent au mausolée de Galla Placidia." *Cahiers archéologiques* III (1948), 29–39.

―――. *Histoire littéraire des grandes invasions germaniques*. Paris, 1948. [Text of 3d ed., Paris, 1964, is little changed.]

―――. "Les lacunes de la correspondance entre Saint Augustin et Paulin de Nole." *RÉA* LIII (1951), 253–300.

Courtois, Christian. "Auteurs et scribes: Remarques sur la chronique d'Hydace." *Byzantion* XXI (1951), 23–54.

―――. "Les politiques navales de l'empire romain." *Revue historique* CLXXXVI (1939), 17–47, 225–59.

―――. *Les Vandales et l'Afrique*. Paris, 1955.

Coville, Alfred. *Recherches sur l'histoire de Lyon du V^me siècle au IX^me siècle (450–800)*. Paris, 1928.

Crome, J. E. "Il vetro dorato della croce di Desiderio." *Felix Ravenna* LXXXI (1960), 117–23.

Czúth, Béla, and Szádeczky-Kardoss, Samu. "Bagaudák az Alpokban" ["The Bagaudae in the Alps"], Resumé in *Bibliotheca Classica Orientalis* IV (1959), 280–81.

Dahn, Felix. *Die Könige der Germanen.* Vol. V. Würzburg, 1870. Vol. VI. 2d ed. Leipzig, 1885. Vol. XI. Leipzig, 1908.

———. *Urgeschichte der germanischen und romanischen Völker.* 2 vols. Berlin, 1881.

Dannenbauer, Heinrich. *Die Entstehung Europas von der Spätantike zum Mittelalter.* Vol. I. Stuttgart, 1959.

Dantier, Alphonse. *Les femmes dans la société chrétienne.* 2 vols. Paris, 1879.

Dawson, Christopher. *The Making of Europe.* New York, 1956.

Degrassi, Attilio. *I fasti consolari dell' impero romano.* Rome, 1952.

———. "L'iscrizione in onore di Aezio e l' 'Atrium Libertatis.' " *Bullettino della Commissione Archeologica Communale di Roma* LXXII (1946–48), 33–44.

Deichmann, Friedrich Wilhelm. *Frühchristliche Kirchen in Rom.* Basel, 1948.

Delbrueck, Richard. *Die Consulardiptychen und verwandte Denkmäler.* Berlin and Leipzig, 1926–29.

———. "Portraets byzantinischer Kaiserinnen." *Römische Mitteilungen* XXVIII (1913), 310–52.

———. "Der spätantike Kaiserornat." *Die Antike* VIII (1932), 1–21.

———. *Spätantike Kaiserporträts.* Berlin, 1933.

Demangel, R. *Contribution à la topographie de l'Hebdomon.* Recherches françaises en Turquie, vol. III. Paris, 1945.

Demougeot, Émilienne. "À propos des interventions du pape Innocent Ier dans la politique séculière." *Revue historique* CCXII (1954), 23–38.

———. "Attila et les Gaules." *Mémoires de la Société d'Agriculture, Commerce, Sciences et Arts du Département de la Marne* LXXIII (1958), 7–41.

———. *De l'unité à la division de l'empire romain 395–410.* Paris, 1951.

———. "Les invasions germaniques et la rupture des relations entre la Bretagne et la Gaule." *Le Moyen Âge* LXVIII (1962), 1–50.

———. "Note sur la politique orientale de Stilicon de 405 à 407." *Byzantion* XX (1950), 27–37.

———. "Notes sur l'évacuation des troupes romaines en Alsace au début du Ve siècle." *Revue d'Alsace* XCII (1953), 7–28.

Dennis, Holmes V. M. "Another Note on the Vandal Occupation of Hippo Regius." *JRS* XV (1925), 263–68.

Dennison, Walter. "A Gold Treasure of the Late Roman Period from Egypt." In *Studies in East Christian and Roman Art,* by Walter Dennison and Charles R. Morey. New York, 1918. Pp. 87–166.

De Salis, J. F. W. "The Coins of the Two Eudoxias, Eudocia, Placidia, and Honoria, and of Theodosius II., Marcian, and Leo I., Struck in Italy." *Numismatic Chronicle,* n.s., VII (1867), 203–15.

Diehl, Charles. *Ravenne: Études d'archéologie byzantine.* Paris, 1886.

Diesner, Hans-Joachim. "Die Lage der nordafrikanischen Bevölkerung im Zeitpunkt der Vandaleninvasion." In *Kirche und Staat im spätrömischen Reich.* Berlin, 1963. Pp. 127–39 [= *Historia,* IX (1962), 97–111].

————. "Die Laufbahn des Comes Africae Bonifatius und seine Beziehungen zu Augustin." In *Kirche und Staat im spätrömischen Reich.* Berlin, 1963. Pp. 100–126.

————. *Der Untergang der römischen Herrschaft in Nordafrika.* Weimar, 1964.

————. "Zur Datierung der Augustinbriefe 228–231." In *Kirche und Staat im spätrömischen Reich.* Berlin, 1963, Pp. 91–93 [= *Forschungen und Forschritte,* XXXV: 6 (1961), 184–85].

Dill, Samuel. *Roman Society in the Last Century of the Western Empire.* 2d ed. London, 1933.

Dominicis, M. Antonio de. "Il problema dei rapporti burocratico-legislativi tra 'occidente ed oriente' nel basso impero romano alla luce delle inscriptiones e subscriptiones delle costituzioni imperiali." *Istituto Lombardo di Scienze e Lettere, Rendiconti,* Cl. Lett. e Sci. mor. e stor., LXXXVII: 2 (1954), 329–487.

Dopsch, Alfons. *The Economic and Social Foundations of European Civilization.* London, 1937.

Dressel, H. "Erwerbungen des Königlichen Münzcabinets in den Jahren 1890–1897 (antike Münzen)." *Zeitschrift für Numismatik* XXI (1898), 210 49.

Du Cange, Charles du Fresne. *Historia Byzantina Duplici Commentario Illustrata.* 2 vols. Paris, 1680 [= 1963].

Duchesne, Louis. *The Churches Separated from Rome.* New York, 1907.

————. *Early History of the Christian Church from Its Foundation to the End of the Fifth Century.* Vol. III. New York, 1924.

————. *Fastes épiscopaux de l'ancienne Gaule.* 3 vols. Paris, 1900–1915.

Dvornik, Francis. *Early Christian and Byzantine Political Philosophy: Origins and Background.* 2 vols. Washington, 1966.

Dyggve, Ejnar. *Ravennatum Palatium Sacrum: La basilica ipetrale per cerimonie: Studii sull' architettura dei palazzi della tarda antichità.* Copenhagen, 1941.

Eicke, Hermann. *Geschichte der westgotischen Könige seit Alarichs Tod.* Leipzig, 1944.

Ensslin, Wilhelm. *S.v.* "Maiorianus," *RE* XIV: 1 (1930), 584–90.

————. *S.v.* "Marcianus" (34), *RE* XIV: 2 (1930), 1514–29.

————. *S.v.* "Maria" (3), *RE* XIV: 2 (1930), 1712–13.

————. *S.v.* "Maximus" (32), *RE* XIV: 2 (1930), 2543–45.

————. *S.v.* "Placidia" (1), *RE* XX: 2 (1950), 1910–31.

————. *Die Religionspolitik des Kaisers Theodosius d. Gr.* Sitzungsberichte Bayer. Akad. Wissen., Phil.-hist. Kl., 1953, Heft 2. Munich, 1953.

————. [Review of] A. Alföldi, *Untergang der Römerherrschaft in Pannonien,* Vol. II. *Philologische Wochenschrift* XLVII (1927), 842–52.

————. "Das Römerreich unter germanischer Waltung, von Stilicho bis Theodorich." *Das neue Bild der Antike* II (Leipzig, 1942), 412–32.

————. "Valentinian III." In *Menschen die Geschichte machten,* ed. by P. Rohden and G. Ostrogorsky. I (Vienna, 1931), 223–28.

————. "Valentinians III. Novellen XVII und XVIII von 445." *Zeitschrift der Savigny-Stiftung,* Rom. Abt., LVII (1937), 367–78.

————. *S.v.* "Valentinianus" (4), *RE* VIIA: 2 (1948), 2232–59.

————. "War Kaiser Theodosius I. zweimal in Rom?" *Hermes* LXXXI (1953), 500–507.

————. "Zum Heermeisteramt des spätrömischen Reiches, II, III." *Klio* XXIV (1931), 102–47, 467–502.

Farioli, Raffaela. "Ravenna paleocristiana scomparsa." *Felix Ravenna* LXXXII (1960), 5–96; LXXXIII (1961), 5–88.

Fattorusso, Joseph [i.e., Giuseppe]. *Wonders of Italy.* Florence, 1953.

Fiebiger, Otto, and Schmidt, Ludwig. *Inschriftensammlung zur Geschichte der Ostgermanen.* Denkschriften der Kaiserlichen Akademie der Wissenschaften in Wien, Phil.-hist. Kl., LX: 3. Vienna, 1917.

Francisci, Pietro de. "Per la storia del senato romano e della curia nei secoli v e vi." *Rendiconti della Pontificia Accademia Romana di Archeologia,* 3d ser., XXII (1946–47), 275–317.

Freeman, E. A. *Western Europe in the Fifth Century.* London, 1904.

Frend, W. H. C. *The Donatist Church: A Movement of Protest in Roman North Africa.* Oxford, 1952.

Fuchs, H. *Der geistige Widerstand gegen Rom in der antiken Welt.* Berlin, 1938.

Fustel de Coulanges, Numa Denis. *Histoire des institutions politiques de l'ancienne France.* Vol. II. Rev. ed. by Camille Jullian. Paris, 1891.

Gabba, Emilio, and Tibiletti, Gianfranco. "Una signora di Treviri sepolta a Pavia." *Athenaeum* XLVIII (1960), 253–62.

Gabotto, Ferdinando. *Storia della Italia occidentale nel medio evo (395–1313).* Vol. I. Pinerolo, 1911.

Galassi, Giuseppe. *Roma o Bisanzio.* Vol. I. 2d ed. Rome, 1953.

Ganshof, F. L. "Notes critiques sur la patrie des Nibelungen." *Revue belge de philologie et d'histoire* XIV (1935), 195–211.

Gaudemet, Jean. *L'église dans l'empire romain (IVe-Ve siècles).* Histoire du droit et des institutions de l'église en occident, edited by Gabriel Le Bras, Vol. III. Paris, n.d.

————. "Société religieuse et monde laïc au bas-empire." *Iura* X (1959), 86–102.

Gautier, E.-F. *Genséric, Roi des Vandales.* Paris, 1951.

Gelzer, Matthias. *Studien zur byzantinischen Verwaltung Ägyptens.* Leipzig, 1909.

Gentili, Ruggero. "La rivalità fra Ezio, Felice e Bonifacio e l'invasione dei Vandali in Africa." *Il mondo classico* V (1935), 363–72.

Gibbon, Edward. *The Decline and Fall of the Roman Empire.* Edited by J. B. Bury. Vol. III. London, 1901.

Gigli, Guido. *La crisi dell' impero romano.* Palermo, 1947.

――. "La flotta e la difesa del basso impero." *Memorie della Accademia Nazionale dei Lincei,* Cl. scienz. mor., stor. e filolog., 8th ser., I (1946), 3–43.

――. *Il regno dell' Imperatore Teodosio.* 2 vols. Rome, 1963–65.

Gitti, Alberto. *Ricerche sui rapporti tra i Vandali e l'impero romano.* Bari, 1953.

Goetz, Walter. *Ravenna.* Leipzig, 1901.

Gordon, C. D. *The Age of Attila.* Ann Arbor, 1960.

Goubert, Paul. "Le rôle de Sainte Pulchérie et de l'eunuque Chrysaphios." In *Das Konzil von Chalkedon,* edited by A. Grillmeier and H. Bacht. I (Würzburg, 1951), 303–21.

Grabar, André. *L'empereur dans l'art byzantin.* Paris, 1936.

――. *Martyrium: Recherches sur le culte des reliques et l'art chrétien antique.* 2 vols. and album of pls. Paris, 1943–46.

Grégoire, H. "Miettes d'histoire byzantine." In *Anatolian Studies Presented to Sir William Mitchell Ramsay.* Manchester, 1923. Pp. 151–64.

Griffe, Élie. *La Gaule chrétienne à l'époque romaine.* Vol. II, pt. 1. Paris, 1957.

――. "La pratique religieuse en Gaule au Ve siècle: Saeculares et sancti." *Bulletin de la littérature ecclésiastique* LXIII (1962), 241–67.

Grisar, Hartmann. *History of Rome and the Popes in the Middle Ages.* Vols. I–II. London, 1911–12.

Grosjean, Paul. "Notes d'hagiographie celtique." *Analecta Bollandiana* LXXV (1957), 158–226.

Grosse, Robert. *Römische Militärgeschichte von Gallienus bis zum Beginn der byzantinischen Themenverfassung.* Berlin, 1920.

Grumel, V. "L'Illyricum de la mort de Valentinien Ier (375) à la mort de Stilicon (408)." *Revue des études byzantines* IX (1951), 5–46.

Güldenpenning, Albert. *Geschichte des oströmischen Reiches unter den Kaisern Arcadius und Theodosius II.* Halle, 1885.

Güldenpenning, Albert, and Ifland, J. *Der Kaiser Theodosius der Grosse.* Halle, 1878.

Gütschow, Margarete. "Grabungen in Ravenna." *Gnomon* III (1927), 126–27.

Haenel, Gustav. *Corpus Legum ab Imperatoribus Romanis ante Justinianum Latarum.* Leipzig, 1857.

Haller, Johannes. *Das Papsttum: Idee und Wirklichkeit.* Vol. I. 2d ed. Esslingen am Neckar, 1962.

Hanfmann, G. M. A. *Roman Art.* Greenwich, Conn., 1964.

Hartke, Werner. *Geschichte und Politik im spätantiken Rom.* Klio, Beiheft XLV. Leipzig, 1940.

Hartmann, Ludo Moritz. *Geschichte Italiens im Mittelalter.* Vol. I. Gotha, 1897.

Hassebrauk, G. *Westrom zur Zeit des Aëtius, 425–454.* Programm; Braunschweig, 1899.

Hatt, J. J. *Histoire de la Gaule romaine (120 avant J.-C.—451 après J.-C.).* Paris, 1959.

Helbling, Hanno. *Goten und Wandalen.* Zurich, 1954.

Hill, P. V.; Kent, J. P. C.; and Carson, R. A. G. *Late Roman Bronze Coinage.* London, 1960.

Hirschfeld, Otto. "Die römische Staatszeitung und die Acclamationen im Senat." *Sitzungsberichte . . . Berlin,* 1905. Pp. 930–48.

His, Rudolf. *Die Domänen der römischen Kaiserzeit.* Leipzig, 1896.

Hodgkin, Thomas. *Italy and Her Invaders.* 2d ed. Vol. I, Pt. 2; Vol. II. Oxford, 1892.

Holder-Egger, Oswald. "Untersuchungen über einige annalistische Quellen zur Geschichte des fünften und sechsten Jahrhunderts." *Neues Archiv der Gesellschaft für Ältere Deutsche Geschichtskunde* I (1876), 13–120, 213–368.

Hollister, C. Warren. "Twilight in the West." In *The Transformation of the Roman World,* edited by Lynn White. Berkeley, 1966. Pp. 179–205.

Holmes, T. Scott. *The Origin and Development of the Christian Church in Gaul.* London, 1911.

Hopkins, Keith. "Eunuchs in Politics in the Later Roman Empire." *Proceedings of the Cambridge Philological Society,* no. 189 (1963), 62–80.

Hoxie, Albert. "Mutations in Art." In *The Transformation of the Roman World,* edited by Lynn White. Berkeley, 1966. Pp. 266–90.

Hutton, Edward. *Ravenna: A Study.* London, 1913.

Jalland, Trevor. *The Life and Times of St. Leo the Great.* London, 1941.

Janin, R. *Constantinople byzantine.* 2d ed. Paris, 1964.

Jörs. *S.v.* "Citiergesetz." *RE* III: 2 (1899), 2608–12.

Johnstone, P. K. "Vortigern and Aetius—A Re-appraisal." *Antiquity* XX (1946), 16–20.

Jones, A. H. M. "The Decline and Fall of the Roman Empire." *History* XL (1955), 208–26.

———. *The Later Roman Empire, 284–602: A Social, Economic, and Administrative Survey.* 3 vols. and portfolio of maps. Oxford, 1964. 2 vols. Norman, Okla., 1964.

———. "Over-Taxation and the Decline of the Roman Empire." *Antiquity* XXXIII (1959), 39–43.

———. "Were Ancient Heresies National or Social Movements in Disguise?" *The Journal of Theological Studies,* n.s., X (1959), 280–98.

Kaufmann, Georg. *Deutsche Geschichte bis auf Karl den Grossen.* 2 vols. Leipzig, 1880–81.

———. "Ueber das Foederatverhältniss des tolosanischen Reichs zu Rom." *Forschungen zur deutschen Geschichte* VI (1866), 433–76.

Keller, Rudolf. *Stilicho.* Diss. Jena, 1884.

Kent, J. P. C. "Gold Coinage in the Later Roman Empire." In *Essays in Roman Coinage Presented to Harold Mattingly,* edited by R. A. G. Carson and C. H. V. Sutherland. Oxford, 1956. Pp. 190–204.

Kidd, B. J. *A History of the Church to A. D. 461.* Vol. III. Oxford, 1922.

Kienast, Dietmar. *Untersuchungen zu den Kriegsflotten der römischen Kaiserzeit.* Bonn, 1966.

Kirsch, Johann Peter. *Die römische Titelkirchen im Altertum.* Paderborn, 1918.

Kirschbaum, Engelbert. *The Tombs of St. Peter and St. Paul.* Translated from the German by John Murray. London, 1959.

Koch, Julius. "Claudian und die Ereignisse der Jahre 395 bis 398." *RhM.* n.s., XLIV (1889), 575–612.

Koethe, Harald. "Zum Mausoleum der weströmischen Dynastie bei Alt-Sankt-Peter." *Roemische Mitteilungen* XLVI (1931), 9–26.

Kornemann, E. "Galla Placidia." In *Grosse Frauen des Altertums.* 4th ed. Bremen, 1952. Pp. 314–54.

Krautheimer, Richard *et al. Corpus Basilicarum Christianarum.* Rome, 1937 ff.

Kromayer, Johannes, and Veith, Georg. *Heerwesen und Kriegführung der Griechen und Römer.* Munich, 1928.

Kruse, Helmut. *Studien zur offiziellen Geltung des Kaiserbildes im römischen Reiche.* Studien zur Geschichte und Kultur des Altertums, XIX: 3. Paderborn, 1934.

Ladner, G. B. "The Impact of Christianity." In *The Transformation of the Roman World,* edited by Lynn White. Berkeley, 1966. Pp. 59–91.

Lana, I. *Rutilio Namaziano.* Turin, 1961.

Lanciani, Rodolfo. *The Destruction of Ancient Rome: A Sketch of the History of the Monuments.* New York, 1903.

―――. *Pagan and Christian Rome.* Boston, 1892.

―――. "Ricerche topografiche sulla città di Porto." *Annali dell' Instituto di Corrispondenza Archeologica* XL (1868), 144–95.

―――. *Wanderings in the Roman Campagna.* Boston, 1909.

―――. *Wanderings through Ancient Roman Churches.* Boston, 1924.

Larsen, J. A. O. "The Position of Provincial Assemblies in the Government and Society of the Late Roman Empire." *CP* XXIX (1934), 209–20.

―――. *Representative Government in Greek and Roman History.* Berkeley, 1955.

Latouche, Robert. *Les grandes invasions et la crise de l'occident au V<sup>e</sup> siècle.* Paris, 1946.

Lear, Floyd Seyward. *Treason in Roman and Germanic Law.* Austin, 1965.

Leclercq, H. *S.v.* "Galla Placidia." *Dictionnaire d'archéologie chrétienne et de liturgie* VI: 1 (Paris, 1924), 248–75.

Lécrivain, C. *Le sénat romain depuis Dioclétien à Rome et à Constantinople.* Paris, 1888.

Lepper, J. L. M. de. *De Rebus Gestis Bonifatii Comitis Africae et Magistri Militum.* Diss. Cath. Univ. of Nijmegen. Breda, 1941.

Levison, Wilhelm. "Bischof Germanus von Auxerre und die Quellen zu seiner Geschichte." *Neues Archiv der Gesellschaft für Ältere Deutsche Geschichtskunde* XXIX (1904), 95–175.

Lewis, Archibald R. *Naval Power and Trade in the Mediterranean A.D. 500–1100.* Princeton, 1951.

———. *The Northern Seas: Shipping and Commerce in Northern Europe A.D. 300–1100.* Princeton, 1958.

Lichtheim, Miriam. "Autonomy versus Unity in the Christian East." In *The Transformation of the Roman World,* edited by Lynn White. Berkeley, 1966. Pp. 119–46.

Liebeschuetz, W. "Did the Pelagian Movement Have Social Aims?" *Historia* XII (1963), 227–41.

Lizerand, Georges. *Aetius.* Paris, 1910.

Lot, Ferdinand; Pfister, Christian; and Ganshof, F. L. *Les destinées de l'empire en occident de 395 à 888.* Paris, 1928.

Lot, Ferdinand. "De la valeur historique du De excidio et conquestu Britanniae de Gildas." In *Medieval studies in Memory of Gertrude Schoepperle Loomis.* Paris, 1927. Pp. 229–64.

———. "Du régime de l'hospitalité." *Revue belge de philologie et d'histoire* VII (1928), 975–1011.

———. *La Gaule: Les fondements ethniques, sociaux et politiques de la nation française.* Paris, 1947.

———. *Les invasions germaniques: La pénétration mutuelle du monde barbare et du monde romain.* Paris, 1935.

———. "La 'Notitia Dignitatum Utriusque Imperii.' " *RÉA* XXXVIII (1936), 285–338.

———. *Nouvelles recherches sur l'impôt foncier et la capitation personelle sous le bas-empire.* Paris, 1955.

Loyen, A. "Les débuts du royaume wisigoth de Toulouse." *RÉL* XII (1934), 406–15.

———. *Recherches historiques sur les panégyriques de Sidoine Apollinaire.* Paris, 1942.

———. "Traité de fédération imposé aux Wisigoths par l'empire." *RÉL* XII (1934), 31.

Lugli, Giuseppe. *Roma antica: Il centro monumentale.* Rome, 1946.

MacMullen, Ramsay. *Enemies of the Roman Order: Treason, Unrest, and Alienation in the Empire.* Cambridge, Mass., 1966.

———. "Roman Bureaucratese." *Traditio* XVIII (1962), 364–78.

———. *Soldier and Civilian in the Later Roman Empire*. Cambridge, Mass., 1963.

Manganaro, G. "La reazione pagana a Roma nel 408–409 d. C." *Giorn. it. fil.* XIII (1960), 210–24.

Manitius, M. "The Teutonic Migrations, 378–412." *CMedH* I (1911), 250–76.

Marrou, Henri-Irénée. "L'épitaphe vaticane du consulaire de Vienne Eventius." *RÉA* LIV (1952), 326–31.

Martroye, F. *Genséric: La conquête vandale en Afrique et la destruction de l'empire d'occident*. Paris, 1907.

———. "Saint Augustin et la compétence de la juridiction ecclésiastique au Vᵉ siècle." *Mémoirs de la Société Nationale des Antiquaires de France* LXX (1911), 1–78.

———. [Stilicho's "regency" for Honorius], *Bulletin de la Société Nationale des Antiquaires de France*, 1916, pp. 202–6.

Maull, Irmgard. "Le zecche nell' antica Ravenna." *Felix Ravenna* LXXXIV (1961), 79–134.

Mazzarino, Santo. *Aspetti sociali del quarto secolo*. Rome, 1951.

———. *La fine del mondo antico*. Milan, 1959.

———. *Serena e le due Eudossie*. Rome, 1946.

———. *Stilicone: La crisi imperiale dopo Teodosio*. Rome, 1942.

McGeachy, John Alexander. *Quintus Aurelius Symmachus and the Senatorial Aristocracy of the West*. Diss. Chicago, 1942.

Meer, F. van der. *Augustine the Bishop*. Translated by Brian Battershaw and G. R. Lamb. London, 1961.

Meier, Christian. *Res Publica Amissa*. Wiesbaden, 1966.

Meiggs, Russell. *Roman Ostia*. Oxford, 1960.

Menéndez Pidal, Ramón, ed. *Historia de España*. Vol. III. Madrid, 1940.

Meyer, Wilhelm. ". . . epistulae imperatorum romanorum ex collectione . . . Avellana . . . editae." [*Göttingen Universität*.] *Index Scholarum*, Winter, 1888–89, pp. 3–41.

Minuzzi, Marta. "La spilla di Ténès con ritratto di Aelia Flaccilla." *Felix Ravenna* LXXXIII (1961), 99–108.

Momigliano, A. *The Conflict between Paganism and Christianity in the Fourth Century*. Oxford, 1963.

Mommsen, Theodor. "Aetius." *Gesammelte Schriften* IV (Berlin, 1906), 531–60 [= *Hermes* XXXVI (1901), 516–47].

———. "Stilicho und Alarich." *Gesammelte Schriften* IV (Berlin, 1906), 516–30 [= *Hermes* XXXVIII (1903), 101–15].

Morosi, Giuseppe. *L'invito di Eudossia a Genserico*. Florence, 1882.

Moss, H. St. L. B. *The Birth of the Middle Ages 395–814*. Oxford, 1935.

Müntz, Eugène. "The Lost Mosaics of Ravenna." *AJA* I (1885), 115–30.

Musset, Lucien. *Les invasions: Les vagues germaniques*. Paris, 1965.

322 · *Bibliography*

Myres, J. N. L. "Pelagius and the End of Roman Rule in Britain." *JRS* L (1960), 21–36.

Nagl, M. Assunta. *Galla Placidia.* Studien zur Geschichte und Kultur des Altertums, vol. II: 3. Paderborn, 1908.

Nesselhauf, Herbert. "Patrimonium und res privata des römischen Kaisers." *Historia-Augusta-Colloquium, Bonn, 1963* (Bonn, 1964), pp. 73–93.

Nischer-Falkenhof, Ernst. *Stilicho.* Vienna, 1947.

Oost, S. I. "Aëtius and Majorian." *CP* LIX (1964), 23–29.

———. "Count Gildo and Theodosius the Great." *CP* LVII (1962), 27–30.

———. "Galla Placidia and the Law." *CP* LXIII (1968), 114–21.

———. "The Revolt of Heraclian." *CP* LXI (1966), 236–42.

———. "Some Problems in the History of Galla Placidia." *CP* LX (1965), 1–10.

Ostrogorsky, George. *History of the Byzantine State.* New Brunswick, N.J., 1957.

Pace, Biagio. *I barbari e i bizantini in Sicilia: Studi alla storia dell' isola dal sec. V. al IX.* Palermo, 1911.

Palanque, Jean-Rémy. "Collégialité et partages dans l'empire romain aux IV^e et V^e siècles." *RÉA* XLVI (1944), 47–64, 280–98.

———. "L'empereur Maxime." In *Les empereurs romains d'Espagne.* Colloques internationaux du Centre National de la Recherche Scientifique. Paris, 1965. Pp. 255–63.

———. *Essai sur la préfecture du prétoire du bas-empire.* Paris, 1933.

Pallu de Lessert, A. Clément. *Fastes des provinces africaines sous la domination romaine.* Vol. II. Paris, 1901.

Paribeni, Roberto. *Da Diocleziano alla caduta dell' impero d'occidente.* Bologna, 1941.

Pasolini, Pier Desiderio. *Ravenna e le sue grandi memorie.* Rome, 1912.

Pavan, Massimiliano. *La politica gotica di Teodosio nella pubblicistica del suo tempo.* Rome, 1964.

Picotti, G. B. "Il 'Patricius' nell' ultima età imperiale e nei primi regni barbarici d'Italia." *Archivio storico italiano,* 7th ser., IX (1928), 3–80.

Piganiol, André. "La Gaule au temps d'Attila." In *Saint Germain d'Auxerre et son temps.* Auxerre, 1950. Pp. 119–33.

———. *L'impôt de capitation sous le bas-empire romain.* Chambéry, 1916.

———. [Review of] Santo Mazzarino, *Aspetti sociali del quarto secolo. Journal des savants* 1955, 5–15.

Platner, S. B., and Ashby, Thomas. *A Topographical Dictionary of Ancient Rome.* Oxford, 1929.

Rémondon, Roger. *La crise de l'empire romain de Marc-Aurèle à Anastase.* Paris, 1964.

Richmond, Ian A. *The City Wall of Imperial Rome.* Oxford, 1930.

Rivoira, G. T. *Lombardic Architecture: Its Origin, Development and Derivatives.* Translated by G. McN. Rushforth. Vol. I. London, 1910.

Romanelli, Pietro. *Storia delle province romane dell' Africa.* Rome, 1959.

Romano, G. *Le dominazioni barbariche in Italia (395–1024).* Milan, n.d. [1909?].

Rougé, Jean. *Recherches sur l'organisation du commerce maritime en Méditerranée sous l'empire romain.* Paris, 1966.

Rubin, Berthold. *Das Zeitalter Justinians.* Vol. I. Berlin, 1960.

Ruggini, Lellia. "Ebrei e orientali nell' Italia settentrionale fra il IV e il VI secolo d. Chr." *Studia et documenta historiae et iuris* XXV (1959), 186–308.

―――. *Economia e società nell' 'Italia Annonaria': Rapporti fra agricoltura e commercio dal IV al VI secolo d. C.* Milan, 1961.

―――. [Review of] V. A. Sirago, *Galla Placidia e la trasformazione politica dell' occidente. Athenaeum* XL (1962), 373–91.

Salvatorelli, Luigi. *L'Italia medioevale dalle invasioni barbariche agli inizi del secolo XI.* Milan, n.d.

Scevola, Liliana. "La basilica di S. Giovanni Evangelista a Ravenna." *Felix Ravenna* LXXXVII (1963), 5–107.

Schild, Wilhelm. *Galla Placidia.* Diss. Halle-Wittenberg. Halle, 1897.

Schmidt, Ludwig. "Bonifatius und der Uebergang der Wandalen nach Afrika." *Historische Vierteljahrschrift* II (1899), 449–62.

―――. *Geschichte der deutschen Stämme bis zur Ausgang der Völkerwanderung.* 2d ed. 2 vols. Munich, 1934–40.

―――. *Geschichte der Wandalen.* 2d ed. Munich, 1942.

Schöndorf, Kurt A. *Die Geschichtstheologie des Orosius.* Munich, 1952.

Schultze, Victor. *Geschichte des Untergangs des griechisch-römischen Heidentums.* 2 vols. Jena, 1887–92.

―――. *Konstantinopel (324–450).* Leipzig, 1913.

Schulz, Fritz. *History of Roman Legal Science.* Oxford, 1953.

Seeck, Otto. *S.v.* "Priscus Attalus" (19), *RE* II (1896), 2177–79.

―――. *S.v.* "Bonifatius" (1), *RE* III (1899), 698–99.

―――. *S.v.* "Bucellarii," *RE* III (1899), 934–39.

―――. *S.v.* "Candidianus" (3), *RE* III (1899), 1472–73.

―――. *S.v.* "Castinus" (2), *RE* III (1899), 1761–62.

―――. *S.v.* "Constantius" (9), *RE* IV (1901), 1099–1102.

―――. "Das deutsche Gefolgswesen auf römischen Boden." *Zeitschrift der Savigny-Stiftung für Rechtsgeschichte,* Germ. Abt., XVII (1896), 97–119.

―――. *S.v.* "Eudokia" (2), *RE* VI (1909), 912.

―――. *S.v.* "Eudoxia" (2), *RE* VI (1909), 925–26.

―――. *S.v.* "Flaccilla" (3), *RE* VI: 2 (1909), 2431–33.

————. *Geschichte des Untergangs der antiken Welt.* Vols. V–VI. Berlin and Stuttgart, 1913–21.

————. *S.v.* "Honorius" (3), *RE* VIII: 2 (1913), 2277–91.

————. *S.v.* "Iovinus" (5), *RE* IX: 2 (1916), 2012–13.

————. *Regesten der Kaiser und Päpste für die Jahre 311 bis 476 n. Chr.* Stuttgart, 1919.

————. *S.v.* "Serena" (2), *RE* IIA (1923), 1672–73.

————. *S.v.* "Stilicho," *RE* IIIA (1929), 2523–24.

Segrè, Angelo. "Essays on Byzantine Economic History: I. The *Annona Civica* and the *Annona Militaris.*" *Byzantion* XVI (1942–43), 393–444.

Seppelt, Franz Xaver. *Der Aufstieg des Papsttums von den Anfängen bis zum Ausgang des sechsten Jahrhunderts.* 2d ed. Munich, 1954.

Sestan, Ernesto. *Stato e nazione nell' alto medioevo.* Naples, 1952.

Seston, William. "Une interprétation nouvelle du mausolée de Galla Placidia à Ravenna." *Association Guillaume Budé: Congrès de Nice, 24–27 avril, 1935.* Paris, 1935. Pp. 234–35.

————. "Le jugement dernier du mausolée de Galla Placidia à Ravenne." *Cahiers archéologiques* I (1945), 37–50.

————. "Verfall des römischen Reiches im Westen: Die Völkerwanderung." In *Propyläen Weltgeschichte,* edited by Golo Mann and Alfred Heuss. Vol. IV. Berlin, 1963. Pp. 487–603.

Sievers, G. R. *Studien zur Geschichte der römischen Kaiser.* Berlin, 1870.

Sinnigen, William G. *The Officium of the Urban Prefecture during the Later Roman Empire.* Rome, 1957.

Sirago, Vito Antonio. *Galla Placidia e la trasformazione politica dell' occidente.* Louvain, 1961.

Solari, Arturo. "Dissidio costituzionale alla morte di Valentiniano III." *Rendiconto delle sessioni della R. Accademia delle Scienze dell' Istituto di Bologna,* Cl. sci. mor., 3d ser., X (1936–37), 11–45.

————. *Il rinnovamento dell' impero romano.* 2 vols. Milan and Genoa, 1938–43.

————. "Tolleranza verso il paganesimo nella prima metà del sec. V°." *Philologus* XCI (1936), 357–60.

Stein, Ernst. "Beiträge zur Geschichte von Ravenna in spätrömischer und byzantinischer Zeit." *Klio* XVI (1920), 40–71.

————. *Histoire du bas-empire.* Vol. I. 2d ed. by Jean-Rémy Palanque. Bruges, 1959.

————. "Die Organisation der weströmischen Grenzverteidigung im V. Jahrhundert und das Burgunderreich am Rhein." *Römisch-Germanische Kommission* XVIII Bericht (1928), 92–114.

————. *Untersuchungen über das Officium der Prätorianerpräfektur seit Diokletian.* Vienna, 1922.

―――. "Untersuchungen zur spätrömischen Verwaltungsgeschichte." *RhM* LXXIV (1925), 347–94.

―――. "Der Verzicht der Galla Placidia auf die Präfektur Illyricum." *Wiener Studien* XXXVI (1914), 344–47.

Stevens, C. E. "Gildas Sapiens." *EHR* LVI (1941), 353–73.

―――. "Marcus, Gratian, Constantine." *Athenaeum,* n.s., XXXV (1957), 316–47.

―――. *Sidonius Apollinaris and His Age.* Oxford, 1933.

Straub, Johannes. "Christliche Geschichtsapologetik in der Krisis des römischen Reiches." *Historia* I (1950), 52–81.

―――. "Parens Principum: Stilichos Reichspolitik und das Testament des Kaisers Theodosius." *La nouvelle Clio* IV (1952), 94–115.

―――. "Die Wirkung der Niederlage bei Adrianopel auf die Diskussion über das Germanenproblem in der spätrömischen Literatur." *Philologus* XCV (1943), 255–86.

Stroheker, Karl Friedrich. "Politische Kräfte in der Auflösung des weströmischen Reiches." *Orpheus* I (1954), 68–75.

―――. *Der senatorische Adel im spätantiken Gallien.* Tübingen, 1948.

Suerbaum, Werner. *Vom antiken zum frühmittelalterlichen Staatsbegriff.* Münster, 1961.

Sundwall, J. *Weströmische Studien.* Berlin, 1915.

Symons, A. J. A. *The Quest for Corvo: An Experiment in Biography.* Penguin ed. Baltimore, 1966.

Tengström, Emin. *Donatisten und Katholiken: Soziale, wirtschaftliche und politische Aspekte einer nordafrikanischen Kirchenspaltung.* Göteborg, 1964.

Thierry, Amédée. "Aëtius et Bonifacius." *Revue des deux mondes,* 1851, part III, pp. 276–310.

―――. "Aventures de Placidie." *Revue des deux mondes,* 1850, part IV, pp. 863–79.

Thompson, E. A. "A Chronological Note on St. Germanus of Auxerre." *Analecta Bollandiana* LXXV (1957), 135–38.

―――. "The Foreign Policies of Theodosius II and Marcian." *Hermathena* LXXVI (1950), 58–75.

―――. *A History of Attila and the Huns.* Oxford, 1948.

―――. "Olympiodorus of Thebes." *CQ* XXXVIII (1944), 43–52.

―――. "Peasant Revolts in Roman Gaul and Spain." *Past and Present* II (1952), 11–23.

―――. "The Settlement of the Barbarians in Southern Gaul." *JRS* XLVI (1956), 65–75.

―――. "The Visigoths from Fritigern to Euric." *Historia* XII (1963), 105–26.

―――. "The Visigoths in the Time of Ulfila." *Nottingham Mediaeval Studies*

V (1961), 3–32 [= *The Visigoths in the Time of Ulfila*. Oxford, 1966. Pp. 25–63.]

―――. *The Visigoths in the Time of Ulfila*. Oxford, 1966.

―――. "Zosimus on the End of Roman Britain." *Antiquity* XXX (1956), 163–67.

Tillemont, Louis Sébastien le Nain de. *Histoire des empereurs*. Vols. V and VI. Venice, 1732–39.

Toynbee, J., and Perkins, J. W. *The Shrine of St. Peter*. New York, 1957.

Treitinger, Otto. *Die oströmische Kaiser- und Reichsidee nach ihrer Gestaltung im höfischen Zeremoniell; Vom oströmischen Staats- und Reichsgedanken*. Darmstadt, 1956.

Twyman, Briggs. "Aëtius and the Aristocracy." Unpublished seminar paper. Univ. of Chicago, 1966.

Ulrich-Bansa, Oscar. *Moneta Mediolanensis (352–498)*. Venice, 1949.

―――. "Note sulle monete dell' Augusta Aelia Licinia Eudoxia." *Numismatica e scienze affini* I (1935), 25–31.

―――. "Le ultime monete della zecca di Aquileia romana." *Aquileia nostra* XVIII (1947), 3–12.

Van Millingen, Alexander. *Byzantine Constantinople: The Walls of the City and Adjoining Historical Sites*. London, 1899.

Vercauteren, Fernand. "Note sur la ruine des villes de la Gaule d'après quelques auteurs contemporains des invasions germaniques." *Mélanges Bidez* II (Brussels, 1934), 955–63.

Vielliard, René. *Recherches sur les origines de la Rome chrétienne*. Macon, 1941.

Voetter, Otto. *Römische Münzen und Medaillons*. Vienna, 1903.

Vogt, Joseph. *Der Niedergang Roms: Metamorphose der antiken Kultur*. Zurich, 1965.

Voigt, Karl. *Staat und Kirche von Konstantin dem Grossen bis zum Ende der Karolingerzeit*. Stuttgart, 1936.

Voirol, A. "Münzdokumente der Galla Placidia und ihres Sohnes Valentinian und Versuch einer Chronologie der Münzprägung unter Theodosius II. (408–450)." *Verhandlungen der Naturforschenden Gesellschaft in Basel* LVI: 2 (1945), 431–45.

Wallace-Hadrill, J. M. "Gothia and Romania." *Bull. of the John Rylands Library* XLIV (1961–62), 213–37.

Wes, M. A. *Das Ende des Kaisertums im Westen des römischen Reichs*. The Hague, 1967.

White, Donald A. *Litus Saxonicum: The British Saxon Shore in Scholarship and History*. Madison, 1961.

White, Lynn, ed. *The Transformation of the Roman World: Gibbon's Problem after Two Centuries*. Berkeley, 1966.

Wieacker, Franz. *Recht und Gesellschaft in der Spätantike*. Stuttgart, 1964.

Wietersheim, Eduard von. *Geschichte der Völkerwanderung.* 2d ed. by Felix Dahn. Vol. II. Leipzig, n.d.

Wilser, Ludwig. *Die Germanen: Beiträge zur Völkerkunde.* Vol. II. 3d ed. Leipzig, 1919.

Wolff, Hans Julius. *Roman Law: An Historical Introduction.* Norman, 1951.

Wulff, Oskar. *Altchristliche und byzantinische Kunst.* Vol. I. Berlin, 1918.

Wurm, Gustav. *De Rebus Gestis Aetii.* Diss. Bonn, 1844.

Zachariae von Lingenthal, K. E. "Ein Erlass des Praefectus Praetorio Dioscurus vom Jahre 472 oder 475." *Monatsberichte der K. Preussischen Akademie der Wissenschaften zu Berlin,* 1879, pp. 159–69.

Zeiller, Jacques. *Les origines chrétiennes dans les provinces danubiennes de l'empire romain.* Paris, 1918.

Zeller, Joseph. "Das Concilium der Septem Provinciae in Arelate." *Westdeutsche Zeitschrift für Geschichte und Kunst* XXIV (1905), 1–19.

# INDEX

Achilleus, bishop of Spoleto, 158, 161

*Adaeratio,* 27

Adrianople, Battle of, 40, 41

Aëtius: origin, family, appearance, character, early career, 212–14, 258; hostage to Goths and Huns, 187, 214; reliance on Huns, 187, 202, 212, 250; and Apollinaris Sidonius, 236; and Frigeridus, 236; and Merobaudes, 212, 236, 238; and Procopius, 213; *cura palatii* under John, sent to Huns for assistance, 187, 214; arrives with Huns in Italy, 189; Placidia's dislike of, 190, 232; drives Goths from Arles, 189–90; Placidia plots against, 190, 210, 212; career in Gaul in 425–31 A.D., 212, 214, 228; and conspiracy against Boniface, 221 n.; activities in 432 A.D., 228; growing power of, 228, 230, 278, causes Felix' death, 229; does not move against throne, 230; succeeds Felix, 228, 230; defeated by Boniface, 233, 251; flees to Huns, 233; agreement with Huns, 233–34; attains supreme command, 202, 234, 235, 251; made Patrician, 234; sends Attila a secretary, 234 n.; marries Pelagia, 235; political power and alliances, 235–38; Petronius Maximus his enemy, 236; interference in finances, 237; occupied with affairs of Gaul, 238, 239–40, 241; second consulship, 240, 244; attitude toward Germans, 240; and first treaty with Geiseric, 241–42; overshadows Valentinian III, 190, 243, 251, 252, 257; great reputation of, 249–50; Cassiodorus on, 257–58; object of honors and intrigues, 258; spends much of 440's in Italy, 258; collects troops against Vandals, 260; and second treaty with Geiseric, 261–62; opposition to engagement of Eudocia and Huniric, 262–63, 287; transfers Burgundians to Savoy, 279; settles Alans in Gaul, 279; friendship with Attila cooling, 280, 281; unparalleled honor of third consulship, 280; some opposition to, 282, 298; and Attila-Honoria affair, 285–86; rusticates Majorian, 287, 293; compels Valentinian to swear friendship and betroth younger Placidia to Gaudentius, 287, 293; and Frankish succession, 295; and "Battle of Châlons," 296; advice to Thorismund, 296; poor showing against Attila in Italy, 297, 298; question of fourth consulship, 299 n.; reasons for downfall, 299–300; Valentinian and Heraclius slay, 198, 300–302; verdict on his murder, 301–2

Aëtius, Eastern General, 299

Africa: retrenchment of boundaries, 2; revolt of Firmus in, 43; social and religious disorders in, 78, 224; grain for Rome, 93, 101, 119, 120, 227; Alaric wishes to control, 93, 95, 101; plan taken up by Wallia, 138; importance to Rome, 145–56, 225, 226, 227, 252, 257, 263; church in, 150 n., 158; Boniface uses as power base, 173; expeditions to, to dislodge Boniface, 222–23

Africa Proconsularis, 242

Alans, 75, 111, 132, 153, 239, 279, 296

Alaric: serves against Eugenius, 59; grievances against Empire, 68; paramount chief or king of Visigoths, 68; campaigns against Empire, 68, 69; invades Italy, 70; agreement with Stilicho, 70, 75, 78; enters Noricum and demands payment, 78, 87; joined by other barbarians, 87; presses demands after Stilicho's death, 87; first march on Rome, 82,